THE STORY OF
HUMAN
COMMUNICATION

About 15,000 years ago, a man who may have looked something like this sat in a nearly dark cave in southern France or northern Spain painting or carving exquisite pictures of animals. Even in those early years, humans stood clearly apart from other animals, many of which were larger and fiercer. A large cortex gave humans the brain power to plan the future and evaluate the past. They were the only animals capable of looking at a limestone wall of a cave and imagining a picture of an animal there, or looking at a bone or rock and imagining a likeness of a person or an animal carved from it. Most important, humans were the only animals to develop a verbal language, a subtle form of communication that made their ideas and memories portable and exchangeable. Early humans left behind a legacy for future generations to see, read, and communicate to others. Thus this artist stands quite properly at the beginning of the story of human communication. (From The Dawn of Man, eds. Andrews, Harvey, Ridder, and Stringer, illus. Burian. Abrams, 1978, p. 141.)

THE STORY OF
HUMAN COMMUNICATION

CAVE PAINTING
TO MICROCHIP

Wilbur Schramm

1817

HARPER & ROW, PUBLISHERS, New York

Cambridge, Philadelphia, San Francisco, Washington,
London, Mexico City, São Paulo, Singapore, Sydney

Sponsoring Editor: Phillip Leininger
Project Editor: Donna DeBenedictis
Text Design: Janice Noto
Cover Design: Karen Salsgiver
Cover Photo: Computer-scanned image by Michael Ross.
   Original photograph from Bildarchiv Foto Marburg, Art Reference Bureau.
Text Art: Vantage Art, Inc.
Photo Research: Mira Schachne and Katherine Vuignier
Production Manager: Jeanie Berke
Production Assistant: Brenda DeMartini
Compositor: ComCom Division of Haddon Craftsmen, Inc.
Printer and Binder: R. R. Donnelley & Sons Company
Cover Printer: New England Book Components

THE STORY OF HUMAN COMMUNICATION: Cave Painting to Microchip

Library of Congress Cataloging-in-Publication Data
Schramm, Wilbur Lang.
   The story of human communication.

   Bibliography: p.
Includes index.
1. Communication—History.   I. Title.
P90.S382   1988   001.51'09   87-11919
ISBN 0-06-045799-6

87   88   89   90   9   8   7   6   5   4   3   2   1

CREDITS

TEXT

Chapter 1   Pages 4–7, from The *Testimony of the Spade,* by Geoffrey Bibby. Copyright ©
1956 by Geoffrey Bibby. Reprinted by permission of Alfred A. Knopf, Inc.

Chapter 2   Pages 27–28, from *History of Mankind,* Vol I by Jacquetta Hawkes and Sir Leonard
Wooley, pp. 4–5 of "Prehistory," by Jacquetta Hawkes. Copyright © 1963 by UNESCO.
Reprinted by permission of Harper & Row, Publishers, Inc.

Chapter 3   Page 34, adapted from "Nonverbal Communication," by Randall Harrison, in
Handbook of Communication, eds. Ithiel Pool and Wilbur Schramm. Rand-McNally, 1973.
Reprinted by permission of Houghton Mifflin / pp. 40–43, based on an article about a paper
given by Julian Jaynes at the 1975 convention of the American Psychological Association, as
reported in the *APA Monitor.* Used by permission.

Chapter 5   Page 68, from *The Culture of Cities,* by Lewis Mumford. Harcourt Brace
Jovanovich, 1938. Reprinted by permission of the publisher / pages 69, 70, from *History of
Mankind,* Vol I by Jacquetta Hawkes and Sir Leonard Wooley, pp. 466–467, 807, and 818 of
"The Beginning of Civilization," by Sir Leonard Wooley. Copyright © 1963 by UNESCO.
Reprinted by permission of Harper & Row, Publishers, Inc. / pp. 74–75, from "Schooldays,"
in *From the Tablets of Sumer,* by S. N. Kramer. Falcon's Wing Press, 1956.

Chapter 6   Page 86, "That which makes the tongue speak . . . ," from *the Ten Principal
Upanishads,* W. B. Yeats and Shri Purohit Swami (translators). Reprinted with permission of
Macmillan Publishing Company. Copyright 1937 by Shri Purohit Swami and W. B. Yeats,
renewed 1965 by Bertha Georgie Yeats and Anne Butler Yeats. Reprinted by permission of
Michael B. Yeats and Macmillan London Ltd and Benares University / pp. 89–91, from *Lives:
The Dryden Plutarch,* rev. by Arthur Hugh Clough. J. M. Dent (London), 1910.

Chapter 7   Pages 109–110, 112, from *Cosmos,* by Carl Sagan. Copyright © 1980 Random
House, Inc. Reprinted by permission of the publisher.

Chapter 13   Pages 248–251, adaptations of seven tables from *Electronic Media,* by Christopher
H. Sterling. Copyright © 1984 Christopher H. Sterling. Reprinted and adapted by permission
of Praeger Publishers.

Chapter 14   Page 256, from *Popular Culture and High Culture: An Analysis and Evaluation of
Taste,* by Herbert J. Gans. Copyright © 1974 by Basic Books, Inc., Publisher. Reprinted by
permission of the publisher.

Chapter 15   Page 289, from *Public Opinion,* by Walter Lippmann. Copyright 1922, renewed
1950 by Walter Lippmann.

Chapter 16 Pages 295, 299–300, from *The Other Government,* by W. L. Rivers. Universe Books (N.Y.), 1982. Reprinted by permission of the author.

Chapter 17 Pages 314–315, from "Public Relations: The Invisible Sell," by Robert Heilbroner. In *Harper's* magazine, 6/1/57.

Chapter 19 Page 341, from *Process and Effects of Mass Communication,* by Arthur C. Clarke. Reprinted by permission of the author and the author's agents, Scott Meredith Literary Agency, Inc., 845 Third Avenue, New York, New York 10022 / p. 347, from *Future Shock,* by Alvin Toffler. Reprinted by permission of Random House, Inc.

ILLUSTRATIONS*

Chapter 1 Opener, Neg. #317638, Courtesy Department Library Services, American Museum of Natural History / p. 3, "The White Lady," in *The Dawn of Man,* eds. Andrews, Harvey, Ridder, and Stringer, illus. Burian. Abrams, 1978, p. 138 / p. 4, from *A History of Communications,* by Maurice Fabre. Hawthorn Books, 1963 / p. 5, "Maps of Lascaux . . . ," in *The Creative Explosion,* by John E. Pfeiffer. Copyright © 1982 by John E. Pfeiffer. Reprinted by permission of Harper & Row, Publishers, Inc. / p. 10, "The Sorcerer," Neg. #329853, Courtesy Department Library Services, American Museum of Natural History. / p. 13 (top), photo "Achuleian Ax," in *The Ascent of Man,* by Jacob Bronowski. Reprinted by permission of Lee Boltin Picture Library / p. 13 (bottom), "Baton (#1)," Neg. #39686, Courtesy Department Library Services, American Museum of Natural History / p. 14, "Clay Bison Sculpture," Neg. #291156, Courtesy Department Library Services, American Museum of Natural History / p. 15, from *The Ascent of Man,* by Jacob Bronowski.

Chapter 2 Opener (top), photo by Leakey expedition, courtesy of Mary Leakey and the National Geographic Society; (bottom) photo courtesy NASA / p. 23, "Cosmic Calendar: December," from The *Dragons of Eden: Speculations on the Evolution of Human Intelligence,* by Carl Sagan. Copyright © 1977 by Carl Sagan. Reprinted by permission of Random House, Inc. / p. 25, adapted from *Prehistory to Present Day: A Bibliography of Communication,* title essay by Wilbur Schramm. Howard Marsh Center, University of Michigan Press, 1979.

Chapter 3 Opener, *Homo habilis,* from *The Dawn of Man.* Abrams, 1978, p. 26 / p. 45, Egyptian hieroglyphs, in *A History of Communications,* by Maurice Fabre. Hawthorn Books, 1963.

Chapter 4 Opener, Egyptian Scribe, photo courtesy The Metropolitan Museum of Art, Rogers Fund, 1948. (48.67) All rights reserved. / p. 55, in *From Cave Painting to Comic Strip,* by Lancelot Hogben. Chanticleer Press, 1949 / p. 56, from *The Alphabet: A Key to the History of Mankind,* by David Diringer. Philosophical Library, 1948, p. 40 / p. 57, from *A Living Language: Chinese Characters* (pamphlet). Palace Museum, Taipei (p. 1) / p. 58, drawn by Professor An-Chih, in *From Cave Painting to Comic Strip,* by Lancelot Hogben. Chanticleer Press, 1949, p. 80 / p. 62, from *A Living Language: Chinese Characters* (pamphlet). Palace Museum, Taipei (p. 2) / p. 60, from *The Great Cultural Traditions,* by Ralph Turner.

*An attempt has been made to obtain permission from all suppliers of illustrations used in this edition. Some sources have not been located, but permission will be requested from them upon notification to us of their ownership of the material.

Chapter 5   Opener, from *The Great Cultural Traditions,* by Ralph Turner / p. 72, from *The Great Cultural Traditions,* by Ralph Turner.

Chapter 6   Opener, from *Orbis Sensualis Pictis,* by Comenius / p. 88 (top and bottom), from *The Great Cultural Traditions,* by Ralph Turner.

Chapter 7   Opener, map of eastern Mediterranean, from *Cosmos,* by Carl Sagan. Copyright © 1980 by Carl Sagan. Reprinted by permission of Random House, Inc. / p. 106, courtesy of the members of the staff of Isotope Institute, in *From Cave Painting to Comic Strip,* by Lancelot Hogben. Chanticleer Press, 1949, p. 104.

Chapter 8   Opener, from *From Cave Painting to Comic Strip,* by Lancelot Hogben. Chanticleer Press, 1949 / p. 124 (top and bottom), from *From Cave Painting to Comic Strip,* by Lancelot Hogben. Chanticleer Press, 1949 / p. 129, from *A History of Communications,* by Maurice Fabre. Hawthorn Books, 1963.

Chapter 9   Opener, provided by Museum of Modern Art, Film History Section.

Chapter 11   Opener, front page of *The New York Times,* April 16, 1912. Copyright © 1912 by The New York Times Company. Reprinted by permission / p. 170, front page of the *New York Herald Tribune,* November 25, 1963. Reprinted courtesy Queens Library–N.Y. Herald Tribune Morgue.

Chapter 12   Opener, from *The American Image: Photographs from National Archives, 1869–1960* / p. 193, from *From Cave Painting to Comic Strip,* by Lancelot Hogben. Chanticleer Press, 1949 / p. 194, from *From Cave Painting to Comic Strip,* by Lancelot Hogben. Chanticleer Press, 1949 / p. 200, from *The American Image: Photographs from National Archives, 1869–1960* / p. 202 (top row), International Museum of Photography, George Eastman House; (middle row, left), UPI/Bettmann Newsphotos; (middle row, right, and bottom row), Brown Brothers / p. 204, from *A History of Communications,* by Maurice Fabre. Hawthorn Books, 1963 / p. 206, Museum of Modern Art / Film Stills Archive / p. 209, from *Stay Tuned: A Concise History of American Broadcasting,* by C. H. Sterling and J. M. Kittross. Wadsworth, 1978.

Chapter 13   Opener, "Radio Listeners in Panic, Taking War Drama as Fact," from *The New York Times,* October 31, 1938. Copyright © 1938 by The New York Times Company. Reprinted by permission / p. 223 (top left and right), AP / Wide World Photos; (bottom) UPI / Bettmann Newsphotos / p. 227, courtesy Culver Pictures, Inc. / p. 229, from Culver Pictures Inc.

Chapter 14   Opener, Charlie Chaplin in *The Kid,* from Wide World.

Chapter 15   Opener, from *A History of Communications,* by Maurice Fabre. Hawthorn Books, 1963.

Chapter 16   Opener, UPI / Bettmann Newsphotos / page 294, Wide World.

Chapter 17   Opener, advertisement, *Harper's Weekly,* 1885, from Culver Pictures Inc.

Chapter 18   Opener, from the Collections of the Henry Ford Museum and Greenfield Village, Dearborn, Michigan.

Chapter 19   Opener, IBM Corporation / page 342, page from article by Arthur C. Clarke, "Extra-Terrestrial Relays," from *Wireless World,* October 1945 / p. 353 (top and bottom), courtesy NASA / p. 355, courtesy NASA.

C O N T E N T S

We now stand at a point in time that historians and scientists think may be the beginning of an Age of Communication, or, as some prefer to call it, an Age of Information, in which communication of information may be the chief source of human productivity in the same way as practical science and industry were chief sources during the Industrial Revolution. This provocative theory gives us cause to think that some examination of and reflection on the remarkable history of communication is timely and worthwhile.

The Story of Human Communication relates a history that began about 25,000 years ago when the people of Earth emerged from prehistory and left us the oldest surviving records of their communication—the cave paintings and figurines. The story continues through the development of language, writing, printing, the mass media, and the ways of exchanging and using information that have made the recent centuries of human communication so distinctive—political communication and public opinion, scientific communication, mass entertainment, advertising and public relations, development communication, and new patterns in news coverage. It concludes with some thoughts on the new importance of microelectronics, including the computer and space communication, and what an Age of Communication might be like if we are indeed entering upon one.

Because communication is such an enormous topic, we have supplied, in addition to reference notes and indices, study aids such as "Suggestions for Further Reading" and "Questions to Think About." There are frequent "Time Capsules" —lists of dates to set the narrative in historical continuity. Illustrations have been used where they promised to be helpful. Quotations introduce each chapter to give us some idea of what great writers and thinkers have said about the various topics covered. Selections, many of them contemporary to the narrative, have been introduced to put "flesh and blood on the bones of history"—for example, descriptions of ancient schools in Sumeria and Sparta, charts of how written letters and alphabets grew into their present form, contemporary accounts of the first demonstration of television, and the like. Tables have been included to provide informative statistics—for instance, data on the distribution of newspapers, radio, and television throughout the world.

The Story of Human Communication is not limited to one medium or one country. Rather it is designed for an introductory course on human communication, as found in departments of communication or other related departments. We hope it will be useful also as supplementary reading in other courses that touch on human communication, and especially that it will be helpful, with or without formal use, to students and others who are interested in communication and want to learn more about it and its significance in modern life.

ACKNOWLEDGMENTS

I want to thank many people, more than can be named in this space, who have contributed to the making of this book. I would like to mention from Harper & Row: Phillip Leininger, my editor, and Barbara Cinquegrani, who took over that responsibility after Phil's departure; Donna DeBenedictis, who handled the editorial production of the book; Katherine Vuignier, who was especially helpful with the illustrations; and other specialists, many of whom I never saw or spoke with, who skillfully guided the design of the volume and the preparation of the visual materials. I would also like to thank the following reviewers of the manuscript: Warren Agee, of the University of Georgia, whose guidance is especially evident in the section on public relations; Michael Emery, of California State University, Northridge; and C. A. Giffard, of the University of Washington. The ideas and criticisms of the late Ithiel de Sola Pool of M.I.T. were helpful over the years as were those of the late Jacques Kayser of the Institut de Presse, University of Paris. Among others who contributed comments and suggestions were Emeritus Professors Lyle M. Nelson and Wallace Stegner, and Steven Chaffee, all of my old "home" at Stanford University. Others to whom I am beholden are Hidetoshi Kato, Gashukuin University, Tokyo; David G. Hawkridge, British Open University; Jack Lyle, Boston University; and Godwin C. Chu, the East-West Center.

In acknowledging the help of all these friends and supporters, I also must mention my family, who have been kind and forgiving for many years toward an "alleged" author in their midst. Let me share with you an incident from family records: One afternoon my son came home from play, his face sweaty and his head doubtless full of hits, runs, and errors. He put his baseball cap down on my writing table, picked up a chapter I had been struggling with, and curled up in a lounge chair to look at the forbiddingly long manuscript. After a few moments he handed down an opinion. "You know, Dad," he said, "this is kind of interesting."

I hope for some comments on this present book that I shall value as much as that one.

Wilbur Schramm

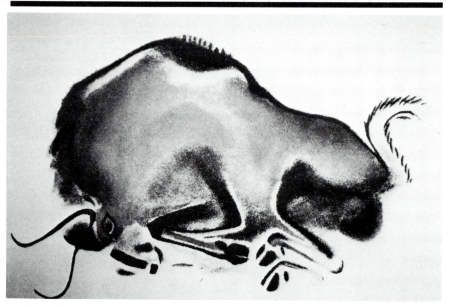

A charging bison, from the Altamira cave in Spain. This reproduction is by the Abbé Breuil, who spent much of his life trying to preserve the cave paintings for persons who might never see them.

THE DAWN YEARS

What's past is prologue.

WILLIAM SHAKESPEARE, THE TEMPEST

I feel the summer in the spring.

CHIPPEWA SONG, TRANSLATED BY FRANCES DENSMORE

*I*magine yourself transported, let us say, 15,000 years into the past. You are in the hills of southern France. You can look down on a little stream, the Vézère, and gaze westward at a broadening valley where the Dordogne River flows toward what we now know as the Bordeaux wine country, not far away. Several hundred miles to the north lies Paris, but Paris was then merely a few huts beside the Seine and a few caves in Montmartre. There, people huddle against the cold of the fourth Ice Age and the threat of large animals.

The sun has not yet warmed the chill out of the icy wind. You can see wisps of smoke coming out of the caves, where people are probably warming their hands and faces around wood fires. Then one of the men of the settlement guides you to a cave.

EXPLORING THE ANCIENT PAINTED CAVES

This must be a rather special cave because it seems not to be used as a dwelling. You have to climb to reach the entrance as you do for most caves, because they are made by water flowing downward. Therefore, you start high and descend. You stumble in the darkness; there are no windows, no slits in the walls. You slide down a steep embankment, then move forward across a dirt floor where water stands in puddles. All in the dark. You feel and stumble. Your guide brings a makeshift lantern, a ladle filled with burning animal fat, but still you see only shades of darkness. The guide leads you back into the hill, then stops, holding his lantern high. As your eyes become accustomed to the flickering light, the whole wall in front of you begins to blaze with color.

Earthy colors—yellows, browns, and blacks—predominate, but pinks and whites shine in the lamplight as well. You are looking at an animal scene painted on the limestone wall. Two lines of animals seem to be moving away from you toward the interior of the cave. It is as though you have been caught up in a parade and are being drawn irresistibly forward out of the great hall where you are standing into the narrower passage ahead of you.

For a while you are aware only of the ensemble of animals and the warm colors. Then you begin to see individual animals, creatures so lifelike that you are at first startled. Some of them are drawn with such a curve of movement, such sweeping strokes, that you almost expect them to walk or run out of the picture. You are in the cave at Lascaux.

Perhaps not until the moving picture came into use did humans feel a more convincing sense of movement from a picture than we get from some of the paintings in the 200 or so caves in southern France and northern Spain. High on the wall of a cave at Altamira, in the Cantabrian Mountains of Spain, is a remarkable painting of a buffalo. Poised to charge, with all four feet gathered under it, eyes fixed straight ahead, muscles tight, the animal is ready in the next instant to leap ahead toward an enemy. It is hard to recall any picture that gives a more convincing impression of pent-up force, action about to happen. Some of the slightly later prehistoric paintings in Africa have the same sense of action. For example, the famous White Lady, clad in white, dances lightly across a cave in southeastern Africa where the Bushmen once lived. In another cave painting, a band of hunters, bows and arrows at the ready, chase a herd of food animals across a plain. These artists of 10,000 to 20,000 years ago were not amateurs or beginners, nor could they very likely have been the first artists in their tribes. They painted with sophistication and grace. They drew with confidence. There must have been a long line of artists before, and perhaps after, them; it simply happened that these pictures survived until our time and were rediscovered, whereas others faded out or were destroyed or are among the hundreds that must still lie buried in undiscovered caves or pits.

If you went to the cave at Lascaux today, you would probably not be admitted without special permission. The moisture brought in by human visitors and the strong exhibition lights stimulated colonies of green algae that began to disfigure

The White Lady, painted about 9000 years ago and discovered in a cave in the Drakensberg Mountains of southeastern Africa. This famous portrait has been reproduced in a painting by Burian and has appeared in The Dawn of Man.

and fade the pictures. Many of the most famous caves therefore have had to be closed to the public. The paintings of Lascaux, like those of the other caves, had lain safe for thousands of years, unseen by humans and preserved in a constant temperature and humidity. Then someone found the cave—four French boys and their dog are said to have discovered Lascaux by investigating a small hole in the hillside—and as soon as tourists flocked in, the pictures began to fade. But if you were seeing them 15,000 years ago, the colors would be brilliant and the lines sharp, and you would have the same thrill as the first viewers had, although we can hardly expect the pictures to mean to us all that they meant to the cave dwellers.

Of one thing we can be reasonably sure: These pictures were not simply art for art's sake, and they were not painted on cave walls solely to make the artist's reputation. There is more behind them than that. The cave paintings still bear evidence of group planning or social purpose. For whatever reason, they were a part of the social intent of the cave dwellers.

These lively hunters, like the White Lady, were found on the wall of a cave in the Drakensberg Mountains of Africa.

Discovery of the Caves of Lascaux

Here is an interesting account by Geoffrey Bibby of how the famous caves of Lascaux were discovered by four teenage boys out for adventure.[1]

> The afternoon of Friday, September 12, (1940) was warm and sunny, and on such a day even the recent defeat of France and the occupation of half their country could not weigh heavily on the spirits of four fifteen-year-old boys who, that afternoon, were out combing the woods of Lascaux on the estate of the Countess de La Rochefoucauld not far from Montignac in the Dordogne. Their terrier, Robot, was even more infected with high spirits and dashed hither and yon through the scrub oak, investigating every sound and scent. Suddenly it disappeared into a cranny among a tumbled mass of stones, and did not return.
>
> The situation was exactly the same as at Altamira seventy-two years before. But seventy-two years can make a difference, even in the outlook of teen-age boys. Montignac lies only fourteen miles from Les Éyzies, and the boys were familiar with the possibilities latent in undiscovered caves. Their former schoolmaster, Léon Laval, was himself an enthusiastic archaeologist and had frequently impressed upon his pupils that they should be on the lookout for cave entrances in their wanderings over the limestone hills. It was for this reason that their equipment on this occasion included an electric torch.
>
> The acknowledged leader of the four boys and the owner of Robot,

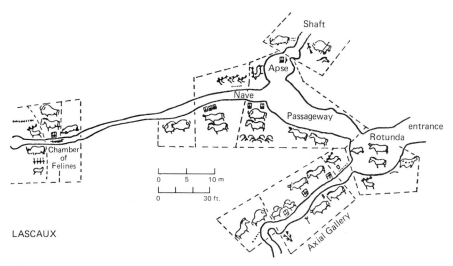

LASCAUX

Sketch of the layout of the caves of Lascaux and of the type of art found along their walls.

Ravidat, determined to follow the dog, undeterred by the hollow sound of dislodged stones rolling and falling a considerable distance. He subsequently wrote an account of the afternoon's events for his former schoolmaster, the schoolboy phraseology of which gives a vivid account of the thrill of discovery.

I succeeded in penetrating five or six metres, vertically, head first. . . . At that point I lit my torch and looked around; but I had scarcely taken a step when I lost my balance and rolled to the bottom. I picked myself up, bruised and battered, and relit the torch, which I had had the presence of mind to keep my grip on.

Seeing that the descent was not too dangerous I called my three pals to come down, advising them to take great care.

Once reunited we started exploring the cavern, looking to right and to left. We made slow progress as the torch was not working very well. In this way we crossed a large hall and, meeting no obstacle on our way, reached a passage, narrow but quite high. It was there that, lifting the torch high, we saw by its trembling light many traces of different colours.

Intrigued by these designs we began to inspect the walls carefully and to our great surprise discovered there many figures of animals of a respectable size. It was then that the notion struck us that we had discovered a cave with prehistoric paintings. Encouraged by this success we went through the whole cave, making discovery after discovery.

Our excitement was indescribable. A band of savages dancing a war dance could not have expressed themselves more vividly. Thereupon we made a solemn promise not to tell anyone of our discovery for the moment, and to return on the next day with more powerful torches.

The next day, laden with equipment, the four boys left Montignac at ten-minute intervals, so as not to excite suspicion, and again penetrated to the cave.

The wonders that met their eyes under the powerful light of four torches beggar description. Along the snow-white limestone walls animal succeeded animal as far as the eye could reach. The blacks and reds and yellows of the paintings stood out as though they had been completed the day before. Horses, stags, bison, wild cattle were portrayed in endless series. Across the domed ceiling sprawled four colossal bulls in jet black, three times life size, their curved horns almost meeting at the highest point of the dome. To one side of the main cavern a succession of stags' heads clearly portrayed a herd swimming over a lake; on the other side a file of shaggy ponies cantered along the wall. Two wild goats were on the point of meeting in head-on collision. One of the largest beasts portrayed on the cavern wall defied identification. It was a large ruminant with a humped neck, with large black spots on its white body, and with two extremely long straight forward-pointing horns springing from its forehead.

From the main cavern two galleries ran off, their walls and ceilings similarly covered with scores of painted animals. At a bend in one of the galleries the boys found the first action picture in all the Palaeolithic, a drawing of a man falling beneath the charge of a wounded bison. Beside this scene was an outline portrait of a two-horned rhinoceros.

Confident now that the newly discovered cave was not merely a true prehistoric site but one that surpassed in richness every other site in the Périgord, the four boys returned to their homes, still determined to preserve their secret from the damage that might be caused by unregulated hordes of sensation-hunters. The next day being Sunday, they took no action, but on Monday morning Marshal, another of the four, called on M. Laval and told him of the discovery. The middle-aged schoolmaster was accustomed to youthful exaggeration and not disposed to embark on a hazardous and ex-hausting excursion for what might well, as he says, have been nothing more than some curiously shaped natural stone formations. He proposed that another of his ex-pupils, an art student, should accompany the youths and make some drawings of the figures.

These drawings left no doubt in Léon Laval's mind. Here was something of the first importance. He set off at once for the cave. On arrival he had some qualms at the prospect of crawling into the entrance hole, which was scarcely more than two feet wide. But, he tells us, shamed by a farmer's wife who had followed them up and who expressed the firm intention of "going down to have a look," he wriggled in and slid down among the stalagtites. A glance was sufficient. Here was a discovery that could not, should not, be investigated by an amateur, however experienced. Instructing the boys to establish a twenty-four-hour guard at the entrance and to let no one descend, Laval hurried back to Montignac and sent a telegram to the Abbé Breuil.

THE CAVE PAINTINGS AND PREHISTORIC COMMUNICATION

Why the Art Was Put in Caves

Why are the pictures in dark caves? Why not in places where light would fall on them? Why are many of them in dark recesses where one can reach them only by paddling through water or crawling through tiny openings? Probably because early humans wanted to put them where not everyone could see them. Why are some of them in deep pits where they can be viewed only by an extraordinary effort, or placed where they can be seen only from a certain angle or in a certain illumination? Probably because early humans wanted viewing them to be an extraordinary experience.

What the Pictures Were Used For

We have reason to be grateful that the cave art was put where it was, because in the open light the pictures would almost certainly have faded back into the rock by this time.[2] But it is unlikely that the cave artists put their pictures in the caves to preserve them. There are two possible explanations for the cave art beyond the fact that it was art. One is magic—"sympathetic" magic, the kind in which a picture or a figure substitutes for a living thing, and whatever one does to the substitute acts on the living creature it represents. This is the idea behind the voodoo practice in which pins are stuck into a doll so that they will supposedly be felt by the person whom the doll represents. Thus, by casting magic over the picture of a deer or a buffalo the hunters could be more confident of success in bringing a real deer or buffalo home from the hunt.

A more likely explanation for the cave art is education: The pictures were probably used in the ceremonies that initiated the young men of the tribe to the mysteries, totems, and rituals of the group. Almost every primitive culture had an initiation ceremony, in which adolescents learned some of the tribal secrets and, by enduring physical pain or exhaustion, proved that they were ready to take on the responsibilities of adults. Thus, for example, the sons of Polynesian chiefs had to undergo the painful practice of tattooing from waist to ankles.

Standing up to the fear of darkness and the unknown must have been one way to prove bravery. However, the Paleolithic elders probably designed and decorated their caves less to make their young men prove something about themselves than to teach them something in a way they would not forget. These Paleolithic schoolboys had no textbooks or classrooms, but they had to learn quickly some vital lessons: the history and beliefs of their people, the ways and means of providing food to keep the people alive, the signs by which they could read messages in the natural world around them. These lessons had to be presented in such a way that they would engrave themselves lastingly on the young adults' memories. What better way to do so than to use the dramatic background of the dark cave, a situation where every experience was necessarily new, largely unexpected, and impressive? A teacher could drag a picture out of the darkness into that experience by simply leading the learners to the place where they could view it or shining a light on it from the proper angle. An elder could reveal a picture to a boy by having him climb into a deep pit or crawl through a narrow passage, where he would suddenly see a picture that looked larger than life and frighteningly real. An initiate would be unlikely ever to forget that experience, and such may have been precisely the intent of teaching in that way and that place.

If you look carefully at the ground in caves where the floor has been damp and soft, you may see not only footprints but also the imprints of boys' buttocks in the clay in front of the pictures. Here is where they may have sat while the elders of the tribe instructed them and revealed the secrets handed down from generation to generation. In some of the caves there are also marks of dancing feet, where ceremonies must have been conducted. There are chapellike rooms with both pictures and reliefs. Thus the pictures were probably symbols of great magic and perhaps of great secrets. Whether viewed as the first cathedrals or the first school halls, these caves were places of beauty, probably used for communicating belief. Like the cities of the Middle Ages or the villages of New England, the first human communities that have left us any communication were built around the most beautiful and most sacred things humans could create. The painted caves were as near the heart of Paleolithic life as were the cathedrals and the white churches to other ages of humankind.

The Only Picture-Making Animals

The prehistoric cave paintings are probably the oldest examples of human communication that have come down to us out of the past. We cannot be sure of that because it is not possible to date the pictures exactly or to say with confidence that they were older or younger than some of the smaller art pieces that now sit in our museums or in the less well-known caves. A remarkable picture of a mammoth is cut—engraved, we might say—in the wall of a cave at Les Combarelles, in France, the work of an anonymous artist who must have had to squat with a lamp in one hand in one of the farthest and smallest recesses of the cave. Other anonymous artists shaped the irregular walls of caves into low relief pictures. Still others carved female figures out of bone, antlers, ivory, or soft stone, or shaped them out of clay, and some of these statuettes may well be older than the animal paintings in the caves—perhaps 30,000 rather than 15,000 years. The fact that they are invariably female, and that many of them show the bulges of pregnancy, leads us to believe that they may have been fertility charms, used to encourage reproduction. Most of the female figurines—called Venuses by art historians—are stylized. They may have been carved from models, for it would have been easier for a Paleolithic artist to create such a human figure from a model than from memory, but most do not appear to be realistic portraits of individuals. Only a few—one found at the base of the Pyrenees, one in the rich hoard of art uncovered at Dolni Vestonice in Czechoslovakia, for example— seem to have been attempts at portraits. On the other hand, most of the animal paintings were highly realistic; some, like the bison of Altamira, breathtakingly so. Only a few examples exist of imaginary animals or figures combining human and animal characteristics. Some archaeologists have thought that these represented the priests or shamans who were later referred to as "masters of the hunt" and perhaps were the religious leaders who presided over the religious rites in the cave. There are only a few definitely human figures except for the little statues. Some of them are apparently engaged in adventure dramas with animals, one or two of them with sex organs erect, either to identify clearly the sex of that kind of actor or to convey a sexual connotation not entirely obvious to the modern viewer of these pictures. In addition to all these pictorial communications there are hundreds of little markings and scratchings in the pictures or on the same wall with them. Some of these can be seen as crude early attempts at picture writing—hieroglyphs. Others are simply classified as unrecognizable. Were these nonrepresentational drawings the first attempts at writing? No one today can be certain.

   Why have humans been the only picture-making animals? True, there was a chimpanzee, housed in an American zoo, who developed a taste for making abstract pictures with finger paint, and his creations enjoyed a considerable vogue and sold for as much as $100. But his drawings were abstractions of line and

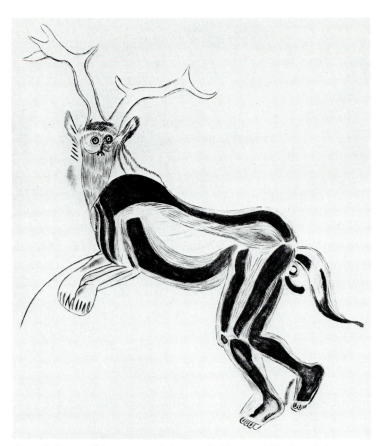

One of the mystifying cave paintings copied by the Abbé Breuil. Most of the cave art is highly realistic rendering of the kinds of animals the cave dwellers saw on their hunts. A few, however, are not realistic and seem to have meaning related in some way to the rituals conducted in the cave. This picture, combining animal and human features, has been called The Sorcerer.

color; he made no attempt to draw any living creature or any scene in nature. In other words, he never became a representational painter, and, so far as we know, neither has any other animal except the human animal. Why, then, did the Cro-Magnon people of Europe and other tribes in other parts of the world, 10,000 to 20,000 years ago, suddenly develop the skill of painting and carving lifelike representations of humans and animals? It must have taken a remarkable leap of the imagination to be able to look at a piece of bone and envisage a human figure carved out of it with a sharp stone. It must have taken a remarkable advance in skill and taste to be able to look at the limestone wall of a cave and be able to imagine the lines and colors on it that would stand for a mammoth or a bison or a human being.

A PREHISTORIC RENAISSANCE

What kind of people were these who communicated by art, long before they learned to write?[3] You would have seen them, if you had visited Lascaux at the time we are imagining. They were a bit hairy for modern taste, but much of that was protection against the cold. On the whole they were quite modern looking. If you were to dress them in modern clothing and take them walking down a modern street they might attract no more attention than any other person who bore the marks of outdoor living and athletic activity. Their ancestors, 50,000 years before them, had low foreheads and bulging brows; these people had high foreheads and no bulge over the eyebrows. Their brain cavities must have been about as big as those of modern humans— about 1400 cubic centimeters, twice as large as the braincase of Peking man or other hominids who stood earlier in the path of human descent. It was the enormous cortex growing in this enlarging skull that must have made it possible for humans to survive among larger, stronger animals, to develop language, to organize in societies, to conceive of religion, and finally to paint the marvelously beautiful things on the walls of their caves.

They had language, perhaps the greatest human achievement. Human language was portable. It could be detached from the immediate surroundings at which one pointed or shook a fist. It could be handed over to one's friends, one's children, or their children. It could carry not only the simple messages of gestures and facial expressions, but also the messages of abstract ideas that set humans apart from the other animals. It enabled human animals to think about questions that began with "why" and "what if," "when" and "how much," "if . . . then," and to deal much more profoundly with "how." More than anything else it was language that made it possible for humans to outlast their chief animal competitors and to impose something they called civilization on the earth.

They had fire. They found how to capture it (perhaps about the time of Peking man), how to preserve it for later use. They could use it not only to resist the glacial cold, but also to cook, to explore in the darkness, to frighten away predatory animals, to drive other animals into traps so that they could be captured and some of them tamed.

They had tools, a considerable variety of them. For several hundred thousand years, the Achuleian ax, or its equivalent, was about the only important tool humans had. Then, sometime between 10,000 and 20,000 years ago, there came a great burst of toolmaking, and humans learned how to make awls, knives, needles, levers, bows and arrows, spear throwers, harpoons, and dozens of other instruments of survival and aggression. It is hard to believe that the hand and eye skills that entered into the paintings and the figurines were not related to the skills that entered into the making of new and ingenious tools.

They had art—graphic and plastic art, as we have seen. If they were able to make lovely paintings and sculptures, and inasmuch as they already had a flexible and extensive language, then they must also have had verbal art. Who can believe that people who could produce the bison of Altamira, the White Lady of Africa, and the best of the Venuses could not also produce poems and stories? "All of antiquity," Fabre said, reviewing what we know about it, "resounds with tales told and retold by anonymous voices."[4] How much have we lost from the human record because there was no way to preserve speech or writing? Have we lost, perhaps, a primitive Homer, an early Thucydides? Everything we know of other Stone Age societies tells us that stories, poems, and folk history were an important part of the lives of such communities, along with dancing and song, which they must have had.

Furthermore, they had worked out at least the elementary problems of living together in societies. Some of their societies were apparently as small as a dozen people, others as large as several hundred. An average might have been about 25 or perhaps 50. The people in these groups seem to have worked out a division of roles. The men were the hunters; the women were the principal gatherers of berries and fruits, the makers of clothing, and probably the cooks. The groups must have had leaders, selected for specific activities on the basis of their ability to perform those activities and show others how. There is good reason to think that the privilege of leadership was earned rather than inherited, for hunter-gatherer civilizations are typically egalitarian. Thus, the best hunters must have been chosen to be leaders of the hunt. The old people who knew most about the tribe's history and traditions must have become custodians of that lore. Others became keepers of the tribe's magic and religion. (It is likely that they were not sole custodians, however. For example, the audiences in an Indian village today take upon themselves the right to correct any minor "holy man" when he is reciting the holy books.) As time went on, roles must have become more and more specialized. Some persons must have been specially trained to perform specific tribal functions; persons in whom an important skill was highly developed

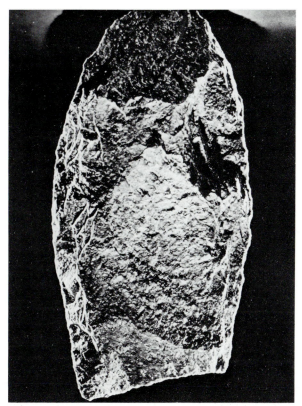

The Achuleian ax. For 300,000 years or more this was the chief tool and weapon of early humans. Not until about 50,000 years ago did carved and decorated tools appear.

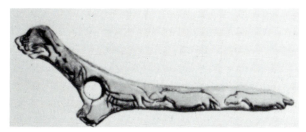

At the time of the cave paintings in Europe, highly decorated implements also began to appear. This is a baton, *apparently an award given to an individual for distinguished accomplishment or high position.*

Clay sculptures of bison in the Tuc d'Audoubert cave in southern France.

were probably designated as teachers of that skill; and so forth. By the end of the Paleolithic age, humans had worked out ways of living and working together and ways of planning so that the skills and intelligence of the group could be pooled in the general interest and the strength of all shared for the good of each.

Humans were also learning to move around their planet, preparing to take command of the places and resources that suited them best. In the early Ice Ages they usually retreated from the winter and the huge ice heaps that spread from the Arctic as far south as present London and Berlin in Europe, New Jersey and Iowa on the American continent. By the end of the fourth Ice Age, however, they were no longer in a mood to retreat. They moved into the caves, where caves were available, in the winter, and went looking for good hunting and fishing places in the summer. But they did more than that. They were venturesome enough to explore and hunt, in any season, along the edge of the glaciers. They explored and to some degree settled all the continents. They crossed many of the water barriers, either when the oceans were low, as they were in the Ice Ages, or where their crude rafts or dugout canoes could travel. Whether they knew it or not, they were looking ahead toward the time when humankind would move freely around the earth, carrying goods to trade, knowledge to share, and sometimes weapons with which to fight.

On the whole, we have to conclude that this period, the time to which you have gone back in imagination to see the caves when their paintings were still new,

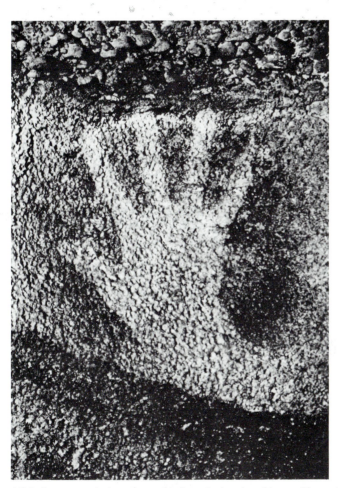

With the cave paintings, humankind put its hand on history. There are actually a number of handprints preserved in the soft limestone of the caves. This one was probably made by someone viewing the pictures 13,000 to 15,000 years ago. It comes from El Castillo cave in Santander, Spain.

was a quite remarkable age in human history. It saw the first known appearance of high-quality art. It marked the first age of technology, signified by the number of new tools. It was the time when humans had organized their own living groups and were beginning to use their unique cranial weapon, a high intelligence never before seen on earth, to explore around them, undertake new tasks, and face new problems. Without too much exaggeration we can call it a kind of prehistoric renaissance, a period of flowering similar in many ways to the Renaissance that came thousands of years later, and pointing ahead, as did that later renaissance, toward even greater things to come.

On some of the Paleolithic cave walls, beside the pictures, are the imprints of human hands, preserved through the years by the hardening limestone. To one who has seen those caves and considered the culture they represent, the handprints seem symbolic of something far greater than the Cro-Magnons who pressed their hands there. For during that age when they left us, among other inheritances, the cave paintings, humankind put its hand on history.

SUGGESTIONS FOR FURTHER READING

A most helpful and informative book about the cave paintings by an author who has himself walked, climbed, and slid through many of the caves is *The Creative Explosion: An Inquiry into the Origins of Art and Religion,* by John E. Pfeiffer (New York: Harper & Row, 1982). *Four Hundred Years of Cave Art,* by l'Abbé H. Breuil (London: Montignac, 1952), is the written legacy of a man who spent much of his life painting reproductions of cave paintings so that they could be seen realistically by persons who had never seen the caves themselves. Another very attractive book includes some of the cave art and some imaginative reconstructions of how early humans and their dwelling places probably looked, so far as we can judge from fossils, tools, and other remains. It is the *Dawn of Man* (New York: Abrams, 1978), beautifully illustrated by Zdenek Burian, edited and adapted by Peter Andrews, Robin Harvey, Colin Ridder, and Christopher Stringer. An excellent reference on the prehistory of humans is appropriately entitled *Prehistory,* by Jacquetta Hawkes (New York: Harper & Row, 1963, reprinted by Mentor, 1965. The page references in this book are to the Mentor edition.) This is the first volume of the UNESCO *History of Mankind.* A general book on the history of human communication is Maurice Fabre, *A History of Communications* (New York: Hawthorn Books, 1963). This is vol. 9 of the New Illustrated Library of Science and Invention (Paris), and is adapted from the French by Peter Chaitin. About half of the 112 pages are illustrations, many of them in color. Another general book, also liberally illustrated, is Lancelot Hogben, *From Cave Painting to Comic Strip* (New York: Chanticleer Press, 1949). Among other useful books on this period are John E. Pfeiffer, *The Emergence of Man* (New York: Harper & Row, 1978); and Andre Leroi-Gourhan, *Treasures of Prehistoric Art* (New York: Abrams, 1967).

QUESTIONS TO THINK ABOUT

1. Most of the cave paintings are skillfully done—some of them of very high quality indeed—and do not look like the first pictures an artist would paint. What do you suppose happened to the practice paintings?
2. Why are most of the pictures of animals and very few of humans?
3. Why are so many of the cave paintings put in awkward places—where they cannot be seen except with artificial light, where viewers have to crawl under a very low ceiling or climb into a hole or something of that kind? They must have purposely been made hard to view. Why?
4. What do you think these paintings were used for? To communicate what to whom? To teach the traditions and beliefs of the tribe? For magic? Totemism? For some other purpose?
5. Taking into account all you have learned about the kinds of humans who lived at the time of the paintings, what would you say are the characteristics that distinguished them from the animals that lived at the same time? They painted representational pictures. They made tools and decorated some of them. They had, already at that time, a sophisticated language. They could make and preserve fire. What else?
6. If prehistoric humans could make such impressive paintings, what other artistic things could they probably do? Dance? Sing? Make poems? Decorate tools? What else?

TIME CAPSULE

The big bang	15,000 million years ago*
Formation of earth	4,400
Life on earth	4,100
Oldest fossils	3,700
First cells with nuclei	3,200
First invertebrates	600
First vertebrates	500
Plants begin to colonize land on earth	430
Appalachians formed	250
Dinosaurs on earth	230–140
Birds	170
Flowering plants	135
Rocky Mountains formed	75
First primates	72
South America cut from Africa	65
Alaska cut from Asia	45
Himalayas and Alps formed	30
Hominids	15
Humans	1 (plus or minus some millenia)

*All these figures are in *millions* of years. They are necessarily approximate.

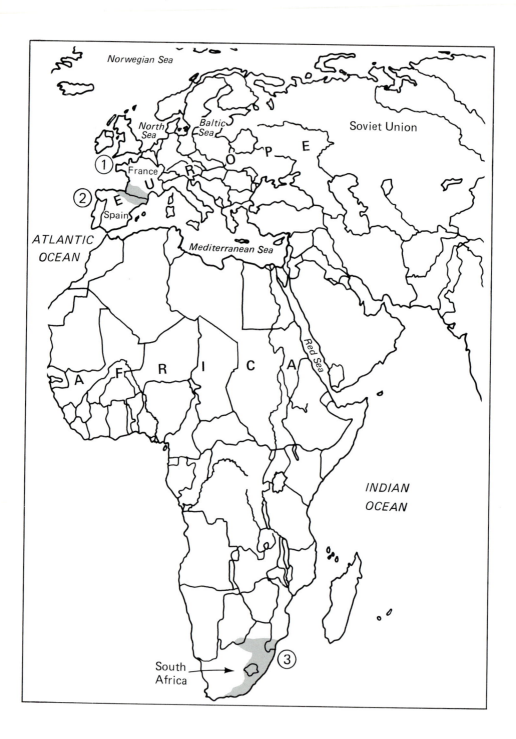

Where did the cave paintings come from?

The most productive caves are indicated on the map on page 18 by numbers: (1) the caves of southwestern France, including Lascaux and Niaux; (2) the caves of northeastern Spain, including Altamira and Santander; and (3) the caves of the Drakensberg Mountains of southeastern Africa.

What is a long time? Above: *a hominid footprint from Tanzania about 3.6 million years ago, photographed by the Leakey expedition.* Below: *a human shoe print from the moon, 1969.*

HOW LONG IS A LONG TIME?

The world is very old, and human beings are very young.
CARL SAGAN, DRAGONS OF EDEN

Mankind is poised midway between the gods and the beasts.
PLOTINUS

Although it seems a very long time since our oldest records of human communication were painted on cave walls or carved in bone, those years look much shorter in the long view of history. Let us therefore turn aside for the moment from the story of the cave painters and the figurine carvers and try to put human communication into a time perspective.

What is a long time? For a small boy it may be the hour he has to wait after eating before he can go to swim. For an impatient driver it may be the seconds before the traffic light turns from red to green. For an old man or woman it may be the years of a life. A long time is relative, not absolute.

The longest time we know anything about is the time since the "big bang," which supposedly took place about 15 billion years ago, plus or minus 1 or 2 billion years. Exactly what happened at that time, or how, or why, we are far from certain about. But whatever happened, the nuclear forces of the universe apparently gathered themselves into an almost incomprehensible mass that exploded from a central point and blew everything out in all directions at a speed near that of light. We must assume this, because whatever happened is so far beyond our ability to map, and so far beyond the translation capacity of optical telescopes and radio telescopes, that we really know very little about what it was. We do know, however, that a great event took place and that the approximate time measure between that event and the present is about 15 billion years. There must have been something before the big bang, of course. Something must have happened to assemble all those materials that so mysteriously blew up. But that chapter in the universe is still closed to us. Did Time and Universe really begin there, or did the big bang simply destroy all the records of what went before it?

THE COSMIC CALENDAR

Compared to the lifetime of the universe, the history of human communication is infinitesimally brief. How can one compare 20 thousand with 15 billion? It makes little sense to talk about one ten-thousandth of one percent. The only very good way to handle a difference like that is to conceive it in units that we can comprehend. This is what Carl Sagan did when he wrote about the history of the universe in *Dragons of Eden*.[1] He took familiar measures—the months and days in the calendar year. Then he expressed those enormous numbers of years in terms of days of the month and year, starting with the big bang on January 1, cosmic time.

Even so, it takes a long time to leaf through the calendar to human history. By Sagan's cosmic calendar, the Milky Way galaxy to which our sun belongs must have come into existence about May 1—about 10 billion years ago. Our own solar system, centering on the sun, probably originated about September 9—between 4 and 5 billion years ago. The earth itself must have been formed about September 14, just over 4 billion years in the past. Then comes the first date that seems very close to us—September 25, about 4 billion years ago. That was when life began to form on the earth.

September 25 seems very close by our time to midnight of December 31, which by the cosmic calendar stands for today. But it is actually nearly 4 billion years! Each cosmic month equals 1.25 billion years. Thereafter, life on earth moved ahead at a maddeningly slow pace according to the human way of keeping time, but quite speedily by Sagan's cosmic calendar. The oldest rocks we have found on earth seem to date back to October 2. The oldest fossils we have discovered would be dated October 9, between 3 and 3.5 billion years ago. These were apparently bacteria and blue-green algae. The first cells with nuclei, which paved the way for the emergence of fish and animals, are dated November 15. On the calendar of the universe we have now passed through 10½ months. Our own galaxy (the Milky Way) is lighting our own skies in the summer nights. Our own sun is shining. Our own planet is circling the sun. But even at this late time, over 13 billion years since the origin of the universe, there are still no signs of fish or animals or flowers or trees on the earth.

What was happening elsewhere in the universe during these millions of years before our planet developed its blanket of oceans and flora, and thus became what our astronauts have called the blue planet? It is hard to conceive of a situation in which life would develop on only one planet out of billions. Have living things indeed appeared on other planets, in other systems, during the years before Earth was formed, and before it acquired inhabitants? If so, have any of them evolved into what we know as human form? Have any of them developed an intelligence comparable to human intelligence? Indeed, how many of them may have far exceeded human intelligence? The answers to these questions will have to wait until we receive the first message from distant space, and meanwhile the facts are hidden in the dim past and the almost unimaginable distance.

As Sagan wrote in beginning the lectures in which he presented his cosmic calendar, "The world is very old, and human beings are very young." How young becomes apparent when we fill in the calendar for the imagined cosmic month of December.

Cosmic Calendar
DECEMBER

Sunday	Monday	Tuesday	Wednesday	Thursday	Friday	Saturday
	1 Significant oxygen atmosphere begins to develop on earth.	2	3	4	5 Extensive vulcanism and channel formation on Mars.	6
7	8	9	10	11	12	13
14	15	16 First worms.	17 Precambrian ends. Paleozoic era and Cambrian period begin. Invertebrates flourish.	18 First oceanic plankton. Trilobites flourish.	19 Ordovician period. First fish, first vertebrates.	20 Silurian period. First vascular plants. Plants begin colonization of land.
21 Devonian period begins. First insects. Animals begin colonization of land.	22 First amphibians. First winged insects.	23 Carboniferous period. First trees. First reptiles.	24 Permian period begins. First dinosaurs.	25 Paleozoic era ends. Mesozoic era begins.	26 Triassic period. First mammals.	27 Jurassic period. First birds.
28 Cretaceous period. First flowers. Dinosaurs become extinct.	29 Mesozoic era ends. Ceflozoic era and Tertiary period begin. First cetaceans. First primates.	30 Early evolution of frontal lobes in the brains of primates. First hominids. Giant mammals flourish.	31 End of the Pliocene period. Quatenary (Pleistocene and Holocene) period. First humans.			

Dr. Carl Sagan's month of December in the calendar of the universe (1 month = 1.25 billion years).

Not until December 1—1.25 billion years ago, nearly 14 billion years after the big bang—did the earth have any significant amount of oxygen in its atmosphere. Not until December 16, only 600 million years in the past, did the first invertebrates—worms—appear. The trilobites we find so often in ancient fossil deposits were in the ocean by December 18; the first fish, by December 19. By December 20, plants began to appear on land. By December 21, some of the sea animals moved out of their natural habitats and began to live on land. (Some of them, like the dolphin, did not like what they saw and moved back to the water.) Insects appeared. The first dinosaurs were terrorizing smaller creatures by December 24. These great reptiles faded out of history, for reasons not fully known, after a few cosmic days, and mammals appeared (about December 26, somewhere in the vicinity of 200 million years ago). The first birds appeared (December 27), and flowers began to cover the ground (December 28). The first primates (the family line of humans) were in existence by December 29, and on December 30, Sagan could record on his calendar, the first hominids (probable ancestors of humans) were present on earth. Then, on December 31, Dr. Sagan was able to end his cosmic calendar with two important words: *first humans!*

HUMANKIND'S DAY ON EARTH

Not until the last day of the last month! The complete history of humans would fit into the last ten seconds of December 31 on Sagan's calendar. Ten seconds of the imaginary calendar year!

But humans are older than their recorded history. A good guess is that humans have been on earth for a million years. This is hard to calculate, because we keep digging up fossils recognizable as hominids, but we have only the size and shape of the fossil, rather than behavior, with which to judge its humanness. Furthermore, no one has ever defined *human* exactly. Two million might be a better guess for the age of humans. But a reasonable estimate is that humankind's day on earth might be reckoned as 1 million out of 15 billion years. Thus the chapter on earth-humans does not bulk very large in the history of the universe.

Following Sagan's example in setting the history of the universe to equal one calendar year, let us imagine that humankind's day on earth equals one clock day—24 hours. Then one hour of that day would equal 41,667 years; round it off to 42,000. One minute of that day would be about 694 years; round it to 700. And one second would be about 12 years. This is the imaginary clock we shall be dealing with. When we start this clock at midnight, it will be 1 million years

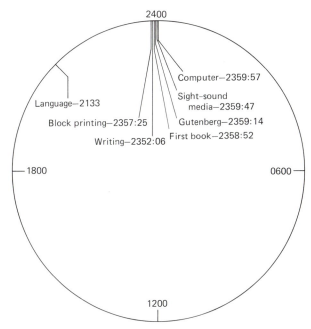

A 24-hour clock for humankind's day on earth (24 hours = 1 million years).

ago. Twelve o'clock noon will be 500,000 years ago. When the instrument reaches midnight a second time, we are in the now, looking into the future.

Start the clock: one second after midnight. We have very little historical evidence for the first 18 hours.[2] There are fossils and a few flaked rocks that might be primitive tools. Some of the fossils have human characteristics, but their brain cavities are less than half as large as the brain of modern humans. The tools are mostly shaped by water or made by flaking one rock with another. If we could step back for a few minutes into the time that passes so quickly on the clock, for example if we could visit humans of 500,000 years ago—as in Chapter 1, where we imagined a visit to the cave painters of 15,000 years ago—we would certainly find them less desirable neighbors than the Cro-Magnon cave painters. Their foreheads were much lower; their brows bulged over their eyes. We might not have been able to identify human ancestors amidst the other hominids. Rather than standing out from other primates, they were still running the race for survival against animals that looked and acted very much like them. Unlike the Cro-Magnons, if dressed in modern clothing they would probably not have looked modern on a modern street. They lived in groups ranging in size from a dozen to a hundred or more. They lived where they could retreat from the cold, and during the rest of the year moved around, following herds of animals to good hunting grounds. Whether they painted anything, we do not know; if they carved anything, it must have been crude work. And there is one thing we are fairly sure of: Whatever vocal communication they had must have been mostly animal cries and nonverbal signals; it was a bit early for language. We would probably not have heard words. But they had fire. Peking man may have been the first of our ancestors to master it. This early human was a member of the strain we call Pithecanthropus, along with Java man, Heidelberg man, and other famous beings whom we have met only as fossils.

If you could have traveled in humankind's day on earth, you would undoubtedly have been impressed by the scenery. That day was geologically dramatic. Four times in that million years the polar ice caps spread southward and in many cases joined other glaciers from the more southerly mountains of Europe, Asia, and North America. In some places, these ice blankets seem to have been 10,000 feet thick. Between ice ages, the land warmed again, and in some periods produced tropical forests in what is now the North Temperate Zone. Fossil remains of alligators have been found in such places as South Dakota. During that million years the earth writhed and wrinkled, creating the Himalayas, the Andes, and the Rockies. Not long before, the Himalayas had been a trough in the Asian earth, occupied by water that geologists have called the Sea of Tethys. Then came intense geologic pressure from the south, causing the earth's crust to buckle, and raising the planet's highest peaks. What was left of the Sea of Tethys became the Mediterranean.

You would not have seen huge populations of humans during most of that day. For one thing, the individual life span apparently averaged only about 30 years. Furthermore, a population of hunters and gatherers had to move constantly from hunting ground to hunting ground, and could not afford to settle down and create farms and cities. And the recurring periods of glaciation helped to keep population low. During those times, much of northern Europe would be like northern Canada or Alaska today, unable to support large numbers of settlers. It has been estimated, for example, that at one time the total population of England must have been about 250. And the total human population was not very large. There were more orangutans than humans on earth, and the baboon population exceeded the human by perhaps 50 times.

It is reasonable to think that much of the first half—perhaps the first three-quarters—of humankind's day on earth must have been taken up largely with learning to live in the rough and challenging Pleistocene period, when four separate ice sheets swept down and the great mountain ranges curled and uncurled. Humans learned to keep warm, first with animal skins and later with fire; to make homes in caves; to become quick and skillful hunters and gatherers. There was communication, of course: How could animals live together without communication? But much of it must have been nonverbal.

Verbal communication came slowly to replace the animal cries and grunts, the well-understood gestures, and the stones put down to mark paths and trails. Certainly the first great step in human communication, probably the greatest intellectual achievement in all of human history, was language. Language must have existed, at least in a primitive form, 100,000 years ago. We are guessing at that; we have no choice except to guess, because oral language leaves no writing behind it. There may have been some verbal communication as much as a million years ago; in any case, sounds must have grown into words very slowly. Thus it is likely that language developed over a long time, and at different rates in different places. Therefore, some languages may have been in use much earlier than others. But the evidence, as we shall see in Chapter 3, is on the side of late rather than early development, and there is good reason to think that the great steps forward in language came not far in time from what in Chapter 1 we called the prehistoric renaissance—the explosion of technology in toolmaking and the explosion of art in painting and carving.

If we say that humans had language 100,000 years ago, that would be the equivalent of 9:33 p.m. on our clock—21 hours, 33 minutes after the dawn of humankind's day on earth.

Humans moved out of the painted caves. They ceased to be chiefly hunters and gatherers, pursuing game animals and gathering fruits, berries, and grain where they could be found. Rather than making their homes where food abounded, they found ways to make it abound where they wanted to live. They discovered a hybrid of wheat they could carry with them and plant. They domesticated guard dogs whose ancestors had recently been wolves, and milk and pack animals whose ancestors had been wild goats. As the ice shelf withdrew into the north, humans found their way around the world. During the later ice ages, sea levels had changed as much as 400 feet. There was a dry footpath between Asia and America, which humans crossed in two great surges of population. Over the new pathways and the old animal trails, humans wandered around their unknown world, finding places to hunt and gather and, after a while, places to settle. It is hard to conceive of how little the world was settled, even at the end of the fourth Ice Age: perhaps two persons per square kilometer in northern Europe, 160 persons per acre even in the first Middle Eastern cities.

According to the distinguished historian Jacquetta Hawkes,

> What it will prove most important to remember is that our species did not only inherit from the past its bodily equipment, dominated by its subtly elongated brain, but also highly charged emotional centers and all the strange

furniture of the unconscious mind. Man emerged bringing with him hate, fear, and anger, together with love and their joy of love in their simple animal form. He also brought the social heritage of family affection and group loyalty. Today some of us believe (while others do not) that among the most elusive and yet the most precious heirlooms of all were shadowy deep-seated memories of the experience of the evolving animal line during the vast stretches of its history, memories which enrich and unite modern man by throwing up from the unconscious the images and ideas that inspire our arts and help to make them universally evocative. . . . There can be no question, whatever construction we put upon them, these mental and emotional inheritances which man received from the prehuman past were to provide a most potent force in the creation of culture.[3]

But let us remember that humans also brought with them into the light of history tools to replace the Achuleian ax, which had been the chief weapon for 300 centuries; weapon throwers and needles and sharp knives and the first metal work, and art on the tools and the homes as a kind of message to those who would follow; the art of living together in groups, learned in the wandering during prehistory. Most important of all, perhaps, they brought the art of writing—furnishing a memory for humans so that it was not necessary to try to carry all the past in their heads and they could focus on the new as easily as on the old. With these new social and scientific tools they created books and libraries, they invented villages and towns and cities; and from these came schools and science and all the great civilizations that spread from the Fertile Crescent over the globe.

THE RECORDED HISTORY OF HUMAN COMMUNICATION

Disregarding whatever may have been the meaning of the undecipherable and nonrepresentational symbols on some of the cave walls, we can say that writing came into use, probably in Sumer, between 5000 and 6000 years ago. If language was the greatest intellectual achievement of humans, writing was our greatest invention. Greater than the invention of the wheel or the plough, greater than the concept of the number zero developed by the ingenious Hindu mathematicians, greater than the invention of the telephone or the motion picture or the telegraph. Greater than the computer. Greater because it freed humans from being dependent only on what old people could remember, from being able to communicate only as far as the voice could carry or the signal fire could be seen; greater because it built a bridge into the measureless distance and the endless future.

When did writing come into the history of humans? About 7 minutes before midnight on the clock of humankind's day. In other words, human creatures were on earth about 23 hours and 53 minutes of their day before they learned to write.

The next great step in human communication technology was printing. Block printing was in use over 1900 years ago, but Gutenberg and his printers did not put out their first books until about 1450. Thus the Gutenberg kind of printing came only in the last minute of the last hour of the 24, the earlier printers only in the last 3 minutes of that Day.

Printing and the electronic media were, in a sense, a déjà vu activity. That is, humans kept returning to the old path. We learned to write with beauty and skill, and then invented machines that would let us write faster and more efficiently (although no more beautifully) so that we could live in an age of reading, duplicating, and printing. We learned to paint the bison on the dark wall of the cave, and then developed an apparatus that would make moving pictures of bison as they really look to us. We found a way to construct a handmade megaphone, and then built an electronic megaphone that would let us talk not merely to the next hill, but to the next continent if we wished. We found ways to watch the dance in distant villages without traveling there, and to listen to drums even in the next country without cupping our ears. Therefore printing and the first stage of electronics were not so revolutionary as language or writing, but they are the kinds of communication we chiefly write about today. And they all have come into being in the last minute of our day.

A newer, more revolutionary development is microelectronics. Its greatest product is the computer. As we shall have occasion to say later, this development promises to make such changes in human life and thinking as have perhaps never come out of communication since the introduction of language and writing. And when has this new communication technology come into use? The communication satellite dates to 1945, the modern computer to 1946, and the solid-state devices, such as the transistor and the chip that made microelectronics possible, to 1947. In other words, what we think of now as our most exciting new communication machines have all come into use in the last four seconds of our human day.

It is clear, then, that the long times which we sometimes ascribe to communication history are in perspective very short times. Humans are new things on earth, but human communication is still newer. Another characteristic of human communication is also clear. Just as human beings are only a step from the primates who lived in trees, so our communication is only a step from the snarls, calls, grunts, and gestures of animal communication. Modern humans have come into the world of computers and microelectronics and libraries and television (in which we have a very short history) from a very long history among other animals and other primitives. We are newly human. New communicators. We bring with us an inheritance from prehuman years far longer than our experience in human years, and this inheritance affects how we use our modern communication and what we believe is worth doing with it.

One reason we seem to be surrounded by such a rush of new developments in communication and such a flood of symbols is that communication has helped to cement the connection of ideas and knowledge. The history of human communication is really a history, not of action, but of interaction. As Leonard Woolley says, the history of communication cannot be attributed to any region or any people: "No single region provided all the techniques essential for civilized life. The new materials that are lacking in one country had to be imported from another and with them came the knowledge of techniques; because of the need for international trade of this sort, new ideas originating in one area spread quickly and easily, to be adopted and improved upon by the independent genius of different people. Civilization is indeed due to diffusion, but more of ideas than of models, and not from a single source but from many."[4]

Soedjatmoko offers the following comment about the present situation: "The industrial and industrializing countries are all clearly unprepared for the future. . . . No nation, rich or poor, powerful or weak, can work out its salvation in isolation. The answers we are looking for cannot be found by any single culture alone. They can only be found together. In both success or failure, the role of communication may well be crucial."[5] The role of communication, then, is what we want to examine.

SUGGESTIONS FOR FURTHER READING

This chapter leans heavily on Carl Sagan's brilliantly written *Dragons of Eden: Speculations on the Origin of Human Intelligence* (New York: Ballantine Books, 1977), especially the section "The Cosmic Calendar," pp. 13–17. Among other books about the time span of the universe are Boeke and Kees, *Cosmic View: The Universe in Forty Jumps* (New York: John Day, 1957), and some of Dr. Sagan's other writings, notably the book that came out of his immensely popular television program, *Cosmos* (New York: Random House, 1980), and his earlier book, *The Cosmic Connection: An Extraterrestrial Perspective* (New York: Doubleday, 1973).

Among books on the origin and development of human life are Arthur Kornberg, *DNA Replication* (San Francisco: W. H. Freeman, 1980), and a Scientific American Book, *Evolution* (same publisher, 1979). Also interesting is Theodosius Dobzhansky, *Mankind Evolving: The Evolution of the Human Species* (New Haven: Yale University Press, 1962); also L. Orgel, *Origins of Life* (New York: Wiley, 1973).

A somewhat different approach will be found in Isaac Azimov, *Extraterrestrial Civilization* (New York: Fawcett, 1979). Also worth reading, even by persons who saw the much-praised Bronowski television program *Ascent of Man,* is Jacob Bronowski's book of the same title (Boston: Little, Brown, 1973).

QUESTIONS TO THINK ABOUT

1. Bronowski writes: "Every human action goes back in our animal origins; we should be cold and lonely creatures if we were cut off from that blood-stream of life. Nevertheless, it is right to ask for a distinction: What are the physical gifts that man must share with the animals, and what are the gifts that make him different?" How would you answer that question?
2. Scientists believe that our earthly civilization has been changing for the last several hundred years at an increasing rate of speed, much faster than ever before. Does this suggest any prediction for the next millenia of humans on earth?
3. Suppose you were looking for life on a planet somewhere in our galaxy. What kind of life would you expect to find? A duplicate of what we have on earth?
4. In light of what you have read in this chapter, how would you explain to someone the meaning of "a long time"? For example, "15 billion years"?

He walked the earth 30,000 years ago.

THE BIRTH OF LANGUAGE

The evolution of verbal concepts opened the door to all further achievements of man's thoughts.

JULIAN HUXLEY

Language is the best show man puts on.

BENJAMIN WHORF

It is no accident that *community* and *communication* have the same linguistic root. One cannot exist without the other. Whenever animals have clustered together, sharing the acts of daily life, they have found ways to communicate.

HUMAN COMMUNICATION BEFORE VERBAL LANGUAGE

There was human communication long before there was language or speech or even meaningful sound. The first highly developed language systems probably made little use of the vocal mechanism. Communication must have been tactile or visual, in some cases olfactory. It must have depended on body movements—posture, gesture, facial expression, movements of hands and fingers and feet. It no doubt included signals not requiring words—like a fire on a hilltop—and monuments —such as a mound to indicate a burial site, a pile of stones to mark a path. All nonverbal.

Randall Harrison has described nonverbal communication in terms of four *codes,* meaning patterns of signs:[1]

1. *Performance codes.* Under this heading Harrison includes nonverbal signs expressed through bodily action: facial expressions, eye movements and eye contact, gestures, posture, touch, smell; and all the nonverbal signs related to speech, such as the quality, pitch, and tempo of voice, pauses, laughter, sighs, and grunts.
2. *Artifactual codes.* Here he lists clothing, cosmetics, status symbols, art objects, room decoration, architecture, and so on.
3. *Media codes.* These refer to headline size, position within the newspaper or on the page, use of color, close-up or long-range shots, music or other sound effects, order of presentation, and the like.
4. *Contextual codes.* These codes signify time and space use. They include close-up or faraway conversation and appearance of an office—for example, clean versus cluttered desks, calendar on desk, phone on desk, and the other things that indirectly describe what the occupant of an office does, and how.

Now, which of these might apply to the centuries before humans learned to talk, the ages that have been dreamed of as "silent"? We can begin by crossing out most of number 3: There were no mass media in those days. Similarly, number 2, artifactual codes, must have meant less in 500,000 B.C. than today. There was no Dior, then, no Gucci, and if there were any cosmetics, we don't know what they were. The shaman may have worn a special costume. We can imagine an early man picking up shiny stones (in South Africa perhaps he picked up diamonds) and bringing them home to decorate his cave or hut, but art objects must have been scarce and uncommon indeed. If there was architecture, it must have been utilitarian in the case of huts or selective in the case of caves—the biggest cave with the best view over the valley where food animals might be seen in time to alert the hunters.

Look at number 4. There were no desks or telephones, of course, yet contextual codes may have conveyed important meaning earlier than we imagine. Having a parent close at hand was probably as reassuring to a child then as now. Where one stood in the presence of someone else may have been as meaningful then as now.[2] Today we find that Latin Americans and southern Europeans tend to stand closer together when they converse than North Americans and the British. Anthropologists are full of stories about what happens when representatives of these two groups try to have an important conversation—one, feeling more comfortable at a respectful distance, retreats, while the other, more comfortable at close range, presses closer, even hops over the desk or chases the first down the hall. We have no way of knowing from how long ago these behaviors have been inherited, but it may well be that the distinctions between "your space" and "my space" may be among the oldest nonverbal signals of communication.

It is evident, then, that performance codes must have been the chief source of nonverbal signs in the era before verbal language. Eliminate the signs relating to speech, and you have some idea of how humans must have communicated a half million years ago.

WHY HUMANS BECAME VERBAL

Mario Pei, in his delightful book *The Story of Language,* estimates that as many as 700,000 distinct elementary sign combinations can be produced in this way, a number which, he says, would be quite sufficient to provide the equivalent of a highly developed modern language. And he asks a question that tantalizes us as we speculate upon what happened in the dawn years of humans on earth, and also how communication might be developing on other planets: Why did human communication go the way of speech and words and language, rather than body signs and nonverbal concepts? "Granted a different historical development," Pei says, "it is conceivable that the human race might have reserved its oral passages for purposes of eating and breathing only, and developed an entirely different machinery for the transfer of meaning."[3]

There have been recent examples of unspoken language. Some North American Indian tribes developed sign language so that representatives of different tribes could sit in council together. The Boy Scouts devised a sign language of their own, based upon this Indian lingua franca, so that they could communicate during international jamborees. Deaf people learn to use sign language skillfully, and the remarkable deaf and blind child Helen Keller proved that it was possible to establish effective communication, and even to learn to write, without either sound or sight, once she discovered the magic talisman that everything had a name! The whole history of communication demonstrates how relatively easy it is to substitute one muscular combination for another and how seldom interpersonal communication depends upon a single such combination. The scholars who study extrasensory perception, far-out and unscientific though they may seem, are on the track of such an alternative development in human communication. It is their belief that the limitations of eye and ear, touch, voice, and movement may eventually be overcome by establishing relationships that require none of these traditional mechanisms.

How did humans happen to go the way of speech rather than gesture? One possible answer is that the complex and abstract content of language is easier to translate and easier to master with verbal signs than with nonverbal ones. It must be easier, for example, to learn calculus and explain the principle of indeterminacy without having to rely entirely on nonverbal symbols. Speech sounds must have added immensely greater subtlety and flexibility to the repertoire of gestures.

But there is a simpler, more practical answer: Communication by speech left both hands free. This was Darwin's explanation, and it is one of the reasons for thinking that the high point of language development may have been related to the high point of toolmaking. Furthermore, the supposed advantages of sign language for intertribal and intercultural communication may not have proved very effective in practice, for even nonverbal signs have quite different significance in different cultures, and without words it is not always easy to explain these differences. For example, an American audience is likely to hiss a performance they think is bad, whereas a European audience is likely to whistle loudly. On the other hand, an Asian audience is likely to hiss its approval of a performance. A European girl, walking down a street in America, might interpret boys' whistling at her as a sign of disapproval—unless someone had previously explained to her the significance of an American "wolf whistle." Thus the road to speech may have led away from some of the uncertainty and indefiniteness of the other road.

THE ORIGIN OF LANGUAGE

The plain truth is that we do not know why the road to speech was taken, and we have no very good way to find out. How can we study the origin of language? No primitive communities that have not yet developed language are now available for study. We can study infants before they begin to talk, of course, and there have been a few "wolf children" who are believed to have spent much of their childhood with animals rather than humans, but this is hardly the same as studying primitive humans before anyone around them had developed language. In four cases, men who were powerful enough to do this kind of thing have carried out experiments intended to show what language a child would speak if isolated entirely from human beings. These men included an Egyptian pharaoh, an Indian emperor, Frederick the Great of Prussia, and King James IV of Scotland. King James thought the child would surely begin to speak Hebrew because—he reasoned from the Bible—that was the language in which Adam and Eve communicated. Unfortunately, all four children died too early to prove anything except that infants need companionship.[4]

We can also study animal communication. In the case of intelligent animals such as dolphins, whose brains are about as large in proportion to the rest of their bodies as humans', there is some hope of being able to penetrate the interspecies difference and even to gain some idea what problems may arise, some time in the future, in trying to communicate with beings from another world. And it is evident that dolphins, and probably whales also, do communicate by means of their whistles and their sonar signals.

Actually, however, we have no real evidence on the development of human language before humans began to write it down. Sumerian language records go back somewhere between 4000 and 3500 B.C., Babylonian and Assyrian records to about 3000 B.C., Chinese to about 2000 B.C. Many culture groups have had no written language at all until missionaries or anthropologists arrived, in the eighteenth or nineteenth century, and wrote down, with some European alphabet, what they thought they heard.

One way to work back toward the origin of language is to study the earliest written records and the few archaic words and sentences quoted by early writers, and try from these to reconstruct still earlier languages. This is much like the way paleontologists have used fossil skulls or bone fragments of ancient living creatures. For example, it is now possible to say quite a bit about the Ur-language that is supposedly the parent tongue of all the Indo-European languages. Linguists accomplished this by working backward from commonalities in Sanskrit, Persian, Greek, Latin, Old German, Hindustani, and other languages on that family tree. No single fragment of the parent Indo-European language exists, but scholars think they know quite a bit about the people who used it. Apparently these people were familiar with horses, bears, and wolves; they knew snow, and pine, willow, and birch trees; they seem to have had both copper and iron. This would seem to locate ancient users of the language in the Copper-Stone Age, probably before 3000 B.C., and very likely on the Iranian plateau or the shores of the Baltic Sea. We therefore hypothesize settlers from the early Indo-European communities fanning out into southern Asia, the countries north of the Mediterranean, and ultimately all of Europe, carrying with them words, syntax, and semantics that have differentiated into tongues now spoken by more than a billion people.

But even when we carry the story back as far as ancient Indo-European, we are still very far from the origin of language. That language must already have been well developed at the earliest stage when we can conjecture anything about it. As a matter of fact, every primitive culture we can study today has a language adequate to its needs; none of them is just beginning to develop language. We have to attempt other ways to reach back toward the beginnings. One of these is to try to learn how the brain deals with language. Thus, Noam Chomsky, the M.I.T. scholar whose linguistic theories have been influential in the last two decades, believes that the language faculty of the brain is a "fixed function . . . characteristic of the species—one component of the human mind which maps experience into grammar."[5] He conceives of a "Property P" in all grammars that is a precondition of learning the language, and probably a human language faculty related to it that is genetically determined rather than learned. With the aid of this faculty, human beings can translate what they hear into a form which they can readily code and understand. If so, there must be a particular stage of development at which the human animal can handle Property P. However, there are certain problems in conceiving of a human language faculty that is genetically determined and still will work for languages as different as, say, German and Chinese. No such language faculty has been isolated.

Neurologists have been able, on the other hand, to identify the small areas in the left hemisphere of the brain that are chiefly involved in language. They are Wernicke's area, which lies at or near the region of the cortex where hearing seems to register, and Broca's area, which lies near the region that seems to be related to the speech mechanism. Damage to either area severely affects the ability to handle language. When something happens to Wernicke's area, it limits the ability to comprehend language and to a lesser extent the ability to produce language. Damage to Broca's area, which seems to recode the information received from Wernicke's into articulated form, results in poorly spoken, slow, difficult speech and grammatical inadequacies. Thus we are able to say that development of these areas must have taken place before humans could have mastered language. But all these areas of the brain seem to exist in even the most primitive people today. Perhaps more sophisticated study of ancient fossilized skulls will give us some idea when these areas developed, but as yet this hope has not been realized.

Animal studies may also be able to throw some light on questions of origin. Recent research reported from the Yerkes Regional Primate Center has suggested that cross-modal perception may be one of the first neurological developments necessary for language and speech. Apes learn quickly to match visual with tactile inputs, but monkeys do not. For example, apes that are allowed to see an object through a window and to touch two objects of different shapes that they cannot see through another opening can easily match the shape they see to the shape they touch. This ability is apparently acquired somewhere between the evolutionary stages represented by the lower and the higher primates. Further studies of the higher animals may ultimately help to establish an evolutionary cutoff point after which the language faculty is possible.

Actually, most animal vocalizations are different from human speech. The entire vocal repertoire of rhesus and squirrel monkeys can be elicited by electrical stimulation of points along the limbic system of the brain. Yet no rhesus or squirrel monkey speaks. Even though speech may have stemmed from the emotional and grammarless cries of hominoid animals, as many scholars have suggested, still by some means or other these cries had to be transferred from the brain's limbic system to the cortex, where they could be processed in the areas mentioned, before they resulted in speech. The spectacular growth of the human cortex during human-kind's million years may also yield some information on when language could have come into use.

Human language has another quality that seems to distinguish it from the vocalizations of animals. As Pei says, dogs have apparently been barking, cats meowing, lions roaring, and donkeys braying since time immemorial in about the same way.[6] But even in the few thousands of years during which we have written evidence of the nature of language, humans have constantly been devising new sounds and words, transmitting them to other members of society, constructing new sentences, and communicating new ideas and experiences in ever more sophisticated ways. Human language, in other words, seems to have the ability to evolve. Languages are born, live, and die. In fact, we suspect there are more "dead" languages than live ones—perhaps 4000 as compared to 3000. Thus the seeds of development and change seem to be born into human speech, but not into animal sounds.

Furthermore, human speech is detachable; its signs can be carried around and used to talk about something that is not present. They can be used to talk about the past that is not seen and the future that is unknown. They stand for something. Most of the social signals of the higher primates, it has been pointed out, are not semantic; they do not stand for something else. They are more like the cry of a newborn infant than they are like the speech of human adults. The remarkable thing is that something in the newborn human infant, something that we do not yet fully understand, enables it within two years to demonstrate the language faculty, and within the two years following to achieve one of the greatest intellectual accomplishments of its life: to comprehend the idea of names and the concepts of words and meanings—to learn a language.

How did human language originate? We keep returning to that question, as scholars have done for years. We think we know how present-day human infants learn a language: They imitate and are encouraged to do so, increasingly rewarded as they master social use of the language. But before there was language there were no language speakers to imitate. The time-honored theories of language origin are no more than myth dressed up in amusing names. There is, for instance, the bow-wow theory—that humans imitated sounds of the animal world and used them as language elements. That is, early humans may have called the dog a "bow-wow" or "woof-woof" or something of the kind. Left unexplained is how that developed the concept that objects have names. There is the pooh-pooh theory—that language grew out of expressions of pleasure, pain, anger, and fear like those of the other animals. But it is a long step from a scream or a growl to words differentiating, relating, and explaining those emotions. There is the yo-heave-ho theory—that language grew out of the sounds of physical exertion. There is the theory, credited first to Darwin, that language grew out of the sounds made by human animals in playing with their vocal mechanism. It makes as much sense as any of the others to conjecture that some of this playing was associated with certain events or feelings and thereafter the sounds came to be used to recall those associations. Plato believed that language came out of "inherent necessity," which doesn't explain much, and Aristotle suggested that it arose from "agreement" among people, which falls short of explaining how people without language could come together to agree on one. Each of these theories lacks one or more essential steps. How did humans, but not other animals, learn to transform their animal vocalizations into names and symbols? How did humans, but not other animals, come to feel the need to have a system of sounds that was detachable from a present situation, and how did they learn to respond to such a need?[7]

One thing we know for sure is that every human, barring severe brain damage, is born with the ability to learn a language. We can be reasonably sure that this remarkable quality did not appear suddenly. Either genetically or socially, there could hardly have been a sudden emergence of the language faculty. It must have come from a long neurological evolution and a long social evolution in a favorable learning situation.

Ashley Montagu suggests that toolmaking tied in with big-game hunting may have provided that kind of favorable situation. If so, language may have grown up slowly and gradually over a million years, or even more. This has been a fairly common estimate—that rudimentary language may be a million years old.

HUMAN LIFE AND HUMAN LANGUAGE

Julian Jaynes, a Princeton psychologist, has challenged the idea of the great antiquity of language.[8] Jaynes thinks that speech would not be necessary for transmitting the rudimentary skills of toolmaking and therefore sees no reason why highly developed language would have to have existed a million years ago. Speech might actually get in the way: This basic skill learning might better be accomplished, as children learn many skills today, by modeling and practice. A more likely time for language to appear, Jaynes thinks, would be during the fourth Ice Age, which lasted from about 70,000 B.C. to 10,000 B.C.

This was a time when history seemed really ripe for such a development, a time when speech must have had survival value. During the fourth Ice Age the bitter cold and increased frequency of migrations were challenging the very existence of human animals, forcing them to adapt to new conditions. They needed all the help they could muster. During this period, the increasing use of tools would make it desirable for humans to free their hands from gestural communication so as to be better able to work on and with tools. Migration into unfamiliar lands and northern climates, with long nights and long winters, would have made it more difficult to use visual signals. Hunting by night, living in dark caves, humans would probably find out that voice signals which may have been largely incidental to main activities might take over some of the functions of visual and tactile signals. Or so Jaynes hypothesizes. He thinks that voice signals would have assumed a new importance by the end of the Middle Pleistocene, perhaps 150,000 B.C. If speech were indeed cast in a new role, then one would expect to see a reflection of new communication in new social behavior. Jaynes finds this in the explosion of toolmaking around 40,000 B.C. Beyond that, his hypothesis requires some evidence that the human brain would have developed sufficiently, by that time, to process language. Here the hard evidence is scant, but skull measurements and evidence from behavior indicate that this stage in development must have been reached at least 100,000 years ago, perhaps much earlier. By that time the limbic functions mentioned earlier as the source of animal cries must have been in the process of being transferred to the enlarging cortex, and consequently the sounds could be used for more flexible and sophisticated purposes.

Some evidence for this comes from studies of primates and of handedness. Lesions in the areas of the cortex that are involved in human speech apparently do not impair the vocalization of monkeys, although they have very serious effects on human language. This difference implies that the transfer of some vocal functions to the cortex took place in humans before it did in some of the other primates. It is noteworthy also that the language and speech areas of the human cortex are in the left hemisphere, and that fine control of the right hand is also centered there. Most of the lower primates show no signs of hand dominance, whereas the great majority of humans are right-handed. Is it too long a leap to relate the implications of this difference to the development of human speech? Scholars (for example, Steklis, Harnad, and Lancaster) believe that they detect changes in tool design, when tools began to proliferate, which indicate that most of the newer tools seem to have been made for right-handed individuals.[9] If this is indeed the case, if there was a new emphasis on right-handedness at the time of the explosion of toolmaking in the fourth Ice Age, then there may well have been a corresponding development also of other areas in the left hemisphere, and this development would probably include the linguistic control centers.

So Jaynes's hypotheses have a certain face validity, and they suggest a long slow development of human speech and language followed by a dramatic advance in the years of the fourth Ice Age.

Jaynes's theories concerning the process of language development are at least as far from the typical beliefs as are his conclusions concerning the time of development. The usual concept has been that names came first. Give an object a name, and that name can be carried around in place of the object so that one can talk about it rather than having to point to it. Therefore the utility of language would become quickly apparent. But Jaynes sees it happening another way. The first long step toward language, he believes, was the modification of existing cries to carry special meanings. "Imagine a cave dweller screaming 'wahee!' at the approach of a sabre-tooth tiger," said the report of the meeting at which Jaynes detailed his theory. "The intensity of such a signal would probably correspond to the intensity of the danger—perhaps in its ending phoneme. . . . The sight of a distant tiger might result in a much less intense cry and a different ending, such as the more relaxed 'wahoo.' It is these endings [Jaynes thinks] that became the first modifiers meaning near and far. And the next step toward syntactic language would be separating the endings from one particular cry and attaching them to another with the same indication."

The next stage, he believes, would be the age of commands. These could have been modifiers separated from the cries they modified. To any hunting party the usefulness of a new cry like "ee" to mean "come nearer," and a cry like "oo" to mean "go farther away" would be obvious. After commands would come nouns—animal or life nouns probably first, then names of things, finally people names—and after them, verbs and other parts of speech and ever more varied sentences.

Jaynes estimates that the age of modifiers lasted until about 46,000 B.C., when the development of superior tools became evident. The age of nouns may have coincided with the cave paintings of animals, about 20,000 B.C., and the mysterious scratchings on the walls of these caves that have been interpreted by some scholars as humans' first attempts at writing. Names of things may have come into use with the development of pottery, pendants, and ornaments, and names of people must have been in common use by the time ceremonial burials became common, perhaps not long after 10,000 B.C. This time scheme, as we have said, is quite different from earlier estimates, but at present Jayne's ideas make as much sense as any dealing with the early history of language.

WHERE HUMAN LANGUAGE DEVELOPED

We are not yet able to say with any confidence whether human language developed in only one place. Gottfried Leibnitz was one of the first modern scholars to advance the hypothesis of a single parent tongue,[10] but others also have contended that the story of the Tower of Babel, whether literally true or not, was at least a metaphor for what actually happened. They believe there was a single protolanguage that all people used until they moved apart and their speech became less and less intelligible between groups. These scholars support this position chiefly with two kinds of evidence—the existence of language families, indicating interrelation and increasing differentiation, and a series of extraordinary resemblances in pairs of languages where there may be reason to suspect historical contact. For instance, the mysterious pre-Japanese Ainu language, spoken by only a few thousand persons whose ancestors were apparently on the Japanese islands before the Japanese, calls the number 80 "four twenties," precisely as does the French language—*quatre-vingt*. The word *puss,* or some near equivalent, is used to refer to a cat not only in Europe, but also in Arabia, North Africa, and southern India. And today Polynesian children on the islands of Samoa use an elementary school reading book entitled *O le Pusi Uliuli*—or *The Black Cat.*

The most common viewpoint today, however, is that, whereas human beings may have come into being in one place (Africa is now the most commonly suggested birthplace), language probably developed in more than one place on earth and a comparatively few parent languages each fathered a large number of offspring. We have already mentioned the Indo-European group, which is the largest family of languages on earth although it does not have the largest number of people as members. The largest number of language users belongs to the Sino-Tibetan family, and the largest number of speakers of any language speak Chinese. Another large family includes the Arabic and Semitic languages; another, the Slavic tongues of the Soviet Union; still another, the Dravidian languages of southern India. Certain other language groups do not fit into any of the large families. Among these, to mention an example or two, are the ancient languages of Australia, Malay, and some of the Pacific islands. The present map of languages, therefore, seems to favor at least a small number of independent language births, although a single dramatic Babelian division could have happened—less likely in one afternoon than in tens or hundreds of thousands of years.

Despite the climate of uncertainty over the early history of human language, there are certain things about the chronicle of humans and language that can be said with confidence. One of these is that language is a living, growing, changing organism. Ralph Waldo Emerson called it "a city to the building of which every human being brought a stone." All of us contribute to it by our daily utterances and our responses to the utterances of others. We live with language change, although it is sometimes hard to see unless one can look back at what was written several centuries ago or listen to a recording from long ago. The more sedentary, the less mobile a community, the less change takes place in its language. The more mobile it is, the more it borrows and adapts. Overall, the rate of change in human languages in the last several thousand years has been extraordinary. The language spoken in England not more than a thousand years ago is a foreign language to English speakers today. Someone has said that the English left a different language in each country they colonized, and this has obviously been not because they brought different languages, but because the language changed in use. George Bernard Shaw was being only partly facetious when he remarked that England and America are "two countries separated by a common language."

Would language changes be less or more today if there had not been the enormous acceleration of travel and communication since the Renaissance? It is hard to say. Were it not for the sharp and subtle tool of language, there would probably never have been the developments that accelerated travel and the world-wide expansion of telecommunications, satellites, computer circuits, broadcasting, and, of course, print. The nations of the world have been moving closer together. On the one hand, this should encourage the languages to move closer together, to share words and phrases and to have more bilinguals. On the other hand, it should encourage more change in any given language.

Perhaps we have been wrong in emphasizing the things we do not know about language at the cost of things we think we do know. Whether human language developed very early, as Montagu thinks, or mostly in the last 70,000 years, as Jaynes believes, is not really the essential matter. Whether it took place when humans learned to distinguish the endings of cries like "wahee" and "wahoo" is not of great importance. What is important is that of all the steps humans took in the million-year climb up the mountains of communication, language was the longest one and had the greatest effect. It gave us a better way to receive, process, store, retrieve, and communicate information. It gave us a better tool with which to think and therefore to gain an advantage over competitors. For the last million

When symbols like these began to appear, humans were in a second chapter of language development. These are Egyptian hieroglyphs carved in wood, sometime around 3000 B.C.

years Planet Earth's thinking animals have been locked in combat with time and space, natural forces, and other animals. Humans found that one of the greatest weapons was information. We chose, purposely or unwittingly, a path that led us toward making information readily portable and preservable, transportable farther than we ourselves could go, conservable for our fellows and inheritable by our children. Every major step along this path has brought a major change in our way of living. The history of language and, indeed, of communication in general has therefore been less a history of technology than a social history of the long march of humankind and society.

SUGGESTIONS FOR FURTHER READING

One of the most readable books in an extensive literature on the development of language is Mario Pei, *The Story of Language,* rev. ed. (Philadelphia: Lippincott, 1965). Another useful title is Philip Lieberman, *On the Origin of Language: An Introduction to the Origin of Human Speech* (New York: Macmillan, 1975). A 914-page collection of papers, many of them on language development, is *Origins and Evolution of Language and Speech,* edited by S. R. Harnad, H. D. Steklis, and Jane Lancaster (New York: *Annals of the New York Academy of Science,* vol. 280, 1975). Two older classics are Otto Jespersen, *Language, Its*

Nature, Development, and Origin (New York: Henry Holt, 1922); and Edward Sapir, *Language: An Introduction to the Study of Speech* (New York: Harcourt Brace Jovanovich, 1921).

QUESTIONS TO THINK ABOUT

1. What must have been the limits on human communication before language was developed?
2. Why, do you think, did humans take the verbal rather than the nonverbal route in developing their language?
3. What do you see as the advantages and disadvantages of an alphabetical versus a nonalphabetical language?
4. Some scholars believe that human language originated in one place on earth, others that it originated in more than one place. What is your opinion?
5. Hogben gives a sample of a section of an intelligence test once used in England, which illustrates some of the problems that scholars have in trying to understand a language for which they have no dictionary or interpreter. You might like to try solving this "unknown" language. Here is the test:

> The sentences below are in a foreign language, and their meanings are given in English. In each English sentence a word is underlined, and you have to underline the word which corresponds to it in the foreign sentence. You can do this by comparing the sentences with each other. . . . Notice that the foreign words are not always in the same order as the English words.

Ek piyala chae.	A cup of <u>tea</u>.
Yih chae bahut achchhi hai.	This <u>is</u> very good tea.
Chae bilkul taiyar hai.	Tea is <u>quite</u> ready.
Kab taiyar karoge?	When <u>shall</u> you make <u>ready</u>?
Main bahut pyasa hun.	I am <u>very</u> thirsty.
Bahut achchhi hai.	It is very <u>good</u>.
Yih mera rumal nahin hai.	<u>This</u> is not my handkerchief.

TIME CAPSULE

Homo habilis (e.g., Leakey discoveries)	2,000–1,000*
Hand axes	900
Java man	600–500
Fire	500
Peking man	500–400
Neanderthal man in Europe	70–35
Great burst of activity in toolmaking, art, agriculture, etc.	50–?

*All these figures are in thousands of years ago.

Homo sapiens sapiens (modern humans)	30–?
Cro-Magnons (including the cave painters in Europe)	25–10
Height of painting at	
Lascaux	15
Altamira	12
Drakensberg (the White Lady)	9
Fired pottery	7
Bronze Age	5.5

An Egyptian scribe. The young man who modeled for this statue was probably one of the first professionally educated people in the history of human communication. He undoubtedly had gone to scribe school, where he learned to read and write letters and documents for others. He kept records of the government, of families, and of transactions; he wrote down the history of the nation; and recorded laws, legends, and lessons. In other words, he had been trained to use what was perhaps the greatest human invention—writing.

THE INVENTION OF WRITING

Writing is the memory of the ages of man.
MAURICE FABRE, A HISTORY OF COMMUNICATIONS

The ink of the scholar is more sacred than the blood of the martyr.
MUHAMMAD

*I*n the last 14 minutes (cosmic time) of humankind's day on earth, two things happened that made a great difference in human communication. The first was related to communication but to other social forces also; it was the establishment of villages, and later of cities, where the situation was favorable for communication to develop rapidly. The second was one of the major changes in communication: the invention of writing.

FROM HUNTING AND GATHERING TO VILLAGES AND AGRICULTURE

For most of their million years on earth humans had been hunters and gatherers. They ate a high-protein diet of wild animals and fish, supplemented by such wild berries, fruits, and grains as they could find. It was a hard life. Much of their time was spent hunting or moving from hunting ground to hunting ground. On the other hand, it was exciting—much more so than tending the crops on a farm. Today's popularity of hunting as recreation gives us an idea of how Mesolithic people, after they became farmers, must have missed the old days.[1]

Even in the hunting and gathering period some humans had begun to domesticate animals. The first such animal was probably the dog, which came from the wolf family. It would have been interesting to see how Paleolithic humans went about taming these first wild creatures. Domestication of cattle also began rather early, for cattle could be easily captured around the water holes and streams where humans as well as animals drank. Cows were apparently not the first milk animals, however. That distinction went to the goat which, like the sheep, is supposed to have originated in Asia. As time passed, therefore, some of the families and tribes of hunters and gatherers supported themselves partly as shepherds, driving their animals with them between hunts. This arrangement had the special advantage of making meat or milk protein available to them when hunting was bad or winter immobilized them. And when the time came to move into villages, they found that some of their domestic animals could help them plow the soil.

Thus, in the last 10,000 of humankind's million years, additional kinds of living patterns began to be seen among these early humans. There were the hunters and gatherers, as there had been for centuries. There were groups who were full- or part-time shepherds. Still others belonged to what has been called the hoe culture, meaning that they farmed very small plots of land though without the help of plows or draft animals. The yield from their gardens was not very large, and there was always the conflict between the need to hunt, the need to farm, and the need to defend against scavenging birds and vegetarian animals. Then, not long after 8000 B.C., the first villages began to appear—in Iranian, Arabian, Syrian, Armenian, and North African areas where previously there had been only hunters and gatherers.

The cultural and psychological impact of settling an early village was significant. The hunter-gatherer groups or tribes had ranged in size from less than a dozen to a hundred or more. A typical village would range in size from several hundred up to several thousand. Therefore, more people saw more of each other than they had been accustomed to see in the old hunting days. More communication went on. More people did the same things, and therefore had more common experiences to talk about. Village people traveled less and hunted less often than the smaller tribal groups had done. Because they spent more time together they began to develop new social institutions and arrangements. A village of several hundred needed a government. A village of several hundred would find a school easier to establish than would a tribe of a dozen or two. Hunters and gatherers owned very little personal property—the animal skins they wore, their spears and axes, but very little else. Most other property was held in common. In the village, however, it became important to keep a record of who owned what. When fears about intermarriage began to surface, it became important to keep records of family genealogies. When farming began to produce the bulk of the village food, it became useful to know the day of the year so that the best planting days would not be missed. In other words, moving into the village created more uses for communication, and more communication encouraged more institutions and cooperative arrangements that in turn encouraged still more communication.

This was the setting out of which writing emerged. This, and the ancient roots of behavior that humans brought with them out of the dim centuries when they were fighting for survival among other animals. If we search for the ancient base of writing we are likely to find it in the human search for a memory that would be better than one's own. There is very little evidence that writing was either sought or used at first to send messages far away. Rather it was needed and sought after to keep the record. Before there was writing, the knowledge that made hunting more efficient—the record of the tribe, the wisdom of the wisest, the skills of the most skillful—were passed from generation to generation only by word of mouth and example. If they were to endure, someone had to remember them. History, as Fabre pointed out so eloquently, was the remembered word.[2]

But who remembered? The archives, the libraries, the encyclopedias, existed only in the memories of the aged. The role of "Rememberer" for the group must have been one of great importance among all preliterate humans. It is important even today among people who do not have a long written tradition. Alex Haley, in *Roots,* tells how his quest for information about his ancestors led him to old people in Africa who could recite from memory 20 generations of the members of a family.[3] Anthropologists who studied the Pacific islands near the beginning of this century found people on those islands who could recall a chief's ancestors for hundreds of years, along with each generation's accomplishments and troubles. Religious persons in the Indian subcontinent recite verse after verse from the holy books for hour after hour, almost without end.

THE INVENTION OF WRITING TO REPLACE THE MEMORY ROLE

The ability to retain and pass along the archives of a people was neither a casual skill nor a responsibility casually conferred. Individuals must have been carefully selected and painstakingly prepared for memory roles. The American Indians gave the task to their shamans or priests. The Polynesians intensively trained the young who were to be given custody of legends, myths, prayers, and family records. They had to pass examinations, and indeed faced an examination from every audience, because the faculty of oral memory was valued by everyone, and no one hesitated to compare his or her memory of the legendary or ancestral past with that of the official Rememberer. Eskimo shamans and African healers were depended on to remember the magic of the culture, the formulas to cure illness, and the incantations to bring rain, success in hunting or fishing, or victory in battle.

If you have ever thought of the early centuries of humans as quiet, disabuse yourself of that notion. They must have resounded with voices of rememberers and reciters, storytellers and teachers, just as life today is full of the sights and sounds of the mass media. The earliest written works that have come down to us are also full of such voices. Much of the Old Testament of the Hebrew scriptures is made of the stories, sermons, and poems of narrators and preachers, many of whose names were lost before their words were committed to paper. The *Iliad* and *Odyssey* reveal their origin in oral literature, and the Anglo-Saxon epic *Beowulf* is so close to the oral tradition that there is even confusion between two *Beowulfs* that must have come from different but parallel traditions. Students of many early cultures have been amazed by the number and variety, sometimes by the contradictions, of tales and legends that have come down to the present through hundreds or thousands of years of repetition. For example, 200,000 to 250,000 stories have been recovered from the African oral tradition.

The long yearning for a usable memory, then, was among the pillars on which the invention of writing was built. Another was the art of what we have called the prehistoric renaissance. Whether or not any of the scratchings on the cave walls beside the pictures were really attempts at writing, the skills developed by artists in that time clearly pointed the way toward the skill of writing. And because much writing began with pictures—pictographs—the representational art of the cave painters was on the main road to the development of writing.

THE EMERGENCE OF WRITING

Representational art was not the only road, however. The nonrepresentational decorations on the tools also provided some examples to be copied in early writing. Not all written symbols grew out of representation of things. Some things could not be drawn pictorially; therefore, more abstract symbols came to be used where more appropriate. Other sets of symbols grew out of the early need to count and measure. Our surviving use of *foot* as a linear measure, and of *hand* as a measure of the height of animals, suggests one of the early ways humans went about designing units of measurement.

Our calculus textbooks still carry an echo of ancient mathematics, for *calculus* comes from the Latin word for pebble, and a handful or sackful of pebbles was undoubtedly one of the first mathematical remembering machines. Another such device was a notched stick, and our surviving pattern of tallying by fives—卌— is a way of recording numbers whose origin probably came from notches on sticks. Even today some Chinese numbers suggest this same origin: for example, — =

☰, meaning 1, 2, 3. Another way of recording numbers was to tie knots in a string. Before he marched away on a difficult mission against the Scythians, Darius gave his Ionian soldiers a strap with 60 knots in it. He told them to untie one knot each day. If he had not returned by the time they undid the sixtieth knot, they were to sail home without him. The practice of knotting a string was developed to such a level of complexity by some of the early Indian people of Peru—using colored threads in different combinations and knots of different kinds in different combinations—that a special caste of knot readers was required to interpret the messages.

By all odds the most impressive things humans left behind them on their path to writing were the astronomical observatories and calendars found all over the peopled world, from China to England, Egypt to Scandinavia, Australia to the Andes. It may seem strange that humans, before they had writing, were nevertheless good enough astronomers to build a Stonehenge in southern England where the sun casts a shadow exactly on the line of two marker stones when it rises on the morning of the summer solstice, or to design the prototype of a temple at Karnak where the sun shines directly down the main avenue of columns as it sets on the evening of the summer solstice, or to make a lunar calendar of 360 days and measure a solar year of 364.25 days.[4]

As we rediscover with every generation, an illiterate is not necessarily stupid. The centuries during which writing was struggling to be born were not dull, uneventful, or unproductive. They now look rather empty on the pages of history, but that is because no one was writing the history on those pages. They may have seemed uneventful when communities of toolmakers huddled together against the cold of the Ice Age, but to the historian of human communications, those years seem surprisingly active. Pictures were appearing in caves; new technology was being carved into tools; masks were proclaiming totems and magic; Karnak and Stonehenge and less elaborate creations were keeping the calendar; symbols of counting were in use and obviously being used; Rememberers, custodians of information, were quite properly among the most important members of society. And then, about 5500 years ago, humans had an insight into written communication similar in quality to the insight that resulted in language. The earlier insight had told us that everything could have a name, represented by a sound, and that other sounds could be used to establish relationships among names. The later insight suggested that every name could have a picture or some other kind of pictorial symbol to represent it, and that humans could learn what sound these pictorial symbols stood for, and thus read language in them. Once this step was reached, the rest of the lingual development process was mostly mechanical. Humans had invented the idea of writing and reading.[5]

RELATIONSHIP BETWEEN EARLY WRITING AND PICTURES

Most, but not all, early writing came directly from picture making. As we shall see, the further writing developed, the less representational it became, and the more nonrepresentational symbols were co-opted for it. Some language systems—like the runes used by the early Celtic population of Britain—were not pictorial at all, but simply sound codes, as unrepresentational as telegraphy. But the earliest forms of written language were largely derived from pictures. The earliest well-developed system of writing seems to have been cut with a wedge-shaped tool in clay tablets. The center of this kind of work was Assyria, and it dates back to approximately 3500 B.C. Four hundred years later, hieroglyphs came into use in Egypt. For the most part, these were painted or drawn on papyrus, a paperlike substance made from a plant that grew along the Nile. These two systems are the most famous examples of what we have come to call pictographic writing, although pictographs have been found in many places throughout the world.

A pictograph has three distinguishing qualities. Like the cave paintings it is a picture of an object, although stylized and simplified so that it can be drawn or carved quickly. Second, a pictograph abstracts meaning from the picture. For example, a pictograph of an arrow or a spear does not necessarily refer only to that tool; it may be used to convey the idea of threat or conflict in general. Third, a pictograph usually represents a sound.

Thus, for example, a hieroglyph of a bird with long wings apparently stood for the sound *pa* as you will see from the illustration. It would have been theoretically possible to develop either hieroglyphs or cuneiform to the point where they could represent all spoken language apart from the pictures they carried. However, neither cuneiform nor hieroglyphs became a true alphabet. This development took place a little later, in neighboring countries on the eastern shore of the Mediterranean.

Nevertheless, the evolution of all early languages was from pictographs toward less representational symbolic coding, as the illustrations show. Consider the evolution of Assyrian cuneiform in the illustration. Originally the fish was quite realistic, as were the head, food, and water. But it was not easy to cut realistic pictures with a wedge in clay. Furthermore, it took too long. You can see from the figure what happened. The pictographs became less realistic, and some of them were combined. You will notice that the signs for head and food were combined so as to mean *eat,* but even these signs were hard to recognize at a later stage.

The same progression from realism to symbolic coding can be seen in the evolution of Chinese writing, which came into use about 2000 B.C. and has outlasted all other forms of picture writing. Notice how the primitive picture of the mountains gradually loses its pictorial quality over the centuries, but retains even to the present the upward thrust of the lines and the three peaks. And see how

Hieroglyphic

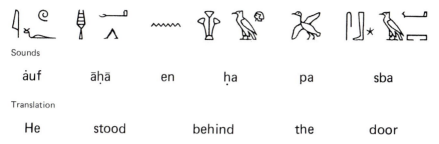

Sounds					
áuf	āḥā	en	ḥa	pa	sba

Translation					
He	stood	behind	the	door

Hieroglyphic characters, sounds, and translation.

the rain picture gradually loses detail but still suggests a sky and small particles. You will remember the weather forecast symbols on some modern pictographs, which we all readily understand.

Pictographic writing is far ahead of pictures for rapid communication, because it is simplified and units can be combined to require less drawing. For example, instead of drawing five men or five eagles, the writer can combine the symbol for man or eagle with the symbol for five, and do the job with two characters rather than five or ten. In place of having to draw one pictorial figure for cow and one for bull, the Chinese found it possible to combine a symbol for the bovine family with a highly stylized male or female symbol. The bovine symbol at that stage of the language looked like this: Ψ (the horns can be clearly seen). The male symbol was ⅃ (not too far from the biologic male symbol ♂). Combined, the result was Ψ⅃ = *bull*.

CHARACTERS, SYLLABARIES, AND ALPHABETS

These new forms of writing were an enormous advance upon communication by pictures or knots or drums or even the spoken word alone, because they could be saved through time and sent through distance. Consequently, anyone desiring a government career in Egypt or Assyria had to learn to write. The wedge-shaped cuneiform characters provided a memory for the history, science, and literature of one part of the Middle East, and grew into the great library of Babylon. The successors to hieroglyphs provided a memory for Egyptian learning and grew into the great library of Alexandria. Chinese writing proved to be a national treasure beyond price, because it held that large and diverse nation together for thousands of years in a condition of remarkable stability; every literate Chinese read the same

Original pictograph	Pictograph in position of later cuneiform	Early cuneiform	Classic Assyrian	Meaning
				heaven god
				earth
				man
				pudenda woman
				mountain
				mountain woman slave–girl
				head
				mouth to speak
				food
				to eat
				water in
				to drink
				to go to stand
				bird
				fish
				ox
				cow
				barley grain
				sun day
				to plow to till

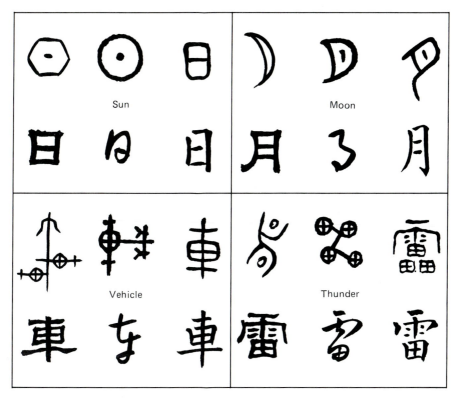

How Chinese characters developed from pictographs to modern forms. The sun and moon are obvious; the "vehicle" may be something like a chariot.

language and thus had access to the same culture even though spoken Chinese differentiated into dialects that kept Cantonese speakers from understanding spoken Mandarin, and Mandarin speakers in the Beijing area from understanding Cantonese.

Two great cultures in different parts of the world developed pictographs, and from these and other sources languages grew which humans could learn to read efficiently. But there was still another step to be taken in the evolution of modern languages. For Western languages, especially, it was necessary to develop alphabets.

The pattern has always been the same whenever an alphabet has come into

---

The evolution of Assyrian cuneiform. All systems of writing followed the same general path of development from pictographs to symbolic characters. This was cuneiform writing impressed on clay tablets and is therefore a bit more difficult to make realistic, but even so some of the early patterns remain.

being. First there were descriptive devices independent of language. These were the cave paintings, grave monuments, trail markers, masks, knots, and the like. The second step was the development of pictographs—pictures representing sounds. When each pictograph came to represent a sound as well as an object or an attribute of the object, then it was possible by means of the stylized characters (most of them no longer looking much like pictographs) to represent and recall the sounds of the spoken language. When the written language had developed to the point where each sign represented the sound of a spoken syllable, then another step toward an alphabet could be taken: the making of a syllabary. A syllabary had certain obvious advantages. Fewer signs were necessary; rather than having a new symbol for each

Another illustration of the development of Chinese writing from pictures to characters. Notice that the character meaning mountain *retains the three peaks of the original.*

word, a limited number of syllable sounds could be combined to make any number of words. Cuneiform writing turned into a syllabary. So did Phoenician, Hebrew, Aramaic, and other Mediterranean writing related to the Egyptian. So also did the Hittite that gave rise to the Aegean syllabaries—the long-mysterious Linear A and B of Crete, the Cypriot-Minoan, and others. When the people of Japan took over the already venerable Chinese word signs, they too made a syllabary of them. By this time, invention was under way on many fronts, with numerous people working on the same idea. In 1700 B.C., the alphabet was an idea whose time had come, like printing from alphabetical metal type in the fourteenth and fifteenth centuries and the telephone in the 1870s.

By 1550 B.C. there was evidence of alphabetical writing among the Canaanites, Phoenicians, and Hebrews. The importance of these new forms was not the creation of a system of letter signs (we have perhaps put too much emphasis on that), but rather the *idea* of the alphabet—that each phoneme, each smallest sound of the spoken language could be represented by one letter sign and thus the whole language could be written by combining relatively few signs. Greek had 24 such signs; Latin, 23; the present "Roman" alphabet used for English, 26. Some languages require 30-plus signs; others (notably Pacific island languages), as few as 14. The power of the alphabet idea can be illustrated by the fact that a Chinese child (whose language has no alphabet) must master thousands of signs; a syllabary requires hundreds; an alphabet, 20 or 30.

In its pure form, therefore, one sign of an alphabet always represents one sound, and always the same sound. In practice, this purity has not been maintained. This is nowhere more evident than in English, where dialect changes and literary formalism together have corrupted the principle of one letter, one sound. As a result the language has become harder to read than formerly, and dozens of innovators have been led to propose reformed spelling and reformed alphabets. George Bernard Shaw has been said to be responsible for the tongue-in-cheek suggestion that the word *fish* might quite properly be spelled *ghoti*—*gh* as in *enough, o* as in *women,* and *ti* as in *action!*[6]

The Phoenicians, Canaanites, and Hebrews used no vowels in their alphabets. The Greeks, with their clear and systematic thinking, introduced vowels into the alphabet they borrowed (apparently from the Phoenicians) so as to leave no doubt which vowel sound was intended. By the time the poems of Homer were written down, about 800 B.C., they were put into an alphabet which, with only slight changes, the schoolchildren of Western countries have used ever since. Through the Greek Catholic church, this same alphabet was adapted for the Slavic languages and became the Cyrillic alphabet of Russia and eastern Europe. Thus today we can read the writings of Lenin, the newspaper *Le Monde* of Paris, road directions in Brazil, advertisements in North America, the Maori Bible in

THE ALPHABET

EGYPTIAN	SINAITIC	PHOENICIAN	ARAMAIC	KHAROSTHI	HEBREW	SABAEAN	BRAHMI	GREEK	LATIN	ENGLISH
					א			Λ	A	A
					ב	ח		β	B	B
					ג			Γ	CG	CG
					ד			Δ	D	D
					ה			E	E	E
								Γ	F,V	F,V
								I		Z
					ח			B	H	H
		⊗	⊗				⊙	⊗		(Th)
								S	I	I,J
								K		K
								L	L	L
								M	M	M
							⊥	N	N	N
								X	X	(X)
					ע			O	O	O
								Γ	P	P
								M		(S)
					ק			φ	Q	Q
					ר			P	R	R
					ש			ξ	S	S
					ת			T	T	T

A parade of alphabets over time and distance. Some of the relationships are quite obvious. For example, the Egyptian hieroglyphs that foreshadowed English H and O are quite similar to the later forms.

New Zealand, and a government notice in Kenya, all printed in letter signs that can claim descent from the pictographs of Egypt, the syllabaries of Phoenicia, and the alphabet of Greece.

THE GREATEST HUMAN INVENTION

There were countless fascinating side trips from the road we have been following. For example, there was the choice of reading from left to right, right to left, or both. The earliest Greek writing followed the Phoenician (as do Arabic and Hebrew today) in reading from right to left. Then, about the sixth century B.C., perhaps with the intention of making reading easier on the eyes, the Greeks adopted for a short time the method of reading alternately from left to right and right to left. They called it *boustrophedon*——"as the ox plows." As in plowing, at the end of every line that had been read from left to right, the reader would find that the next line had been written from right to left. This did not last long, for reasons that can be imagined. But why thereafter the Greeks wrote exclusively from left to right, a custom in which they were followed by all who adapted their alphabet, is something we do not know. The Chinese for centuries wrote in columns down the page, beginning at the right side of the page and moving column by column to the left. Until recently, their books have begun where Western readers would have expected the back cover to be. Since 1949, however, the People's Republic of China has downplayed both the down-the-page and the right-to-left customs and is mostly printing in horizontal lines, like the West, left to right.

What does this 20,000-year history (which Hogben appropriately called "From Cave Painting to Comic Strip"), and particularly the decisions about use of an alphabet, mean to humans?[7]

Clearly one result of developing alphabetical writing was to win a victory for the verbal as opposed to the pictorial element in the language. Therefore it is interesting to look at the history of human communication in larger perspective and ask whether the great expansion of pictorial communication in the twentieth century has now, after so many centuries, swung the pendulum back from the word to the picture. And if the development of alphabetic, verbal writing in the years after 1700 B.C. made so much difference in human social history, can we expect any comparable effect from a reversal?

These questions can be postponed for now, but let us consider another topic about which we have perhaps said too little: the communication history of China, where language and writing developed in a different way from that of the European and Mediterranean nations, and where the evolution of writing went only as far as word signs. The handicaps of stopping the evolution at that point are obvious. They may be suggested by a few comparisons. An English-language typewriter with 44 keys can write any English sentence, including all the letters, numbers, and punctuation marks. A Chinese typewriter, to carry out a similar job in the Chinese language, would need to command at least 8000 or 9000 characters or their equivalent. Even with this resource, the typewriter could produce only about one-fourth the words in a typical Chinese dictionary. Western schoolchildren can learn the alphabet in a few days, read elementary material in a year, and write fairly well in two or three years. Chinese students spend much of their time for many years learning to read and write their language. Their calligraphy is not merely utilitarian, like Western schoolchild writing; it aims at being an art form. And if they want to master classical Chinese literature, they face nearly a lifetime of study.

But this is not the whole story. Chinese writing has retained enough of the pictorial element to make the experience essentially different from that of reading

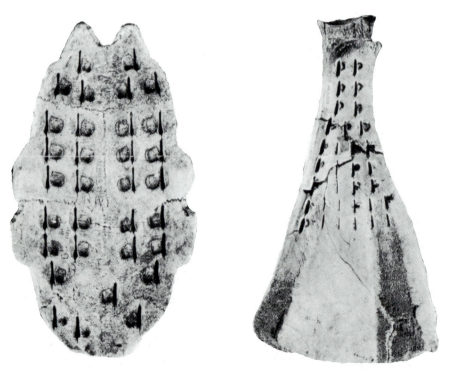

The earliest Chinese writing available to us is on oracle bones, *used by soothsayers of the Shang dynasty (1766–1122 B.C.) to foretell the future. The bones were put into a fire and consequently cracked; a prophecy was made from the characters through which the crack passed.*

a European language. That is to say, Chinese writing is more than an adaptation of the spoken tongue. A Chinese, hearing a word sound, may well have to consider what word sign it refers to. There are only approximately 300 syllabic sounds in Chinese, but most of them are represented by more than one written character. If the same sound is represented by more than one word sign, each word sign will have a different meaning. Thus, for example, two Chinese whose family names are pronounced in the same way and transliterated with the same combination of letters into English may have quite different written names in Chinese. Even another Chinese cannot distinguish the names without seeing them written out. When, say, a foreign man comes to China to live for a time, he is often given a Chinese name that sounds somewhat like his English language name, but to the Chinese people around him his manufactured Chinese name will have a special meaning because of its associations with the ideographs that are used for it. In other words, the writing itself carries an important part of the meaning of the language and consequently contributes to the richness of the experience of reading.

One can reflect also upon the social result of a system of word signs like Chinese writing. The Phoenician-Greek-Aramaic alphabet makes it relatively easy for written languages to differentiate into dialects, because the spoken tongue is in command and the written signs follow easily and flexibly the changes in spoken language. But, as we have suggested, the written language of China, difficult though it is to learn to read and write, has been an element of solidarity for its people. It resisted change. The speech of north China and of south China came to sound quite different, but both north and south Chinese *read* the same language. Fabre suggests another effect of the alphabet-less nature of Chinese. "The complexity and static nature of the Chinese script," he says, "was reflected for thousands of years in the formal, tradition-bound, serene life of the Celestial empire."[8] In other words, he is suggesting that the signs humans write affect the values and standards they live by.

This is really an early version of the Whorf-Sapir hypothesis,[9] that what humans know and feel depends on the language from which they learn. Whether or not that hypothesis can be confirmed in the case of China, there is no doubt that writing itself, the system, the skill, the art of writing, has enormously affected human life. With language and writing in hand, humans had paid the tuition for their own education. "Civilization is not evolution," Hogben wrote in one of his most provocative passages. "It is the record of the self-education of one of the most highly teachable members of the brute creation."[10] The invention of writing provided a long-term memory for these teachable animals. Thus they could conserve their intellectual resources, save what needed to be saved without having to keep all the details in their heads, and devote their major energies to advancing knowledge. Furthermore, writing gave humans an efficient way to share their knowledge, to pool their insights and discoveries, so that all people could begin to climb from the highest step any of them had previously reached. More humans could take part in discovery; more could profit from self-education. No longer would human animals have to spend most of their time in a cave, wondering what was out there beyond the firelight.

SUGGESTIONS FOR FURTHER READING

A very useful book on the Bronze Age in general is Leonard Woolley, *The Beginnings of Civilization,* second volume in the UNESCO History of Mankind (New York: Harper & Row, 1965). An old favorite in this same area is Ralph Turner, *The Great Cultural Traditions* (New York: McGraw-Hill, 1941). On the development of writing, specifically, see David Diringer, *The Alphabet: A Key to the History of Mankind,* 3rd ed. (New York: Funk & Wagnalls, 1968); also Oscar Ogg, *The 26 Letters* (New York: Crowell, 1948). Especially good on the families of writing is H. Jensen, *Sign, Symbol, and Script* (New York and London: Allen and Unwin, 1970).

QUESTIONS TO THINK ABOUT

1. "Once writing came into existence, urbanization became possible." Can you explain this?
2. What must have been some of the first uses that human society made of writing?
3. How would you go about designing a typewriter for a language (like Chinese) that has no alphabet?
4. You probably remember that *boustrophedon* writing was used for a while in Greece and other places around the Mediterranean. This is a kind of writing in which lines run alternately from left to right and right to left. The name comes from the Greek word for an ox plowing a field. Why, do you suppose, was that style abandoned after a century or so?
5. It has been said that there was improvement in self-reliance with the invention of writing. Why should this be the case?

TIME CAPSULE

"Neolithic revolution"	50,000*
End of fourth Ice Age	8,000
Agriculture, village formation	8,000–6,000
Cities in Sumer	4,500
Bronze Age	3,500
Earliest known writing	3,500
Cities in Egypt	3,300
Scribe schools flourish	3,000

*These dates are years B.C.

Papyrus begins to replace clay tablets for writing	2,500
Phonetic alphabet	1,580
First book-length writing, Egyptian *Book of the Dead*	1,350
Public library in Athens	530
Parchment, vellum used for writing	200
First publishing house (handwritten books), in Rome	100

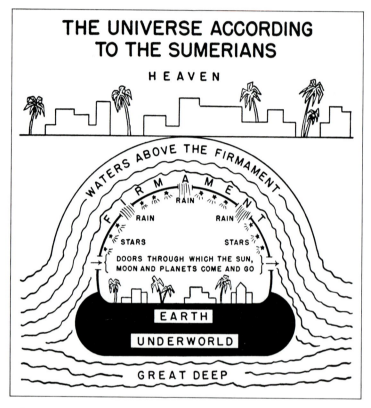

What the universe looked like to the Sumerians. Apparently the first people to use writing, they established some of the first great cities and one of the first school systems.

INSTITUTIONS OF COMMUNICATION: THE CITY

Mind takes form in the city.

LEWIS MUMFORD, THE CULTURE OF CITIES

The city functions as the special organ of social transmission.

PATRICK GEDDES AND VICTOR BRADFORD

*F*or thousands of years before there were any cities, towns, or villages, small family and tribal groups wandered the earth, avoiding large fierce animals and finding shelter, water, and hunting grounds where they could. Some of them made homes in caves, more of them in woodlands. They manned lookouts to spot animals and enemies. They moved away from the arctic ice and the winter weather. Many of them became nomads, traveling fairly regular routes each summer and winter with their few domesticated pack or food animals. Some such groups learned to plant and cultivate small gardens along the route, and after a long time, a few of them began to stay with their gardens and establish small villages where water, hunting grounds, and lookouts were plentiful.

What such a Neolithic village looked like can be seen in a recent exhibit in the Smithsonian Institution in Washington, D.C. It describes an oasis in an area that is part of present-day Jordan, not far east of the Dead Sea. The oasis, called Babh-elh-Dra, was famous for its good water. Caravans would stop there, perhaps spend a night or two, and then move on. Just before 3000 B.C., however, one group decided to move into Babh-elh-Dra, not to visit but to stay. They cultivated fields around the oasis, acquired farm animals, built huts, and maintained a village for a thousand years. Then Babh-elh-Dra passed from human records, the farms went back to desert, houses crumbled and disappeared. But archaeologists discovered the site where the village had been, and the Smithsonian reconstructed it in miniature from the remaining walls and artifacts so that visitors could see what a Stone Age village looked like.

FROM CAVE TO VILLAGE TO CITY

The feature that distinguished a village like Babh-elh-Dra from the camps occupied by similar people along similar paths was the permanency provided by agriculture. In planting season people cultivated the same fields; in harvest season they harvested the same plots. The characteristic that gave Babh-elh-Dra a different appearance from the camps along the roads was the huts, the shelters, the walls—in other words, the architecture. Agriculture and architecture were the first two great practical arts, and it was agriculture and architecture that anchored the first settlements to fixed places in the previously unmapped Neolithic world. On that foundation some of the villages grew into towns, and a few of the towns into cities.

According to Lewis Mumford,

> Cities reflect the peasant's cunning in dominating the earth. They are a product of the earth. Technically they but carry further his skill in turning the soil to productive uses, in enfolding his cattle for safety, in regulating the waters that moisten his fields, in providing storage bins and barns for his crops. Cities are emblems of that settled life which began with permanent agriculture; a life conducted with the aid of permanent shelters like orchards, vineyards, and irrigation works, and permanent buildings for protection and storage.[1]

But the city, as it developed toward the end of the 8000 B.C. to 5000 B.C. period, was of special importance to the people of the time, beyond that it contributed to agriculture and architecture. Mumford describes it eloquently: The city, he said, became the

> point of maximum concentration for the power and culture of a community. It is the place where the diffused rays of many beams of life fall into focus, with gains in both social effect and significance. The city is the form and symbol of an integrated social relationship; it is the seat of the temple, the market, the hall of justice, the academy of learning. Here in the city the goods of civilization are multiplied and manifolded; here is where the issues of civilization are focussed.[2]

WHAT COMMUNICATION MEANT TO THE CITY

What transforms the "passive agriculture regime" of the village into the active institutions of the city? Mumford does not believe that the difference is merely one of magnitude, density of population, or economic resources. Rather, the "active agent" is a "factor that extends the area of social intercourse, communication and communion; and that so creates a common underlying pattern of conduct and a common set of physical structures." In other words, the city was one of the great transducers and transformers in human history. "The city is both a physical utility for collective living," Mumford says, "and a symbol of those collective purposes that arise under such favorable circumstances. With language itself, it remains man's greatest work of art."[3]

Thus the city is a place of exchange, a transmission valve between the earthiness of the peasant village and the sophisticated art and thought of civilization. As the institutions and processes of the city honed and polished the values and practices of the villagers and nomads, so did the rural backgrounds of the villagers and nomads feed the city. In the city, people learn the requirements and take advantage of the rewards of collective living, trading ideas and customs, imitating what they admire, following what they find rewarding, perfecting what they value. In a sense, then, in the same way that a clan or a tribe built its cooperative life on communication, a city is an institution of communication, but an immensely more complicated institution. When we study the workings of a city, we necessarily study human communication.

Primitive humans emerged from the Stone Age as jacks-of-all-trades. They had learned to do what they needed done. When they joined with others to form a village, each had to play a cooperative role in the society and also to find a specialized role—supposedly what he or she could do best and thereby best compete in. According to Woolley,

> Specialization of this sort must have started very early and by degrees, but with the introduction of metal it became essential, for metal working is a skilled job requiring a long apprenticeship, and it is an all-time job; indeed, as the growing population of the city assured a regular consumers' market for manufacture of all kinds, the various trades became ever more exclusive in their demands on the workers' time. It is true that agriculture remained the most important factor in the economy of the state, so much so that most, even of the city dwellers, would have their own vegetable gardens or paddocks large enough to supply fodder for a few animals, but very often the care of the garden would be entrusted to hired labour or to a tenant who shared in its produce; the ordinary citizen was a craftsman, a smith, a potter, a carpenter, or shopkeeper, and, as the scope of business increased, a merchant. In most of the countries there was no standing army; war meant the raising of a citizen levy, and that would be only after the gathering of the harvest, in "the season when kings go forth to war," so that in the early days, at least, soldiering was not a profession; but even then there was need of a cadre of regular officers, and the king would have his personal bodyguard around him, with the result that a military class did exist and was to become more important as imperialistic policies developed.[4]

In a theocratic state the priesthood was bound to figure largely. The head of each household would continue to conduct the services and the sacrifices of domestic gods, but the ritual of state worship was the business of the government. Woolley continues:

> Thus, the King might be himself the god, or represent the god, or be the high priest, but in any of these functions he would probably be surrounded by a regular order of ministers. Where the distinction between religious and lay authority did not really exist, but religion gave its sanction to the civil power, there the civil service, if not actually identical with the priesthood, was bound to be recruited mainly from the ranks of the clergy. With the introduction of the art of writing a new feature was added to the social aspect. It must be remembered that writing was a temple invention and therefore first practiced by the priests. It had to be taught, and the priests were perforce the teachers, but as the advantages of writing were realized others than professional priests would join the temple schools; a certain number of business men would acquire the new learning, but most of them, too busy to learn for themselves, would be ready to utilize the services of professional writers, and to meet their need there arose a regular class of scribes, public notaries and letter-writers, whose literary attainments would further recommend them for the minor posts of government.[5]

Thus humans came out of the dawn years equipped with a nonspecialized form of labor and accustomed to living with a very small in-group whose shared values and morality were passed on unchanged to the younger generation. They entered a society where change was all around. They had to accustom themselves to a division of labor, a specialization and professionalization of responsibilities, a society in which for their own good they had to belong to a class—priests, soldiers, merchants, scribes, or laborers. They had been accustomed to making the kind of world they wanted to live in, and within the bounds of their physical surroundings and given the small independent group they belonged to, they could do just that. But the new society they came into was tightly organized both by tradition and by people more powerful than they. Early humans had seldom found it necessary to concern themselves with the ownership of private property; aside from clothing and perhaps an ax for hunting, almost everything was owned in common. In the new society into which these people graduated, the right to private property was very important; in fact it became necessary to mark property with the owner's seal or name, and to seek goods that were preferred and hence more valuable than others. Caves were no longer there for the taking; property, too, could be owned privately. Authority was no longer only as broad as the small living group; it came down from a ruler and extended over an entire city or state. With it came rules and laws, the obligation to pay taxes and serve in the army, and so forth. With it came money, replacing the ability to hunt or gather berries with the ability to pay for food. When collected in sufficient amounts, money represented capital to be used for investments as large as property. So when humans moved into the milieu of cities, they left a simple uncomplicated way of life for a highly complicated and interactive one.

CITY LIFE AND EARLY USES OF WRITING

With so much more communication flowing, and so many clans and family groups living side by side in the larger community, one of the first problems that arose was the need to certify the ownership of property. Consequently, almost as soon as humans learned to work with metal they learned to make engraved personal seals. These might mark a bottle or a jar, or be used to identify a package. Any owner of property therefore required a personal seal. The city itself—especially the Sumerian city, where the city's god owned the land and its produce and where the temple was the chief storehouse of riches—was the chief user of such seals.

Thus the first widespread urban need for writing was to record ownership of property, and the first source of writers and scribes was the clergy, but both the uses and the users spread rapidly. Three thousand years ago, scribes kept court archives, officers in the army wrote down their reports, supervisors in the mines kept records of products, and, as Turner noted, "merchants in almost every important city in Egypt and the Fertile Crescent found writing a necessary aid in business; although some of them may have employed scribes, many of them undoubtedly were able to read and write."[6] Still another interesting expansion of writing took place first in the court, where courtiers began to make stories and poems and to write them down for the pleasure of others. Consequently, the need for learning to write extended beyond the clergy, beyond the need to identify property ownership, beyond the scribe who wrote for those who could not write, through the mercantile community, through much of the civil service, and to the courtiers for whom the ability to write and create literary materials became one requirement of being an educated person.

Another need for writing and another source of new words and names arose from travel. In the first millennium B.C., ships plied the Mediterranean, and some went into the seas to the east. They carried merchants, mercenaries, sailors, travelers, explorers, and representatives of courts and rulers. It was a bit too early for any extensive contact with China, but already some ships were sailing to and from India, and the land and sea traffic was impressively large between Mesopotamia and the eastern Mediterranean. The Greeks borrowed the Balylonian system of weights and measures, along with the related vocabulary. Homeric words for *gold, tunic, ax,* and *hour* were borrowed from Babylon, and terms for *messenger, camel, brick, hoe,* and *pine* from Assyria. Plato used the Babylonian names for the planets. The Greek temple column was clearly influenced by the palm and

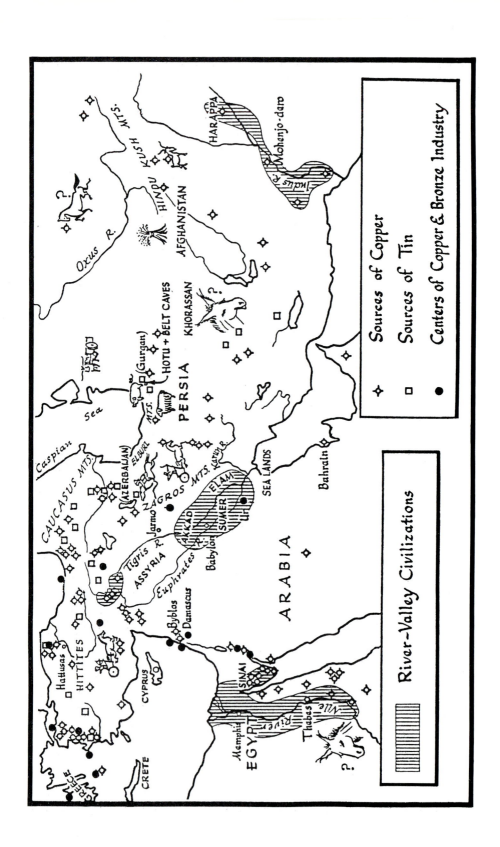

HARAPPA

Mohenjo-daro

Indus R.

HINDU KUSH MTS.

Oxus R.

AFGHANISTAN

KHORASSAN

HOTU + BELT CAVES

(Gurgan)

PERSIA

ELBURI MTS.

Caspian Sea

Bahrain

CAUCASUS MTS.

(AZERBAIJAN)

ZAGROS MTS.

ELAM

Jarmo

AKKAD SUMER UR

SEA LANDS

Tigris R.

ASSYRIA

Babylon

Euphrates R.

Byblos

Damascus

ARABIA

HITTITES

Hattusas

Sinai

CYPRUS

Memphis

EGYPT

Thebes

Nile River

Nile

CRETE

GREECE

Sources of Copper

Sources of Tin

Centers of Copper & Bronze Industry

River-Valley Civilizations

lotus patterns of Egyptian columns. And it is clear that the early centers of Greek letters, whence the skills of writing and reading spread, were modeled on Egyptian temple schools.

THE CITY'S NEED FOR SCHOOLS

Religion, education, business, government, travel, and art all found a common interest in encouraging the growth of communication skills, especially the skill of writing. The first professional role to emerge from the skill of writing was that of the scribe, and the first educational institution to be centered upon it was the primary school. In the Bronze Age this was the temple school. All priests who aspired to serve in the temple had to learn to read and write. As the civil service came to need more scribes than could be provided from among the temple priests, others who were not priests also began to attend the schools. As those engaged in business came to see the need for detailed written records, and as illiterates found it was possible to hire scribes to write letters or official documents for them, the market for scribes proliferated, and some private schools for scribes came into existence beside the official temple schools. These two sources began to produce a variety of scribes—both junior and high scribes, scribes of the temple, royal scribes of the palace, scribes who served as high officials of government, scribes who specialized in specific types of administration, schoolmasters, and notaries public. These professionals, of course, were in addition to many citizens who felt the need of an education without relating it directly to their business or profession.

Because the scribe school was one of the first types of education that supplemented instruction by the family or the clan, and was perhaps the pioneer method by which the city perpetuated its values and laws, it may be interesting to try to sum up what we know about how these early classrooms were run. One of our best reconstructed examples dates from about 1780 B.C., in Ur of the Chaldees. It was in a private house, built around three sides of a courtyard. The house had apparently been remodeled to provide space for a schoolroom, and it may have belonged to a priest because it contained a very large chapel in addition to the usual kinds of living rooms. The space remodeled for classrooms suggested that it was a small school—perhaps 20 to 25 students. In the courtyard and the study rooms were found nearly 2000 clay tablets with writing on them. Several hundred of these were the small round type used for student practice—on one side the teacher's own

---

This map suggests the significance of the Bronze Age to the great things that were happening at that time. More specifically, it points to the relationship of the fertile river valleys where writing was invented, and the availability of metal where the first great cities grew up.

writing, and on the other side the student's attempt to reproduce it. Many tablets contained religious texts presumably to be committed to memory. There were also multiplication tables, square root and cube root formulas, practical problems in geometry, and the like. Thus the school was more than merely a scriptorium; it offered at least some elements of a general education.

Who taught the school? So far as we can find out, there was a staff headed by the "school father," or as he might be called today, the headmaster. He had technical assistants—"the scribe of mathematics" or "of mensuration," "the man in charge of drawing," "the man in charge of Sumerian (language)," "the man in charge of the whip," "the man in charge of the school regulations." And there were one or more "big brothers" (senior pupils acting as tutors).

From the descriptions that have come down to us, we can surmise that discipline was strict; the whip was used frequently. The course of study was very long—it is usually described as lasting from childhood to maturity. So far as we know, only boys attended the scribe school. There is evidence of the existence of female scribes, but how and where they were trained is not known. Furthermore, all available evidence indicates that most of the boys who attended the school were sons of high officials or upper-class businessmen. After the boys had been in school for about two years they were qualified to become junior scribes, which entitled them to participate in the instruction of the younger boys, helping these boys with their assignments, correcting some of the written work, and using the stick when that was considered necessary.

An insight into school life 20 centuries ago is contained in a tablet called "Schooldays," found with the other tablets in the school we have been describing. Here are some selections:

> What did you do at school?
> I reckoned up my tablet, ate my lunch, fashioned my new tablet, wrote and finished it. Then they assigned me my oral work and in the afternoon they assigned me my written work. When the school was dismissed, I went home, entered the house, and found my father sitting there. I told my father of my written work, then recited my tablet to him, and my father was delighted.
> [Another day.] When I awoke early in the morning I faced my mother and said to her, "Give me my lunch. I want to go to school." My mother gave me two rolls and I set out. In the school the "man on duty" said to me: "Why are you late?" Afraid, and with my heart pounding, I entered before my teacher and bowed. But the teacher was correcting the student's tablet of the day before and was not pleased with it, so gave him a caning. Then the overseer "in charge of the school regulations" flogged him because "you stared about in the street," and again because he was "not properly dressed," and other members of the staff caned him for such misdemeanors as talking, standing up out of turn, and walking outside the gate. Finally the headmaster told him, "Your handwriting is unsatisfactory," and gave him a further beating.[7]

The account does not end here, and it is perhaps worth recording that the ending is happier. But this is the kind of school day to which the young students were being invited when they sat in the courtyard and waited to hear the master say,

> Come, my son. You shall sit before my feet. Now I am going to talk to you. Open your ears.

Rather more important, however, is that something of this kind was going on in every one of the early civilizations that were striving to master and share the skill of writing, upon which skill they were building a base of more general education—science and mathematics, later history and philosophy.

THE CITY AND LEARNING

From the cave to the Acropolis of Athens is a very long way; we sometimes tend to give early humans less credit than they deserve for how fast they traveled that road. Yet, viewed close up, it was a slow, difficult trip. For example, ancient scientists really had very little science. They experimented carefully and patiently, but when they found a satisfactory way to do something, they simply recorded it and stopped there. They usually did not consider the principles behind what they had done or try to think of ways to improve it. (We are not talking now about the best of the Ionian scientists—like Aristarchus—who, in the last few centuries before the Christian era, began to create some really sophisticated science.) Master potters at Nineveh in the seventeenth century B.C. could make glazed earthenware by a process that could be followed exactly by a modern potter, with the same result. Yet the ancient potters apparently devoted very little thought to how they accomplished the result, and certainly no thought to devising a formula to explain the chemical reaction they were achieving. The Egyptian mathematicians were no more theoretical than the Assyrian potters. But in earlier years the basis of scholars' calculations was usually simple addition, and they were always looking for practical results that could be applied to daily life; once they achieved those, they gave little attention to how the method could be simplified or perfected—or more deeply understood. Consequently their mathematics was inadequate for thinking about astronomy, although that was a topic that interested early scientists very much.

One of the survivals of the Stone Age was a set of demoniac explanations—for example that illness, good fortune, and bad fortune were all closely related to magic. Laws were thought to come from gods rather than being worked out by humans for their own best good. The practice of medicine was also related to magic rather than biology or chemistry; a doctor was brought in usually to placate an angry god or combat a malignant power, and the medicine prescribed was more likely intended to make the situation unpleasant for the possessing demon than pleasant for the sick body. In medicine, as in law and government, early humans were rather more likely to accept what they saw around them than to question it. An example is the circumstance that nowhere, so far as we have been able to discover, before the end of the Bronze Age had humans reached the stage of questioning and analyzing that made them ask why people were not equal before the law and before their fellows. The institution of slavery was universally accepted, even in the golden age of Athens. The gods had decided that not all persons should have an equal opportunity upon earth, and what the gods had decided was the law.

It was a very long way from the isolated life of the cave or the early villages to the busy cities, where ships and caravans arrived from and departed for distant lands, carrying unfamiliar cargoes and unfamiliar ideas. It must have seemed a great distance indeed between the small groups of 25 to 1500 who lived together at the end of the Stone Age to the hundreds of thousands who crowded together into the masonry streets and houses of the cities; from the hunting parties sneaking up on herds of animals to the city markets supplied by the rice and wheat fields of Eurasia. It must have seemed a long way from the schooling at the parent's knee or imitation of the most skilled hunters to the formality of the temple schools of Sumer, Assyria, and Egypt, and a still longer path to the olive groves of Athens where a few chosen young men walked and talked with Socrates.

Because there was no writing at the beginning of the long road we are talking about, it is hard to say how different the written arts were in the Bronze Age from the corresponding oral arts of the earlier time. Yet we know that some of the oldest surviving Egyptian documents from the Bronze Age were used to sum up a thousand years of learning for the guidance of the pharaohs. Communication among individuals by letter was quite common in Babylon. Egyptians writers created a form of fiction that can hardly be described other than as the short story. And almost as soon as tablets and scrolls began to be used for purposes other than records or testimony to ownership, poems of extraordinary quality and beauty began to appear in handwriting—poems that remind us again of how many great poets we may have missed in the millennia when there was language but no writing.

WHAT EARLY LITERATURE SOUNDED LIKE

What did Bronze Age poetry sound like? Below is a poem that has come down to us from the Twelfth Egyptian Dynasty (about 1900 B.C.). Some scholars have called it "Dialogue of a Man Weary of Life and His Soul," but poetry of this quality does not need a title any more than it needs the author's name which is, of course, lost in the dim past.

Death is in my eyes today
As when a sick man becomes whole,
As when walking abroad after illness.

Death is in my eyes today
Like the scent of myrrh,
Like sitting beneath the boat's sail on a breezy day.

Death is in my eyes today
Like the smell of water-lilies,
Like sitting on the bank of drunkenness.

Death is in my eyes today
Like a well-trodden road,
As when men return home from a foreign campaign.

Death is in my eyes today
Like the unveiling of the heaven,
As when a man attains there to that which he knew not.

Death is in my eyes today
Like the desire of the man to see his home
When he has passed many years in captivity.[8]

Wisdom literature—the proverbs of a nation—was strong in the Middle Eastern countries as we can judge from the selection of the book of Proverbs to be one part of the Hebrew Old Testament. One example that may not be familiar to you is this proverb from Babylon:

There is a disease for which there is no physician; it is to have no food to eat.[9]

And here is one from China:

The world is invariably possessed by him who does nothing.[10]

Finally, here is a Chinese poem dating from somewhere in the neighborhood of 1100 B.C. and reminiscent of the homesickness to be found in the famous S'zu poems of 2000 years later. The author is a soldier who has been away on a campaign:

When we went away
The millets were in flower.
Now that we are returning
The snow falls and the roads are all mire.
The king's business was very difficult
And we had no leisure to rest.
Did we not long to return?
But we were in awe of the orders in the tablets.[11]

The variety of written work suggested by the surviving tablets from the first and second millennia B.C. is startling, extending as it does from Sumerian epics to Egyptian history, and including the narratives which have come down to us under such names as Homer. But the whole period was quite varied and remarkable. The Pyramids were rising beside the Nile. Babylon was enjoying its hanging gardens. The "great city Shang" was rising in western China long before the first Chinese writing appeared on the oracle bones. And even greater monuments were becoming known in southern Asia and Europe. These included a phenomenal group of philosophers and scholars. In Iran there was Zoroaster; in India, Gautama Buddha; in China, Confucius; in Greece, that remarkable group of men including Aristarchus, Euclid, Pythagoras, Socrates, Sophocles, Plato, and Aristotle. It is hard to believe that a distribution of intellectual strength like that could have happened purely at random. It was a remarkable period these men lived in. In fact, if you could have walked through the streets of southern Europe, Egypt, Mesopotamia, and southwestern Asia 2500 years ago you would have seen more than great cities—you would have seen great civilizations also. For where there had been hunters' caves 10,000 years before, then agricultural villages, then cities, now civilizations had appeared. Where there had been savages and primitives, now there were civilized people.

CITIES AND CIVILIZATION

Originally the term *civilization* was derived from the term for city and meant a way of life characterized by cities. Later it came to be broader than urban life and was used to refer to the whole life of a people, especially to a high level of culture. This was the way in which Arnold Toynbee used the word.[12] Toynbee's conception of how civilizations came to grow was that people were challenged in such a way as to evoke creativity in their leaders. He found this challenge largely in physical changes, chiefly in desiccation—the drying up of the land and the advance of the desert. Thus, Egypt and Mesopotamia, for example, had once been green and fertile; then the winds and the temperature changed, sand overran the fields and forests, and inhabitants of the newly desiccated areas were forced to overcome new obstacles and find new ways to feed themselves and live the kinds of lives to which they aspired.

Toynbee's explanation is by no means the only one. Other scholars suggest an almost opposite explanation: that when resources were brought to a point where there was some surplus, then people had time to use their intellectual and artistic as well as their physical abilities, and consequently the great cities of the Bronze Age flowered.

Why it happened, however, is of less importance than the fact that it did happen. The cities flowered, communication flowed through and between them, and around them arose the world's first great civilizations.

Those of us who as schoolchildren studied Homer, the dialogues of Plato, the geometry of Euclid, and the Greek drama are almost inevitably drawn to think of the city of Pericles and Pheidias as our example of the civilizations of that period. And Athenian Greece was truly a remarkable example of what humans could accomplish only 10,000 years out of the cave and only a few thousand years past their first conquest of writing. Instead of talking of the great men of Athens, however, it may be well to say something of the schools of Athens in order to show how they differed from the earlier temple schools of Egypt and Sumer.

Unlike many other cities and states of this period, the Athenian government did not support the schools, although it took a healthy interest in what they taught. But there were no public schools or public school teachers in Athens; the schools were privately owned and the pupils privately paid for.

The Athenian boy usually entered school at about the age of 6. For the next eight years, he learned to read and write, read great amounts of poetry and history, and memorized selections from great men. During all this time, he spent about as much time training his body, through sports and exercises, as he spent training his mind. From ages 14 through 18, the student continued his study of literature but also was introduced to elementary science and mathematics, as well as other subjects of his and his teacher's choice. When the student was 18 he usually entered the military service for two years. Then he went back to schools of higher learning. These had originated in the temple schools of Sumer and Egypt, but the Greeks being what they were, their schools soon took on a character of their own. Many of them took the form of philosophical discussion groups—to hone the sharp mind, some of the observers said, and, others added, to exercise the healthy mind along with the healthy body. Perhaps the largest number of these were operated by the Sophists, and the usual procedure was for a group of young men to attach themselves to the discussion group that was led by one or more men whom they especially admired. The Sophists had the most groups and the most students, but the best-known teachers were Socrates, Plato, and Aristotle.

As we have said, it seems very far from the caves in the hillside to the magnificent Acropolis in Athens, a very long time from the young men of the tribe imitating the great hunters in the fourth Ice Age to the young men of Athens discussing truth and beauty with Plato in the groves of academe in the fourth century B.C., a very long leap from the ceremony in front of the cave paintings to the drama by Sophocles in the Theatre of Dionysus. But that is probably the wrong way to think about the difference. It was a long way but an unbroken road.

Athens, even at its height, was a city of contrasts. Contemplation could exist side by side with conflict, beauty side by side with sordidness. Socrates and his pupils could discuss philosopher-kings while the leaders of Athens were planning imperialism. The young men of Athens were learning to be soldiers as well as philosophers. Athens was a man's town, it has been said more than once—a city of soldiers home from the wars, a city of sailors ashore—in some circles intellectually awakened, in others bawdy, and in still others both intellectually awakened and bawdy. And when it was called a "man's town" that was not wholly complimentary, for Athens was a city where the goddesses were idealized in the temples and the Winged Victory was presented as a woman, and still the women lived apart from the men in the female quarters of houses, were restrained from speaking to men on the street, and in fact seldom saw a man except the head of the household and a few relatives. The best women, proclaimed Pericles, were those about whom the least, good or bad, could be said.[13]

Athens was therefore not so much on a different road from Lascaux and Altamira as it was farther along that road. Could the 175,000 freemen of Athens, the 125,000 slaves, have created the kind of civilization they did without the background of communication that flowed from the cave paintings through Sumer and Egypt into the Peloponnesus and Attica? It seems very unlikely. Many of the men of Athens were more scornful than they may have had reason to be. Blunt, plainspoken Socrates made fun of book learning just when, for the first time, books were becoming cheap and plentiful and his countrymen were beginning to fill them with poems, drama, history, and philosophy that, 1700 years later, printers, scholars, and librarians were seeking out as the finest in Western culture. The freemen of Athens depended upon foreigners (metecs) to do their business for them, and still developed, because of their skill with communication, probably the most efficient exchange economy and the most vigorous economic enterprise yet seen in the Western world. In Athens, for a few centuries, some of the great currents of the Western world—Lascaux, Sumer, Egypt, Babylon, and others—came together and left an impact on all civilizations that came after them. Those were the years when Plato registered for all time what historians have called the prototype portrait of a college president, Aristotle the prototype of a research director, Pericles of a city builder, Aristarchus of a scientist, Sophocles of a national artist. This remarkable constellation of genius, Turner said, was the "first self-conscious thinkers" on the road from Lascaux to the present. "They raised the intellectual issues and problems which first released men from the pattern of primitive thinking. . . . They defined the concepts and the methods of Western thought for the next two thousand years."[14]

SUGGESTIONS FOR FURTHER READING

Several of the outstanding books on the development of cities have been written by Lewis Mumford, notably *The Culture of Cities* (New York: Harcourt Brace Jovanovich, 1938). For a general treatment of Bronze Age history, including the growth of cities, see the *Cambridge Ancient History,* edited by J. B. Bury et al. (Cambridge, England: Cambridge University Press, vols. 1 and 2, 1923–1927). In this field typically most of the literature concentrates on one country per book. For example, see L. Woolley, *Excavations at Ur: A Record of Twelve Years Work* (London: Allen and Unwin, 1954). Also A. J. Evans, *The Palace of Minos: A Comparative Account of the Successive Stages of the Early Cretan Civilization as Illustrated by the Discoveries at Knossos* (4 vols., Oxford, 1921–1935). Also *The Code of Hammurabi, King of Babylon: The Oldest Code of Laws in the World,* translated by C. H. W. Johns (Chicago: University of Chicago Press, 1904). Early Chinese cities are treated in H. G. Creel's *The Birth of China: A Study of the Formative Period of Chinese Civilization* (New York: Fungar, 1954). For Greek cities, see A. E. Zimmern, *The Greek Commonwealth* (Oxford, 1931).

QUESTIONS TO THINK ABOUT

1. Mumford asks a rather rhetorical question: "What transforms the passive agricultural regime of the village into the active institutions of the city?" Answer it.
2. Would you say that the need for communication creates a need for the city, or that the city creates a need to communicate? Or both?
3. What elements of the city, in addition to the large number of people living close together, stimulate communication?
4. Why were there no cities before writing came into use?
5. Explain the following statement by Mumford: "Mind takes form in the city."

TIME CAPSULE

First cities in Tigris Euphrates triangle	3,500*
In Egypt	3,000
In Indus Valley	2,500
In Crete—Knossos	2,300
Phonetic alphabet	1,500
First large Chinese dynasty—Shang	1,500
"Great city of Shang"	1,500
Athens	700
Rome	200
Olmec cities, west coast of Mexico	200

*These dates are years B.C.

Thus thou hast seen in short, all things that can be shewed, and hast learned the *chief Words* of the *English* and *Latin Tongue.*	Ita vidisti summatim res omnes quæ poterunt ostendi, & didicisti *Voces primarias Anglicæ* & *Latinæ Linguæ.*
Go on now and read other good *Books* diligently, and thou shalt become *learned, wise,* and *godly.*	Perge nunc & lege diligenter alias bonos *Libros,* ut fias *doctus, sapiens,* & *pius.*
Remember these things; fear God, and call upon him, that he may bestow upon thee the *Spirit of Wisdom.* Farewell.	Memento horum; Deum time, & invoca eum, ut largiatur tibi *Spiritum Sapientiæ.* Vale.

The last page of Orbis Sensualis Pictis *(The Visible World). This textbook by Comenius was probably the first made especially for audiovisual teaching—Piaget called it "an experiment in improving education never since matched by a single man." Comenius was born in Moravia in 1592, became a bishop, and spent much of his life wandering through Europe avoiding the Thirty Years' War while he taught and wrote. He wrote treatises on the philosophy of education and textbooks illustrating his theories.*

INSTITUTIONS OF COMMUNICATION: THE SCHOOL

Upon the education of the people of this country the future of this country depends.

BENJAMIN DISRAELI

Only the educated are free.

EPICTETUS

*W*e have touched briefly on schools in Chapter 5 because the school is such an obviously important communication element in the development of the city. In the following pages we are going to concentrate on the development of the school itself.

Approximately half of all the professional communicators in the world are connected in some way with schools. They may teach first graders to read or fourth graders to recite the multiplication tables. They may keep ledgers. They may write or publish or sell textbooks. They may be renowned scientists. But in some way or other they are engaged in the sometimes puzzling and often controversial kind of activity we call education.

THE PRACTICALITY OF EARLY EDUCATION

Education makes for change or for fixity. In general, prehistoric education must have been on the side of fixity. Its essential task was to contribute to survival. To this end it was expected to transmit the culture of the tribe to its new members, so that they could grow up as desirable members of the group. They had to learn what was expected of them, what was out of line, what was admirable, what contributed to solving the problems a tribe or a clan faces. How were these things learned? Basically, by doing. From the earliest possible year, the children were brought into the daily tasks and duties of the family. They learned tasks by observing and by doing them. As they grew older they graduated to the broader activities of the tribe. When they gained more experience, they were given more and more responsibility for supervision or leadership.

Thus, the curriculum of such a school must have been relatively unchanging, because the culture itself changed so little. The teachers were not strangers from the outside, they were not even trained experts; they were the fathers, mothers, and neighbors. Children would first learn to sew by watching their mothers do it or learn from their fathers to recognize the tracks of animals. The next step was to identify the most skilled of the tribespeople and let the children learn from them by observing, by helping, and ultimately by cooperating. Thus the best hunter would be responsible for bringing up the best hunters in the next generation. The priestly and ritualistic secrets would be passed on to a few selected children who would in turn pass them on to another generation, thus creating a line of priests. This is the way that the prehistoric schools must have developed from a process of absorbing lessons from one's own family life to a process of learning from the most skilled tribesmen and tribeswomen.

The goal was essentially practical. The skills to be learned were the skills the tribe needed most. Even after the scribe schools came into being, there was little sign of what Kramer, writing about the tablets of Sumer, called "the scientific urge—the search for truth for truth's sake."[1] If there was a break in the solid practicality of the ancient school it must have come with the puberty rites, when the young people of the tribe were taken to the sacred places and secretly taught the myths, history, rituals, and values of their people, which were not essentially practical, but rather imaginative, religious, and magical. This, more than any other part of primitive education, was regarded as the essence of bringing youths into the culture and preparing them for adult participation.

Not for many thousands of years must questioning and discussion have bulked very large in school time. The function of school was to produce solid skills rather than fresh ideas. When writing came into existence, the goal was to make scribes and, later, government workers. Out of this scholastic goal came schools like the one in Sumer that we described in Chapter 5. Not until the time of the great philosopher-teachers of the fifth and fourth centuries B.C. was there any clear indication that practices and values were being questioned rather than merely learned.

EDUCATION IN THE MIDDLE EAST

The first scribe schools we know anything about were in Sumer.[2] As a matter of fact, the first large collection of written documents was discovered in a Sumerian city called Erech—something over 1000 tablets with economic and administrative information, and a few that had apparently been used for memorizing word lists. Like Sumer, Egypt and Mesopotamia sent selected children to study writing. Egyptian schools were under the supervision of the priests. There was one type of formal school for future scribes, another for priest trainees. Boys entered school at age 5 and studied writing and reading until 16 or 17. Scribe trainees were given practical experience beginning at 13 or 14 in the particular office for which they were being prepared. Priesthood training began at the temple college at age 17. Discipline and study were rigid. Memorizing, drill, and practice in writing were the chief methods.

In Mesopotamia there were schools for scribes and schools for priests. The schools for priests were said to have been as numerous as the temples themselves.

EDUCATION IN CHINA

China's formal educational system began a bit later than those of the Middle Eastern countries we have been taking about, but very early set some new directions.[3] From the very first, Chinese schools seemed to have emphasized ethical and moral values and public service. Thus the ancient Chinese virtues of filial piety and respect for the elderly were ingrained in Chinese children for generations before Confucius and Mencius. Furthermore, from very early in the history of China one of the responsibilities of the state was considered to be to select and prepare the most talented students for government service so that they could maintain the ethical and moral foundations of the society. In later times this selection process developed into the elaborate Chinese examination system, the prototype of all civil service examination systems in the world. The system selected the ablest young people for important government service and gradually reduced the class by competitive examinations, until only three top students were left, and they had their final examinations before the emperor himself.

During the later Chou period (771–221 B.C.) cities and urban civilization appeared in China, commerce flourished, and a group of distinguished philosopher-scholars appeared, at almost the same time as Socrates, Plato, and Aristotle in Greece. It was a period of political instability and declining power of the king, but a remarkable period for education and philosophy. The scholars organized themselves into groups that later historians called "The Hundred Schools" to debate how best to cure the ills of the state and achieve again a happy way of life. This was a remarkably creative period in Chinese thinking when Taoists, Confucianists, and Mo-ists organized their own schools (much in the spirit of the schools of Socrates and Plato and the Sophists) and produced philosophical, political, and moral writing that were later regarded as the classics of China. This inheritance flowered during the Han Dynasty (206 B.C.–A.D. 220) when the classics became the core of education, and historians, poets, artists, lexicographers, and literary critics were extraordinarily active and productive. At that time the development of rag paper further stimulated the publication of creative work, and the old and new classics became the core curriculum of a national university, which at one time had 30,000 students! Three degrees were given, corresponding roughly to our bachelor's, master's and doctor's—*hsiu tsai* (cultivated talent), *ming ching* (understanding the classics), and *chin-shih* (the highest).[4]

EDUCATION IN INDIA

The ancient civilization of India must have begun its schooling very much like those we have talked about. Religion was always a strong core for the curriculum. For example, here is a section from one of the ten principal Upanishads, the early textbooks from which the Indian students studied. "These books have Spirit for theme," it begins. And later:

> That which makes the tongue speak, but needs not tongue to explain, that alone is Spirit; not what sets the world by the ears.
> That which makes the mind think but needs no mind to think, that alone is Spirit; not what sets the world by the ears.
> That which makes the eye see, but needs no eye to see, that alone is Spirit; not what sets the world by the ears.
> That which makes the ear hear, but needs no ear to hear, that alone is Spirit; not what sets the world by the ears.
> That which makes the life live but needs no life to live, that alone is Spirit; not what sets the world by the ears.
> If you think you know much, you know little. If you think that you know it from study of your own mind or of nature, study again.[5]

After the Aryan invasion in the second millennium B.C., however, the people were divided into strong castes, and their education depended somewhat on this membership. The Brahmans were prepared to be priests and scholars, the Ksatriyas nobles and soldiers, the Vaisyas farmers and traders, and so forth. In general, the first years of education were at home. At the age of 8 a Brahman boy went through the upanayana (thread) ceremony, which signaled the beginning of his formal education. Ksatriya children had this ceremony at 11, Vausyas at 12. After that, the boy left his parents' house and went to study in his teacher's home, usually in the forest. The teacher treated him like a son and charged nothing for his services, although the student was expected to do some housework, tend the cattle, and keep the sacrificial fires burning. Throughout his student years, the student dressed simply, ate frugally, slept on a hard bed, and maintained celibacy. His schooling usually lasted 12 years, at the end of which he could attend a university (when the educational system had developed to the point where it included universities). There he could extend his education as long as he wished, and some Brahmans were literally lifelong students.

In the years after 500 B.C. the influence of Buddha and Mahavira, both of whom taught in the language of the people, challenged the exclusivity of the Brahmans and brought greater variety to Indian education. The Buddhists, however, established a monastic tradition and offered limited opportunities to students in their monasteries. Therefore, lay schools were needed in greater numbers. Buddhists began to offer secular as well as religious training, and elementary education (in addition to secondary and university) was offered for the first time to large numbers of students. The most notable flowering of Indian learning, however, took place between the fifth and ninth centuries, when their research institutes and universities were doing much of the world's most productive thinking about science, mathematics, and astronomy. We shall have more to say about these later.

EDUCATION IN GREECE

We come to Greece in this brief survey of how schooling developed in the early centuries of writing.[6] Both the Greek language and the Greek school system apparently derived from the Mycenaean civilization of 1400 to 1000 B.C., which in turn grew out of the civilization of Minoan Crete. These early Greek life patterns were basically of an oriental type, much like Egypt, Sumer, and the like, and we can assume that the first teaching must have emphasized the training of scribes. However, when Crete fell and the transformation of the Mycenaean civilization to Greek concepts had been carried out, then the Greek schools reappeared looking quite different than they might have been expected to look on Crete.

The epic poems of Homer, the *Iliad* and the *Odyssey,* set a standard for Greece much as the stories and ballads of knighthood influenced England. They built a tradition of knightly valor, warrior kings and leaders, manliness, skill at sports, and

THE WORLD ACCORDING TO THE SUMERIANS

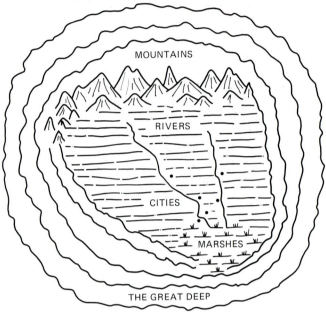

MOUNTAINS

RIVERS

CITIES

MARSHES

THE GREAT DEEP

THE WORLD ACCORDING TO HERODOTUS

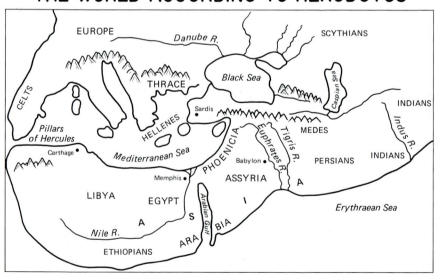

EUROPE

Danube R.

SCYTHIANS

Black Sea

Caspian Sea

THRACE

CELTS

INDIANS

Sardis

Pillars of Hercules

HELLENES

MEDES

Indus R.

Carthage

Mediterranean Sea

PHOENICIA

Euphrates R.

Tigris R.

PERSIANS

INDIANS

Babylon

LIBYA

EGYPT

ASSYRIA

A

Memphis

Erythraean Sea

A

S

Arabian Gulf

I

Nile R.

ARA

BIA

ETHIOPIANS

similar goals which were less valued in many of the other countries we have mentioned. Furthermore they set up a tradition of the "perfect Greek man" as one who possessed a balanced combination of wisdom, strength, and bravery.

A second characteristic which helped shape the Greek school system was the organization of Greece, not into a national system, but rather into a group of city-states, each with its own traditions, values, and ways of administering government. Needless to say, this arrangement invited each school to implement its own ideas of education. So when Thucydides said, "We are the school of Hellas," referring to Athens, he was wrong, for there were many schools of Hellas and they taught many different things.

Perhaps the extreme example would be Sparta. Even in the very early years of classical Greece there was a fundamental distinction between the militaristically disciplined schools of Sparta and the schools of Athens that were less interested in producing soldiers than in producing the *kalos kathagos* (the wise and good man). Later there was a rift almost as deep between two types of Athenian education, and we shall return to that later.

The best way to get an idea of education in Sparta is to read it from Plutarch himself. Here are a few paragraphs from Plutarch's "Life of Lycurgus,"[7] which help to explain not only why Sparta was a military power, but also why Sparta typically won more than half the medals at the Olympic games.

> It was not left to the father to rear what children he pleased, but he was obliged to carry the child to a place called Lesche, to be examined by the most ancient men of the tribe who were assembled there. If it were strong and well proportioned, they gave orders for its education, and assigned it to one of the nine thousand shares of land; but if it were weakly and deformed, they ordered it to be thrown into the place called Apothetae, which is a deep cavern near the mountain Taygetus, concluding that its life could be no advantage either to itself or to the public, since nature had not given it at first any strength or goodness of constitution. For the same reason the women did not wash their new-born infants with water, but with wine, thus making some trial of the habit of body—imagining that sickly and epileptic children sink and die under this experiment, while the healthy become more vigorous and hardy. Great care and art were also exerted by the nurses; for, as they never swathed the infants, their limbs had a freer turn and their countenances a more liberal air; besides, they used them to any kind of meat, to have no terrors in the dark, nor to be afraid of being alone, and to leave all ill-humour and unmanly

<hr>

This is how much human ideas of the world had changed in the 2000+ years between the times the Sumerians and the Greeks were dominant forces in civilization. The world of the Sumerians was curled tightly around the Tigris and the Euphrates and the cities on their banks. By the time of Herodotus, the western part of Asia, the north of Africa, the south of Europe (even the Danube river) were known, as also were perhaps ten Kingdoms.

crying. . . . The Spartan children were not in that manner under tutors purchased or hired with money, nor were the parents at liberty to educate them as they pleased; but as soon as they were seven years old, Lycurgus ordered them to be enrolled in companies, where they were all kept under the same order and discipline, and had their exercises and recreations in common. He who showed the most conduct and courage amongst them was made captain of the company. The rest kept their eyes upon him, obeyed his orders, and bore with patience the punishments he inflicted; so that their whole education was an exercise of obedience. The old men were present at their diversions, and often suggested some occasion of dispute or quarrel that they might observe with exactness the spirit of each and their firmness in battle.

As for learning, they had just what was absolutely necessary. All the rest of their education was calculated to make them subject to command, to endure labour, to fight and conquer. They added, therefore, to their discipline as they advanced in age—cutting their hair very close, making them go barefoot, and play, for the most part, quite naked. At twelve years of age their undergarment was taken away, and one upper one a year allowed them. Hence, they were necessarily dirty in their persons, and were not indulged the great favor of baths and oil except on some particular days of the year. They slept in companies, on beds made of the tops of reeds which they gathered with their bare hands, without knives, and brought from the banks of the Eurotas. In winter they were permitted to add a little thistle-down, as that seemed to have some warmth in it.

At this age the most distinguished among them became the favorite companions of the elder; and the old men attended more constantly their place of exercise, observing their trials of strength and wit, not slightly and in a cursory manner, but as their fathers, guardians, and governors; so that there was neither time nor place where persons were wanting to instruct and chastise them. One of the best and ablest men in the city was, moreover, appointed inspector of the youth, and he gave the command of each company to the most discreet and most spirited of those, called Irens. An Iren was one that had been two years out of the class of boys; a Melliren, one of the oldest lads. . . . This Iren then, a youth twenty years old, gives orders to those under his command in their little battles, and has them to serve him at his house. He sends the oldest of them to fetch wood, and the younger to gather pot-herbs; these they steal where they can find them, either slyly getting into gardens, or else craftily and warily creeping to the common tables. But if any one be caught, he is severely flogged for negligence and lack of dexterity. They steal, too, whatever victuals they possibly can, ingeniously contriving to do it when persons are asleep or keep but indifferent watch. If they are discovered, they are punished not only with whipping, but with hunger; indeed, their supper is but slight at all times, that, to fence against want, they may be forced to exercise their courage and address. This is the first intention of their spare diet; a subordinate one is to make them grow tall. For when the animal spirits are not too much oppressed by a great quantity of food, which stretches itself out in breadth and thickness, they mount upward by their natural lightness, and the body easily and freely shoots up in height. This also contributes to make them handsome; for thin

and slender habits yield more freely to nature, which then gives a fine proportion to the limbs, whilst the heavy and gross resist her by their weight.

 The boys steal with so much caution, that one of them having conveyed
a young fox under his garment, suffered the creature to tear out his bowels
with his teeth and claws, choosing rather to die than to be detected. . . . .

Athens never adopted the extreme militarism of Sparta. Rather, from the
Homeric tradition of the *Iliad* and *Odyssey* it adopted a sort of knightly ideal of
a balance of wisdom, strength, and bravery, and there was for a long time no formal
educational system in Athens to implement it. Parents were free to bring up their
children as they chose. The overall goal of this education was civic responsibility.
At the age of about 20, the Athenian man dedicated himself to his country, served
two years in the military, and thereafter was free to seek such further education
from private teachers as he could be accepted for or pay for.[8]

Athenian schools grew out of the palaestra, which began as a gymnasium for
children, and gradually added music, dance, and poetry. Later a school was established—third in time as in importance Mansfield noted—in which the child learned
to read, write, and count.

We must remember that humanistic and democratic as Athens was in comparison to Sparta, it was never a true democracy. Perhaps one out of ten Athenians
was permitted to take part in the political activities of the city; the others were
slaves or aliens. Therefore, Athens was a place of high intellectual privilege for
people of high privilege. It was the School of Hellas for less than one in ten of
the young men (considerably less than one in ten of the young women) who could
afford to go through the best private schools of the city and at the appropriate time
share the wisdom of the great thinkers of Athens. Great art, great thinking, great
knowledge, an ideal of the noble life, and beauty such as has seldom been equaled
elsewhere were available to the fortunate ones.

The Two Strands of Greek Education

In the great centuries of Socrates, Plato, and Aristotle, two contrasting models of
education were available to the fortunate few in Athens. So great is the reputation
of the Socratic group and Socratic teaching today that we sometimes forget they
had serious and effective competition in their own time.

The controversy was over the function and usefulness of education. On one
side were Socrates and Plato, who were concerned chiefly with the ability of their
students to deal with great ideas and think noble thoughts. On the other side were
the Sophists, professional educators, who were concerned with teaching political
effectiveness. They were quite willing to teach for pay and to train for commercial
success and political effectiveness. They advertised. They gave lectures for money.

Above all, they offered practical results: the preparation of successful statesmen. They pretended, said Grover,

> neither to transmit nor to seek for the truth concerning man or existence; they simply offered a formula for success in political life, which meant, above all, being able on every occasion to make one's point of view prevail. Two principal disciplines chiefly made up the program: the art of persuasion, or dialectic, and the art of speaking, or rhetoric—the two most flourishing humanistic studies of antiquity. The Sophists founded these studies by distilling their general principles and logical structures, thus making it possible to transmit their theory from teacher to pupil.[9]

Socrates, as we might imagine, was alarmed and shocked by this kind of pedagogy. He doubted that virtue could be taught, especially for money, and felt that the goal of education should not be power or efficiency, but rather the disinterested search for the absolute, for wisdom, and for virtue.

These two points of view clashed head on in the fourth century (Plato opened his academy in 387, and Socrates his school in 390). The results of the contest cannot be expressed well as a score. The Sophists won financially. Plato won by the reputation of his books. Socrates lost by being sentenced to death.

But the young people who won the opportunity to study with Socrates, Plato, or Aristotle must have won some of the world's finest teaching. Seldom would such a class have been a lecture course. More often it was a walk through the Grove of Academe, responding to the talk of the master.

For example, Socrates himself apparently taught chiefly by asking questions. An instance is the following passage from a dialogue on "The Education of Women," in which the old master used the question method to expose preconceived ideas to the light of reason.

> **SOCRATES:** Are dogs divided into hes and shes, or do they both share equally in hunting and in keeping watch and in the other duties of dogs? Or do we entrust to the males the entire and exclusive care of the flocks, while we leave the females at home, under the idea that the bearing and suckling of their puppies is labor enough for them?
>
> **STUDENT:** No, they share alike; the only difference between them is that the males are stronger and the females weaker.
>
> **SOCRATES:** But can you use different animals for the same purpose, unless they are bred and fed in the same way?
>
> **STUDENT:** You cannot.
>
> **SOCRATES:** Then, if women are to have the same duties as men, they must have the same nurture and education?
>
> **STUDENT:** Yes.

SOCRATES: The education which was assigned to the men was music and gymnastic.

STUDENT: Yes.

SOCRATES: Then women must be taught music and gymnastic, and also the art of war, which they must practice like the men.

STUDENT: That is the inference, I suppose.

SOCRATES: I should rather expect that several of our proposals, if they are carried out, may appear ridiculous.

STUDENT: No doubt of it.

SOCRATES: Yes, and the most ridiculous thing of all will be the sight of women naked in the palaestra, exercising with the men. . . .

STUDENT: Yes, indeed, according to present notions the proposal would be thought ridiculous. . . .

SOCRATES: Not long ago . . . the Hellenes were of the opinion, which is still received among the barbarians, that the sight of a naked man was ridiculous and improper; and when first the Cretans and then the Lacedaemonians introduced the custom, the wits of that day might equally have ridiculed the innovation.

STUDENT: No doubt.

SOCRATES: But when experience showed that to let all things be uncovered was far better than to cover them up, and the ludicrous effect to the outward eye vanished before the better principle which reason asserted, then the man was perceived to be a fool who directs the shaft of his ridicule at any other sight but folly and vice, or seriously inclines to weigh the beautiful by any other standard but that of the good.

STUDENT: Very true.

SOCRATES: First, then, whether the question is to be put in jest or in earnest, let us come to an understanding about the nature of woman: Is she capable of sharing either wholly or partially in the actions of men, or not at all? And is the art of war one of those arts in which she can or cannot share? That will be the best way of commencing the inquiry and will probably lead to the fairest conclusion.

STUDENT: That will be much the best way.

SOCRATES: Shall we take the other side first and begin by arguing against ourselves; and in this manner the adversary's position will not be undefended?

STUDENT: Why not?[10]

The challenge of this sort of teaching can hardly be missed. For a corresponding example from Plato read the Allegory of the Cave from book VII of *The Republic*. *The Republic* was concerned with the problems of preparing citizens for the state. Just as there are three dominant human qualities—reason, spirit (will), and appetite—said Plato, there are also three classes into which the citizens of a free state may be divided. The purpose of education is thus to determine the part of society into which every individual should be assigned according to his or her ability and character. Such an assignment of citizens will contribute both to their happiness and to the good of the state. In *The Republic,* the chief interest was in the preparation of philosopher-kings to lead the state.

We may suppose that Aristotle also taught in much the same way as his master, Plato, and Plato's master, Socrates. We know him, however, chiefly for his long and tightly argued books which, when made available after so long, helped stimulate the Renaissance in Europe. As an example of Aristotle's way of thinking, we can cite his famous definition of tragedy from *The Art of Poetry,* which introduces the idea of dramatic catharsis.

> We are to to reserve until later any more extended discussion of the Epic, that form of poetry which employs hexameter verse, and of Comedy, and are to deal first with Tragedy, the main topic of the present treatise. As a preliminary, we may frame a definition of the essence of Tragedy, in the main by putting together things already said.
>
> A Tragedy, then, is an artistic imitation of an action that is serious, complete in itself, and of an adequate magnitude, so much for the object which is imitated. As for the medium, the imitation is produced in language embellished in more than one way, one kind of embellishment being introduced separately in one part, and another kind in another part of the whole. As for the manner, the imitation is itself in the form of an action directly presented, not narrated. And as for the proper function resulting from the imitation of such an object in such a medium and manner, it is to arouse the emotions of pity and fear in the audience; and to arouse this pity and fear in such a way as to effect that special purging of and relief (catharsis) of these two emotions which is the characteristic of Tragedy.[11]

Note how systematically Aristotle presents, point by point, the elements of his definition: What is the subject matter? what is the medium of presentation? what is the manner that distinguishes tragedy? and what gives tragedy its impact and effect?

EDUCATION IN ROME

Roman education began with a strong familial tradition.[12] Children were taught by their parents, and the boy, in particular, spent a great deal of time with his father, being instructed in and observing adult behavior. The father typically took his son along with him to serve as a sort of page during public appearances, even in the Senate. The family chapter of education usually ended at age 16, when the young man donned the toga, the garment of adulthood, and was apprenticed to some old friend of the family for a year of experience in public life. Then came two or more years of military service, the first as an ordinary soldier to learn to obey, the second as an officer to learn to lead. As Rome took more of a leading part among Mediterranean countries and became better acquainted with the Greek tradition, however, this custom of family education began to be replaced in part by teaching of the Greek language and Greek thought. Greek teachers came to be important in Roman schools, and the curriculum moved more and more toward bilingual study of the two cultures. Perhaps the outstanding characteristic of Roman education was a seriousness of purpose and thought and a deep concern with public affairs. Law and rhetoric, with scholars like Cicero and Quintilian leading the way, were the fields in which Roman education made the most lasting impression.

CHRISTIAN EDUCATION AND ABELARD

The Roman educational system began to disintegrate after the barbarian invasions of the fourth century. Christian schools developed slowly and at first offered little more than religious preparation for future priests and monks. But in a few places (Ireland was an example) the lamp of learning burned, and lay students as well as religious novitiates were admitted to study. Among the most distinguished of these church schools were the "bishop's schools," which were operated in connection with cathedrals and open to some members of the laity as well as the future clergy. Until about the tenth century the Christian church, through its monasteries and cathedral schools, offered the chief opportunities to young people seeking an education. It has been noted that the cathedral schools reproduced some of the patterns of the Roman grammar schools and in turn supplied a model for European grammar schools of post-Renaissance years. But only in a few teachers was the tradition of questioning, discussion, and intellectual search, set by the Athenian Academy, maintained.

One of these teachers was Abelard, whose fame as an educator may be remembered less well now than the sensational account of his love affair with his pupil Heloise. Abelard, however, taught in the tradition of the Greek masters, as the following example will show. In the early years of the twelfth century he prepared a sort of study text which he called *Sic et Non* (Yes and No). Exactly how he taught it we cannot be sure, but it must have been the basis of discussion and questioning and been intended to sharpen the skills of logic and impel young students to exert themselves in the search for truth among contradictions. He said,

> I wish to collect various sayings of the [Church] Fathers which occur to my memory and which, because of the apparent contradiction in them, present a

problem. They impel young readers to exert themselves most eagerly in the search for the truth, and render their minds more acute by means of the inquiry. This investigation is in fact the first key to wisdom, that is to say, assiduous or frequent inquiry, which is very strongly advocated by that most far-sighted of all philosophers, Aristotle, when he says in exhorting the studious, "Perhaps it is difficult to express oneself with confidence on such matters unless they have been discussed. To entertain doubt concerning some of them is not without advantage." For it is through doubting that we arrive at inquiry and through inquiry we perceive the truth.[13]

With this intent, he collected sayings of the saints in which they had contradicted each other or raised serious questions of truth. He set down something over 150 such propositions, of which the following are examples.

> That faith is based on reason, and the opposite.
> That faith is of things not seen, and the opposite.
> That Divine Providence is the cause of things happening, and the opposite.
> That nothing happens by chance, and the opposite.
> That all things are possible to God, and the opposite.
> That God knows all things, and the opposite.
> That without baptism with water nobody can be saved, and the opposite.
> That the sins of the fathers are visited upon the children, and the opposite.
> That it is permitted to marry more than once, and the opposite.
> That a man may kill himself for some reasons, and the opposite.
> That it is permitted to kill men, and the opposite.[14]

It is apparent that such classes with Abelard must have led to intense and exciting argument. What was said in those classes might have attracted the attention of the shepherds of the church, who wondered what would be happening to their flock.

THE UNIVERSITIES

There were some educational bright spots in the so-called Dark Ages of European education, but the really bright spots of that educational period were in India and the Muslim countries where the flourishing universities and truly distinguished research centers far outshone education in Europe.

Aryabhata was the greatest mathematician of the fifth century. He developed and introduced the use of decimals and the concept of zero. Other Indian scholars were responsible for leading-edge developments in botany, astronomy, and medicine. Half a dozen large universities provided home and workplace for these leading scholars. The University of Nalanda, for example, had several thousand teachers and students, and it was said that more than 1500 teachers discussed more than 100 different dissertations every day. Nalanda attracted students from many foreign countries, but gave an entrance examination so difficult that no more than two or three out of ten applicants could pass it and be admitted. The University of Nalanda was supported by the revenues from more than 100 surrounding villages. More than eight branches of medicine, including surgery and pediatrics, were said to be practiced there. Scholars specialized in subjects as varied as civil engineering and philosophy.

From India the infection of learning spread to the Muslim scholars and the universities they established in the Middle East, North Africa, and Spain. Scholars at these lively Muslim universities calculated the angle of the ecliptic; measured the size of the earth; calculated the procession of the equinoxes; invented the pendulum clock; explained, in the field of optics and physics, such phenomena as refraction of light, gravity, capillary attraction, and twilight; used the globe in teaching the geography of a round earth; and developed observatories for the empirical study of the heavenly bodies. They made advances in the use of drugs, herbs, and foods for medication; established hospitals with a system of interns and externs; discovered the causes of certain diseases and developed correct diagnoses of them; proposed new concepts of hygiene; made use of anesthetics in surgery with newly innovated surgical tools; and introduced the science of dissection in anatomy. They furthered the scientific breeding of horses and cattle; found new ways of grafting to produce new types of flowers and fruits; introduced new concepts of irrigation, fertilization, and soil cultivation; and improved upon the science of navigation. In the area of electricity, Muslim scholarship led to the discovery of such substances as potash, alcohol, nitrate of silver, nitric acid, sulfuric acid, and mercury chloride. It also developed to a high degree of perfection the arts of textiles, ceramics, and metallurgy.

This was what was happening in India and the Mediterranean countries while Europe was experiencing its Dark Ages. But the lights were about to go on again in Europe. Two new phenomena appeared in European education in the eleventh and twelfth centuries. First, there was a new confidence in rational thought as a means of solving problems, particularly those raised by the conflict of authorities. Second, a number of teachers with exceptional talents attracted scholars from the farthest ends of Europe. Abelard was one, in fact one of the foremost, of these. Around such teachers grew up the first universities in Europe. By the twelfth century the doctors at Salerno, the lawyers at Bologna, and the theology students at Paris were organizing into higher educational groups governed by chancellors. Soon these groups established their own statutes and degree requirements. The first universities were societies of students and teachers—guilds, they were most typically called then. At first the organization was quite loose; then gradually these guilds established codes of procedure and requirements and usually were sanctioned by a political or religious authority. Some became so well known that sanctioning was not considered necessary.

The first European university is a matter of dispute. Although Salerno (medicine) and Bologna (law) were probably teaching before Paris, the establishment of the University of Paris, which served as a model for much of north Europe and England, will do as well as any for a starting date. The University of Paris came into existence, beside the cathedral of Notre Dame on the Ile de la Cité, between 1150 and 1170, although it had no written statutes until 1208, and no rector until later than that. It had four faculties: three "superior"—theology, canon law, and medicine—and one "inferior"—arts. The university year was in two terms—from St. Remi (October 1) to Lent, and from Easter to St. Pierre (June 29). The courses were in some cases lectures, but more often the explication of texts (critical and interpretive reading of classics). Three degrees were available: the *determinatio,* or baccalaureate, conferring the right to teach under the supervision of a master; the *licendia docendi,* the right to teach, obtainable after the age of 21; and the doctorate, which was conferred only after a public examination and which signified entrance into the society of masters.

Oxford began in the twelfth century, Cambridge a little later in the same century. Heidelberg was chartered in 1386 and Salamanca in 1346, and gradually societies of students and masters spread over Europe and into the New World. Far away and much later (1636), a university was founded on the banks of the Charles River in Cambridge, Massachusetts, named after its first donor—John Harvard.

But when Harvard was founded, the Renaissance was over and national attention was turning to the establishment of elementary and secondary schools, built around the new products of printing. Therefore, a good place to pause in this long trip would be with Paris, and to look back from that point over the 25,000 years of education we have been reviewing.

TWENTY-FIVE CENTURIES OF EDUCATION

The first educational pattern we looked at was the kind that might have existed around the cave paintings: the family maintaining its ways of life by teaching them to its children. Then the most skilled persons in the community were co-opted to teach their special skills—hunting, sewing, and the like—to the younger people. Then came writing, and a few children were sent to learn to read and write as an aid to those who could not. This school for scribes expanded into a school for religious and government service. In China the preparation for government service turned into one of the most intensive and demanding systems of national examinations ever put into use, and it led to the preparation of many leaders for the government. In the centuries of the great virtuoso teachers, a few specially selected youths were given the opportunity of studying with them. And the next step after the development of individually distinguished scientists and philosophers was the gradual growth of universities and institutes of research and advanced study, in India and the Muslim states, beginning about 500, then in Western Europe, beginning about the twelfth century.

Two trends stand out from this pattern. Education began with instruction for all children, given by the family itself. After that, education became increasingly elitist and selective. The best hunters, the best potential scribes, and the most promising young thinkers were given the opportunity of education. Only a handful of Athenians got to study with Socrates. And when the universities came into being, they too were elitist schools, aimed at the ablest and most promising.

Second, whereas the earliest goal of education had been to maintain the status quo by teaching the children to walk in the steps of their elders, increasingly education came to be used rather to question the status quo, to improve upon it if possible, to add to knowledge rather than merely implanting it, and, especially with the philosopher-teachers, the research institutes, and the universities, to review and challenge existing practices in the bright light of reason.

The next step would be predictable even if we had no further history to examine. For one thing, more people would need and want the benefits of education, and it would therefore become less an elitist activity. This is what happened after the Renaissance and the political revolutions when nations decided that all their people, not merely a few selected ones, should have the opportunity to learn what they needed to learn. The result was national public school systems and the spread of schools beyond the cities to the peasant villages. Second, it would be predictable that education would be asked more and more not merely to teach what had become customary and accepted, but also to question humankind's picture of the universe and concept of the ideal society. This has been precisely the direction education has taken in recent centuries.

SUGGESTIONS FOR FURTHER READING

No reader of this book needs to be told that the historical literature on education is extensive or that it is mostly restricted to one country per book—for example, education in early Egypt or ancient Greece or Ming China or the United States of America after 1800, and the like. For instance, readers will see in this chapter that one of the most ancient clay tablets still in existence reports on what happened in the schools of old Sumer, that Plutarch was deeply interested in the educational system of Sparta, that Plato recorded much of what is believed to be Socrates' teaching in Athens, and that Abelard left behind many of his class topics. Given this richness and diversity of reference materials, a good starting place is the long article on History of Education in the *Encyclopaedia Britannica*. John Emerson Baker is author of the article in the 14th edition.

QUESTIONS TO THINK ABOUT

1. "Early education was essentially practical." Is this no longer true, and, if so, what brought about the change?
2. Apparently a student to be taught by Socrates did not need textbooks. Why are they necessary today?
3. What would you say were the social goals of education in old Sumer? In ancient China? Ancient Greece? The United States today?
4. It has been said that the effect of scribes on how people set down their ideas was something like the effect of the invention of the typewriter. To what extent is this true?
5. Of course we have no written record of what creative literature was like before writing, but writing must have made a difference when it was invented. What kind of difference, would you say?

TIME CAPSULE

First contemporary accounts of schools, in Sumer (Schools were established soon after writing reached any area.)	ca. 3800–3500 B.C.
Early universities	
University of Al-Azhar (Cairo)	970 A.D.
Bologna	1200
Paris	1150–1170
Oxford	ca. 1200
(Its first college was University College.)	1249
Cambridge	ca. 1230
Valladilid (chartered in)	1346
Heidelberg (chartered in)	1386
Santo Domingo	1538
Harvard	1636

FOR THE RECORD

Pleasurable Methods Must Be Devised in the First Stages of Teaching

Desiderius Erasmus (ca. 1466–1536)

Progress in learning a language is much furthered if the child be brought up amongst people who are gifted talkers. Descriptions and stories are impressed the better if to good narrative power the teacher or parent can add the help of pictorial illustration. The same method can be more particularly applied to the teaching of natural objects. Names and characteristics of trees, flowers, and animals can be thus learnt; specially is this plan needful where the creature described is wholly unfamiliar to the child, as for instance the rhinoceros, the tragelaphus, the onocratalus, the Indian ass, and the elephant. A picture is shown, containing an elephant, in combat with a dragon. At once the class shows curiosity. How shall the master proceed? He states the Greek and Latin names for elephant, giving the Latin genitive as well. He then points to the trunk, giving the Greek and Latin for it, and the purpose of the organ: he will explain that the elephant breathes as well as feeds by its means. The tusks are next dealt with, the uses and rarity of ivory; if possible he will produce something made of it. The dragon is shown to be of the large Indian species. He states the Greek and Latin equivalents for 'dragon,' their similarity in form, and their feminines. He will instil the fact that between the dragon and the elephant there is, instinctively and constantly, a ruthless war. If any boy is keen for further knowledge in the subject, the Master will add many other facts concerning the nature and habits of these two great beasts. Boys, too, will generally be attracted by pictures of hunting scenes, through which a wealth of information about trees, plants, birds, and animals may be imparted in a most delightful and yet instructive manner. In choosing subject-matter of this kind it is desirable to take some pains to discuss what is naturally attractive to the youthful mind, and discard what is of too advanced a kind. Remember always that youth is the springtime of life, when harvests are sown and flowers bloom.

The Clerk of Oxenford*

A Clerk ther was of Oxenford also,
That un-to logik hadde longe y-go.
As lene was his hors as is a rake,
And he was nat right fat, I undertake;
But loke holwe, and ther-to soberly.
Ful thredbar was his overest courtepy;
For he had geten him yet no benefyce,
Ne was so worldly for to have offyce.
For him was lever have at his beddes heed
Twenty bokes, clad in blak or reed,
Of Aristotle and his philosophye,
Than robes riche, or fithele, or gay sautrye.
But al be that he was a philosophre,
Yet hadde he but litel gold in his cofre;
But al that he mighte of his frendes hente,
On bokes and on lerninge he it spente,
And bisily gan for the soules preye
Of hem that yaf him wher-with to scoleye.
Of studie took he most cure and most hede.
Noght a word spak more than was nede,
And that was seyd in forme and reverence,
And short and quick, and full of hy sentence.
Souninge in moral vertu was his speche,
And gladly wolde he lerne, and gladly teche.

*From Chaucer, *Canterbury Tales*.

Ionia in its great age.

LANGUAGE FOR MATHEMATICS AND SCIENCE

Mighty are numbers; joined with art, irresistible.

EURIPIDES

*H*umans learned very early to count. As a matter of fact, scientists think they have discovered a rudimentary counting sense in animals. If a certain bird's nest contains four eggs, Kramer reports, one may be taken away without disturbing the mother. If two are removed, however, the bird seems to be aware of the difference and usually deserts the nest.[1] Can she count? Lubbock describes a certain species of wasp that supplies the cells in which the young are to be hatched with 5 caterpillars apiece; another species supplies 10, another 15, still another 24. The number is unchanging for each species. In one line the males are smaller than the females, and the mother supplies the cell of the male egg with five victims, the female egg with ten. This, too, is a constant. Does that mean the mother wasp can count?[2]

COUNTING

Do not confuse the development of a number system with the ability to count. Whether or not the number sense is shared with other animals, there is no doubt that primitive humans developed an ability to count at a very early stage. Our observation of existing primitives suggests that they may begin by distinguishing one from more than, then one from two and two from more than two. Some very primitive languages contain no number words at all. More typical, however, are the languages that have words for one and two, and then call everything more than that "a lot," or "many," or "much," or "a heap." It is reasonable to think that primitive humans, in the dawn of language, long before the time of the cave painters, started to learn numbers this way.

As a matter of fact, certain tribes today still have this kind of approach to numbers. Kramer cites the case of one of the tribes of the Torres Straits who had only two number words—*urapun* for "one" and *okosa* for "two." They counted this way:[3]

> 1 = *urapun*
> 2 = *okosa*
> 3 = *okosa urapun*
> 4 = *okosa okosa*
> 5 = *okosa okosa urapun*
> 6 = *okosa okosa okosa*

At that point they gave up with number words and called everything more than six, *ras,* "a lot." You can see why they carried the system no farther than six: Saying 100 would require them to repeat 50 *okosas.* An example of this problem is what the Basuto people of Africa have to say when they express "ninety-nine":[4]

Machoumearobilengmonoolemongametarobilengmoolemong

The next step may well have been tallying, illustrated by our own most common way of keeping track of number totals: ℍℍℍ || = 7. Many early peoples seem to have had tally systems. They typically counted by fives, as we do in the system just illustrated, probably because of the example of five fingers or five toes. Others counted by twos, however, on the model of two eyes, two hands, two legs, and so forth. One tribe of California Indians counted in groups of four, because they apparently took as their model the spaces between the fingers rather than the fingers themselves.

A well-developed system of tallying by fives was used as late as the eleventh century by the Japanese, who had earlier borrowed it from the Chinese. It went like this:[5]

ǀ	ǁ	ǁǀ	ǀǀǀǀ	ǀǀǀǀǀ		T	TT	TTT	TTTT		—	=	≡	≣	≣		⊥	⊥	⊥	⊥
1	2	3	4	5		6	7	8	9		10	20	30	40	50		60	70	80	90

NUMBERS

The importance of a tallying system was that it set up a one-to-one correspondence between a number of things and their numeration. That is, six articles or persons could be checked off against a tally and thus compared with five or eight articles or persons. Once people had a tallying system, they could progress to addition and subtraction and from there to number symbols, which made it easier to use numbers for comparing lengths, sizes, and areas. Early arithmetic and geometry grew mostly out of practical problems. Humans had to count the animals in a herd, measure the size of a piece of land, record the days until the next planting season, and the like. Because the early Egyptians had to recalculate property markers after the

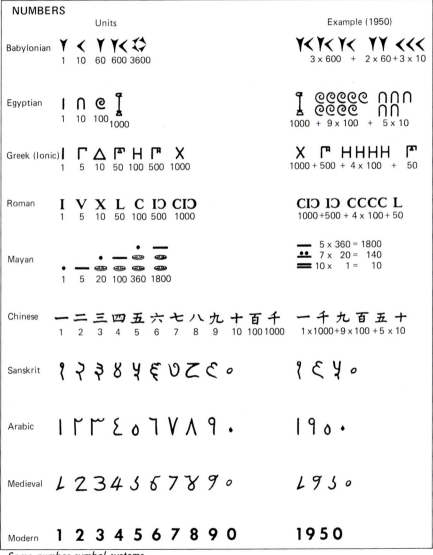

Some number symbol systems.

annual Nile flood, they devised many number words.[6] The Egyptians included number symbols among their hieroglyphs; for example,

1 was a straight line

10 was an arch

100 was a coiled rope

1,000 was a lotus flower

10,000 was a finger pointing skyward

100,000 was a tadpole

1,000,000 was a man with arms outstretched (perhaps in wonder at so large a number!)

Here is how the early Egyptians wrote the number 32,536:

$$\text{{{ ∬ ⦷⦷⦷ ∩∩ ⦀}}$$

Other peoples borrowed number symbols from their word or letter writing. Most of us are familiar with the Roman symbols I for 1, V for 5, X for 10, L for 50, C for 100, and M for 1000. The Greeks also used adaptations of their alphabet to express numerals. Our present numerals are called *Arabic* because we adopted them from the Arabs, although the Hindus also had something to do with their origin.

The following chart shows some of the best-known number symbol systems. You will notice that the number zero begins to appear for the first time with Sanskrit, the language brought by the Aryan invasion of India and used much by the Hindus.

THE LONGEST STEP

An efficient system of number symbols is very important, but it was not the most important step in the growth of a language for mathematics and science. That step was learning to abstract numbers from their referents—to think of "two-ness" and "threeness," rather than of two fish or two rocks, three buffalo or three spears.

In her book *The Main Stream of Mathematics,* Kramer says,

> Some philosophers believe that it may require untold ages for a primitive tribe to conceive the notion that a set of twins, a pair of eyes, and a couple of days are all instances of the general concept "two." What usually happens is that

a tribe evolves a word for "two" to refer to a pair of human beings, a different word "two" for a couple of animals, still another "two" for inanimate objects, and so on. The Thimsian language of a tribe in British Columbia illustrates this very point. . . . There are seven different words for "two," seven others for "three," etc., as far as they count. One set is for animals and flat objects, one for time and round objects, one for human beings, one for trees and long objects, one for canoes, one for measures, and one for miscellaneous objects not in the other six categories.[7]

Alfred North Whitehead wrote on the same subject:

Suppose we project our imaginations backward through many thousands of years, and endeavour to realise the simple-mindedness of even the greatest intellects of these early societies. Abstract ideas which to us are immediately obvious must have been, for them, matters only of the most dim apprehension. For example take the question of number. We think of the number "five" as applying to appropriate groups of any entities whatsoever—to five fishes, five children, five apples, five days. Thus, in considering the relation of the number "five" to the number "three," we are thinking of two groups of things, one with five members and the other with three members. But we are entirely abstracting from the consideration of any particular entities, or even of any particular sorts of entities, which go to make up the membership of either of the two groups. We are merely thinking of those relations between those two groups which are entirely independent of the individual essences of any of the members of either group. This is a very remarkable feat of abstraction; and it must have taken ages for the human race to rise to it.[8]

It did indeed take a long time for humans to arrive at that way of thinking. The oldest mathematical text we have is apparently the Rhind papyrus, supposedly written by an Egyptian priest named Adhmes in the seventeenth century B.C. It is essentially a text on arithmetic, and more than half of it deals with the reduction of fractions. As we find out more and more about early mathematics and mathematicians, we learn with some amazement of how far the Babylonians and Sumerians went with the mathematics of astronomy and geometry. Their findings are now seen to have aided the Egyptians, the Greeks, and later the Indians and the Spanish Muslim mathematicians. For example, the first scholar who discovered the importance to mathematicians of the concept of zero is believed to have been a Babylonian named Naburianu, almost 1000 years before the concept was developed by the Hindus. The Egyptians were great practical geometricians, as their surveys and their observatories proved, but they made little contribution to the theoretical underpinnings of the science. The Greeks were ahead in the theoretical area at the time of Pericles and for a long while beginning about 600 B.C. As a matter of fact, it was the translation of Greek books from 600 B.C. to the time of Christ that fueled the mathematics and encouraged the science of the Renaissance.

THE NUMBER ZERO

There were many bright spots in mathematics and science between the great centuries of Greece and the European Renaissance. The Hindus, for instance, treated fractions in a fresh way. They understood the law of signs. They calculated the value of pi (the ratio of circumference to diameter of a circle). But the really exciting part of Hindu mathematics was the treatment of zero. For centuries, mathematicians—including those in India, such as Bhaskara and Aryabhata—had puzzled over the meaning and use of zero. Even the greatest mathematicians had been unable to think of zero as a number. Diophantos, who lived in the third century and made some of the most significant early contributions to algebra, asked, what number, multiplied by itself, gives itself as an answer? "Obviously one," he answered his own question. We would add, "Zero also." But zero did not exist for Diophantos except as a dash; it was not a number.[9]

Historians have offered various explanations of why the interpretation of zero as a number came more easily to the Indians, with their concepts of nirvana and infinity, than to other people. One significant contribution the Hindu mathematicians made was to show that that any number except zero divided by zero equals infinity. They divided a number by 0.1, then 0.01, then 0.001, and so on, and were able to show that the smaller the number divided into any number the larger the result would be. Thus they concluded that if one could divide by the smallest conceivable number—zero—then the result would be infinitely large. Thus gradually the Hindu mathematicians were able to shed some light on the concept of zero as well as the problems of fractions, which raised other questions bothering the early mathematicians. They were able to conceive of zero as a tenth number and numbers as a ten-place system in which zero could be used to indicate a shift point. The great French mathematician-astronomer Laplace had this to say of the Hindu contribution:

> It is India that gave us this ingenious method of expressing all numbers by means of ten symbols, each symbol receiving a value of position as well as absolute value, a profound and important idea which appears so simple to us now that we ignore its true merit, but its very simplicity, the great ease which it has lent to all computations, puts our arithmetic in the first rank of useful inventions; and we shall appreciate the grandeur of this achievement when we

remember that it escaped the genius of Archimedes and Appolonius, two of the greatest men produced by antiquity.[10]

IONIA

An Early Flourishing of Science

There was a bright period in China about the tenth to twelfth centuries. Among the products of this country, before or during this time, were the astrolabe, gunpowder, the clock, paper and ink, and the first really skillful printing. An astronomer named Kuo Shou-Ching made important contributions to astronomical knowledge. There was another bright period in Spain during the Muslim occupation when Arab and Jewish scholars translated many of the pre-Christian Greek texts and saved them for later use in Europe. But the great place and time for mathematics and science in all the centuries before the European Renaissance was the Ionian islands of Greece during the years between 600 B.C. and the Christian era.

Why Ionia? Carl Sagan asks, "why in these unassuming and pastoral landscapes, these remote islands of the Eastern Mediterranean?"[11] Why not in one of the great rich cities? He tries to explain what lay behind the events in Ionia:

> The Ionians had several great advantages. Ionia is an island realm. Isolation, even if incomplete, breeds diversity. With many different islands there was a variety of political systems. No single concentration of power could enforce social and intellectual conformity in all the islands. Free inquiry became possible. The promotion of superstition was not considered a political necessity. Unlike many other cultures, the Ionians were at the crossroads of civilizations, not at one of the centers. In Ionia, the Phoenician alphabet was first adapted to Greek usage and wide-spread literacy became possible. Writing was no longer a monopoly of the priests and scribes. The thoughts of many were available for consideration and debate. Political power was in the hands of the merchants, who actively promoted the technology on which their prosperity depended. It was in the Eastern Mediterranean that African, Asian, and European civilizations. including the great cultures of Egypt and Mesopotamia, met and cross-fertilized in a vigorous and heady confrontation of prejudices, languages, ideas and gods. What do you do when you are faced with several different gods each claiming the same territory? The Babylonian Marduk and the Greek Zeus was each considered master of the sky and king of the gods. You might decide that Marduk and Zeus were really the same. You might also decide, since they had quite different attributes, that one of them was merely invented by the priests. But if one, why not both?
>
> And so it was that the great idea arose, the realization that there might be

a way to know the world without the god hypothesis; that there might be principles, forces, laws of nature, through which the world could be understood without attributing the fall of every sparrow to the direct intervention of Zeus.[12]

Between 600 and 400 B.C., he says, this great revolution in human thought began. Ionia, he concludes, was the place where science was born.

The first great Ionian scientist was Thales of Miletus, who was able to predict a solar eclipse, to measure the height of a pyramid from the length of its shadow and the angle of the sun above the horizon (which is the same way we have measured the height of the mountains on the moon), and to prove theorems, foreshadowing Euclid. Another Ionian was Theodorus, the master engineer of ancient times. He was said to be responsible for developing the key, the ruler, the carpenter's square, the level, and the lathe. He also made notable contributions to the skill of bronze casting. Bronze was used in the Middle East as early as 10,000 years ago but was not very practical until people learned how to extract it from the minerals in which it was found. That happened about 5000 B.C. The process of extracting copper was discovered a few centuries after that, and later on some of the copper and bronze findings were applied to working with steel. Perhaps the outstanding achievement of the ancient world in working with hard alloys was the Japanese steel sword, which dated to about 800 B.C. and was a model for such work for centuries.

But back to the Ionian scientists. It is hardly necessary to mention the name of Euclid, whose books were resurrected and exerted a great influence on geometry during the European Renaissance. Eratosthenes was able to estimate the circumference of the earth (which he did not think was flat) within two or three percent. Hipparchus mapped the constellations. Archimedes was probably the greatest mechanical genius until the time of Leonardo. Ptolemy named the stars, understood the precession of the equinoxes, and devised an apparent explanation for the motion of the planets. Pythagoras contributed far more than the Pythagorean theorem that all today's mathematics students study. Hippocrates, the most famous physician of ancient times and author of the physician's oath which all medical students still repeat as a part of their graduation ceremony, was another of the Ionian group. Still another was Democritus, who conceived the idea of the "ultimate particle," which he called the atom. Here are his theories on the structure of matter.

1. There is nothing but atoms and space; all else is an impression of the senses.
2. Out of nothing comes nothing; nothing which is can be reduced to nothing. All change is merely an aggregation or separation of parts.
3. Nothing happens by chance or intention, everything through cause and of necessity. The laws of nature inhere in the mere combination of atoms.[13]

In many respects the most forward-looking of the astronomer-mathematicians was Aristarchus, who was probably the first distinguished scientist to hold the view that the sun rather than the earth is the center of the solar system, and the planets go around the sun rather than the earth.

What a constellation of scientific stars these Ionians represented! But the result of their science was ultimately a disappointment.

What Happened to Ionia

What happened scientifically on the Ionian islands was a genuine shock to most of the people in neighboring countries who knew about it. Even to the most brilliant of the Athenians in Plato's and Aristotle's time, the universe and the human race were operated and controlled by gods and demons. They believed the sun was a god, not a hot stone. They believed in thinking about the natural world around them, not doing experiments on it. They felt that science was something for slaves to do, not the free citizens of Athens. And then suddenly they found on their doorsteps in the eastern Mediterranean a group of articulate scholars like Anaxagoras who believed that "everything was made of atoms; that human and other animals had sprung from simpler forms; that diseases were not caused by demons or gods; that the Earth was only a planet going around the Sun. And that the stars were very far away."[14] It was impossible for them to accept the idea that the sun might be so large as actually to be larger than the Peloponnesus (the part of the Greek peninsula where Sparta was located). It was incongruous for them to hear from the Ionian scientists that "neither we nor our planet enjoys a privileged position in nature," which Sagan calls the "heritage of Aristarchus,"[15] and which, as we know, continued to be denied almost until our own time.

As a result, the Ionian scientists were ignored or scorned or punished. Pericles brought the brilliant Anaxagoras to be his own adviser, and soon Anaxagoras was thrown into prison for impiety. Plato is thought to be responsible for having all the books of Democritus—who believed in atoms—burned, and in fact not even one book of Democritus still exists. What was happening among the scholars of Athens was incompatible with what was happening on the Ionian islands. As the historians now record, Ionian science came toward its end. The tide turned away from experimental and naturalistic science, and even though some of it continued in the great library and research institute in Alexandria, for the most part it was little heard of for 1500 years. As a matter of fact, Kepler was persecuted and jailed in the sixteenth century for about the same beliefs that got Anaxagoras into jail in Athens. As late as our own century it was widely believed that the Milky Way is the only galaxy in the universe, and it took real courage for the Harvard astronomer Harlow Shapley, in 1921, to suggest that our solar system might be actually out near the edge of the Milky Way galaxy rather than at its center. We have only to look at the Dark Ages to find impressive evidence of what happened to the best thought of Ionia.

What if the bright light of early science in Ionia had not flickered out when it did? Sagan asks that question in his book *Cosmos:*

> What if science and the experimental method and the dignity of crafts and the mechanical arts had been pursued for 2000 years before the Industrial Revolution? What if the power of this new mode of thought had been more generally appreciated? I sometimes think we might then have saved ten or twenty centuries. Perhaps the contributions of Leonardo would have been made a thousand years ago, and those of Albert Einstein 500 years ago. . . . If the Ionian spirit had won, I think we—a different "we," of course—might by now be venturing to the stars. Our first survey ships to Alpha Centauri and Barnard's Star, Sirius and Tau Cen would have returned long ago. Great fleets of interstellar transports would be under construction in Earth orbit—unmanned survey ships, liners for immigrants, immense trading ships to plow the seas of space. On all these ships there would be symbols and writing. If we looked closely, we might see that the language was Greek.[16]

We are not yet ready for the stars, Sagan says—"but perhaps in another century or two, when the solar system is all explored (and) we will also have put our own planet in order, we will have the will and the resources and the technical knowledge to go to the stars."[17]

From what did not happen in Ionia as well as from what did, we can draw a communication lesson. Ignorance and prejudice and misplaced authority closed around the great scientists of Ionia and kept them from communicating what they knew. The absence of communication is therefore as powerful as its presence. It may have cost you and me a thousand years of intellectual growth.

What Ionian Science Has Meant to Us

What is the importance of the invention of what Whitehead calls "almost perfect technical efficiency in the manipulation of numbers"?[18] We might think of computers and modern electronic calculators, but certainly they did not exist when the Ionians were estimating the orbits of the planets. But a highly efficient abacus was already in use at the time of the Greeks, and many centuries earlier than the abacus there was a kind of protoabacus, a so-called counting machine that worked as shown in the following illustration. Here is how the number 1740 would be registered on the abacus:

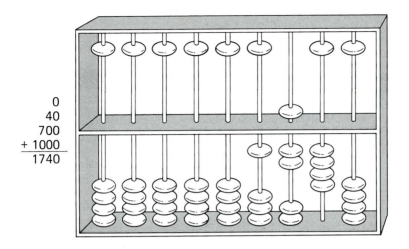

It was not machines like this, however, that were responsible for the mathematical thinking of the Ionians. It was the fact that a few humans learned to think generally and abstractly about the things and relationships surrounding them and thus could state relationships that would have general rather than particular application. Quoting Whitehead again, "Mathematics supplied the background of imaginative thought with which the men of science approached the observation of nature. Galileo produced formulae, Descartes produced formulae, Huyghens produced formulae, Newton produced formulae."[19]

Thus, by enabling human thought to move into abstractions, mathematics has not taken it away from practicalities. Let us quote again from Whitehead: "Nothing is more impressive than the fact that as mathematics withdrew increasingly into the upper regions of ever greater extremes of abstract thought, it returned back to earth with a corresponding growth of importance for the analysis of concrete fact."[20] Because there was great mathematics in the seventeenth century, the eighteenth century was mathematically minded and the platform was laid for the Industrial Revolution of the nineteenth. Because of the development of generalized understandings in those centuries, in the twentieth century we have computers and sophisticated electronics and satellites.

SUGGESTIONS FOR FURTHER READING

Most of the general treatments of communication history such as Lancelot Hogben's *From Cave Painting to Comic Strip* (New York: Chanticleer Press, 1949) have chapters on the development of mathematics and science. A useful collection of essays and papers on the subject is James R. Newman, ed., *The World of Mathematics* (New York: Simon & Schuster,

4 vols., 1956). A briefer book with a historical emphasis is Edna E. Kramer, *The Main Stream of Mathematics* (New York: Oxford University Press, 1952). The titles on the history of science are legion.

QUESTIONS TO THINK ABOUT

1. Why do we have ten numerals rather than, say, 8 or 12 or 5? If we did have a system with 12 numerals, where would zero appear?
2. Can you write the numerals for the present year in some of the languages represented in chart on page 105—for instance, Egyptian, Greek (Ionic), Roman, Chinese, and Arabic?
3. Why is it important to have a rule for the position of numbers?
4. Why, would you say, have Arabic numbers come into use in so many countries of the world?
5. What special requirements for number systems are created by (a) writing, (b) printing, (c) worldwide commerce, and (d) computers?
6. Although the Arabs and Hindus in the Middle Ages had the mathematical sign for square root, plus and minus signs came into use only in the fifteenth century, and multiplication and division signs only in the sixteenth century. Why would these four very common signs have come into use so late, and the square root sign so early?

TIME CAPSULE

Adhmes (Rhind papyrus)	9th century B.C.*
Thales	636–546
Pythagoras	ca. 582–ca. 507
Anaxagoras	ca. 500–ca. 428
Empedocles	ca. 495–ca. 435
Hippocrates	ca. 460–ca. 470
Democritus	ca. 460–ca. 370
Plato	ca. 427–ca. 347
Aristotle	384–322
Euclid	ca. 300
Aristarchus	ca. 310–ca. 230
Archimedes	ca. 287–ca. 212
Ptolemy	2nd century A.D.
Aryabhata	ca. 539–?
Other distinguished Indian mathematicians	400–650

*Readers should be warned that early Greek biographical dates are rather hazy, and that different reference books are likely to give different dates for the Greeks in this list. The source of these biographical dates is the *Concise Columbia Encyclopedia* (New York: Columbia University Press, 1983).

Copernicus	1473–1545
Galileo	1564–1642
Kepler	1571–1630
Descartes	1596–1650
Pascal	1623–1662
Newton	1642–1727

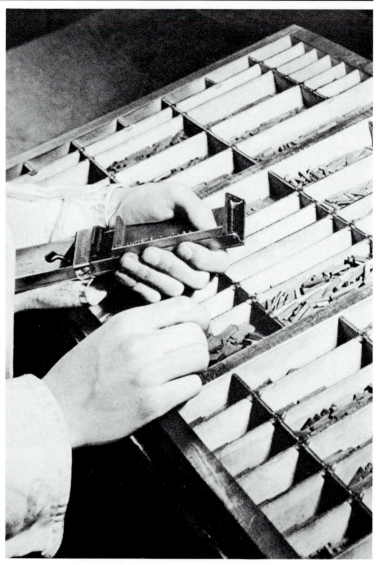

Setting type. These skillful hands are making use of what we might call the third great development in human communication. Note that this printer is working with a type case that contains 26 letters, 26 capitals, and a few punctuation marks, rather than the 8000 or more characters with which the earlier Chinese printers had to work.

THE DAY OF THE PRINTER

[No one] needs to be told at length how printing contributed to the diffusion of knowledge previously transmitted by oral tradition, how much more the master-printers and bookmakers from Gutenberg to Benjamin Franklin contributed to the making of our language habits than all the professors of their time, how much the trade in reading matter contributed to the great enlightenment of the four centuries that followed. . . . Literacy is today a medical diagnosis.

LANCELOT HOGBEN

The Printing-press may be strictly denominated a Multiplication Table as applicable to the mind of man. The art of printing is a multiplication of mind.

RICHARD CARLILE

If a date could be set for the invention of printing, it would be long before 1450, when tradition has it that printed matter had begun to come from the press of Johann Gutenberg in Mainz, Germany. Printing, as we know it, was a long time coming into use, and came to Europe mostly from China and Korea. Rag paper and good ink were available in China by the year 200 A.D. or perhaps earlier. A few hundred years later, documents were being printed from carved wooden blocks; the oldest surviving book so printed was produced about 700 A.D. Six hundred years later, more or less, the art and convenience of printing from movable type—one character on each piece of wood, metal, or hard clay—was discovered and put to use, apparently in Korea. Thus every essential element of the printing process was available to Gutenberg and his colleagues in 1450, and they supplied the one missing element by adapting the European wine press for use in the print shop.

Therefore, if a date could be set for the invention of printing it would be long before Gutenberg's work in 1450. There is even some doubt as to how much part Gutenberg himself played in the events of those years around 1450. Whatever the precise details may be, he stands in the story of human communication as a symbolic figure rather than a discoverer, and 1450 stands as a date of fruition rather than one of innovation.

PRE-CHRISTIAN ERA PUBLISHING

There was an impressive amount of printing and publishing before 1450, even before the beginning of the Christian calendar.[1] Nearly half a million clay tablets have been found that were "published" in cuneiform writing in the countries east of the Mediterranean. Many of them were made before 2000 B.C., and many came from the libraries of Babylon and other ancient cities. The royal libraries in Alexandria were estimated to hold 490,000 scrolls in the third century B.C. There still survives a complete book, the Egyptian Book of the Dead, inscribed on papyrus in 1350 B.C. The *Acta Diurna,* which was posted at various places in Rome to carry official news and announcements, particularly the acts of the Roman Senate, and which consequently has some claim to be considered the first newspaper, began publication in 131 B.C. As early as 100 B.C., the Sosii brothers in Rome, using armies of scribes, were publishing, copying, and selling books in editions that would have been considered quite respectable in size even in the early decades of printing. Horace was one of the Sosii authors. Papyrus had been in use for writing as early as 2500 B.C. in Egypt, and parchment in Greece by 150 B.C. Thus, before the beginning of the Christian era, public libraries, publishers, books, a protonewspaper, papyrus and parchment, ink, rudimentary copyright laws, and even some instances of official censorship were all in existence.

EARLY DEVELOPMENTS IN EAST ASIA

Beginning with the Christian era, center stage shifts to China. During the Han dynasty, in a year traditionally recorded as 105, a court eunuch named Ts'ai Lun reported to the emperor on a new process for making writing material. Silk paper was too expensive; papyrus and bamboo strips were too clumsy; parchment required a great number of animal skins—for example, to print one copy of Gutenberg's Bible on parchment would have required 170 skins. But Ts'ai Lun (or some inventor whom he sponsored) had learned a lesson from the wasp, which chews various types of vegetable fibers and, when they are moist, presses them into a light, smooth material for its nest. So the Chinese tried different fibers and combinations of them: tree bark, rope, rags, even fishnets. They soaked these in tubs, pounded them with mallets, passed them through a sieve, and pressed them into thin sheets to dry. Either Ts'ai Lun or his younger contemporaries perfected ways to make the paper absorb ink efficiently. They tried adding different substances for sizing. The best additive they found was starch flour, usually in the form of a thick paste. (Some centuries later, gelatin was found to be a still better material for sizing.) The resulting paper was relatively inexpensive, light in weight, and easy to handle and to write upon.

For the historic date 105, we have only the record of the Han historian. The first clearly datable paper that survives in China was made in the year 264 A.D., from precisely the kind of materials Ts'ai Lun had specified. And in 1931 the Swedish archaeologist Folke Bergman, exploring a Han ruin, discovered what very possibly may be the oldest sheet of paper in the world. It was stashed away with other materials, including a number of manuscripts written on wood, some of which could be dated. Most of the pieces of wood, for instance, seem to date from about the year 95. On the latest of them was written "5th day of the 1st moon of the 10th year of Yung-Yuan," or February 24, 98. We cannot assume that all the manuscripts were stored away as soon as they were written or that the sheet of paper was put in the cache at exactly the same time as the other items, but the probability is that the paper was hidden away at the same time as or shortly after the other items and that the wooden manuscripts were not very old when put away. If so, the ancient sheet must have been manufactured soon after, or even before, Ts'ai Lun's paper.

The development of paper gave China a long start in making use of the new art of writing. Ink from lampblack had been available since about 100 B.C. Between the years 175 and 183, standard texts of the Chinese classics were being cut in stone and multiple copies of ink rubbings made from them. About the fifth century it became common practice to use seals made of wood for stamping charms on paper. Seals and stamps, of course, had been in use since at least the second millennium B.C., and a high level of skill had been attained in engraving them. In the late seventh or early eighth century—during the Tang dynasty, which has often been compared to the Renaissance in Europe—these seals and stamps evolved into good block printing. Outlines of written characters were cut out of a smooth wooden block, the raised parts were inked, and an impression was recorded by pressing the block and a sheet of paper tightly together. So common did block printing become that about the year 770 the Japanese empress Shotoku ordered one million Buddhist charms, in Sanskrit language and Chinese characters, to be printed from wooden blocks for use by the faithful. In 835, printing was mentioned for the first time in extant Chinese literature, and the earliest complete block-printed book that survives was printed in 868. Then the Sung dynasty (960–1280), just as it had done with such other products as the magnetic compass, gunpowder, and porcelain, developed and put into wide use what the more creative Tang dynasty had conceived. These were two remarkable dynasties, one more creative, the other more productive. The Sung published dynastic histories, the Chinese classics, commentaries on the classics, dictionaries, books on medicine, botany, and agriculture, and belles lettres—over 500 volumes, some in large editions. The quality of block printing was very high in this period. And this was while Europe was in the darker part of what we somewhat unjustly call the Dark Ages.

THE SLOW SPREAD OF THE CHINESE DEVELOPMENTS

Why did these developments in China take so long to reach the West?[2] Part of the reason may have been Chinese secretiveness, part of it the uncommonness of travel and trade. Marco Polo apparently missed seeing much of the printing industry, although he did notice that the Chinese were using paper money. It was the Muslims who first made use of the Chinese developments in printing. At the battle of Talas, near Samarkand, in 751, they seem to have captured some Chinese printers and from them learned the secret of making rag paper. They set up their own paper mills in Samarkand, and the industry spread over the Muslim territories and even into Moorish Spain. But it took another four centuries for the method to come into use in Europe. In any case, not until about 1275 did the first papermaking centers grow up in Italy, and it was 50 to 75 years more before they appeared in France and Germany. The Italians made a substantial contribution to the process by using gelatin for sizing, and the Germans by using water power to operate the mills and mash the vegetable fibers. By the end of the fourteenth century there was an ample supply of fiber paper in Europe to replace the far more expensive and harder-to-print-on parchment. But that was 12 centuries after the process had become familiar in China. And in the meantime China had been experiencing its own renaissance 500 years before the Renaissance in Europe.

While paper slowly made its way from central Asia into the Muslim countries and across the Mediterranean to Western Europe, a still greater secret was known in Asia and apparently not exported. In the eleventh century, between 1041 and 1048, movable type was invented there. The first account of it appears in a book by Shen Kua, who was born in 1030 and lived to record many of the innovations of the Sung period, including the magnetic compass. His account of this landmark in typography bears all the marks of an eyewitness, and you will enjoy reading it.[3] Although the story is too long to reproduce in this book, here is a brief summary:

> Pi Sheng, "a man of the common people," was the inventor, Shen said. He made type of baked clay in which he cut characters "as thin as the edge of a copper coin." Each character was a single piece of type. He put them into an iron frame for printing and stored them—20 copies or more of the frequently used characters—in wooden type cases marked with labels. This sounds very much like a modern hand-set print shop, and his discovery could have been earthshaking but apparently was not. "When Pi Sheng died," says the account, "his font of type passed into the possession of my cousins and up to this time it has been kept as a precious possession." Thus it became a family keepsake rather than a national resource.

Another such event took place about 1313 in China. A magistrate named Wang Cheng caused about 60,000 characters to be carved, each on its own wood block. He also invented type cases that revolved around a vertical axis, so that the enormous number of different characters could be readily stored and retrieved. He used these to print the records of his district, and he had hoped to use the same font to publish a large book on agriculture but found that artisans had already begun to cut large wood blocks for this volume. So, rather sadly, he "laid the type aside to await another opportunity"—which, we can assume, never came.[4]

Another lost opportunity was suggested by an archaeologist's discovery of several hundred pieces of hardwood type on the floor of a cave in Tun-huang, west of the Gobi Desert. They have been dated as approximately 1300. Therefore, apparently the art of printing with movable type was being practiced at the beginning of the fourteenth century even far from the population centers of China.

But the tantalizing feature of this discovery is that the language there was Uighur, which is descended from Aramaic and is alphabetical. Thus it would seem that the stage was set in China for printing with movable type using a limited number of alphabetical characters rather than the 8000 or so necessary to print in

Chinese. But apparently the time was not ripe: The Uighurs were not printing in their own language; the language of the movable type found in the cave at Tun-huang was Chinese.

Now the scene shifts to Korea. Movable type seems to have come into use there, and apparently there were early experiments with casting it in metal. It is claimed that a book was published there from movable type as early as 1241, and there is no doubt whatsoever that a government type foundry was established in 1403. Korean historians commonly give this latter date for the introduction of movable metal type. The best writers in Korea were put to work to design the type for the new foundry. At least three separate fonts were made, and many books were printed. But as in the other two incidents, there was a curious result. Like the Uighurs, the Koreans had a phonetic alphabet—it was apparently available before 1403—but they did not use their own alphabet for printing with their own movable type. Why? Apparently because Chinese was the literary language of Korea, and it was felt that the literary treasures of the nation should be preserved in the traditional language.

So this is the stage that printing in Asia had reached before Gutenberg. DeVinne comments, "The inventor of printing did not invent paper and did not originate engraving on wood. He was not the first to print upon paper, he was not the first to make printed books, it is not certain that he made the first printing press, it is not probable that he was the first to think of or make movable type."[5]

EARLY EUROPEAN PRINTING

The record of printing in Asia throws a slightly different light upon the invention of printing in Europe. Not that what happened in Mainz and other European centers of printing about 1450 and in the decades immediately following was any less significant, but rather it was significant for a different reason. What did actually happen in the Gutenberg years? The first thing to note is that Gutenberg and his fellow European printers of the fifteenth century were in the right place at the right time.

All the ingredients for a successful printing industry were at hand.[6] All the mechanical aspects of printing except an efficient press were inherited from Asia. For the one missing ingredient, the printers of France, Germany, and Italy had only to look around them at the wine presses in European vineyards.

Skills related to printing and bookmaking were also abundant in the fifteenth century. For centuries, Christian monks, working patiently in their scriptoria, had kept alive the art of bookmaking; indeed, they had maintained a standard of careful illumination and well-drafted pages that printed books would have a hard time equaling. Just how many block books were circulating in Europe before 1450 we do not know—the number was certainly far less than the outpouring of such books in Asia—but there seems no doubt that there were master printers before Gutenberg, although most of them may have been producing playing cards and shrine cards rather than books. A new trade in pictorial reproduction was helping to support artists. Metal workers had mastered the art of making stamps and dies, and among goldsmiths and jewelers were many skilled engravers who put letters or illustrations on the stamps. Gutenberg was first employed by a goldsmith. Thus a group of skilled trades and arts was gathering around the early printers, ready to take on larger assignments.

In the fourteenth and fifteenth centuries, a new urban class of merchants, traders, and artisans had emerged to share power with the landed aristocracy. Many of them became highly prosperous and could afford to pay for information. They needed information—literacy to read accounts, navigation books and almanacs to steer a valuable cargo safely from port to port, handbooks of military science, quick reports on prices and sales in faraway markets. The middle class was demanding the right to share with the nobles and the clergy the skill of reading. Education, which had been largely the responsibility of the church, was now expanding out of the monasteries, and lay schools were becoming available. Universities were coming into being. Oxford, as we have said, was founded in 1167, the University of Paris a bit earlier, and 50 other universities in the next two centuries. There was a new birth of interest in the Greek and Roman classics, and a rising interest in science spurred by the new mathematical inputs from India and the Muslim worlds. As lay society needed more printed materials on education, business, science, and politics, so did the church need many copies of indulgences, prayer books, and scriptures. In other words, there was a wide sense of need as well as resources to meet the need and pay for it.

Let us not forget one other resource of great importance—an alphabet in common use throughout Europe. Consequently there was no need, as there would have been in China, to cast 8000 different items of type.

In other words, when Gutenberg appeared on the scene the social situation was set for a cultural explosion. In the next century that explosion took place. What Gutenberg actually had to do with it is rather mysterious.

GUTENBERG

He was born Johannes Gensfleisch zur Laden, probably a year or two before 1400. His father called himself Friele Gensfleisch zur Laden zum Gutenberg, the

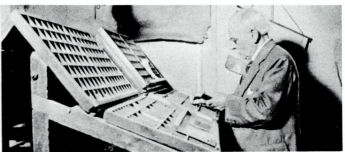

The effect of having an alphabet. **Top:** *a type case for Chinese characters.*
Bottom: *a type case for English.*

last name being that of the family home, and Johann took the name of the house for his own, with the result that he appears in history as Johann or Johannes Gutenberg. His family was one of the patrician clans of Mainz, a city known for its artisans in precious metal. His father worked for the mint of the archbishop, and for this and other reasons we think that young Gutenberg must have become familiar with the goldsmith's craft. But there is not much on paper to prove that. In fact there is not much on paper about him in his own time at all. His signature or designation as printer or publisher appears nowhere on any piece of printing. Most of the contemporary biographical information about him comes from records of lawsuits or loans. In 1436 he was sued for breach of promise and for slander. In 1439 he was sued by two partners with whom he had contracted to "teach them all his arts and enterprises," and who found the terms too stiff. Gutenberg won the suit, and some of the testimony which has been preserved reveals interesting details of the work he and the partners had been engaged in. It was expensive; it required the purchase of lead and other metals; it somehow involved a press and "forms" (*formen* was a common word also for type); and during the trial a goldsmith testified that he had earned 100 gulden from Gutenberg for activities related to printing. There is nothing more direct than that in the record; Gutenberg seems to have been rather secretive about what he did. The records of loans, foreclosures, and taxes do not tell much, although it is interesting to record that he paid a tax on the contents of his wine cellar, while he lived in Strasbourg, and the cellar in 1439 contained about 420 gallons. Several of the loans and suits mention "work on the book," or equivalent, but never what book or even exactly what kind of work. Was the book the 42-line Bible? Perhaps the most interesting of the loan cases was a suit against Gutenberg by Johann Fust in 1455. The verdict went against Gutenberg, who was unable to pay, and his "equipment and stock passed into the hands of Fust." The printing firm of Fust and Schöffer (Fust's son-in-law) became one of the best known in Mainz. Gutenberg died in 1468 at the age of about 70, and his printing equipment went to a Dr. Conrad Humery. This brief account is in inverse proportion to the size of the literature on Gutenberg, which runs to many volumes, but none of the literature contains much direct evidence on his career as a printer.

A single leaf of a poem, issued probably about 1445, and a set of indulgences issued in the early 1450s have been ascribed to Gutenberg, but without any hard evidence. The famous 42-line Bible, one of the magnificent accomplishments of early European typography, appeared in 1455 or 1456 in "150 paper copies and 30 on vellum," according to Pollard.[7] It is popularly called the Gutenberg Bible and is regarded as the first fine example of the new art of printing, but here again the evidence of how it came to be is not very clear.

The indication is that it was published by Fust and Schöffer, whom Gutenberg had supposedly served as designer and printer before the relationship was broken off by the lawsuit in 1455. Gutenberg's name appears nowhere in the Bible or in any acknowledgment accompanying it. Johann Schöffer, the grandson of Jacob Fust and son of Peter Schöffer, claimed later that the book was solely

A page from the 42-line Bible.

the product of Fust and Schöffer, and Gutenberg had nothing to do with it or with the invention of printing. Yet as Robert Lechene notes in the *Britannica* perhaps the most convincing argument of all comes from this same young Schöffer who worked so hard to deflate Gutenberg's reputation. Says Lechene, "Though Schöffer claimed from 1509 on that the invention was solely his father's and grandfather's, the fact is that in 1505 he had written in a preface to an edition of Livy that 'the admirable art of typography was invented by the ingenious Johann Gutenberg at Mainz in 1450.' It is assumed that he inherited this certainty from his father, and it is hard to see how a new element could have persuaded him to the contrary after 1505, since Johann Fust died in 1466 and Peter Schöffer in 1502."[8]

So if we want to cite one name, it should probably be Gutenberg. But the name matters less than what happened after printing from movable metal type came into use in Europe. What happened was that lines of force converged on Western Europe. Some of them had come from far away and long ago, such as paper and ink from China in the second century. Some were relatively recent, such as the growth of the new merchant class and a bursting sense of the need for literacy and information. In the middle of the fifteenth century someone, probably several people, gathered these forces together into a critical mass and set off a cultural explosion that is still reverberating. Gutenberg and the 42-line Bible are merely symbols of those developments, which soon reached far beyond any one man or one book.

A TIDAL WAVE OF SOCIAL CHANGE

A tidal wave may be a better description than an explosion of what happened after the coming of movable metal type and a press to Europe. And, in fact, what Gutenberg (or someone else) started in Mainz about 1450 is no easier to summarize than a tidal wave. But it might have started with an explosion, and we think of the mysterious big bang of 15 billion years ago. The coming of metal type printing to Europe was a cultural and social big bang. If we ask why the explosion was so much larger and louder than the earlier and more innovative discoveries in China, the only reasonable answer is that the explosive materials were assembled and ready to a greater degree in Europe than in China. If we ask why we hear so much more about Gutenberg and printing in Europe in the fifteenth century than about earlier printers in China, we must remember that Gutenberg and his fellow printers lived in—helped create—a reading and writing society.

What we can say about how type was cast and set, inked and impressed in the middle of the fifteenth century, therefore, is far less interesting than what came about when the printed pages began to be lifted off the type. Within a few decades the number of books in the Western world increased almost exponentially. In England, to take an example, 13 new editions of books were published in 1510. In 1580 there were 219; in 1800, about 600; today, about 14,000 a year. And the editions grew steadily larger. The 1455 Bible, as we have noted, was printed in 150 copies on paper, 30 on vellum. Yet in the first decades of the sixteenth century, 34 different editions of Erasmus's *Adagia* were printed, with 1000 or more copies each. Hogben cites some telling figures about religious publishing. In the first half of the 1700s, the British Bible Society was able to publish the previously unheard-of number of 480,000 copies of the Bible; 480,000 in 50 years. Yet in the first three decades of the twentieth century, the Foreign Bible Society published in England a total of 237 million Bibles!

The printing press, in effect, unchained the books that, during the Middle Ages, were kept for use principally in the monasteries and castles. Thousands of booksellers set up shop. University libraries and special libraries grew up; later came public libraries. In America, rich men such as Andrew Carnegie put a considerable part of their fortunes into establishing libraries for free use in all except the smallest towns and villages. And as the tidal wave of books moved outward from the printing centers of Europe and North America, some of the dreams for a new kind of education began to come true. Education for all children, literacy for all adults, came to be within reach. Before the age of print, Abelard and two books could start a university. Unfortunately the flatbed presses of fifteenth- and sixteenth-century Europe could not duplicate Abelard, but the books could be duplicated, and were. As the supply of books grew, so did the number of learned people and teachers, schools and universities. Universal public education came into existence early in the nineteenth century, and illiteracy retreated and all but vanished in the Western world.

With literacy and expanding public education came a notable widening of horizons and interests. Merchants and traders, always interested in opportunities and prices in distant places, now found they needed such information faster. Couriers and printed news bulletins brought it. Travel followed trade, and news followed travel. Newsbooks began to circulate, describing events in recent months. News sheets of a more timely nature followed the newsbooks, and these led to the first newspapers, soon after 1600. Before long, Baron Reuter was operating a news service, with carrier pigeons (rather than wires or satellites) carrying news bulletins across the English Channel.

News opened long-closed windows on government and lawmaking. Public opinion became something that political leaders had to take into account. News and education opened doors, for the first time, to participation in public affairs by a broad segment of the public. And so Europe and America had their centuries of unrest and revolution, during which power was transferred from the titled gentry to different segments of society. If it seems farfetched to relate the French and

An early print shop.

American and British revolutions to the 42-line Bible that came off the press in Mainz in 1955, it is less farfetched to relate them to news sheets, newspapers, and political tracts, all of which could be printed inexpensively and in large numbers, thanks to the techniques and methods introduced about the time of the 42-line Bible.

The new abundance of printed works rekindled the excitement of rediscovery of the Greek and Roman literary, philosophical, and scientific classics. These had never been entirely forgotten, never lost, but the privilege of meeting the fine minds of antiquity had been limited to a few people in each age. Now the classics became again generally available to all who could read and wanted to read the best. And with the classics of the great Mediterranean countries came the mathematical contributions of the Indians, Muslims, and Arabs, a new set of numbers to replace the clumsy alphabetized numbers of the Greeks and Romans, and a new view of algebra to add to Euclid's geometry and lay the basis for calculus and modern mathematics. The art of printed illustration contributed to the study of botany and anatomy, and thus to medicine and natural science, and also to map making, so a new picture of the earth and its inhabitants came slowly into being.

The appetite for printed illustrations was one of the phenomena of printing's early years. Book illustrations and decoration had reached a very high level with the monks but had been restricted to only a few readers. So popular were printed illustrations that a book by Schedel in 1493 appeared with something over 1800 illustrations but only 645 *different* ones. The same pictures were used over and over again with different labels—sometimes identified as a view of one city, sometimes another.

A new emphasis on the visual element of human communication is one of the greatest influences of print. Reading is a skill that makes great demands on the eye, none on the ear. Consequently it makes no use of all the nonverbal cues and implications of oral communication. Furthermore the very nature of language requires that facts and ideas be expressed in a consecutive, linear, verbal way rather than the simultaneous, holistic way in which we absorb a nonverbal visual experience. Because one reads mostly by oneself, individual rather than group behavior is encouraged, solitary rather than discussion learning. As a result of substituting reading for listening and seeing, therefore, we should expect some fundamental changes in human ways of thinking and behaving. These propositions are hard to test in the midst of all the other influences that have impinged upon humans since 1450, but they have strong face validity.

We have mentioned some of the changes that printing has helped to bring about in people and society but have said nothing about developments in printing itself. The system used in 1450 was complete and mature, and changed in no fundamental way for several hundred years. Then changes began to come swiftly. The metal press came into use in 1795, the power press shortly after 1800, the rotary press in 1811. This made the process of stereotyping feasible, and pages and forms could be printed from a mold rather than from type. Wood pulp paper came into use in the 1880s. About this same time the linotype was perfected, and it was followed by other types of typesetting machines. Photoengraving and fine-screen platemaking were followed by rotogravure in the 1890s. But the developments that would really have startled Gutenberg came in the twentieth century with offset printing and photocomposition. The results of these have been that "hot lead" processes have all but disappeared from many printing plants; that photographic processes have offered a new feasibility to small printers, specialized printers, and nonalphabetic languages; and, beyond all this, that by means of facsimile a printed page may now be delivered miles away into a home, office, or school without the intervention of any printing machinery except electronic and chemical processes. As the *Encyclopaedia Britannica* notes almost ruefully, "the whole history of printing is a progression away from those things that originally characterized it: lead, ink, and the press."[9]

Two more effects, or echoes, of the explosion in printing must be mentioned. One is the advent of what one might call personal printing. We need only mention the typewriter, with what it has accomplished as a swifter substitute for handwriting, and the now almost universal ability to duplicate typewritten or printed copy with photocopy or stencils, so that everyone can in effect become a publisher.

The other effect is less recent but even more significant. To live as an author before the invention of printing, a person had to have a rich patron, a job apart from writing, or independent wealth. In other words, it is was almost impossible to make a living directly from one's writing. As a result, until the Middle Ages and for some time thereafter, relatively few persons wrote. When printing came into use, however, and especially when copyright laws became effective in the early eighteenth century, authors could collect royalties on the sale of their books. The result was that a new role, of great importance, was added to the communication roles we have listed: printer, publisher, bookseller, teacher, librarian, editor, reporter, and now the role of *author*—one who could now sell one's words and ideas for general reading and draw an income dependent not on the tastes or vanity of a wealthy person or a government, but on the tastes and interests of fellow men and women.

This was the nature of the tidal wave of social change and human development that followed upon the meeting of paper, ink, type, press, and some talented printers in the middle fifteenth century in Western Europe. As a note on the history of human communication, it is well to recall something that Benjamin Franklin did at the end of the eighteenth century. Why did Franklin, scientist, philosopher, author, ambassador of his country, and signer of the Declaration of Independence, choose to identify himself on a public vita not by any of these honorific achievements, but simply as "printer"? Could it have been that his keen eyes (behind the bifocals which he himself invented) saw the importance of the printer's role in Western civilization? And that he chose to ally himself to that broad current, the strands of which came together just at the right time to move history and affect the lives of all people?

SUGGESTIONS FOR FURTHER READING

A basic reference on the history of printing is W. T. Berry and H. E. Poole, *Annals of Printing: A Chronological Encyclopedia from the Earliest Times to 1950* (London: Blandford Press, 1966). In addition to the detailed chronology of persons and events, this book contains a detailed bibliography. Douglas McMurtrie's *The Book: The Story of Printing and Bookmaking* (New York: Oxford University Press, 1943) is a classic in this field. T. F. Carter, *The Invention of Printing in China and Its Spread Westward,* rev. L. C. Goodrich (New York: Ronald Press, 1955), is highly useful on that part of the history. A brief treatment, beginning with 1440, is W. Chappell, *A Short History of the Printed Word* (New York: Knopf, 1970). E. L. Eisenstein's *The Printing Press as an Agent of Change* (New York: Cambridge University Press, 1979) is one of the few books devoted wholly to the social history of printing. A volume with somewhat similar emphasis is S. H. Steinberg. *Five Hundred Years of Printing* (Baltimore: Penguin Books, 1974).

QUESTIONS TO THINK ABOUT

1. Just before 1450 there were supposed to have been only a few ten thousands of books in all of Europe. This was not far different from the number in China in the year 100, and perhaps one-tenth of the number in the library at Alexandria. Why was the number of books relatively so low in medieval Europe?
2. Why did modern printing come into extensive use first in Western Europe?
3. Was there any relationship between the flowering of movable-metal-type printing in Europe in the fifteenth century and the European Industrial Revolution in the nineteenth century?
4. What if radio and television had been discovered before printing? Unlikely though that is, what effect might it have had on the way printing and the two electronic media developed?
5. Presently our need for newsprint is cutting dangerously into the world's supply of timber. Has mass communication any answer for that problem?

TIME CAPSULE

Ts'ai Lun makes rag paper	105*
Paper folded in book form to replace scrolls	150
Arabs learn Chinese secret of making paper	751
Diamond Sutra, first (block) printed book	868
China develops movable type made of clay	1040
Koreans and Chinese make movable metal type	ca. 1400

*These dates are A.D.

Gutenberg at work in Mainz, with movable metal type and new
    type of press   1450
42-line Bible comes off press of Fust and Schöffer, in Mainz   1455
William Caxton establishes first print shop, using Gutenberg's method,
    in England   1470
Aldus Manutius and other printers become active on continent   1475–1500

The oldest surviving print of a television picture broadcast in the United States.

BIRTH OF THE MASS MEDIA

The fact that a printer could produce on the average one volume a day, while a copyist produced two a year, made change inescapable.

ITHIEL DE SOLA POOL

Society is molded by the interaction between media content and the media audience.

WALTER LIPPMANN

*A*t the beginning of Chapter 2 we turned aside from the early history of human communication to put the story in time perspective. Here again, at a turning point in the story, we are challenged to turn aside and ask the probing questions Gauguin wrote on the canvas of one of his Tahiti paintings: Where do we find ourselves? Where have we been? Where do we seem to be going?

Humans have passed through an age of speech, an age of writing, and, more recently, an age of print. In the nineteenth and twentieth centuries the age of print has expanded to include electronics and photography as well as communication organizations of a new kind that we call mass media. A few centuries from now historians may call this not an age of print but an age of mass media.

I am reminded of how my son and I, in the summer when we could get away from city lights, used to watch the stars, galaxy after galaxy, climb out of the west and slide down into the east. We would name such stars as we could and try to pick out the galaxies from the sky full of starlight above us. One night my son asked how old these stars are. I was bemused at the thought of trying to get a child to comprehend billions of years, and so I said, "Very old. Much older than we are. Older than we can count." He thought about that. "I see," he said at last. "I bet these are the old stars going over us now. Our stars will come up later in the evening. The young stars." I smiled at his idea, and yet the more I thought about it the more I found it useful. Consider, for example, the chapters in communication history which we have watched rise like galaxies, ever since the time of cave paintings, and follow each other across the sky. The cave paintings are an infinitely old galaxy to us, but newspapers and television are a new young galaxy. They are *our* stars. We live in the galaxy of the mass media. People who live in our centuries are the first to have seen that galaxy, and it determines how the sky looks to us. We are children of the mass media.

Therefore we are going to devote most of the remaining chapters to the mass media, their institutions, their manifestations, and some of their effects.

WHAT A MASS MEDIUM IS

There have always been media, but not always mass media. All the communication technology and organizations described earlier in this book are media: They all carry information from some source to the senses of receivers. But it is hard to date mass communication farther back than the existence of printing from movable metal type. And even so, it is not easy to draw a line across history and say that on one side are the media and on the other, the mass media. History is a flowing stream that carries with it all that has been experienced and learned and combines it with what is newly learned. Thus it is well to explain here exactly what we mean by mass media.

To be sure, *mass* connotes size: A mass medium ordinarily serves a large number of people. But how large is a large number? Great leaders and orators—Nehru at the Red Fort, for instance—often spoke to more people than read a weekly newspaper. It is clear that size itself is not a sufficient test. How large does an audience need to be to meet the mass media requirement?

We might argue that *mass* is an ill-chosen word. For example, we are more likely to get a sense of mass from being in the crowd in one of Nehru's audiences or in a packed football stadium than from sitting by ourselves reading a newspaper or viewing television, both indisputable mass media. But we have inherited the term *mass media* and will probably continue using it for a long time.

One characteristic of a mass medium is that it circulates the same message to all its audience. Of course, not all readers read the same news or view the same television, hear the same radio or go to the same movies. But when many thousands of people are presented with the same information, from which they can choose as they wish and read into it such meaning as they feel proper, that is a different experience from, say, a telephone conversation. It is an important characteristic of a certain type of communication, no matter what we call it.

With the exception of very small media, such as the old newspapers that were run by one person who served as printer, reporter, and salesperson—with that level of exception, one of the qualities of mass media is that they include an organization whose efforts are dedicated to the production and circulation of communication. Obviously one individual could hardly be called a mass medium, although that individual may be a mass communicator. Furthermore, a mass-media organization can be expected to maintain a continuing communication service, usually at regular intervals. Is a book publishing house, then, a mass medium? It is very hard to say that it is not, even though it does not produce a book, say, every Friday. It serves a mass audience. It is operated by a professional staff engaged in producing a certain kind of communication service. And it has another characteristic that seems to belong to all mass media: Communication technology is interposed between that communicating staff and the intended audience.

In the case of the newspaper and the publishing house, that technology is print; in the case of motion pictures, the technology is photography and projection; in the case of radio, the technology of electronic recording and broadcasting. This is one of the chief reasons why we think of mass media as coming into history during the day of the printer. Print was the first sophisticated communication technology used to send identical messages to large audiences. But here, too, we have problems of definition. How about the telephone? This is a simple but sophisticated technology that permits one person to talk to another with little regard for distance or location. It even permits one person to talk to a number of others, whose phones are connected together, or a whole group (with a conference call) to talk to each other. Yet although the telephone is a wonderfully efficient and convenient tool, we do not usually think of it as a mass medium. Although radio can be used as a telephone (for example, when a plane in flight talks with the airport tower), still we think of mass radio usually as providing a regular service of information and entertainment that is prepared by a staff organization and broadcast very widely by transmitters, antennas or cable, and radio waves.

Thus, when we list the social units we think of as mass media we typically cite newspaper, magazine, and book publishing; motion pictures; radio; television; and sound or sight recording. We may find it useful to include other forms of large-scale communication. Some of the arrangements that seem to be growing out of the computer and other microtechnology less than half a century old may well come to be included in that list. And there are others we do not yet imagine.

Here is a chart that describes a mass medium in simple terms of public and (relatively) private communication:

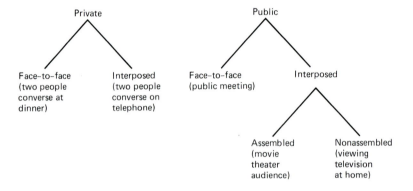

Those we usually think of as mass media are the ones included here as public and interposed media.

THE GROWTH OF MASS MEDIA

From the viewpoint of history, any "new" form of communication is always in some ways new, in some ways old. History, as we have said, is a continuously flowing stream. As we look back over the 15,000 years of human communication about which we know something, we can cite four dates that seem particularly important in the history of the mass media. They all merge into each other and are all distinguished by inventions or other developments in technology.

We know little about the invention of language, of course, but that would certainly be included if it were not shrouded in the mist of prehistory. When we move into recorded history, however, we should mention 3500 B.C., which is a good guess at the date of the greatest human invention, after language—writing. The Sumerian scribes and the Sumerian alphabet stand at the beginning of the history of the mass media as they stand at the beginning of so many other strands in our history. The first date is 3500 B.C., then; and after that the approximate date for the perfection of modern printing, the year 1450. By that time humans had supple and effective languages to work with and widely used systems with which to write them. Furthermore, they had a hunger for regular supplies of information that language and writing could satisfy if they could be circulated widely enough: news, political and economic façt and comment; entertainment and artistic enjoyment beyond that which they had gotten used to in their cities and villages. The printing press and its allied arts provided a way to meet those needs.

The next date of importance is an approximation of the beginning of the Industrial Revolution as it relates to communication—perhaps 1840. This is near the birth of photography and the telegraph, just after the mastery of steam power, which was soon applied to the printing press, and just before the nineteenth- and early twentieth-century discoveries about electricity and optics, which were soon applied to media that existed as yet only in imagination. In other words, this date represents the start of the great century of invention which contributed more to the technology of human communication than any other period in history. Perhaps the greatest invention of the nineteenth century, as Whitehead noted, was the process of invention itself. This process was mastered by all the great innovators who contributed to communication media in that time: Daguerre, Talbot, Morse, Eastman, Bell, Edison, DeForest, and Zworykin, to mention only a few. The mastery of the process was so widespread and the fruits of its use ripened so quickly that humans who came to 1840 with nothing but printed media possessed, a century later, almost all the photographic and electronic media with which we are familiar today.

Almost all. For one date of great importance—rather, several consecutive years of great importance—still remains to be mentioned. If we choose one additional year, it might well be 1947, when the transistor was invented and in its second generation gave birth to the microchip and the other electronic microprocessing that has made so much difference to human communication in the last half century. It might be better to mention *three* years, 1945 through 1947. In 1945 came Arthur Clarke's publication of the theory of the communication satellite, which has done so much to extend the boundaries of human communication. In 1946 came John Von Neumann's treatise on the electronic computer, a remarkable book of theory to which every computer traces its lineage. The computer may well turn out to be the most significant machine in history, and microprocessing (1947) may prove to be the development that made it possible for humans to use the new electronic developments efficiently.

The history of human communication, then, extends from a slow beginning with the development of language over a period of many centuries; to the invention of writing, which was the dominant communication technology for millennia; then to the development and use of modern printing during a period that can be measured in centuries. And after that in a little more than a century, humans learned to apply brilliant new technology to old communication uses, and our modern communication media and machines emerged.

THE DURABILITY OF MEDIA

Looking at the media today reminds me again of my starwatching on a summer night. By the end of the nineteenth century we were familiar with the newspaper and the magazine. Then came the first stars of photography, and by the beginning of the twentieth century the motion picture galaxy was spread out for us to admire. Soon came the first stars of sound communication—the telegraph, the telephone, the first sound-recording methods, and finally the radio. It took a relatively short time for those galaxies to move past. But move past they did, and they were followed by the brightest galaxy of the century—television. Just as 1900 to 1935 or so were dominated by movies, and 1920 to 1950 or so by radio, so television was the dominant new galaxy after 1950. In the 1980s we still have all these media, but ever-newer technology such as the computer, digital data communication, and home recording and communicating of various kinds are beginning to send up a new parade of stars and suggest the advent of galaxies never before heard of.

There is one thing wrong with our comparison of media watching to star watching. The stars rise, sweep across the night sky, and sink behind the western horizon. More than one galaxy is visible at a time, but in a few hours any one of them comes and goes and for one revolution of the earth remains invisible to us. Mass media rise and shine, but they seem not to sink and disappear from our view. All the media that were visible to us from the seventeenth through the twentieth centuries are still here. A mass medium seems never to die. We mean a medium, not a single unit within the media. A single newspaper may go out of business or be absorbed by another newspaper or change its pattern so completely that it seems new. But *newspapers* remain. Despite all the changes that have come to newspapers as a type in 400 years, despite the changes in news styles, news goals, patterns of control and support, appearance and tone, despite the competition of radio, television, and magazines for news and advertising, despite the impact of electronic typesetting, offset printing, and satellite transmission of whole pages, despite such nontechnological developments as the appearance of huge ownership chains, still the newspaper lives and flourishes. When television came into use and took over much of the audience and the advertising support for radio entertainment as well as many of radio's most popular personalities, radio shook with the punch for a while and then discovered it could present other kinds of programs. When several of the most popular and prosperous magazines in the country, such as *Life* and the *Saturday Evening Post,* fell victim to television competition and new advertising concepts, these famous names had to suspend publication, but the magazine as a medium shrugged its shoulders and kept on publishing. Magazines simply went about finding out what kind of content fit their competitive situation better. It was the radio story over again: Instead of concentrating on the leading soap operas and the highest-priced comedians and features, radio began to concentrate on popular music, news, and the kind of information and relaxation a listener wants when, say, driving a car or studying lessons. This has been the recent history of the mass media. Faced with severe competition, a medium has simply moved to a new address. Given the situation, what is the job we can do best? That question has always concerned media when crowded out of an old home. Radio, magazines, and movies have changed. But they have not been killed off.

THE IMPACT OF THE MEDIA

Undoubtedly the first mass media meant something different to the people who saw them in their early years than they mean to us in later perspective. The advent of printing presses meant that great books, which had formerly been chained to the reading desks in monasteries or locked in the collections of a few rich and powerful people, were now available to anyone who could read them. And persons who could not read them had to see to it that their children could learn to read. When print began to be used for news, its impact was felt slowly and for a long time only in the great cities, where the news came faster (although still not very fast) and from farther away. Traders could find out the sales prices from cities across bodies of water or national borders. Ordinary readers learned the names of kings and commanders. Wars were heard about while the fighting was still going on, not only as a part of history.

It took 200 years for the full impact of printing to be felt, 50 years after the first painstaking photographs for cameras to become available to persons other than specialists, another 50 for cameras to become an article tourists typically include in their baggage. Even the inventors of new products were not always sure how to use them. Bell's new telephone was used in England for several years to carry music into homes—a sort of cable radio. Edison for a long time showed no interest in projecting his new moving pictures in a theater; he preferred to put them into machines where passersby could pay five cents to peep in at a sequence that might last two minutes. Whistlers were at first perhaps the most popular performers on Edison's new sound-recording cylinder. When radio came into wide public use, it was a new game, something that even upper school or high school students could play. When I first found out about radio, I made a "cat-whisker" (a fine wire with which to "tune in"), traded some of my more valuable possessions for a cheap pair of earphones, and pressed the catwhisker against different points on a silicon crystal, listening for whatever was on the air. I thrilled to hear a new Louisville station play "My Old Kentucky Home" on a set of bells, although I confess that would not greatly thrill me today. I set my watch to government time signals from Arlington, Virginia. Not exactly earth-shaking, but it did extend my horizon as far as Arlington and Louisville, and sometimes it set me thinking about how those sounds traveled so far through the air and what was happening in my little coil of wire to transform apparently soundless air into the sounds in my earphones.

When television came into use, it was delayed a long time while the equipment was being perfected; then by World War II, which kept industry so busy there was no time to work with an article merely for home use; and then for several more years while the U.S. government decided whether to approve the CBS system, which used a rotating wheel to produce color, or the RCA system, which was wholly electronic. The CBS wheel was said to produce better color, but the RCA design made it possible to receive either color or black-and-white transmissions on the same set. The RCA design won the competition, and television exploded on the sales counters and in the living rooms of Americans. It took only 10 years to put television into 95 percent of American homes. Television picked up many of the most attractive features of earlier media, such as radio and movies, and it was "*the* thing." By 1960, one American was not likely to ask another, "Did you watch television last night?" but rather, "What did you watch on television last night?"

That was how the media were born. They came along faster and faster: from print to movies, 450 years; from movies to television, 50 years. They picked up many of the most attractive features of earlier media. Print made news fast, but radio and television made it much faster. Photography could capture what our eyes saw, but movies could capture it in motion. Television could let us see pictures and movement and hear sound, near or far, even from the surface of the moon or the depths of the sea.

THE IMPORTANCE OF THE MEDIA

Viewed in the perspective of time, some of the excitement fades out of the story of the media but the true stature of these developments stands out more clearly. What happened about 3500 B.C. in Sumeria contributed more to what humans knew or could know than all that happened in the millennia since human history began. What happened in 1450 or a few centuries before or after that contributed as much to human knowledge as all that had happened in the preceding 5000 years. What happened in the nineteenth and twentieth centuries contributed as much as all that had happened since the dawn of recorded history.

What, specifically, did these developments contribute? As the Sumerians had found a device to record knowledge and, albeit slowly and painfully, to transport and exchange it, so did the Europeans of the mass-media centuries find a more effective way to contribute to knowledge and knowing. Instead of clay tablets that lay in schools and libraries in Sumeria, people created books and newspapers that could be reproduced in huge numbers and circulated wherever the language could be read. Instead of training a few selected children to become scribes or courtiers, other people gradually established public schools for the great majority of all children and even educated adults who could no longer go back to school for what they had missed but could have the media bring school to them. As the Mediterranean and west Asian countries had built great storehouses for books and manuscripts, so the mass media put working libraries of print, later of pictures and recorded sound, into even small towns and small schools.

It is perhaps too easy now to think of the mass media in their least lovely aspects—as thieves of time, as ballyhooers of advertising or political candidates, as purveyors of the cheapest content to attract the most people and the least educated ones. One-third of the way through the twentieth century, visitors discovered that front porches were disappearing from the small towns of America. Families no longer spent social evenings on the porch, entertained guests there, or exchanged conversation with neighbors walking past. The center of home life had moved to the living room, where the radio set was and where the television was or soon would be. The new media had an extraordinary effect on family life. Five hundred years ago, when printing was still new in Western Europe and unknown in North America and most of the rest of world, the media occupied a negligible part of one's day. As a matter of fact, there were really no mass media to take up any time. In 1900, before radio and television came into use, the printed media and films as they then existed claimed less than one hour of the average day. Now mass media take up between four and five hours of an average day for an average adult, a little more than that for most children. Radio was the first addition to media fare that made such a difference; when television arrived it cut radio time almost in half but took title to three hours or more itself. This is an extraordinary event. In a few hundred years, humans gave away about five hours a day to communication that did not even exist in 1450 and that hardly existed a century ago. Five hours a day is between one-third and one-fourth of a person's waking time. Many families eat dinner while watching television. Many workers ride back and forth between home and work listening to radio. By the time young Americans are in the twelfth grade they have seen, on the average, 15,000 hours of television. This is more time than they have spent in any other activity except sleeping; more time than they have spent playing or eating. I was less than surprised, therefore, when Marshall McLuhan once said to me, "You are wasting your time studying media in schools; the real education is out here, with the network the teacher and the picture tube the classroom."

The media, therefore, and especially the newest members of the group, have succeeded in altering the routine of human life in a way unprecedented since the time when men ceased to spend most of their time hunting and women most of their time gathering, and families moved into villages and began raising farm crops.

The amount of human life now taken over by the tube may or may not seem like an attractive report. Yet let us not forget that these same media have performed an unequaled service in stretching human horizons and speeding human awareness of what happens beyond those horizons. *Far* and *fast* are the key words to describe what has happened to human knowledge in the last five centuries. Less than two centuries ago, it was possible to fight the Battle of New

Orleans, with considerable losses on both sides, *two weeks after* a treaty had ended the British-American war—simply because the news had not yet come. That sort of thing is hardly conceivable today. Not many decades ago, what was known about Africa or Asia came to us mostly from explorers' adventure books or, a little later, from missionaries' exhortations. Now we have seen and read about these countries, their people, and their leaders. We have seen wars, in color and sound, that have taken place on distant battlefields and served to remind us what war is really like, not what storytellers have said of it. We have seen once-mysterious places like Antarctica. We have seen the col of Everest, the Louvre, Xian, the Upper Nile. We have seen what starvation looks like, triumph and tragedy, new life and new death. We have heard great men and women explain some difficult problems and then answer, or try to answer, difficult questions about them.

Of course, we have had to trust the media that represent us, for although they have become able to look and see and hear for us they still ask us to depend on them for what they look at and listen to. We have found out, in political campaigns and elsewhere, that it is possible to learn to "use" the media. Wittingly or unwittingly, what a reporter writes about or what an editor sends to print, where a reporter points the camera or what pictures an editor selects, the report that is written may or may not be what you or I would consider a fair and balanced report if we really knew enough about it to judge. The other media have the same problem as the press: They may or may not always tell us what we can accept in complete confidence; the ethics of news reporting applies also to radio and television, motion pictures, and book publishing, when they stand between us and the distant world. Yet this fact is inescapable: Far more evidence is now available to bridge the gaps of distance and time, to give us an opportunity to make up our own minds as to what is out there beyond the horizon, and what kind of men and women walk the earth with us, than ever before. It is hard to comprehend the power of the communication media until we realize how much responsibility we delegate to them to know and tell us what we need to know. That is why the advent of the mass media represents one of the important steps in human communication. It is why we have thought it well at this point in our story to stop and look at what has happened, and to ask the question, What is it all about?

SUGGESTIONS FOR FURTHER READING

There is an accurate and helpful summary of mass-media statistics—chiefly on growth, finances, and audiences—which carries the account in most cases into the 1980s: *Elec-*

tronic Media: A Guide to Trends in Broadcasting and Newer Technologies, 1920–1983, by Christopher H. Sterling (New York: Praeger, 1984). This is an update of the Aspen handbook, *The Mass Media,* by Sterling and Haight, and emphasizes the electronic media but does not entirely ignore the other media. A highly readable text, emphasizing print but also taking up the electronic media, is *Media: An Introductory Analysis of American Mass Communication,* by P. M. Sandman, D. M. Rubin, and D. B. Sachsman (Englewood Cliffs, N.J.: Prentice-Hall, 1978). A shorter and less detailed introduction is *Men, Women, Messages, and Media,* rev. ed., by W. Schramm and W. E. Porter (New York: Harper & Row, 1982). Marshall McLuhan's *Understanding Media: The Extensions of Man* (New York: McGraw-Hill, 1964) is relevant here. Other and more specialized approaches include J. Tunstall, *The Media in America* (New York: Columbia University Press, 1977); J. G. Blumler and E. Katz, eds., *The Uses of Mass Communication: Current Perspectives on Gratification Research* (Beverly Hills, Calif.: Sage, 1974); and J. Klapper, *The Effects of Mass Communication* (New York: Free Press, 1960). B. Rosenberg and D. M. White have taken a different perspective in their edited volume, *Mass Culture: The Popular Arts in America* (New York: Free Press, 1964). Two sociological approaches are D. McQuail, *Towards a Sociology of Mass Communication* (New York: Macmillan, 1969); and C. R. Wright, *Mass Communication: A Sociological Perspective* (New York: Random House, 1959). A reader on research and theory is W. Schramm and D. Roberts, eds., *The Process and Effects of Mass Communication,* rev. ed., (Urbana, Ill.: University of Illinois Press, 1974).

QUESTIONS TO THINK ABOUT

1. It has been said that we are children of the mass-media age. Does that tend to make us different from people who lived in pre-mass-media times? If so, in what ways (e.g., opportunity? knowledge? behavior? controls upon us? what else?)?
2. Can you think of a better name than *mass media* for these media and this age?
3. Does a mass medium ever die? Do you see any indication that one of the mass media is likely to change greatly or be replaced in, say, the next half century?
4. Do you think we ought to consider media such as telephone and telegraph, even though they are not really "mass" media, along with newspapers, television, radio, etc.? If so, what should we call this whole group of media that came into use in the nineteenth and twentieth centuries?
5. How much time do you yourself devote to media, and how do you divide it among the media? Is this typical of your friends also?
6. Harold Lasswell specified three functions the mass media perform in society—survey the environment (e.g., news), correlate society's response to the environment (e.g., government and politics), and transmit the social heritage (e.g., education). To these, most later scholars have added the function of providing entertainment. Which of the mass media seem to you to be chiefly involved in each of these functions?

Average Annual Expenditure in American Home for Communication Services (excluding education)

Telephone	$ 225
Newspapers	120
Postal service	116
Television	102
Periodicals	44
Books	42
Radio	26
Disks and tapes	13
Total	$ 688

SOURCE: Ben Bagdikian, *The Information Machines* (New York: Harper & Row, 1971).

The Daily Courant.

Wednefday, March 11. 1702.

From the Harlem Courant, Dated March 18. N. S.

Naples, Feb. 22.

ON Wednefday laft, our New Viceroy, the Duke of Efcalona, arriv'd here with a Squadron of the Galleys of Sicily. He made his Entrance dreft in a French habit; and to give us the greater Hopes of the King's coming hither, went to Lodge in one of the little Palaces, leaving the Royal one for his Majefty. The Marquis of Grigni is alfo arriv'd here with a Regiment of French.

Rome, Feb. 25. In a Military Congregation of State that was held here, it was Refolv'd to draw a Line from Afcoli to the Borders of the Ecclefiaftical State, thereby to hinder the Incurfions of the Tranfalpine Troops. Orders are fent to Civita Vecchia to fit out the Galleys, and to ftrengthen the Garrifon of that Place. Signior Cafali is made Governor of Perugia. The Marquis del Vafto, and the Prince de Caferta continue ftill in the Imperial Embaffador's Palace; where his Excellency has a Guard of 50 Men every Night in Arms. The King of Portugal has defir'd the Arch-Bifhoprick of Lisbon, vacant by the Death of Cardinal Soafa, for the Infante his fecond Son, who is about 11 Years old.

Vienna, Mar. 4. Orders are fent to the 4 Regiments of Foot, the 2 of Cuiraffiers, and to that of Dragoons, which are broke up from Hungary, and are on their way to Italy, and which confift of about 24 or 15000 Men, to haften their March thither with all Expedition. The 6 new Regiments of Huffars that are now raifing, are in fo great a forwardnefs, that they will be compleat, and in a Condition to march by the middle of May. Prince Lewis of Baden has written to Court, to excufe himfelf from coming thither, his Prefence being fo very neceffary, and fo much defir'd on the Upper-Rhine.

Francfort, Mar. 12. The Marquifs d' Uxelles is come to Strasburg, and is to draw together a Body of fome Regiments of Horfe and Foot from the Garrifons of Alface; but will not leffen thofe of Strasburg and Landau, which are already very weak. On the other hand, the Troops of His Imperial Majefty, and his Allies, are going to form a Body near Germefhein in the Palatinate, of which Place, as well as of the Lines at Spires, Prince Lewis of Baden is expected to take a View, in three or four days. The Englifh and Dutch Minifters, the Count of Frife, and the Baron Vander Meer; and likewife the Imperial Envoy Count Lowenftein, are gone to Nordlingen, and it is hop'd that in a fhort time we fhall hear from thence of fome favourable Refolutions for the Security of the Empire.

Liege, Mar. 14. The French have taken the Cannen de Longie, who was Secretary to the Dean de Mean, out of our Caftle, where he has been for fome time a Prifoner, and have deliver'd him to the Provoft of Maubeuge, who has carry'd him from hence, but we do not know whither.

Paris, Mar. 13. Our Letters from Italy fay, That moft of our Reinforcements were Landed there; that the Imperial and Ecclefiaftical Troops feem to live very peaceably with one another in the Country of Parma, and that the Duke of Vendome, who was vifiting feveral Pofts, was within 100 Paces of fa'ing into the Hands of the Germans. The Duke of Chartres, the Prince of Conti, and feveral other Princes of the Blood, are to make the Campaign in Flanders under the Duke of Burgundy; and the Duke of Maine is to Command upon the Rhine.

From the Amfterdam Courant, Dated Mar. 18.

Rome, Feb. 25. We are taking here all poffible Precautions for the Security of the Ecclefiaftical State in this prefent Conjuncture, and have defir'd to raife 3000 Men in the Cantons of Switzerland. The Pope has appointed the Duke of Berwick to be his Lieutenant-General, and he is to Command 6000 Men on the Frontiers of Naples: He has alfo fettled upon him a Penfion of 6000 Crowns a year during Life.

From the Paris Gazette, Dated Mar. 18. 1702.

Naples, Febr. 17. 600 French Soldiers are arrived here, and are expected to be follow'd by 3400 more. A Courier that came hither on the 14th. has brought Letters by which we are affur'd that the King of Spain defigns to be here towards the end of March; and accordingly Orders are given to make the neceffary Preparations againft his Arrival. The two Troops of Horfe that were Commanded to the Abruzzo are pofted at Pefcara with a Body of Spanifh Foot, and others in the Fort of Montorio.

Paris, March. 18. We have Advice from Toulon of the 5th inftant, that the Wind having long ftood favourable, 11000 Men were already fail'd for Italy, that 2500 more were Embarking, and that by the 15th it was hoped they might all get thither. The Count d' Eftrees arriv'd there on the Third inftant, and fet all hands at work to fit out the Squadron of 9 Men of War and fome Fregats, that are appointed to carry the King of Spain to Naples. His Catholick Majefty will go on Board the Thunderer, of 110 Guns.

We have Advice by an Exprefs from Rome of the 18th of February, That notwithftanding the preffing Inftances of the Imperial Embaffadour, the Pope had Condemn'd the Marquis del Vafto to lofe his Head and his Eftate to be confifcated, for not appearing to Anfwer the Charge againft him of Publickly Scandalizing Cardinal Janfon.

ADVERTISEMENT.

IT will be found from the Foreign Prints, which from time to time, as Occafion offers, will be mention'd in this Paper, that the Author has taken Care to be duly furnifh'd with all that comes from Abroad in any Language. And for an Affurance that he will not, under Pretence of having Private Intelligence, impofe any Additions of feign'd Circumftances to an Action, but give his Extracts fairly and Impartially; at the beginning of each Article he will quote the Foreign Paper from whence 'tis taken, that the Publick, feeing from what Country a piece of News comes with the Allowance of that Government, may be better able to Judge of the Credibility and Fairnefs of the Relation: Nor will he take upon him to give any Comments or Conjectures of his own, but will relate only Matter of Fact, fuppofing other People to have Senfe enough to make Reflections for themfelves.

The Courant (as the Title fhews) will be Publifh'd Daily; being defign'd to give all the Material News as foon as every Poft arrives; and is confin'd to half the Compafs, to fave the Publick at leaft half the Impertinences, of ordinary News-Papers.

LONDON. Sold by E. Mallet, next Door to the King's-Arms Tavern at Fleet-Bridge.

The first daily newspaper in the English language.

INSTITUTIONS OF THE MASS MEDIA: NEWS I

We need news for the same reason that we need eyes—to see where we are going.

REBECCA WEST

A people without reliable news is, sooner or later, a people without the basis of freedom.

HAROLD J. LASKI

The purpose of a newspaper is to place the occurrences all together . . . to muster the Newes . . . as it were unto one armie.

THOMAS ARCHER

There was news, of course, before there were newspapers. The hunger for news is as old as humankind: to some extent for curiosity; to a greater extent, for guidance. The earliest tribes selected alert, keen-eyed members to wait on the hilltops and watch for food animals or hostile warriors—and to report what they saw. These watchers were our first news reporters. Just as the shadow of the ancient chiefs and orators falls on every government today, so on every modern newspaper, newscast, or wire news bulletin falls the shadow of those watchers on the hills.

We are talking about a leap of, say, 30,000 years in human history, one of almost incalculable size in the history of news. We live now in a world that has 60,000 newspapers, 8000 of them published daily. These have a combined circulation of about half a billion, at least 2 billion readers.

This is where we are, and we started with watchers on hilltops. How did we bridge that gap?

NEWS BEFORE THE AGE OF PRINTING

Travel, even the tentative wandering and exploration of prehistoric times, must have been one of the first ways that news came. When the earliest wanderers or travelers came home, they would have been quizzed on what they had seen. As people saw more and more strangers and moved farther from home base, the questions would have grown more sophisticated. Ten thousand years ago, when tribes learned to live as farmers rather than as nomads, they had less need of watchers, more need of able reporters. What kinds of crops were being raised in other villages? What improvements were being made in the design of shelters? How were other villages organized and governed?

In the years of writing, the scribes joined the watchers and the travelers in reporting—or recording—events. Scribes were the custodians of the written memory of society—observers, even expediters, of ongoing events. They helped pass the knowledge of events farther than it could be carried by word of mouth. Thus, the skills and tasks of scribes pointed to many of the roles that later became part of mass communication.

Then as now, it was important for news to come fast.[1] One of the early spectacular examples of news delivery was the time the Greek warrior Pheidippides ran from Marathon to Athens to carry a news bulletin to the government of Athens. (The distance, calculated as 26 miles, 385 yards, set the standard for modern marathon races.) His news bulletin was that Athens had defeated Persia in the greatest naval battle of ancient times.

In the first century B.C., apparently at the behest of Julius Caesar, a handwritten sheet called *Acta Diurna* ("the day's actions") was posted outside the Senate chamber and in other prominent places in Rome. The *Acta* carried not only a report on the Senate, but also official announcements and other news of which the government wanted the public to be aware. Thus for a few years, the *Acta Diurna* had a rather good claim to be called a daily newspaper, although it was limited to a few handwritten copies and to days when the Senate met. The chief custodian of news in Rome and most other early states was, of course, the government, but Roman private enterprise was so vigorous that the government could hardly be expected to compete. Just as private publishers hand copied and sold books, so did other entrepreneurs arrange for and sell handwritten newsletters that were circulated to friends and subscribers outside Rome. Not many copies could be made, but it is interesting to see this prototype of modern newsletters 2000 years before the style came into wide use in our own time.

Perhaps the most extensive early activity in news gathering occurred in China. During the Tang dynasty (618–907) a sort of official gazette began to circulate among members of the court. Along with official announcements it carried reports from inspectors who went twice a year to find out for the emperor what was happening in the provinces. This came to be called the *Ti-pao* ("palace report"). It was written by hand or printed from engraved wooden blocks until the seventeenth century, when type was used, and the circulation gradually spread beyond the court to other high-ranking citizens. Toward the end of its history, the *Ti-pao* was called the "Peking Gazette." It lasted until the end of the empire in 1911, making it the longest-lived newspaper in history, although it was not published very frequently or circulated very widely.

With a few exceptions like these, news circulated, before the age of printing, mostly by word of mouth or by private letter. Town criers moved through the streets declaiming official notices, sometimes a few items of news, and occasionally an advertisement or two. In coffeehouses people traded news items they had picked up or read in a letter. Handwritten official announcements were sometimes posted in public places. That is where the news business was in the middle of the fifteenth century, when printing from movable metal type came into use in Europe.

NEWS IN PRINT

The newspaper as we know it is less than 400 years old. It was born in northern Europe from the marriage of powerful social and technological currents. One such current was the growth of commerce, requiring information on prices, availabilities, and needs, sometimes from another country or another continent. A second was the expansion of political concerns beyond the court and nobility to the general public, and beyond the immediate vicinity to the entire country and other countries. All these new interests demanded news.[2]

The initial technological input was, of course, from printing, no longer with engraved wooden blocks but now movable metal type and a press. The real importance of this new technology lay in the changes it encouraged in society. People learned to read. More materials became available to read. More news came, and faster. Reliable records are not available for the century after 1450, but we know that the number of books in Europe increased from some tens of thousands to about 20 million in that time, and we can assume that the number of Europeans able to read at the end of the first century of modern printing must have been several times what it was at the beginning of that century.

The genetics of news might therefore be described as economics plus politics plus printing plus reading, and one or two more elements, for instance, paper (some of which might be used to print more money).

Four hundred years, the lifetime of the newspaper, is a short time in history, but the period included very difficult years for newspapers. For one thing, the printing press of the fifteenth and sixteenth centuries was not the showpiece we see in newspaper plants today. The early hand press could turn out only 100 to 150 copies per hour *of a single sheet.* Typesetting was not mechanized. It took a whole day to set one page of the Gutenberg Bible. The first news sheets were about 8 × 10 inches and were printed on one side of the page. The first newspapers, when newspapers came to be, were one or more such sheets. There were no news agencies. In many cases the first publishers were also the entire news staff. With these resources the pioneering newspapers proposed to cover the world of news.

In post-Gutenberg Europe, as in earlier times, news came first into the possession of the rich and powerful. Governments announced what they wanted their people to know. Exchanges and traders, especially those of the Netherlands, Germany, and France, began to circulate to their clients financial and business newsletters, usually including a few items of straight news. Sailors and travelers shared what they had found out. Coffeehouses were favorite places for such information to be exchanged. Some coffeehouse proprietors gathered what news they could from foreign patrons and read it aloud at a certain hour each day—a custom that foreshadowed radio and television news centuries later. Some marketing centers, and occasionally governments also, prepared news summaries especially for reading aloud. In Italy the price for such a reading was usually a small coin called a *gazeta,* which lent its name to many later news sheets and newspapers—gazettes. Thus sporadic opportunities to exchange news were gratefully accepted, but as printing shops became available, efforts were made to circulate news in print.

News in print began mostly as accounts of one or two events, usually in a neighboring country. Why in a neighboring country? Because governments, in most cases, were afraid of what home-country news might do to political stability. News was safer if it came from far away or if the government itself selected it. Therefore, news sheets were either circulated by "state privilege"—governmental permission—or they were issued surreptitiously without editor's or publisher's name and hawked on the street for a penny or two before the seller could be caught. Every issue of such undercover news sheets bore a different name, even though they might come out of the same print shop. And of course there was no regular publication schedule.

However, the news sheet, official or unofficial, was the first step toward a printed newspaper. News sheets developed rather earlier on the Continent than in England, and earlier there than in America, where settlers were still clearing forests and building settlements. Anthony Smith has summarized rather neatly the stages through which news publishing passed as it moved toward the form of a newspaper.[3]

There was, first, the *relation,* which was an account of a single news event. This almost invariably appeared on a single small sheet, although sometimes, when the news was very important, it could command more than one page. For example, the Battle of Flodden Field was covered by an English publisher in four pages—and in *verse.* Needless to say, this could not have been very speedy coverage.

A second form was the *coranto,* which was a series of events. A favorite use of this form was to combine recent news from one country or several countries—foreign countries, for reasons we have explained. For example, one of the first corantos in England was entitled *Newes from Germany, Italy, and Hungarie.* This, rather than a masthead, would identify the coranto.

A third form was a succession of related events, the *diurnal.* An example of this might be a month's summary of proceedings in Parliament.

Fourth, there was the *mercury,* a bound book of news with title page and cover, most commonly used to summarize the most important news from one country during a period of six months or more. Most of the first news books came from the Continent. Such books were often printed for sale at the trade fairs that occurred usually twice a year. The energy and acumen required to collect and summarize this amount of news was impressive. But it is not the only example of early news reporting that might astonish modern editors: Some of the early news items were written in Latin—not for scholarly reasons, but to leap language barriers.

When anonymous news sheets were hawked (with or without official permission) in the cities, coffeehouse patrons were reading news bulletins with coffee, and summary news books were being issued as often as every six months on the European continent, then European news readers and writers were about ready for another step forward. And it was at this time that an exciting new idea began to be talked about by people who had previously been interested in something less. Why not have a real news*paper?* A newspaper that did not have to depend on government or on a trading center for its news. A paper that could appear regularly—every week, or even oftener, so that the news might be fresh. A paper that would carry the same masthead on each issue rather than try to disguise itself. A paper that would proudly, rather than fearfully, display its editor's and its publisher's names. In other words, a dependable source of news that would be continuously and regularly available, and not be distributed only when it was safe to do so.

Date of First Newspaper (Before 1900) in Different Continents

	Asia	Europe	Americas	Africa	Oceania
Before 1600	618, China	80 B.C., Rome			
1600–1699		1605 (Netherlands, Germany)* 1605 (Belgium) 1610 (Switzerland) 1620 (Austria) 1622 (U.K.) 1631 (France) 1634 (Denmark) 1636 (Italy) 1645 (Sweden) 1661 (Poland)	1689 (U.S.)		
1700–1799	1744 (Indonesia) 1780 (India)	1703 (USSR) 1721 (Hungary) 1737 (Ireland) 1763 (Norway) 1771 (Finland) 1791 (Yugoslavia)	1722 (Mexico) 1729 (Guatemala) 1732 (Costa Rica) 1744 (Peru) 1751 (Canada) 1764 (Cuba) 1785 (Colombia) 1785 (Ecuador)		

*Date is estimated.

Date of First Newspaper (Before 1900) in Different Continents

	Asia	Europe	Americas	Africa	Oceania
				1800 (South Africa)	
			1801 (Argentina)		
					1803 (Australia)
			1804 (Dominica)		
			1804 (Haiti)		
			1807 (Uruguay)		
			1807 (Puerto Rico)		
			1808 (Brazil)		
			1808 (Venezuela)		
		1810 (Spain)	1810 (Chile)		
	1811 (Philippines)				
			1820 (El Salvador)		
		1821 (Greece)			
			1822 (Panama)		
1800–1899	1823 (Pakistan)		1823 (Bolivia)		
		1828 (Romania)			
			1830 (Honduras)		
	1831 (Turkey)				
					1840 (New Zealand)
		1846 (Bulgaria)			
	1851 (Iran)				
		1860 (Czechoslovakia)			
	1861 (Japan)				
				1875 (Egypt)	
	1889 (Burma)				
				1890 (Nigeria)	
				1890 (Ghana)	

THE BIRTH OF THE NEWSPAPER

The newspaper idea was an extremely attractive one, but in the sixteenth century it seemed very far away. The idea came true in the first decade of the seventeenth century. The honor of being the first newspaper has been claimed for the *Nieuwe Tidingen,* said to have been published in Antwerp beginning in 1605. The publisher was Abraham Verhoeven, who apparently developed it out of a commercial bulletin that circulated in Holland and Italy. Verhoeven made good use of

Holland's lively trade relations with the rest of the world; every Dutch ship was a source of foreign correspondence or correspondents. But the date of 1605 has never been confirmed, because no copy of the *Nieuwe Tidingen* exists with a date earlier than 1621.[4]

The birthday of the modern newspaper was probably in the years between 1605 and 1610. The birthplace was probably the Netherlands, Belgium, Germany, or Switzerland—most likely Germany. At least four German papers, in Wolfenbuttel, Augsburg, Cologne, and Strassburg, began to publish between 1605 and 1610. Switzerland began to issue a paper in 1610. Belgium and the Netherlands were at least on the verge of producing a real newspaper at that time. Those dates seem to be reliable. So also are the facts that the first papers were single-page, printed on one side of the page only, and issued weekly. Perhaps the most impressive of those facts is the *regularity* of the publication. The first newspaper, whatever its name, was not very imposing to look at, but it appeared at regular intervals and under the same masthead and the same publisher's name.

It was another ten years before England or Austria produced its first general newspaper: Austria in 1920, England in 1922. France's first paper *(La Gazette,* which later became the official *Gazette de France)* began to publish in 1631. Denmark's first newspaper was dated 1634, Italy's 1636, Sweden's 1645, Poland's 1661. In the American colonies, the first attempt at a newspaper of broad content and general circulation appeared in 1689 and lasted exactly one issue before it was closed down by the colonial governor. This was *Publick Occurrences.* The first newspaper that endured for any length of time in America was the *Boston News-Letter,* a weekly, published "by authority of the Government," beginning in 1704.

Russia's first newspaper was published in 1703. Thus, 100 years after the birthday of the first newspaper (assuming that was sometime between 1605 and 1610), a total of only 12 countries had newspapers that appeared on a regular schedule, and the total of newspapers in all these nations was probably not more than twice that number—an average of two papers per country.

THE HARD LIFE OF THE EARLY NEWSPAPER

A favorite name for newspapers in the early decades of the seventeenth century was *corantos* ("currents" of news). An astonishing number of these corantos reported only news from other countries, which says something about the sensitivity of local governments. Corantos from both Italy and Germany were being published in Amsterdam by 1619, and the first coranto in English was published in Amsterdam, not England. Actually, the first attempt to publish a coranto in England landed the publisher Thomas Archer (who was quoted at the beginning of this chapter) in jail because he had published without permission. A stationer named Nathaniel Butter published the first authorized coranto in England in 1622. The circumstances tell us something about the life of a newspaper publisher in the early seventeenth century. Butter's paper was entitled *Corante, or Newes from Italy, Germany, Hungarie, Spaine, and France.* Not England. Butter's license gave him permission to print news "honestly *translated from the Dutch.*" When Archer got out of jail he joined the staff.[5]

It was religion rather than politics per se that got in the way of much press freedom in the early years—although religion and politics became so intertwined in the sixteenth and seventeenth centuries that speaking of one usually called up the other. Henry VIII of England came to the throne a devout Catholic who felt that one of his regal obligations was to suppress anti-Catholic publications. Four years later he turned against the Vatican and founded the Church of England, with himself as head. One of his new obligations was to suppress *pro-*Catholic books and news sheets.

After a return to Catholic monarchy under Queen Mary, Elizabeth I took the throne and refounded the Church of England. Once again the government frowned on Catholic publications. Then James and Charles, strong Catholics both, came to the throne, and the pendulum swung toward the Catholics again and against their opponents, who called themselves Puritans. John Milton, the most eloquent of the Puritans, wrote, in his *Areopagitica,* a message to the kings and a defense of press freedom that has been quoted ever since:

> Give me the liberty to know, to utter, and to argue freely according to conscience. . . . Though all the winds of doctrine were let loose to play upon the earth, so Truth be in the field, we do injuriously, by licensing and prohibiting, to misdoubt her strength. Let her and falsehood grapple; who ever knew Truth put to the worse in a free and open encounter.[6]

When the Puritans came to power, Oliver Cromwell set up controls even more authoritarian than his opponents had used. And history took an ironic twist: The Puritans named a chief censor of anti-Puritan writings, and the appointee was none other than John Milton, author of the stirring defense of press freedom just quoted.

Historians may some day look back upon this intertwining of religion, politics, and press freedom as a slightly hilarious chapter in the history of journalism. In those days, however, it was not hilarious. It was deadly serious. It put many people in jail—and some of them to death—for journalistic offenses.

On the European continent, the winds of the Reformation were blowing up more censorship and repression. Monarchs decided, for reasons not always clear, that ordinary readers should hear nothing about politics except what their government told them. King James I, for one, decided that news of the Thirty Years' War should not reach the ordinary reader. A revolutionary movement in another country, a long war, an international incident, for example, were not events that most governments wanted brought to the attention of their subjects. And attacks on governments in power were simply not to be discussed.

In those first centuries of news publishing, there were four principal ways to keep the press in line, as the governments saw the line. One was licensing. In England and a number of other countries, publishers were required to obtain a royal patent, which was essentially permission to publish. Second, to obtain such a patent, the publisher had to agree to censorship. The heartily disliked Court of the Star Chamber was founded by England in 1585 to administer these regulations. The publisher of the first regular newspaper in England, in order to obtain his patent to publish, had to promise to submit the text of his weekly one-page news sheet for approval each time he printed. This precensorship was a common requirement throughout Europe. A third way of controlling the press was to impose a tax. For example, the Stamp Act, which was put into effect in 1712 by England and aroused such indignation in the American colonies, required a publisher to pay a tax of one halfpenny for a one- or two-page paper and one penny for a four-page paper. There were also special taxes on advertising. These taxes practically doubled the cost of a paper, and they succeeded in putting a number of publishers out of business and discouraging others from entering. In addition to all those means of controlling the press, there was always the fourth way, threatening to charge a publisher with "seditious libel," which was often interpreted simply as criticism of the government.

The European press grew up in this repressive atmosphere. It is not surprising, therefore, that almost all papers in the seventeenth century published no oftener than once a week, circulated usually no more than 300 copies per issue, and were ordinarily more concerned with foreign than domestic news. But this was changing.

In 1703, the oldest daily still in existence in Europe, the *Wiener Zeitung* (*zeitung* had been adopted as the German word for "newspaper") began to publish in Vienna. From modern printing to the first real newspaper was about 150 years. From the first newspaper to the first daily was almost another century. From that time until the European press stood up, confident about its independence, was, depending on the country, another 150 to 200 years.

At the beginning of the eighteenth century, dailies began to appear throughout Europe. England had its first daily in 1702 and five dailies by 1750. Germany is said to have had a daily paper for a short time in the 1660s, and indubitably had one, in Augsburg, beginning in 1718.

But the European press was not yet on the freeway to freedom. The authoritarian atmosphere in which the press had to function actually lasted rather longer on the Continent than in Britain or America. In France, in the eighteenth century, the death penalty could be imposed for material which threatened to "attack religion, arouse feelings against or pronounce attacks upon the authority of the Government, or undermine due order and tranquility."[7] Even Diderot had to spend 100 days in the dungeon at Vincennes for something he wrote, and one offending printer at Mont-Saint-Michel was put into an iron cage until he died. In Prussia the king for a time forbade the importing of all foreign newspapers. Austria at one time banned 2500 publishers in that country within a period of two years.

With the official papers, things were a bit easier. Renandot, editor of the *Gazette de France,* noted that "the King himself sends me memoranda."[8] But still the *Gazette* had to publish what it was told to publish. For example, it had to "authoritatively refute" Galileo's support of the theory that the earth goes around the sun rather than vice versa. It had also to publish detailed accounts of Galileo's trial and condemnation by the Inquisition in Rome.

In that kind of situation, European editors and publishers did not dare expect smooth traveling. One decade would be upbeat, the next one down. During the French Revolution, the number of newspapers in Paris rose to 350; during the following consulate, it sank to 13; during the empire, to 4. During the revolutionary period of 1640–1659 in England, 30,000 news publications appeared in London—such a decade of journalism as has seldom been seen at any other place and time. Then authoritarian controls closed most of them down again.

This spasmodic but hardhanded control of the press continued, off and on, well into the nineteenth century. The English press suffered from the Six Acts, which provided for more taxes on the press and heavier penalties for seditious libel. France, and all countries conquered by Napoleon, suffered from tough controls; Germany, from the Carlsbad Decrees of 1819 which also tightened controls; America, from the Alien and Sedition Laws, which were aimed at the Republicans (as they were called at that time, although philosophically they were rather closer to modern Democrats). In any case, these regulations made all journalists uncomfortable.

AN OLD CHAPTER ENDS

Gradually, the outlook improved. Sweden, in 1766, became the first country to pass a law guaranteeing freedom of the press. Developments in America also took on a more hopeful cast. An important court case involved John Peter Zenger, a German immigrant printer who had dared to attack in print the administration of the colonial governor of New York and consequently was jailed for seditious libel. An aged but able lawyer, Andrew Hamilton, succeeded in convincing the court that juries, rather than judges, should decide such libel cases. Zenger was acquitted, and 50 years later England revised its own libel law to include this point. About the same time that happened, another mighty blow was struck for press freedom in the United States: The First Amendment to the new Constitution provided that "Congress shall make no law . . . abridging the freedom of speech, or of the press." From that point on, American editors and publishers were among the freest in the world. In England, censorship was restructured and the long-observed licensing system was abolished, just at the end of the eighteenth century.

But the most important development as newspapers moved out of the eighteenth and through the nineteenth century was the appearance of a number of distinguished newspapers—or at least papers that would gain distinction as they grew older. Among these was the *Times* of London, which began in 1788 as *The Great Universal Register*. It soon outgrew the handicap of that name and acquired another official and several unofficial names, the latter including "The Old Reliable" and "The Thunderer." Other famous papers that began to print in the late eighteenth century included the *Neue Zurcher Zeitung,* of Switzerland, which was founded in 1790, and the *Allgemeine Zeitung* of Germany, which first appeared in 1797 and ended up in Frankfurt. In the United States, Henry J. Raymond's *New York Times* was founded in 1851, and in the half century preceding that, the first "penny papers" appeared—edited by distinguished men such as Benjamin Day, James Gordon Bennett, and Horace Greeley. Not only were these papers skillfully edited, they were also highly prosperous. Greeley's *Tribune,* for example, was reaching 200,000 people within ten years of its founding. Along with these widely circulating American papers were a number in England that emphasized excellent writing: among them, Mist's *Journal, The Review, The Tatler,* and *The Spectator,* edited by Defoe, Addison, and Steele, respectively. Whether called newspapers or magazines, they set standards in England for ability to interest and attract large audiences of readers.

Important papers were beginning to appear also in places far from Europe and America. For example, the *Straits Times* was founded in Singapore in 1834 as a weekly and became a daily in 1858. The *Times of India* began to publish in 1838, also as a weekly, and the *Sydney Morning Herald* in 1831. The important Japanese papers and the leading papers of Latin America, Eastern Europe, and the Middle East came along a little later.

With papers like these to represent them, journalists now found it easier to stand tall. Which they did.

AWFUL EVENT

President Lincoln Shot by an Assassin

The Deed Done at Ford's Theatre Last Night

THE ACT OF A DESPERATE REBEL

The President Still Alive at Last Accounts

No Hope Entertained of His Recovery

Attempted Assassination of Secretary Seward

DETAILS OF THE DREADFUL TRAGEDY

[OFFICIAL]

War Department,
Washington, April 15—1:30 A.M.

Maj.-Gen. Dis:

This evening at about 9:30 P.M., at Ford's Theatre, the President, while sitting in his private box with Mrs. Lincoln, Mrs. Harris, and Major Rathburn, was shot by an assassin who suddenly entered the box and approached behind the President.

Newspaper headlines from 1865.

A NEW CHAPTER BEGINS: THE MODERN PRESS

"In 1815," said Anthony Smith, "press freedom in Europe was an idea, an experiment, a fearful dread; by 1881 it had become an enduring institution, its most admired text enshrined in the French Press Law passed in July of that year."[9] The French law began with a sentence which set the tone of a new chapter in newspaper history: *La presse est libre* ("the press is free").

Some countries had anticipated the developments of 1881. The United States of America was one. Norway had proclaimed freedom of the press in its new constitution of 1814 and had established 80 newspapers by 1870. Italy decreed a new order for the press in its constitution of 1848. Canada, which had been handicapped in its journalistic development both by difficulties with the authorities in London and internal squabbling between French and English groups at home, extended telegraph service coast-to-coast in 1850 and began to establish a group of influential and prosperous city papers. Germany swept away its restrictions on the press in 1848 and put them back in 1850, but the papers had acquired new influence and impetus, which flowered toward the end of the century. In 1881 Britain passed a libel law that got rid of the long-resented requirement that newspapers deposit money against possible judgments. The law also freed newspapers from prior inspection of their copy and from much of the fear of being hailed into court for trial on the accusation of criminal libel. Removal of these restrictions encouraged the founding of many more papers, more prosperous and self-dependent papers, and papers that took leadership in socializing the newly literate masses of their countries, providing a political voice for them and advertising support for their businesses.

Something needs to be said about the technological developments in journalism that came with the Industrial Revolution. The printing presses that rode westward in covered wagons to help settle the American continent were the old hand presses, but throughout the cities of America and Europe these were being replaced by powered rotary presses. First powered by steam, then by electricity, these presses made it possible to print thousands of complete newspapers rather than 150 single sheets per hour, which was about the best the older printers could do. Stereotyping made it possible to reproduce photographs. Handsetting of type was replaced to a large extent by the linotype machine. In our own century, of course, electronic typesetting has made both handsetting and linotype setting seem obsolete. Telegraph, telephone, teletype, and radio delivered news to editorial offices farther and faster than ships, pigeons, stagecoaches, railroads, or airplanes could carry it. The typewriter (long before the era of electronic word-processing machines) speeded up newsrooms. And devices such as the electric light made it possible for subscribers to read newspapers—and for journalists and printers to produce them—at night as well as by day. In addition to all these were the challenge and stimulus presented to newspapers by three new media of electronic news and pictures: films, radio, and television.

Thus, in newly comfortable, less threatening, and well-financed surroundings, the journalists of Western Europe and America were at last able to produce the kind of papers toward which they had been struggling for three centuries.

We have been speaking mostly about the European press because that is where most of the giant steps in the early history of the press were taken. Beginning in the latter half of the nineteenth century, however, the road branched off. While the Western European and North American press went on to firm up their own patterns for the elite and the popular press, Russia, the countries of Eastern Europe, and later China restructured their press, in fact created a new press, along Communist lines. Similarly, countries of Asia, Latin America, the Middle East, and Africa, building on the base of some excellent papers already established there and using their lessons from colonial experience, established what we have come to know as the Third World press. And something fundamentally new came to the press when humans learned to record, present, and transmit news—parallel to and sometimes in competition with newspaper news—by moving pictures on a screen and sound through earphones or a loudspeaker. We shall come to these news developments in the following chapters.

SUGGESTIONS FOR FURTHER READING

The most usable volume on the history of the newspaper, viewed internationally, is Anthony Smith, *The Newspaper: An International History* (London: Thames and Hudson, 1979). Of course, Smith allots himself less than 200 pages to cover all the world's press, and therefore gives far less detail than texts limited to one country. The most-used text on American journalism is Edwin and Michael Emery, *The Press and America: An Interpretive History of the Mass Media,* 5th ed. (Englewood Cliffs, N.J.: Prentice-Hall, 1984). Sound, readable, and well illustrated, this book has annotated bibliographies. It gives some attention to other than the printed media and to press developments in other countries, but it makes no attempt to be a world history of journalism. Robert Desmond, *The Information Process: World News Reporting to the Twentieth Century,* 3 vols. (Iowa City: University of Iowa Press, 1978–1982) is an ambitious effort toward a worldwide history of news. There are many books on individual newspapers and editors. A sample is Meyer Berger, *The Story of the New York Times, 1851–1951* (New York: Simon & Schuster, 1951). A survey of a different kind is Louis L. Snyder and Richard B. Morris, *Treasury of Great Reporting* (New York: Simon & Schuster, 1962). A similar collection of recent newswriting is Bryce Rucker's *Twentieth Century Reporting at Its Best* (Ames: Iowa State College Press, 1964). A picture of the press as seen from the inside is to be found in books such as David Halberstam, *The Powers That Be* (New York: Knopf, 1979); A. J. Liebling, *The Press* (New York: Ballantine Books, 1961); Harrison E. Salisbury, *Without Fear or Favor: An Uncompro-*

mising Look at the New York Times (New York: Times Books, 1980); Gay Talese, *The Kingdom and the Power* (also about the *New York Times)* (New York: World Publishing Co., 1969); and an account of the *Washington Post*'s well-known job of investigative reporting on Watergate, by the reporters who did it: Carl Bernstein and Bob Woodward, *All the President's Men* (New York: Simon & Schuster, 1974). A summary picture of *The International News Agencies* has been written by Oliver Boyd-Barrett (Beverly Hills, Calif.: Sage, 1980).

QUESTIONS TO THINK ABOUT

1. How does one describe a newspaper? Suppose that someone asks you what kind of newspaper is—for example—*Le Monde,* what sorts of information would you give in reply? For instance, where is it published? Is it privately or governmentally owned? What is its circulation? What does it look like—how many pages, how many columns, usual makeup, etc.? What kinds of news coverage does it emphasize? What kind of readers does it seem chiefly to cater to?
2. We remarked in this chapter that the first real newspapers did not appear until some years after the beginning of news coverage. What is a "real newspaper"?
3. Why were governments so fearful of what newspapers might do to the power structure if they were not tightly controlled?
4. Are there any places in the world today where news media are under strict political controls?
5. What, if anything, did advertising have to do with lifting controls on the European press?
6. The press in the United States seemed to be able to operate rather more freely in the first half of the nineteenth century than most of the European press. Why?

TIME CAPSULE

Forerunners of the printed press	
Acta Diurna (Rome)	80 B.C.
Ti-pao (China)	618 A.D.
First news sheets on sale in Europe	ca. 1475
First print shop in England (Caxton)	1476
First newspapers on European continent	1605–1620
Corantos first become popular	1620
First regular newspaper in England—*Our Weekly Newes*	1622
Gazette de France	1631
First printing press in American colonies—at Harvard College	1638
Milton publishes *Areopagitica*	1644
First newspaper in American colonies—suppressed after one issue	1690
First English-language daily—*The Daily Courant,* in London	1702
First regularly issued newspaper in colonies—*Boston News-Letter*	1704

The New York Times.

VOL. LXI...NO. 19,596.   NEW YORK, TUESDAY, APRIL 16, 1912.—TWENTY-FOUR PAGES.   ONE CENT

TITANIC SINKS FOUR HOURS AFTER HITTING ICEBERG; 866 RESCUED BY CARPATHIA, PROBABLY 1250 PERISH; ISMAY SAFE, MRS. ASTOR MAYBE, NOTED NAMES MISSING

Col. Astor and Bride, Isidor Straus and Wife, and Maj. Butt Aboard.

"RULE OF SEA" FOLLOWED

Women and Children Put Over in Lifeboats and Are Supposed to be Safe on Carpathia.

PICKED UP AFTER 8 HOURS

Vincent Astor Calls at White Star Office for News of His Father and Leaves Weeping.

FRANKLIN HOPEFUL ALL DAY

Manager of the Line Insisted Titanic Was Unsinkable Even After She Had Gone Down.

HEAD OF THE LINE ABOARD

J. Bruce Ismay Making First Trip on Gigantic Ship That Was to Surpass All Others.

Biggest Liner Plunges to the Bottom at 2:20 A. M.

RESCUERS THERE TOO LATE

Except to Pick Up the Few Hundreds Who Took to the Lifeboats.

WOMEN AND CHILDREN FIRST

Cunarder Carpathia Rushing to New York with the Survivors.

SEA SEARCH FOR OTHERS

The California Stands By on Chance of Picking Up Other Boats or Rafts.

OLYMPIC SENDS THE NEWS

Only Ship to Flash Wireless Messages to Shore After the Disaster.

The Lost Titanic Being Towed Out of Belfast Harbor.

CAPT. E. J. SMITH, Commander of the Titanic.

PARTIAL LIST OF THE SAVED.

Includes Bruce Ismay, Mrs. Widener, Mrs. H. B. Harris, and an Incomplete Name, Suggesting Mrs. Astor's.

A historic front page of the New York Times *devoted entirely to the sinking of the Titanic (paper dated April 16, 1912).*

INSTITUTIONS OF THE MASS MEDIA: NEWS II

The newspaper has a history: but it has, likewise, a natural history. The press, as it exists, is not, as our moralists sometimes assume, the wilful product of any little group of living men. On the contrary, it is the outcome of a historic process.

ROBERT E. PARK

What is to prevent a daily newspaper from being made the greatest organ of social life? Books have had their day—the theatres have had their day—the temple of religion has had its day.

JAMES GORDON BENNETT

[We need] an organ that should be beyond taint of corruption, invulnerable against attacks and inspired by men who feel it their mission to teach the truth that they have acquired by hard toil and bitter suffering.

KARL MARX

*T*o bridge the gap between acts of an opera, composers typically write some special music which they call an entr'acte. Between the first and second parts of our story of the development of the press, we can place a verbal entr'acte written by Anthony Smith.

In the 1880s, all over the world, the newspaper was ready for a new formula. The market was now large enough for the old loyalties between a newspaper and a tiny social group to have lost their meaning; the technology of the industry was such as to make further expansion essential, and this in turn required investment on a large scale. A wholly new audience was waiting to be catered for, but it needed different treatment at the hands of editors and journalists. The newly literate would not read the long ribbons of type reporting hour-long political speeches verbatim without cross-headings. The new gadgetry of the period—from organized pigeons for sports reporting to the telephone—was waiting to fulfill a new journalistic design.[1]

Journalists in different parts of the world responded differently to this challenge. Newspapers in Western Europe and America carried forward the development they had already begun. The Soviet Union, the states of eastern Europe, and China installed a Communist press. The new countries installed such forms of the press as they could and as they thought would speed their national growth and economic development. And then electronic news entered the race.

First let us finish the story we started in the Chapter 10: the growth of the Western press.

THE WESTERN PRESS

The pattern that had been developing in Europe and North America was a twofold kind of press—elite and popular papers—privately owned and fiercely independent of government control.[2]

The Elite Newspapers

By elite papers we mean those that try seriously to provide and interpret the news for opinion leaders and policymakers. We have mentioned some of these papers but there are many others and we can only give examples. In Britain, one thinks of the *Times* of London and the *Guardian,* which started in Manchester and became a national rather than a provincial paper. In France, *Le Monde* and *Figaro.* In Germany, the *Frankfurter Allgemeine* and *Die Welt.* In Switzerland, *Neue Zürcher Zeitung.* In Italy, *Il Corriere della Sera* and *La Stampa.* In Denmark, *Berlingske Tidende. Die Presse* of Austria. *Svenska Dagbladet* of Sweden. *El Pais* of Spain. In Vatican City, the *Osservatore Romano.* And in the United States, the *New York Times,* the *Washington Post,* the *Wall Street Journal,* and the *Los Angeles Times.* Papers like these have been read and admired all over the world.

No one would contend that these are the only elite papers in the countries mentioned, or that these are the only countries that have elite papers. For example, any international list of influential elite papers could hardly omit Japan's *Asahi*

Shimbun or the Soviet Union's *Pravda,* along with numerous others. These names will come up in later pages.

Each of these elite dailies has a quality and personality of its own, but we can make some generalizations about them as a group. They represent a stage in the development of the newspaper that could hardly have been imagined only a few decades before, when newspapers were struggling to subsist on circulations of 300 to 3000 and to resist the stifling controls of government. In the West the elite press has not only gained independence from government control but also achieved the financial stability needed to provide worldwide coverage and interpretation of the news. These papers are read in their own countries for guidance and understanding, and in other countries as a voice of public opinion in their home countries. As public opinion has risen in importance, so has the press risen as a leader and spokesman of it. This is a long step from the years when editors were largely restricted from printing news of their own countries and had to go fearfully to government officials for approval before printing any news of any kind.

The Popular Newspapers

The elite papers in America and Europe appeal mostly to upper-middle-class readers. They are not written for the great mass of readers. On the other hand, the most prosperous dailies in the nineteenth and twentieth centuries have been written precisely for that mass—largely working-class people, the more recently educated, an audience looking for short paragraphs, big headlines, and entertainment along with enlightenment. Some publishers found they could sell that kind of paper for a penny, attract a large readership, and make large profits.

England's first penny paper was the *Daily Telegraph.* Founded in 1861, it was circulating 240,000 by 1879 (at that time the largest circulation in the world). However, popular journalism had already been launched in England by the time the *Telegraph* was founded. As a matter of fact, in 1833 the New York *Sun,* an American penny paper, hired an English newspaper writer, George Wisner, who had earned a nationwide reputation in English for his human interest coverage of London police court news. He transferred this style of writing to New York, and it was in no small degree responsible for the *Sun*'s popularity. Thus English popular journalism was in existence before English penny papers were.

Compared to the penny papers in the United States and the more recent popular press in Europe, the *Telegraph* was a relatively dignified journal. A more striking example of the popular press in England was the *Daily Mail,* founded by Alfred Harmsworth (Lord Northcliffe) in 1896. The *Daily Mail* was the first large British paper designed to support itself mainly by advertising. Consequently, it had to attract a large readership, which it did by appealing to the tastes and needs of

A front page of the New York Herald Tribune *reporting the shooting of Lee Harvey Oswald the same day as JFK is buried.*

the lower middle class and by selling copies to newsboys for resale in the streets. "A penny paper for one halfpenny," it called itself, and indeed it cost more than half a penny to produce: Advertising made up the difference. Harmsworth's basic approach to journalism was "explain, simplify, clarify," from which his paper derived its style of short snappy paragraphs and attractive illustration. Its circulation topped one million by the time of World War I.

Sunday papers and a few evening dailies proved to be most successful examples of the popular press in Western Europe. *Lloyd's Weekly News* reached a million in 1896. *News of the World* actually passed 1.5 million by 1909, and 4 million after World War II. In France, *Paris Soir* passed 2 million in 1938.

The American Press

The American press exemplified the popular newspaper in an even more spectacular fashion. In the United States the newspapers felt responsibility for helping to build the new country. In the East and South the press of the original colonies helped lead public opinion through the colonial revolution, and from this resulted half a century of partisan argument (in what came to be called the party press) between proponents of a strong central government and those who advocated states' rights for the new country. In the American West, after the revolution, newspapers set out to inform and educate the new citizens of the new nation. Almost every settlement of any size soon had its own printing press and weekly newspaper, its own editor and its own printer. These papers were usually short on national or international news, but no other kind of paper knew its audience so well or was so concerned with the problems of its hometown. In 1830 only 26 settlements in all the new American country had as many as 8000 people, but still the country had 65 dailies and 500 weeklies. Even when city papers in the United States were circulating over one million, the number of weeklies continued to grow. As late as the 1920s there were 15,000 weeklies serving country towns, and even now there are about 7600.

The country weekly lived on, but the party press was succeeded in the cities by a popular press.[3] It is common to date this succession to 1833 when Benjamin Day decided to sell the New York *Sun* for a penny a copy rather than the six cents or so typically paid for city papers. He took a paper that had six narrow columns of small type and redesigned it with three wide, easy-to-read columns. Rather than filling the paper with political debate or business news, he filled it with crime, human interest anecdotes, "inside" stories of well-known people, sports, and other exciting stuff readers could drool over. Within three years he was selling 30,000 copies a day.

James Gordon Bennett followed that lead with his New York *Herald* in 1935,

Number of Newspapers and Their Circulation in the United States

Year	Weekdays	Weekday Circulation	Sunday	Sunday Circulation
1920	2042	27,790,650	522	17,083,604
1930	1942	39,589,172	521	26,413,047
1940	1878	41,131,611	525	32,371,092
1950	1772	53,829,072	549	46,582,348
1960	1763	58,881,746	567	47,698,651
1970	1748	62,107,527	586	49,216,602
1980	1745	62,201,840	735	54,671,755
1984	1688	63,340,336	783	57,511,975

SOURCE: American Newspaper Publishers Association, *Facts About Newspapers* (Washington, D.C.: 1985).

"matching the *Sun* crime for crime and sensation for sensation, and then some." Bennett established his own private pony express to bring news from Washington, and found a way to intercept European news in Newfoundland and rush it to New York before the ships could get there.

Horace Greeley's *New York Tribune* soon joined the parade of penny papers. Greeley, however, was serious about news. Rather than digging for scandal and crime, he hired correspondents in 12 cities of North and Central America and depended on them to cover the news for him—fast. He ran a vigorous and uncommonly frank editorial page. And the city people who had been starved for news at six cents per day hastened to buy the *Tribune* for a penny. Indeed, the special weekly edition was selling 200,000 copies by the time of the Civil War.

The *New York Times* also sold for a penny when it was founded, but it was already launched on its career as the elite paper of New York. And high-quality regional papers began to appear in such cities as Chicago, Atlanta, Kansas City, St. Louis, Louisville, Boston, and Baltimore—later in cities farther west, such as Denver, San Francisco, and Los Angeles.

But the greatest excitement still was in the popular press. And perhaps the classical chapter in that story was written by Joseph Pulitzer and William Randolph Hearst.

Pulitzer and Hearst

Pulitzer had made a success of the *St. Louis Post-Dispatch* before he bought the New York *World,* which was at that time a quiet, dignified commercial paper with around 20,000 circulation. In his first issue of the paper, Pulitzer wrote,

There is room in this great and growing city for a journal that is not only cheap but bright, not only bright but large, not only large but truly democratic —dedicated to the cause of the people . . . devoted more to the news of the New than the Old World—that will expose all fraud and sham, fight all public evils and abuses—that will battle for the people with earnest sincerity.[4]

He lived up to this introduction. Two weeks after he took charge, he launched his first crusade—abolish tolls on the Brooklyn Bridge. He attacked Standard Oil, Bell Telephone, and New York Central because they were monopolies. He exposed and denounced tenement conditions, civil service corruption, and political bribery. He made crime stories realistic by photographs and drawings. He sent an expedition to the aid of a pioneer woman captured by American Indians. He sent one of his columnists around the world to try to make the trip in less than Jules Verne's 80 days. Ten years after he took over the *World* the circulation had leaped from 20,000 to 400,000.

But he had a worthy competitor in William Randolph Hearst. Hearst had persuaded his father to make him a present of the *San Francisco Examiner,* and he became publisher of the *Examiner* when he was only 24. But he had learned journalistic lessons from Day and Pulitzer. He filled the paper with scandal, crime news, gossip, and anything else that, as he put it, would make a reader say "Gee whiz!" He hired the best staff he could pry away from other papers, including the first of the so-called sob sisters, who wrote a daily column for the women in the audience. "Does Tight Lacing [of corsets] Develop Cruelty?" was a typical front-page headline of that period. The *Examiner* soon became the most successful paper on the Pacific coast, and then Hearst bought the nearly moribund *New York Morning Journal* and challenged Pulitzer.

His methods were Pulitzer's own, combined with the rough, tough journalism of the West. Hearst hired practically the whole Sunday staff of the *World.* He sent special trains to get reporters and their news back to his paper before Pulitzer could get it. He stole away from the *World* a cartoon called "The Yellow Kid," which was published daily and had become enormously popular. Pulitzer then hired another cartoonist to draw another "Yellow Kid," and the contretemps gave a name to the kind of competition Hearst was engaged in with Pulitzer: yellow journalism.[5] The circulation of the *Journal* went up until it nearly matched that of Pulitzer's *World.*

The most exciting chapter of the Hearst-Pulitzer story came at the time of the Spanish American War. Both publishers were watching the situation closely and trying to stir up sympathy for Cuba. Hearst sent two internationally known correspondents—Frederic Remington, the artist, and Richard Harding Davis, the novelist—to cover events in Cuba. They found not much happening, and Remington wired for permission to return home. Hearst replied: "You furnish the pictures and I'll furnish the war." Soon afterward, the battleship *Maine* blew up in Havana harbor. Both Hearst and Pulitzer filled their columns with indignant comment, and after that there was plenty of war. By that time both papers were selling more than one million copies a day.

Scripps

None of the later chapters of the history of the popular press quite matched for sensation the contest of Hearst and Pulitzer, but at least one more chapter deserves mention. That is the career of Edward W. Scripps.

Scripps was an Illinois farm boy who started his first paper when he was 24. He learned the craft of journalism under his brother, James, who was publisher of the *Detroit News*. From the *News* Edward moved to ownership of the *Cleveland Press* and the *Cincinnati Post*.

That fact itself shows how he diverged from the paths of Hearst and Pulitzer. They were metropolitan publishers, and their flagship dailies were in New York. Scripps preferred to publish in smaller but growing cities. For them he produced a somewhat later version of the penny press—low-priced afternoon papers, "brightly written, easily read newspapers, small in size but big in heart. . . . Closely edited news, human-interest features, fearless news coverage and local crusades, and hard fighting independent editorial opinion constituted the Scripps formula."[6]

Scripps himself described his newspapers as an expression of his sense of responsibility to the working class. "I have constituted myself," he said, "the advocate of that large majority of people who are not so rich in worldly goods and native intelligence as to make them equal, man for man, in the struggle with individuals of the wealthier and more intellectual class."[7] He saw his newspapers as a schoolroom for the working people, the only such available to them. And because he felt that *most* situations were unfair to this large majority, he practiced what some have called a journalism of protest, protesting unfair government, undemocratic politics, inequality of opportunity, and oppressive business controls. Scripps described himself as being in rebellion against society.

But although he was against capitalism and for progressive democracy, as a publisher he was an astute businessman. First he would pick able, ambitious young people to work with him as editors and business managers. He would choose a city where the outlook for business and industry was good but where the newspaper opposition was not very lively. He would put up a few thousand dollars and buy the paper, then send an editor and a business manager to run it. If the paper did not do well, they were replaced. If the paper did not make a profit within, say, ten years, it was sold. But if it did really well, then the new editor and business manager were rewarded with up to 49 percent of the stock. The formula worked so well that at age 36 Scripps could retire to a California ranch and call the editorial shots while his editors and business managers managed the profitable Scripps papers.

IN THE EAST: THE NEW COMMUNIST PRESS

One of the most striking chapters in the history of the European and Asian press was foreshadowed in the press itself. Karl Marx, the Communist party's chief theoretician, edited the *Rhenische Zeitung* in Germany in 1842 and 1843, until it was suppressed. Thereafter, while writing documents like the Communist Manifesto and *Das Kapital,* he served sporadically as a correspondent (for Horace Greeley's *New York Tribune* among other papers!). V. I. Lenin, head of the Bolshevik movement and founder of the Communist party of the Soviet Union, established in 1912 a newspaper called *Pravda* (truth) in St. Petersburg (later appropriately renamed Leningrad) and edited the paper between 1912 and 1917, resourcefully changing the name whenever the paper was closed by the czar's government. When the revolution flared in 1917 he took the paper (with its original name *Pravda*) to Moscow and made it the official publication of the Soviet Communist party. Similarly, Mao Tse-tung edited revolutionary newspapers during some of the time he was laying the groundwork for the 1949 takeover in China, and he was instrumental in establishing *Renmin Ribao* (the people's daily) in Beijing. All these Communist leaders realized the importance of the newspaper to what they were doing, and what happened to the press when the new regimes were established in eastern Europe and Asia was unlike anything else in journalistic history.

In most countries of Europe the press grew up under private ownership and in response to pressures and opportunities offered by the market. In the new political structures created in Russia after 1917, eastern Europe after 1945, and China after 1949, however, a new press pattern was conceived and imposed. There was to be no private ownership of newspapers. Rather, an official paper was to represent the Communist party, another the government, still others the needs and interests of important groups in the population: labor, youth, the army, and so forth. In Russia, *Pravda* represents the party; *Izvestia,* the Supreme Soviet (parliament); *Trud,* labor organization; *Krasnaya Zvesda* (red star), the Red Army; *Komsomolskaya Pravda,* the national youth organization. In each province of the country, this structure is duplicated; that is, there is a paper representing the party, another representing the government, and so on. These provincial papers pass along what the national papers have to say and also translate, interpret, and extend it to fit the local situation and needs.

Even in the countries of Eastern Europe where before 1945 there were privately owned papers, some of them quite distinguished, the Russian system was installed, with the partial exception of Poland, East Germany, and Hungary. In these countries there is no counterpart of *Izvestia,* the government paper, although other papers take over that function. When China joined the parade in 1949, it too established its set of official papers. And like Russia, it created a large and powerful news agency, Xinhua, corresponding to Tass.

The function of this new press was somewhat different from the one served by the Western European press. In the Marxist society, Lenin had said, "A newspaper is not only a collective propagandist and a collective agitator, it is also a collective organizer." Under Joseph Stalin, a Russian editor explained, the press was "the means to maintain contacts with the working masses of our country and rally them around the party and the soviet state." Nikita Khrushchev told a conference of journalists in Moscow: "As soon as some decision [of the party] must be explained or implemented, we turn to you, and you, as the most trusted transmission belt, take the decision and carry it to the very midst of the people." In other words, the press is to be concerned with what the people know and think, and what they do.[8]

News per se, therefore, is not the chief function of the Communist press, as it is of the West European and American press. Rather, its function is the interpretation of news; the selection of news in accord with the goals of the party; and beyond that, the education and guidance of the people. The ideas of private ownership of newspapers, or of an adversary relationship between press and government, do not fit within the Communist philosophy of the press. The press belongs to all the people, although the ordinary citizen does not have the skill or knowledge to run it, and therefore management is delegated to the party. Even though the press is operated *for* rather than *by* the people, special efforts are made to encourage readers to write letters to the editor. The number of letters received by important Soviet papers is phenomenal; *Pravda's* letter bag typically contains more than 1000 letters per day, and 50 professional employees make sure that all these are read and answered or responded to by action. Another way in which the press makes its readers feel that it is *their* press rather than the government's is by inviting local people to serve as correspondents to report on local communities or work groups. These locals are usually untrained as correspondents, but they have been well trained at least to report the good rather than the bad news. A *Christian Science Monitor* writer said after a visit to *Pravda:* "There is no [he should have said "little"] advertising, no crime, no comics, no travel tips, no crossword, no personality columns, no law court reports, no inside gossip from the Kremlin, no late bulletins, no list of international sports results. There also is no pessimism, no despair, no problem that cannot be solved."[9]

The typical Communist paper is a serious paper that works in the tradition of the elite rather than the popular press as those have developed in the West, but it tries to adapt that pattern to large masses of people rather than selected leaders. Circulations of official papers in Russia and China are enormous. *Pravda* and *Komsomalskaya Pravda* both circulate about 11 million copies a day; *Izvestia* is not far behind. Of course, these official papers have a built-in audience in the local officials and cadres who have to read them to keep informed of national policy and doctrine, and changes in the official line. But in most provincial capitals and other large cities there is also an unofficial newspaper that contains a higher proportion of entertainment than the *Pravda*s and *Red Star*s. So the popular press survives to a certain extent even in the Communist system, but is a somewhat different popular press than that of the West.

The Communist press is most certainly a controlled press. No opposition press or voice of opposition in the existing press is permitted. Criticism is permitted, in fact encouraged, but it must be directed at local administrators and their failure to follow good Communist policy and doctrine rather than at that doctrine and its chief custodians. The editors are in almost every case trusted and reliable party members, and Moscow keeps in close touch with them. Glavlit, the Soviet censorship organization, also keeps a close eye on newspaper content. On the whole, the Communist press gives a rather remarkable impression of unanimity and agreement.

Much of this arises from the organization and philosophy of the press, but much can be attributed also to the way the major content of the press comes to it. *Pravda* speaks in the Soviet Union, and its voice is heard everywhere in the land, not only because of its local editions but also because provincial and local papers pick up its line and some of its articles. Tass furnishes not only national and international news but also a guideline as to what should be said about it. In China these same functions are carried out by *Renmin Ribao* and Xinhua. In the Eastern-bloc countries, even though there may be no paper equivalent to *Pravda* in authority, no national news agency comparable to Tass, still the voices of both *Pravda* and Tass are heard there also.

What happened in 1917 and 1949 therefore represents the first planned and deliberate variation from the Western press.

THE PRESS IN THE NEW COUNTRIES

More than 80 countries exist today that were not politically independent 50 years ago. Most of them are products of the movement toward decolonization and nation building that followed the war of 1939–1945. The bulk of them are in the Southern

Hemisphere, and almost all of them are on one of three continents—Africa, Asia, and Latin America—or one of the ocean islands. Together these new countries cast a majority of the votes in the United Nations, and they represent more than half of the world's population.

Many of the new countries had little communication tradition before the last half century, and now they are busy trying to catch up, not only in education, industry, commerce, and political relations, but also in developing their communication systems.

Communication development is enormously different from one to another of these countries, and even within a single country. For example, some countries have no newspapers at all, and some have no dailies. More than half the population in the new countries is illiterate, which helps to explain why the extension of radio has gone rather faster than that of the press. On the other hand, the large urban centers almost all have professionally run newspapers, and some countries—notably those that got an earlier start or have made swifter progress in economic development—have well-developed systems.

For example, the ancient country of India has some truly distinguished daily papers, among them, the *Times of India,* the *Statesman,* and the *Hindu.* Another ancient country, Egypt, has an outstanding paper in *Al Ahram.* Latin American countries, which got a somewhat earlier start than many of the new countries, have a number of strong papers—for example, *O Estado* of São Paulo, *Jornal do Brazil* and *El Globo* of Rio de Janeiro; *La Prensa* of Buenos Aires, which has had a great history; *Excelsior* and *Novedades,* in Mexico City; El Tiempo, of Bogotá, Colombia; *La Nación,* of San José, Costa Rica; *El Universal,* of Caracas, Venezuela; and *El Mercurio* of Valparaiso, Chile, the oldest newspaper in Latin America (founded in 1827).

Another strand of press history is illustrated by some swiftly developing east Asian states which have excellent newspapers. Among these are the *Straits Times* of Singapore (founded in 1845), *Sin Chew Jit Poh* of Singapore and *Nanyang Siang Pao* of Kuala Lumpur (both highly successful Chinese-language newspapers), the *South China Morning Post* of Hong Kong, the *United Daily News* of Taiwan, and *Dong-a-Ilbo* of Seoul, Korea. (Japan, where the level of mass-communication development compares with that of any country in the world, and Australia, where the communication system is also far advanced, do not seem quite to belong with the developing countries, although they are in a developing region. They will be discussed a little later. The People's Republic of China and its official newspaper, *Renmin Ribao,* have already been mentioned in connection with the Communist press.)

The chief problem of the new countries is not with the development of communication in their large cities or with such world-renowned newspapers as we have been mentioning, but rather with the mass of their population, many of whom cannot read and cannot afford to buy broadcast receiving sets. Another problem is the scarcity of technology and of expert training in the field. Some of the countries are advanced in these respects; others are barely starting.

The governments of all these countries realize that an effective communication system is necessary for national growth and strength. Therefore they expect their media to play a full part in nation building. All of them own their broadcasting systems, almost all of them own their own radio stations, and many of them own their newspapers. Many of those that do not have government-owned papers exert the same tight authoritarian control that European papers experienced before the late nineteenth century; some of them have controls identical to the Communist press in Europe and Asia. Furthermore, they are increasingly sensitive about their relationships with the communication systems of the North (North-South has joined East-West as a term for describing international relations.)

This sensitivity has been orchestrated into an international political debate, much of it within the meetings and corridors of UNESCO. The topic of the debate is the desirability or undesirability of a "New World Information Order" (NWIO).[10] This is too complicated an idea to discuss at length here. There have already been half a dozen large international meetings, and the MacBride Commission of internationally known journalists and scholars has reported on the NWIO in a large book. The issues have become emotionalized as well as complicated to an almost unbelievable degree. Let us suggest, however, some of the basic questions that have been raised.

For one thing, no country likes to have a foreigner or a foreign organization in charge of the news that goes out about it or comes into it. The United States found that out before its own news agencies were able to share the news distribution function with the powerful European agencies. Similarly, now, the new Third World countries do not wholly like the existing international news agencies (which basically represent England, France, and the United States) and the correspondents of the foreign press reporting to the rest of the world about them. They feel the picture is distorted in favor of the big countries' interests. The new countries want their *development* stories covered, rather than stories of their train wrecks, political uprisings, disasters, crimes, corruption, and other sensational matters. That is why they try to put their own national news agencies or some other filtering device between the foreign agencies and the local news sources and users.

On the other hand, the Western agencies say their clients are really not much interested in the story of the building of a new gas plant in a developing country. But they *are* interested in stories of disasters and crimes and corruption and revolutions, major or minor. They point out that even Third World readers aren't much interested in development news from elsewhere in the Third World. Furthermore, Western newspeople believe in unimpeded coverage of news as one of the prime tenets of press freedom. Within reason, the international wires that serve Asia will give client countries what they want, but there are limits; and the agencies try to serve all their clients, East or West.

In addition to that, most of the technology of news coverage—the news wires and cables, the satellites, and so forth—is owned by the rich countries of the West. That is especially galling to Third World countries because they feel that as colonies their resources were used by the colonial powers without a fair return. Thus the new countries were not given an opportunity to build up professional skills or technological and financial resources to compete on an even basis with agencies from the richer countries.

Furthermore, Western domination of the news flow is seen by many spokespersons for the Third World (and Soviet) viewpoint as a form of cultural imperialism. It is imposing the Western image of the world on the new countries, and carrying the Western image of the new countries rather than presenting those countries as they see themselves. Just as the colonial powers took the raw materials from colonies for their own uses, so are they now taking news and using it profitably. Or so the critics say. The Third World representatives feel they are entitled to share at least some of this profit and to use their press in promoting their national interests.

The Western news organizations are conciliatory. They recognize defects in their news coverage and are prepared to respond to criticisms. They are willing to consider more favorable rates on use of Western technology by the new countries. They are willing to help the new countries train reporters and technicians. But the idea of government control on use of the news rubs them just as raw as the idea of cultural imperialism rubs the new countries. To the Western press, with its history of government news control in Europe from the seventeenth to the nineteenth century, freedom of the press includes freedom to cover the news—themselves.

Thus what might be a significant push from Western newspeople and news organizations to help their colleagues in the new countries is slowed by ideological differences that will not be quick to disappear.

THE PRESS OF JAPAN AND AUSTRALIA

The situation confronting the press of Australia and, especially, Japan is so different from that of the new countries' press that it seems only proper to insert a separate note about it, even though Japan is an Asian country and the Australian press serves a continent-sized island immediately south of Asia.

Japan has few characteristics of a developing country despite its location and the recency of its communication development. It has the highest living standards in Asia, perhaps the highest literacy level (99 percent) in the world. It circulates more daily newspapers than any other country except the Soviet Union, more copies per capita than any other country in the world. Luter and Richstad justifiably call it "the world's most highly developed press system."

The flagship of the Japanese daily press is the *Asahi Shimbun* ("rising sun newspaper") which circulates over 12 million copies in 18 morning and 10 evening editions. It publishes in Tokyo and four other main offices in Japan. To meet the particular needs and interests of different parts of the country it prints altogether 105 localized editions. It prints also an English-language edition. According to Luter, it has nearly 10,000 employees in five Japanese cities, 23 overseas offices, and 280 domestic news bureaus. It owns 125 automobiles, 82 motorcycles, 53 radio-equipped jeeps, 13 vans for radio-photo transmission, 3 jet airplanes, and 4 helicopters.[11]

In the lively competition that characterizes the Japanese press, *Asahi* and *Yomiuri Shimbun* (meaning "the read and sell newspaper") have traded back and forth the distinction of having the world's largest circulation. At last report, *Yomiuri* was ahead—ahead even of *Pravda* and the largest European newspapers —with nearly 13 million buyers of its morning and evening editions. *Asahi* has over 12 million. Until the last half dozen years, *Mainichi Shimbun* ("daily newspaper") competed on even terms with the others, but it has recently fallen off to about 7 million, which is less than *Pravda* and makes it still the fourth or fifth largest newspaper in the world.

Japan's total circulation of daily newspapers is about 65 million, slightly more than that of the United States and just under that of the Soviet Union. This is about 550 copies per 100 people.

The striking fact about those circulation figures is that the newspapers responsible for them are what we would describe as elite papers. That is, they are serious in tone, aimed at opinion leaders rather than people seeking light reading, corresponding to the *New York Times*, the *Frankfurter Allgemeine*, or the *Neue Zürcher Zeitung*, rather than the popular press. *Yomiuri* has recently included more popular material, which may account for its new leadership in circulation. But no elite paper anywhere else in the world has been able to reach such a level of circulation.

Let us now say a word about the Australian press. The two leading dailies in that country are also serious, elite papers, although some newspeople comparing the Australian and the Japanese papers have said that no Australian could be "that serious." The *Sydney Morning Herald*, founded in 1831 and published as a daily beginning in 1940, is the oldest newspaper in Australia. *The Age*, of Melbourne, is slightly less old and slightly smaller in circulation—both circulate between

250,000 and 300,000. It is more serious about public issues and probably has a stronger influence on leaders of opinion.

It should be noted that these two elite dailies have by no means the largest circulation in Australia. The country has a strong representation of the popular press, many of which sell 400,000 or more per weekday, 700,000 or more on Sunday. This makes the achievement of the very serious Japanese dailies all the more remarkable.

NEWS AGENCIES

The news agency is a journalistic device that, more than any other, binds together the news systems and units of the different countries.[12]

No newspaper or news agency can hope to be entirely self-sufficient in news coverage. Even the small-town weekly finds it necessary to make formal or informal arrangements with certain people to watch for items that would interest the paper's readers. As late as the nineteenth century, the more alert papers in Europe and America had reporters who studied the foreign newspapers and borrowed items of local interest. They met arriving ships and talked with travelers, cultivated relationships with traders and financiers to keep current on financial news, maintained friends in the police and fire departments, the railroads, the hotels, and other organizations whose employees might be knowledgeable about newsworthy events. In some cases these papers paid small sums to people to write newsletters from foreign or state capitals or metropolitan centers. Even so, they often missed important items and details. And therefore they looked for a better way.

Charles Havas, of Paris, found such a way. In 1833 he bought a translating agency in Paris and turned it into a news service. The first product he offered for sale was a systematic search of European papers for items that would be useful to the French press. He hired correspondents in other European capitals and offered news services in countries other than France. He even ran a delivery service by carrier pigeon between Paris, London, and Brussels. In 1856 he began to supply news in return for advertising space so that he could profit from the sale of advertising and of news.

His success and the undoubted usefulness of his service attracted others into the field. One of these was Bernard Wolff who left the Havas organization and started a telegraph news service in Berlin. The German government had just opened a new telegraph line, and Wolff began to use it for the old staples of news exchange —markets, prices, other commercial developments. Then he branched out into political as well as economic news.

The principal German telegraph line ran from Berlin to Aachen. Paul Julius Reuter, another newsman who had learned the business from Havas, set up an office in Aachen, but soon moved it to London. There he started, like Wolff, by supplying the English papers commercial and financial information. He soon expanded this service. In fact, of all the early news agency founders, Reuter may have been the most innovative. He supplied a regular service of news telegrams to any paper that would subscribe to his service, using not only the telegraph, but also carrier pigeons and the transatlantic cables as soon as they became available. He also acquired a considerable corps of correspondents, some of whom traveled while others covered news centers.

As small as these services were, compared to modern news agencies, these three competing agencies found themselves crowding each other. Therefore, in 1870 the three agencies divided the world among them, each taking initiative in serving its country's colonies and other conveniently accessible areas. Because of England's widespread colonial empire and the vigor of the service, Reuter came out with the winner's share.

Meanwhile the metropolitan newspapers in America were also feeling the need for help in covering foreign or other distant news. The cost of covering the Mexican war of 1846–1848 under competitive conditions had proved too much for even the comparatively prosperous New York papers. Therefore, six New York papers formed a cooperative news-gathering organization, the New York Associated Press, to share some correspondents and a large number of stories. This was the first news agency created by cooperating newspapers rather than by a central office. The New York Associated Press grew into the national Associated Press (AP), still with cooperative membership, and signed an agreement with Reuter under which the English agency furnished daily coverage of European news to America, and the Associated Press supplied corresponding coverage of American news to England. When the new Scripps newspaper network grew up far enough, it too felt the need of a news service, and the result was the United Press. As Hearst began to build his chain, the members of that group also discovered the need of a news service, and Hearst formed the International News Service, which later combined with the Scripps service to form United Press International (UPI).

After World War I, the Wolff agency ceased to exist and Havas changed its name to Agence France Presse (AFP). The four remaining agencies—Reuter, AFP, AP, and UPI—competed worldwide for news and clients. The more prosperous papers in many countries subscribed to more than one of these international agencies in order to get wider coverage and a variety of viewpoints.

National news services, and in some cases semi-international ones, have proliferated, especially in the years since World War II. This was the case particularly in the newly independent countries, some of whose news agencies have offered their services internationally. The Soviet socialist ideology almost required the Soviet Union to have its own news service with its own interpretation of events, and so Tass came into being. It served not only the USSR but also Eastern Europe and other papers that wanted to subscribe. China followed the Russian example, and with Xinhua serves all the Chinese press and such other papers as want to receive the service. Japan organized its own agency, Kyodo, with a national and an international wire. The news services of smaller nations, particularly the ex-colonial countries, felt the need to exert more control than before over the news being received by their papers and also the news going out from their countries through the international agencies. For this reason, during recent decades there has been a lively effort to use national agencies as news filters controlled by the government and to exchange news directly between developing agencies rather than through the large international agencies. One experiment along this line was the creation of the Pool of News Agencies in Non-Aligned Countries, for which about 50 of the developing countries provide news, chiefly government handouts. This operation was first managed by Tanjug, the Yugoslav news agency, beginning in 1975, then later transferred to the Tunisian News Agency. This press service has been less than a great success, but some of the dissatisfactions behind it continue to be expressed in the meetings and publications of the New World Information Order, and still remain to be settled.

NEWSMAGAZINES

It would be negligent to omit the newsmagazine from our discussion of printed news media.[13] Although it has characteristics of the newspapers and the very large, very popular magazines such as the *Saturday Evening Post* and *Life,* the newsmagazine is a genre of its own. Ever since it came into being in 1923, when Henry R. Luce and Britten Hadden founded *Time,* it has proved astonishingly successful and has been able to compete both with the newspaper and with broadcast news. There is one important difference, however: Whereas there are thousands of newspaper and broadcasting stations, there is only a handful of newsmagazines.

An essential quality of the newsmagazine is its personality. *Time, Newsweek,* and *U.S. News & World Report* in the United States, *Der Spiegel* in Germany, and perhaps a dozen other newsmagazines throughout the rest of the world have been able to maintain their personalities and prosperity and stand out from other sources of news in their countries.

The personality rests on the way the magazine is put together—on the way in which it is written. A reporter is not sent out to write a news item but is assigned to prepare a "file" on a given topic. That is, the reporter does not try to write a lead for publication and answer in detail the who-what-where-when-how questions a reporter is taught to consider. He or she writes something that more closely resembles narrative, trying, for example, to include interesting details such as appearance, behavior, and quotes. In other words the reporter is not so much trying to summarize as to describe what happened. Often several reporters are sent out to write this sort of thing on the same story. When their files get back to the office, staff researchers check every detail. Then a writer prepares a tentative story from everything at hand. An editor often rewrites that. Sometimes a top editor writes it over again. Every effort is taken to make the story interesting and easy to read, to keep it as short as possible, and still to retain the essential details. In other words, the newsmagazine tries to achieve, in a week rather than a few hours or minutes, some of the vividness and the personality of television, but in type rather than picture and sound. For millions of people in countries that have good newsmagazines, therefore, these publications serve both as a summary of essential news and a pleasant way of absorbing it.

SUGGESTIONS FOR FURTHER READING

Most of the readings suggested in Chapter 10 will apply also to this chapter. Let us, however, suggest a few titles on the press of other countries and on news agencies. Several books edited or written by Merrill provide a good starting point. One is *Global Journalism: A Survey of the World's Mass Media,* edited by John C. Merrill, with chapters by seven other persons (New York: Longman, 1983). Another is John C. Merrill and Harold Fisher, *The World's Great Dailies* (New York: Hastings House, 1980). Francis Williams's *The Right to Know* (Harlow: Longmans, 1969) is a British editor's and broadcaster's look at the media around him, emphasizing chiefly Europe. *Handbuch der Weltpresse,* edited by H. Prakke, W. B. Lerg, and M. Schmolke (Opladen: Westdeutscher Verlag, 1970), also aims at a world review.

The Press in Developing Countries, by E. Lloyd Sommerlad (Sydney: Sydney University Press, 1968), is chiefly concerned with the problems of bringing out a press in the Third World. *Publishing in the Third World,* by P. G. Altbach and Eva-Marie Rathgeber (New York: Praeger, 1980), deals with some of the same problems. D. R. Mankekar, *Media and the Third World* (New Delhi: Indian Institute of Mass Communication, 1979), and Leonard R. Sussman, *Mass News Media and the Third World Challenge* (Beverly Hills, Calif.: Sage, 1977), are on rather different sides of the New World information order argument. The MacBride report, Sean MacBride et al., *Many Voices, One World* (London: Kegan Page, New York: Unipub, Paris: Unesco, 1980), is on all sides of it.

Susumu Ejiri, *Characteristics of the Japanese Press* (Tokyo: Nihon Shimbun Kyokai, 1984), is a useful introduction to that press. Among books on the Latin American press, one thinks of Marvin Alisky, *Latin American Media: Guidance and Censorship* (Ames: Iowa State University Press, 1981). Charles Moses and Crispin Maslog, *Mass Communication in Asia* (Singapore: AMIC, 1978), is a useful brief introduction. *Mass Communication and*

Journalism in India, by D. S. Mehta (Beverly Hills, Calif.: Sage, 1980), is an introduction to that system.

Among the many books on the European press are C. Bellanger et al., eds., *Histoire Generale de la Presse Francaise,* 4 vols. (Paris: Presses Universitaires de France, 1969–); James Curran, George Boyer, and Pauline Wingate, eds., *Newspaper History: Studies in the Evolution of the British Press* (London: Constable, 1978); V. Castronovo and N. Tranfaglia, *Storia della Stampa Italiana* (Bari: Laterza Editori, 1976); M. Lindemann, *Die Deutsche Press bis 1815,* K. Koszyk, *Die Deutsche Presse im 19. Jahrhundert* and *Die Deutsche Presse 1914–1945* (the last three all Berlin: Colloquium, 1966, 1967, 1972); and Alan J. Lee, *The Origins of the Popular Press 1855–1914* (London: Croom Helm, 1976).

On news agencies, see Oliver Boyd-Barrett, *The International News Agencies* (Beverly Hills, Calif.: Sage, 1980); G. J. Robinson, *News Agencies and World News* (Fribourg, Switzerland: University Press of Fribourg, 1981); Graham Storey, *Reuters' Century 1885–1951* (Reuters: 1951), which tells the story from that side; and Victor Rosewater, *History of Cooperative News-Gathering in the United States* (Englewood Cliffs, N.J.; Prentice-Hall, 1930), which tells it from the American side.

QUESTIONS TO THINK ABOUT

1. Look at Merrill's and Fisher's list of elite newspapers in For the Record. How many of them are you familiar with—or, let us say, how many have you read more than once? How many would a person who reads only English be able to read? A person who reads only Russian? Japanese? French? Spanish? German? Italian? Chinese? If Merrill and Fisher had been Frenchmen or Germans, do you suppose the distribution of languages would have been as it is? Judging by the papers in this list you have read, how would you describe a "great daily" as Merrill and Fisher see it?

2. What would you say is the proportion of information versus entertainment in the newspapers you read?

3. What are the different kinds of authoritarian controls that are exerted or have been exerted on newspapers? For example, how do the controls on the Communist press differ from those the European press struggled against during the seventeenth and eighteenth centuries?

4. What are the special problems now faced by Third World countries as they try to develop their press systems?

5. If you are interested, look at the evaluative reports on such famous commissions on the press as the Royal Commission on the Press in Great Britain (1962) and the Hutchins Commission in the United States (1948). What different problems did they focus on?

6. How many different kinds of press system are there in the world? A book that is now rather old but still challenging (*Four Theories of the Press,* by Siebert, Peterson, and Schramm—Urbana: University of Illinois Press, 1956) lists four, but not all readers accept this division. Can you suggest a better one?

Fifty of the World's Great Dailies

ABC (Spain)
Aftenposten (Norway)
The Age (Australia)
Al Ahram (Egypt)
Asahi Shimbun (Japan)
The Atlanta Constitution (U.S.)
The (Baltimore) *Sun* (U.S.)
Berlingske Tidende (Denmark)
Borba (Yugoslavia)
The Christian Science Monitor (U.S.)
Il Corriere della Sera (Italy)
The Daily Telegraph (U.K.)
O Estado de S. Paulo (Brazil)
Le Figaro (France)
Frankfurter Allgemeine (West Germany)
The Globe and Mail (Canada)
The Guardian (U.K.)
Ha'aretz (Israel)
Helsingin Sanomat (Finland)
The Hindu (India)
Izvestia (Soviet Union)
Jornal do Brazil (Brazil)
Los Angeles Times (U.S.)
The (Louisville) *Courier-Journal* (U.S.)
The Miami Herald (U.S.)

Le Monde (France)
Neue Zürcher Zeitung (Switzerland)
The New York Times (U.S.)
Osservatore Romano (Vatican City)
El Pais (Spain)
Pravda (Soviet Union)
Die Presse (Austria)
Rand Daily Mail (South Africa)*
Renmin Ribao (China)
The Scotsman (U.K.)
La Stampa (Italy)
St. Louis Post-Dispatch (U.S.)
The Statesman (India)
Süddeutsche Zeitung (West Germany)
The Straits Times (Singapore)
Svenska Dagbladet (Sweden)
Sydney Morning Herald (Australia)
The Times (U.K.)
The Times of India (India)
La Vanguardia Española (Spain)
The Wall Street Journal (U.S.)
The Washington Post (U.S.)
Die Welt (West Germany)
Winnipeg Free Press (Canada)
The Yorkshire Post (U.K.)

*No longer being published.

SOURCE: John C. Merrill and Harold A. Fisher, *The World's Great Dailies: Profiles of Fifty Newspapers* (New York: Hastings House, 1980).

A farm family in Hood River County, Oregon, listening to the radio. First print, then electronic communication, reached into every home, office, and school. This family had long had the newspaper through rural free delivery. Now, in the early 1920s, it had access to additional news through radio, to the voices of national leaders, music from the Metropolitan Opera and Carnegie Hall, and before long, entertainment that had previously been restricted to cities. The picture was taken by the Federal Extension Service, and that seems particularly appropriate because the smaller boy in the picture grew up to be a distinguished scholar and researcher who studied the process of agricultural development under the auspices of the extension service, and some of his first studies were of the use of radio for development. His name is George Beal.

COMMUNICATION AND THE CENTURY OF INVENTION

The greatest invention of the nineteenth century was the process of invention itself.

ALFRED NORTH WHITEHEAD

What hath God wrought!

SAMUEL B. MORSE

*B*efore we can fill out the story of news we must say something about the other media, in addition to print, that come into that story. This takes us to the nineteenth century and to the subject of invention.

For all technology, and especially communication technology, the latter nineteenth and the early twentieth century was an enormously exciting time. Let us review the record—or at least a small part of it. What did human beings have at the end of that period that they could hardly have imagined at its beginning? They had inanimate sources of power to substitute for human muscles and work animals. Skilled machines to take over for many human skills. New ways to transform matter into such things as synthetics, and previously unknown chemicals. A new insight into medicine and surgery. Electricity to light homes and work places, and to run here and there on wires doing chores for us. New and efficient ways to organize work into cooperative groups. A machine that made it possible for us to leave the earth if we wanted to. And, lest we seem to forget, new communication technologies that extend our senses and our ability to communicate almost beyond limit of distance, and to store what we hear and see and think about almost beyond limit of amount and time. To see what that means, imagine how different life would be today without the telephone, television, and electronic recording. (We leave out the computer and the chip; they came a bit later.)

Probably no other time in history has gathered together such a large and talented group of inventors as the period we are talking about. Yet, no inventor creates technology out of dreams alone. Behind the technological creativity of the so-called Industrial Revolution and its extension into our century were both a rebirth of ancient science and invention and a remarkable group of new scientists who laid down platforms of theory and principle upon which inventors could stand with confidence and look into the technological future.

THE ROOTS OF INVENTION

The foundations of these new scientific platforms were themselves deep in the past.[1] When Francis Bacon named the three developments he felt had been necessary for transforming European society—he said they were the magnetic compass, gunpowder (originally for fireworks, not for guns), and printing—he may or may not have known that all the discoveries he was naming had originated in China. Credit for developing a really usable system of numeration, including zero and Arabic numerals, rests largely with India and the Muslims. The Greeks developed an abstract logical system of mathematics upon which the great mathematicians of the Renaissance and post-Renaissance centuries could build. The Muslim scholars of the Renaissance translated the ancient classics of science as well as philosophy and literature. Some of the artists themselves developed interests broad enough to encompass science and technology; Leonardo da Vinci, for example, put into his notebooks beautiful and imaginative pictures of devices like airplanes which would not be "invented" for another three or four centuries. Still another force behind the age of technology was the restlessness of the Renaissance, with its remarkable history of exploration and development of international trade that brought cultures together and stimulated one group of humans to learn and borrow from others. Together, travel and the circulation of print made it far easier than before for people to know how others lived and to adapt what others had learned.

But it was a new and brilliant group of natural scientists who did the most to break the path to technology. Astronomers such as Galileo and Kepler helped change human ideas of their position in the universe, and in the course of so doing Kepler developed the principles of optics. Electricity and magnetism came to be understood in large part because of the work of Gilbert, Helmholtz, Faraday, and Maxwell, among others. Modern chemistry emerged from the studies of Boyle,

Lavoisier, and others; medicine, from the studies of William Harvey on the circulation of the blood, Pasteur on bacteria, and so forth. Leibnitz invented the calculus, Lobachevsky the non-Euclidean geometry, among other things. Mathematicians such as Descartes, LaPlace, Fourier, and Poisson greatly advanced that field. The idea of a time dimension in biology led to the development of evolutionary theory by Darwin, Wallace, and others. The towering scientific figure of the nineteenth century, however, might be identified as Isaac Newton, and his *Principia* as the great book of theory. But the century should not be described in terms of any one person, or even a few; it was a lively and productive age of science in many fields, and the practical products of its technology reflect this kind of versatility.

One thing that must be kept in mind in thinking about the Industrial Revolution is that there was no gulf between theoretical and practical studies of science such as we are accustomed to. For instance, Lord Kelvin, the great physicist, and Thomas Henry Huxley, the great biologist, were almost equally interested in the theoretical and practical implications of their studies. The best universities and departments in the nineteenth century typically gave courses in practical applications, frequently taught by their best scholars.

With this ferment, it would have been almost impossible for persons interested in applications to miss all the opportunities around them. It was as remarkable an age of technological as of scientific growth. If we want to take a few examples, think of what happened to sources of power—from the steam engine developed by Newcomen in 1711 and improved by James Watt in 1763, to the electric motor, to the internal combustion engine; or to forms of transportation—from the steamboat (using Watt's engine), to the automobile (into which Daimler and Benz, and later, Henry Ford, put the the internal combustion engine and thus created the proto-Mercedes and the "Model T" in the early twentieth century), to the airplane (flown by the Wright brothers in 1905); or building materials—from methods for making iron and steel to methods for making synthetics and plastics; or any one of a hundred other kinds of basic development, such as the electric light. But some of the most remarkable technology of the Industrial Revolution was in the field of communication.

CAPTURING SIGHT ON FILM

Print was so marvelously successful in providing a memory for humans and circulating ideas over space and time that it dominated communication for 400 years in Europe, and longer in Asia. But for all its magic, the age of print lacked the magic of voice and body language and appearance and nonverbal sound. Even when ways were found to reproduce paintings and drawings in print, these were only surrogates for what one sees in life. And there was no way to reproduce and transmit sound except the ancient megaphone, and some devices that seemed more like toys than science—for example, a taut string stretched a hundred feet or so over which sounds like those of speech could be carried. Toy though it was, it gave certain inventors an idea, and they set to work finding out how to transmit really legible speech a really long distance over a string or a wire. The result was ultimately the telephone. For a hundred years before any of the great communication inventions of recent times, scientists and inventors were at work on how to carry live sound farther than a human voice would carry, to record and duplicate and transmit the kind of picture their ancestors had learned 20 millennia earlier to record on cave walls, and to find a way to let humans see what the cave paintings had only suggested—movement.

In a surprising number of instances they worked from the kinds of devices we have called toys. The taut string is an example. Music boxes and mechanical pianos are other examples. One of the most effective of these devices whose evolution stopped just short of the intended goal was the camera obscura, which was developed out of a design from the marvelously fertile imagination of Leonardo da Vinci. It was simply a dark chamber to which light was admitted through a single small hole (in later versions, through a lense). It projected on the wall of the dark room a very clear picture of whatever was happening within sight of the opening. The picture left little to be desired, and it fascinated its users. A suitcase-size model was made and carried by travelers so that they could peer into the case and enjoy the most favorable possible view of the scenery. Lord Byron, for example, carried one with him when he went to Italy. The device is still exhibited in museums and occasionally in a carnival or exposition. But note that it would not *record* a picture, and this is what the inventors were challenged to achieve.

Throughout the Western world people were working to turn this remarkable device into another device that would not only give a sharp picture but also preserve it—in other words, a camera. In the nineteenth and twentieth centuries the center of technological innovation in communication clearly had moved from Asia, where it had been for a thousand years before the European Renaissance, back to the West. When Asia again began to contribute substantially to communication technology it was the electronics industry of Japan that did so, and not until the latter half of the twentieth century. The story of photography began in France.

The invention of photography involved three persons.[2] One was a lithogra-

The camera obscura.

pher, another was a professional scene painter, and the third was a trained scientist. Out of this unlikely combination came the first practical process for making photographs.

The lithographer, Joseph Niepce, lived in a city about 200 miles south of Paris. He depended upon his son to copy drawings on the lithographer's stone. When the son was called for military service, Niepce found his own drawings were unsatisfactory and began to consider how he could use light to help draw the pictures he needed. He tried coating a glass plate with a type of asphalt which, when treated with oil of lavender, changed its solubility in proportion to its exposure to light. Exposing a plate of this mixture from the upper window of his farmhouse, he actually succeeded in making a photograph of his barnyard. This was in 1826, exactly 100 years before the first public demonstration of television. Niepce's dim photo is still preserved carefully at the University of Texas. But an exposure of several hours was necessary to make it, and in that time all the shadows faded out. The process was manifestly impractical.

Niepce's experiment, however, came to the attention of another Frenchman who was interested in photography: Louis-Jacques-Mandé Daguerre. He was the proprieter of the Diorama in Paris, an auditorium to which people came to view enormous paintings (14 × 22 meters) of famous places and events. Daguerre often made his sketches for these scenes with the aid of the camera obscura, which projected scenes on the walls to be painted. He began to wonder how he might

One of the oldest surviving photographs. It required about half an hour to expose this picture.

record the light from the camera obscura and thus eliminate the need to trace the outlines and paint them in later. When he heard about Niepce's photograph he wrote to Niepce, and they worked together on developing a photographic process. After Niepce died in 1833, Daguerre continued trying various chemicals, however, and in 1837 produced a faithful and detailed picture of his studio on a silver-plated sheet of copper that had been exposed to fumes of iodine to make silver iodide, which was light sensitive. The photograph was "fixed" by removing the unaffected silver iodide with sodium thiosulfate.

Thus any of three dates might be chosen to mark the "invention" of photography. The year 1826 might be used because that was the time of Niepce's first photograph. The most often used date, 1839, was the date when Daguerre felt his process was perfected and sold it to the French government in return for life annuities both for himself and for the son of his old collaborator Niepce. Daguerre himself preferred to call his process the making of "heliographs" (sun writing), but it speedily became known over the world by the name of its inventor: daguerreotype. And 1837, when Daguerre made his first sharp pictures by a practicable process, has probably more right to be called the birthday of photography than either 1826 or 1839.

The third member of this trio of inventors was William Henry Fox Talbot, who was English. He was trained as a scientist at Cambridge, but felt himself rather inclined toward the arts. He found, however, that he lacked the talent for drawing landscapes, which was a popular undertaking at the time among university gentlemen, and got the idea of trying to record by chemical means the images he saw in his camera obscura. He actually developed a workable process at about the same time as Daguerre, and his method had certain advantages over Daguerre's in that his pictures—"photogenic drawings" he called them—were on paper and in the form of negatives from which copies could be made. Daguerre's were positives and on glass plates. Talbot reported his process to the Royal Society six months before the French government published details of Daguerre's process—a booklet by Daguerre which attracted so much interest that 30 editions and translations appeared before the end of 1839. So Talbot must be considered along with the other inventors of photography, and this event was like so many other steps in the development of communication technology—an idea whose time had come and on which several talented persons were working at the same time.

The next steps in the development of photography were improvements in lenses and the invention by George Eastman of a fast film, which made it possible to make pictures in a short time—"snapshots." (Daguerre's pictures had required 15 minutes' exposure.) Just beyond these steps, in the late 1880s, came the invention of motion pictures. But certain other developments of importance took place before movies.

TRANSMITTING SOUND ON WIRE

In the first half of the 1870s two inventors in the United States were working, simultaneously but unknown to each other, on the problem of how to send more than one telegraph message at the same time over the same wire. The telegraph had been invented about the same time as photography; as a matter of fact, Samuel F. B. Morse had demonstrated it for the first time publicly in 1837, the very year in which Daguerre had shown his own working model. The telegraph was for communication electronics the same kind of first step as the camera was for communication optics. Morse has perhaps received more credit than he deserves for the telegraph, because the electronic principles had all been set out by two Englishmen, Wheatstone and Cooke, and William Watson had demonstrated a laboratory system 90 years before Morse. A working telegraph was functioning in England not long after Morse had strung a wire from New York to Washington and transmitted the first message (by Morse code), "What hath God wrought!" The telegraph, of course, used the long wire for the signal and the ground for the return arm of the circuit. Until long wires were available (for example, the first Atlantic cable in 1866), therefore, the telegraph was useful mostly for short connections— in a factory or between businesses, between homes (once people had learned the Morse code), and the like. But by the middle 1870s there were over 200,000 miles of telegraph circuits, carrying 31 million telegrams a year between 8500 offices, and individuals in homes everywhere were learning the Morse code so they could "talk" over their own lines. Lines were constantly in short supply, and that is why Alexander Graham Bell and Elisha Gray were working on how to carry multiple messages on the same telegraph wire.[3]

Bell was a Scotchman whose poor health had led his family to emigrate to Canada in 1870. He had spent one year at the University of Edinburgh, but his study there did not include electricity. Gray had worked his way through three years at Oberlin College and had developed several electronic inventions. In the 1870s both these men found that several tones could be sent at once over the same telegraph wire; if that were so, then it would seem reasonable that a great many different tones could be transmitted, and when that became apparent the hunt for a multiple telegraph signal took a different turn. For it seemed wholly likely that the system might transmit enough tones to represent the human voice.

The scientific background had long been available for such a conclusion. It was known that sound is a vibration. Charles Wheatstone, the inventor of the Wheatstone bridge, demonstrated in the 1820s that sounds could be transmitted through rods of glass and metal. Michael Faraday demonstrated in the 1830s that the vibrations in a piece of metal could be translated into electrical impulses. Why did it take so long to move from there to the telephone? The fact is that it is often a long step between theory at this level and its practical application. There had to be an individual between Faraday and Wheatstone, on the one hand, and the American Telegraph and Telephone Company, on the other. That man turned out to be Bell (which is why we have the "Bell" Telephone system today), but it might just as well have been Gray. Both Bell and Gray perceived a practical and profitable use for the physical relationships discovered by Wheatstone and Faraday. They had the kind of minds required to conceptualize science in terms of everyday use— to turn a set of equations into a machine-made instrument on a desk, so to speak. Were there no such individuals 40 years earlier when Wheatstone and Faraday were illuminating the problem? Perhaps not. Or perhaps their attention was elsewhere. Or the time may simply not have been ripe, as it was not ripe for a Gutenberg until the middle of the fifteenth century.

In 1874 Gray built a voice receiver much like the present instrument, containing a vibrating steel diaphragm in front of a magnet. In the same year, Bell designed a comparable receiver using a skin membrane with a piece of iron in the middle to carry the vibrations. In 1875, Bell and his assistant Thomas Watson built two identical instruments, consisting of a vibrating membrane and a coil, one to be used as transmitter, one as receiver. These were tested but did not work satisfactorily, perhaps because the sound was very faint and the surroundings noisy. In the same year, Gray designed a transmitter using a variable resistance circuit with rods moving in water. Bell and Watson worked to improve their device. What Gray did at this time is not entirely clear; he may have lost confidence. But in any case, both men prepared patent papers. On January 20, 1876, Gray filed a notice of intention to apply for a patent. Six days earlier, Bell had filed, not a notice of intent, but a complete patent application. Up to this time neither man had been able to transmit speech successfully by wire. But that six-day difference in filing time made the difference in two careers.

Bell, having priority in application, received his patent on March 7, 1876. He still had not proved that the apparatus he had drawn and described on the patent application would work. But on March 10 he did successfully transmit speech, and this should probably be set down in history as the birthday of the telephone. Into the horn with its transmitting diaphragm he said, "Mr. Watson, come here, I want you." And Watson, his ear to the horn over the diaphragm in the next room, heard and came.

Little by little, Bell and his allies and competitors learned how to make the instrument usable over long distances. When the new telephone was demonstrated in June 1876 at the U.S. Centennial Exposition, it could still transmit only a few hundred feet, and persons who saw the demonstration of the instrument in those first years remarked how Edison and Watson "yelled at each other" over the phone line across the stage. It took several years to develop an efficient system, one of the chief contributions to it being a carbon microphone invented by Thomas Edison. It was 1915 before telephone conversations could be carried across the United States, and 1926 before they could travel across the ocean—and then only by radio.

It is generally said that Bell's patent of March 7, 1876—number 174,165—is the most valuable one ever issued by the U.S. Patent Office. Therefore, it is well to record a few curious facts about it. In 1877 Bell offered to sell it to Western

Union for $100,000. They declined the offer! Another interesting fact is that there was less than complete agreement on the purpose for which to use the telephone. Bell himself expressed some ideas on the future of the telephone in the following letter:[4]

Kensington, March 25, 1878.

To the capitalists of the Electric Telephone Company:

Gentlemen—It has been suggested that at this, our first meeting, I should lay before you a few ideas, concerning the future of the electric telephone, together with any suggestions that occur to me in regard to the best mode of introducing the instrument to the public.

The telephone may be briefly described as an electrical contrivance for reproducing, in distant places, the tones and articulations of a speaker's voice, so that conversation can be carried on by word of mouth between persons in different rooms, in different streets, or in different towns.

The great advantage it possesses over every other form of electrical apparatus consists in the fact that it requires no skill to operate the instrument. All other telegraphic machines produce signals which require to be translated by experts, and such instruments are therefore extremely limited in their application, but the telephone actually speaks, and for this reason it can be utilized for nearly every purpose for which speech is employed.

At the present time we have a perfect network of gas pipes and water pipes throughout our large cities. We have main pipes laid under the streets communicating by side pipes with the various dwellings, enabling the members to draw their supplies of gas and water from a common source.

In a similar manner it is conceivable that cables of telephone wires could be laid under ground, or suspended overhead, communicating by branch wires with private dwellings, counting houses, shops, manufactories, etc., uniting them through the main cable with a central office where the wire could be connected as desired, establishing direct communication between any two places in the city. Such a plan as this, though impracticable at the present moment, will, I firmly believe, be the outcome of the introduction of the telephone to the public. Not only so, but I believe in the future wires will unite the head offices of telephone companies in different cities, and a man in one part of the country may communicate by word of mouth with another in a distant place.

In regard to other present uses for the telephone, the instrument can be supplied so cheaply as to compete on favorable terms with speaking tubes, bells and annunciators, as a means of communication between different parts of the house. This seems to be a very favorable application of the telephone, not only on account of the large number of telephones that would be wanted, but because it would lead eventually to the plan of intercommunication referred to above. I would therefore recommend that special arrangements be made for the introduction of the telephone into hotels and private buildings in place of the speaking tubes and annunciators, at present employed. Telephones sold for this purpose could be stamped or numbered in such a way as to distinguish them from those employed for business purposes, and an agreement could be signed by the purchaser that the telephones should become forfeited to the company if used for other purposes than those specified in the agreement.

It is probable that such a use of the telephone would speedily become popular, and that as the public became accustomed to the telephone in their houses they would recognize the advantage of a system of intercommunication.

In conclusion, I would say that it seems to me that the telephone should immediately be brought prominently before the public, as a means of communication between bankers, merchants, manufacturers, wholesale and retail dealers, dock companies, water companies, police offices, fire stations, newspaper offices, hospitals and public buildings and for use in railway offices, in mines and other operations.

Although there is a great field for the telephone in the immediate present, I believe there is still greater in the future.

By bearing in mind the great object to be ultimately achieved, I believe that the telephone company cannot only secure for itself a business of the most remunerative kind, but also benefit the public in a way that has never been previously attempted.

I am, gentlemen, your obedient servant,

Alexander Graham Bell.

For the first ten years, though, there was strong impetus behind the idea of using the telephone for music and news—in other words, wired radio. Bell went around giving demonstrations that always included singers, instrumental music, and sometimes news bulletins—in addition to Watson and Bell, as we have noted, shouting at each other—which may have been one reason why the use of the new device for music may have seemed more promising than its use for conversation. In Europe, such wired broadcasting was introduced commercially in the 1880s. The crystal ball is sometimes clouded.

In the middle of 1877, when the new instrument was a year old, there were only 209 telephones in use, all in the United States. Most of them were private lines between home and office or between offices. The first exchange was installed in New Haven, Connecticut, in 1878. It served 21 telephones. By 1880 there were 138 exchanges, 30,000 subscribers. By 1887 there were 150,000 telephones in the United States, and considerable numbers also in Canada, Britain, Germany, France, Sweden, Italy, and Russia. We know what has happened since.

A telephone switchboard in the early years of the twentieth century.

Thus the new developments in communicating sound did not begin by providing a memory for sound, as writing provided one for language, print for writing, and photography for seeing. The telephone and the telegraph were used for disseminating the human language and the human voice. The memory device came into being ten years after the telephone, on a day in 1877 when Thomas Alva Edison recited the nursery rhyme about Mary and the little lamb into a machine built around a vibrating needle and a wax cylinder.

RECORDING SOUND

Certainly one of the most remarkable persons in the age of technology was Thomas Edison. It is neither possible nor proper to say that he was the greatest inventor of that age, because it is wrong to try to define *great* in this context. Was he greater than Bell? Was Edison's electric light a greater invention than Bell's telephone? Was he greater than Daguerre? Was his motion picture system a greater invention than Daguerre's still-photographic system? Was he greater than Watt, who perfected the steam engine, or the Wrights, who got the airplane to fly at Kitty Hawk, North Carolina? The question is not really helpful. We can say, though, that Edison produced probably more inventions that have changed human life than any other man of his time. He was a systematic man, a quiet man, deaf for most of his adult life. He had grown up a poor boy, supported himself in his teens by becoming one of the fastest telegraphers working on the railroad system, taught himself to be a scientist, and established at Menlo Park, New Jersey, perhaps the first well-stocked, well-staffed laboratory for invention. Out of that laboratory came the motion picture, the phonograph, the electric light, the storage battery, and countless other devices that have become a part of modern life.

There is no picturesque story connected with Edison's development of the phonograph and phonograph record. As he did with so many other things, he saw the need, researched it, thought out a system he believed would work, tried out countless alternatives until he found one that would work better than others, and built it. He preferred the cylinder record to the disk, so he developed a cylinder coated with wax, which produced a surprisingly good sound through Edison's magnifying horn. And then he had a memory machine for sound. It had a vibrating needle, a wax cylinder, a horn to magnify the sound, and it would say in what was unmistakably Edison's voice, "Mary had a little lamb," or sing in what was unmistakably Caruso's tenor, or read a poem as no one else except Alfred Tennyson could read Tennyson's poetry.[5]

Curiously enough, Edison was surer of the possible uses of his memory machine for sound than of his memory machine for motion, which he developed a little later. Almost at once he sent phonographs and wax cylinders to Europe to record readings by Browning, Tennyson, and other poets. He recorded Johannes Brahms playing a Hungarian rhapsody. People were becoming acquainted with the new machine through nickel and dime machines in amusement parks where they could listen to a short novelty recording—whistlers were great favorites at that time, and so, as always, were bands and comedians. A race was developing to record the great names. This was helped along by the gradual replacement of Edison's wax cylinder by the Gramophone disk, which was easier to make and to handle. Gramophone itself recorded a number of famous instrumentalists and orchestras. Its American affiliate became Victor, which introduced Red Seal records featuring such singers as Enrico Caruso. Pathé, in Paris, still using the cylinder phonograph, recorded Mary Garden and other performers. The Russian Red Label recorded Fyodor Chaliapin. By 1910 about four out of every five records sold were of classical music. Thus it was that the first great impact of the phonograph, following Edison's lead, was to diffuse this kind of music (rather than the "top 40") beyond

the concert hall and the opera house into smaller towns and less affluent homes. The diffusion of popular music came later and was parallel to the development and popularization of radio. For its first decade, at least, the phonograph lived up to many of the hopes that it would contribute to the elevation of musical taste.

CAPTURING MOTION

We have said something about the first steps toward applying the science of optics and the science of electronics to communication. Let us now turn again to optics. And we shall find ourselves again in Thomas Edison's laboratory.[6]

Daguerre's first pictures, as we have noted, required an exposure of 15 minutes to two hours. By 1870, however, lenses and camera mechanisms had been so much improved that it was possible to make pictures with a shutter speed of one-thousandth of a second. When that was accomplished the stage was set for motion picture photography. Having discovered how to record realistically what their greatest artists had previously been able to record on stone or canvas, humans now had an opportunity to record what no human had *ever* been able to record: the sights of motion.

The path to motion pictures was quite as extraordinary as the path to still photography. The story can hardly be told without including the governor of California. In 1872, Governor Leland Stanford (who later founded Stanford University) employed an English photographer to help him win a $25,000 bet. The bet, made in the spirit of the old American West, concerned whether at some time in its gallop a horse has all four feet off the ground. Stanford said it did; the man who bet with him said it did not. So Stanford hired Edweard Muybridge to find out and prove it by photography. Muybridge got the idea of placing 12 cameras at equal distances along a race track, with strings across the track attached to each camera. As the horse broke each string he would trip the camera and record a picture. Thus consecutive pictures were made of a horse galloping, and they showed conclusively that there was a point in the horse's motion when he had four feet off the ground. So Stanford won his bet, and Muybridge collected his fee. But there was a sequel.

Muybridge was fascinated by this set of pictures. He placed the 12 snapshots

---

Some of the communication inventors of the nineteenth century. Top line: *Joseph Niepce and Louis-Jacques-Mandé Daguerre, inventors of photography.* Middle line: *Samuel F. B. Morse, builder of the first operating telegraph; Thomas A. Edison, inventor of the electric light, the phonograph, the motion picture, and the storage battery, among other things.* Bottom line: *Alexander Graham Bell, inventor of the telephone; Guglielmo Marconi, first man to transmit a message by radio across the Atlantic.*

Rotate the disk and the horse seems to gallop.

on a wheel and rotated it in front of a lens and a light. Thus he could show a picture of a horse galloping. The brain, of course, retains the image a little longer than it stays on the screen, and this gives the illusion of continuous motion. By placing 20 and then 40 cameras, rather than 12, along the track, Muybridge could get rid of some of the flicker and make the pictures sharper. In a sense these were the first motion pictures, but the process was still not really feasible. People made picture dishes and picture wheels and rotated them in front of a light, and enjoyed the uncommon experience of watching recorded motion. A Frenchman developed a so-called photographic rifle that took 12 pictures a second on a rotating glass plate, but this too was less than a workable process because, like the wheels, it could record only a few seconds of action.

The next step was George Eastman's invention of celluloid roll film, which for the first time made it possible to record a series of consecutive pictures on the same strip of film. This was a great contribution because with it, a very long series of pictures could be taken at high speed on a medium that could be used without being transferred to a wheel or a dish or some other device to rotate the same set of pictures over and over again.

At that point the scene shifts again to Edison's laboratory in New Jersey. Under Edison's direction, a member of the laboratory staff, William K. L. Dickson, developed a motion picture camera using Eastman's celluloid film. Dickson also invented a peep-show type of viewer for the films he recorded. This was shortly after 1890. Another inventor, Thomas Armat, developed a workable projector for such films in 1896. So Edison had the first motion picture camera, which he called the Kinetograph; the first one-person viewing device, the Kinetoscope, which he patented along with the Kinetograph in 1891; and later a good projector, the Vitascope—in other words, a complete system ready to go to work. He was surprisingly uninterested in taking advantage of his head start into film production, and even in projecting the new moving pictures on a screen. He seemed to think of the new development as a device to supplement the music he could record on his invented phonograph rather than the reverse of that, which proved to be the profitable combination. This was quite at variance with the aggressive attitude he took with his new phonograph. And so the initiative passed into other hands and other countries.

The story of the development of the film industry is not something we can treat here, but we should record that the first moving picture shot on celluloid was made in the Edison laboratory by Dickson, and was entitled *Fred Ott's Sneeze.* It showed a worker in Edison's laboratory who came in with a bad cold and gave out a resounding sneeze in front of the camera. The first of Edison's films that attracted a great deal of publicity was a filmed scene from a Broadway play, *The Widow Jones.* For the record, the title of this little film was *The Kiss.* It showed an actor and an actress in a passionate embrace, and it was loudly hailed as the death knell of public morality—as, later, were also feature films, disks, radio, and television.

Edison's early filmstrips, in the 1890s, were very short, for one thing because he preferred to run the film at 48 frames a second to avoid flicker. The pictures were typically dancing girls or comedy scenes. None of them was projected; none of them lasted more than a few minutes; and they were essentially peep shows, not big-screen movies.

Looking back with the advantage of hindsight, it seems almost incomprehensible that Edison could sit for five years with a world monopoly on the technology required to operate movie theaters and still produce nothing except peep shows. He simply was not interested in projecting films for a theater audience. Therefore, the first important developments in making films for projection came from Europe.

Fred Ott's Sneeze, *which may have been the first movie. Ott was an employee of the Edison laboratory who came to work one day with a bad cold and walked in front of the experimental motion picture camera.*

SENDING SOUND THROUGH THE AIR

The story of radio begins the same way as many of the other technologies we have been reviewing. The science was available: Faraday's work with magnetic fields in the 1830s; Maxwell's mathematical prediction in the 1860s that electromagnetic energy could be propagated at the speed of light; Hertz's test and confirmation of Maxwell's theories in the 1880s. Then an uncommonly persistent Italian inventor named Guglielmo Marconi put Hertz's experiments to practical use and began propagating meaningful telegraphic signals through the air.[7] In the early 1890s he managed to send a wave signal 9 meters, then 275 meters, then 3 kilometers, then in 1901 the 3200 kilometers from England to Newfoundland. That first transatlantic message was simply the letter *s*—three dots in the Morse code—repeated over and over.

At this point radio was simply a telegraph extender and was used for communication with ships at sea. Its greatest impact came when ways were found for it to carry speech. This became possible with the improvement of microphones and receivers, but most particularly when new tubes were developed to amplify very weak currents. Among these was Fleming's diode, which was transformed into the audion tube when DeForest added a grid to it. It served not only as a superb amplifier but also as a replacement for the old spark transmitter. As the technology improved, radio operators listening for Morse code were frequently startled to hear opera singers and musical instruments in their earphones: Laboratories were tinkering with the new devices. In 1915 the American Telegraph and Telephone Company (Bell's old company) was able to transmit quite understandable voice radio from Arlington, Virginia, to Paris. A little later it was found possible to talk back and forth, by voice radio, between ground and airplanes. The quality of transmitted music also improved notably. In 1916 David Sarnoff, who as a Morse code radio operator had copied down some of the messages from the sinking *Titanic,* had become contracts manager for the Marconi Company. (He later became head of the giant RCA.) Sarnoff wrote a prophetic memorandum. Transmitting stations should be built to broadcast music and speech, he said. Radio was becoming more than an experiment. It should become a "music box" for homes. He proposed a

> . . . plan for development which would make radio a household utility in the same sense as the piano or phonograph. The idea is to bring music into the house by wireless.
>
> While this has been tried in the past by wires, it has been a failure because wires do not lend themselves to this scheme. With radio, however, it would be entirely feasible. For example, a radio transmitter having a range of say 25 to 50 miles can be installed at a fixed point where instrumental or vocal music or both are produced. The problem of transmitting music has already been solved in principle and therefore all the receivers attuned to the transmitting wavelength should be capable of receiving such music. The receiver can be designed in the form of a simple "Radio Music Box" and arranged for several

different wavelengths, which should be changeable with the throwing of a single switch or pressing of a single button. The "Radio Music Box" can be supplied with amplifying tubes and a loudspeaking telephone, all of which can be neatly mounted in one box. The box can be placed on a table in the parlor or living room, the switch set accordingly and the transmitted music received. There should be no difficulty in receiving music perfectly when transmitted within a radius of 25 to 50 miles.

The same principle can be extended to numerous other fields as, for instance, receiving of lectures at home which can be made perfectly audible; also events of national importance can be simultaneously announced and received. Baseball scores can be transmitted in the air by the use of one set installed in the Polo Grounds. The same would be true of other cities. This proposition would be especially interesting to farmers and others living in outlying districts removed from the cities. By the purchase of a "Radio Music Box" they could enjoy concerts, lectures, music recitals, etc. While I have indicated a few of the most probable fields of usefulness for such a device yet there are numerous other fields to which the principle can be extended.[8]

We are so accustomed to the existence of such a system that it is hard to think of a time when there was no radio in the home. And Sarnoff's memorandum is so logical and realistic in view of what has happened since that we tend to think of it as a routine idea. But imagine yourself without a broadcasting system and with nothing to make one out of except new electronic devices never tested for such a service; and then consider what a leap of imagination it took to write a memorandum like Sarnoff's. When the world relaxed from World War I, Sarnoff's idea was picked up both in the United States and Western Europe, and thereafter in almost every other country of the world as soon as the technology became available.

Exactly where and when radio broadcasting began has been disputed. Most historians prefer to say it started with station KDKA, Pittsburgh, in November 1920. But whether the first scheduled broadcasts really came from there or from Detroit or elsewhere is less important than the undoubted fact that in at least one country several hours of radio were on the air each day in the late months of 1920. By the end of the 1920s, radio was on the air in 50 countries. Now radio reaches more persons than any other medium.

As new media have come in they have had to find viable places for themselves among existing media, and in general each medium readjusts its content to what it can do better than other media. Thus, motion picture films cut into the monopoly of still photographs as a recorder of visual experiences. The phonograph put a damper on the idea of furnishing music by telephone. Radio staked out its own territory, against both phonograph and telephone, as provider of live music and

The KDKA studio decorated for Christmas, 1922.

speech to homes. When television came, a little later, it caused a major readjustment in existing media, notably radio, film, and print. As we noted in Chapter 9, no medium has gone out of existence when faced by a new medium; it has merely moved over to make room for the newcomer by concentrating on the particular services it can uniquely provide. Thus when television invaded radio's monopoly in offering evening home entertainment, radio became a specialty medium—offering news bulletins, music, and sports, and serving such specialized listeners as motorists who could not watch television while they drove, young people who wanted a background of popular music while they studied or worked, and others who wanted to keep up with more sports than television could bring them.

SENDING MOTION PICTURES THROUGH THE AIR

We have already begun to talk about television, which most persons would think of as the most spectacular of these new communication technologies. But they were all spectacular in their times. People rushed to buy stereopticons so they could look at "real" pictures at home. The excitement of hearing a radio program from a few hundred miles away was certainly greater in the first years of radio than the thrill of hearing one from the other side of the world today. And who can say that giving humans a machine by which they could talk—two-way—to someone of their choice anywhere in the world is any less spectacular than another technological development? But the newness or spectacular quality is not necessarily equal to the social effect. For example, there was very little new about the horseless carriage that Henry Ford put together in a garage at Dearborn, Michigan. Not even the internal combustion engine was new. But Ford's "Model T" and other creations like it created a new industry, made humans more mobile than they had ever been, invented suburbs, and ultimately brought OPEC into existence. Sometimes these inventions came with a flash of insight as, for example, when DeForest put together three wires in a vacuum and thereby made a tube that played an essential part in sending voice and music through the air. Sometimes the inventions came from long painstaking trial and error, as when Edison tried hundreds of substances before finding a suitable filament for the electric light bulb, or a thousand chemical combinations before he was able to put together a working storage battery. The point is that a group of persons appeared in this age of technology who were willing to give much of their lives to the task of translating theory into practice —transforming what scientists had discovered into something humans could use in their ordinary lives.

Television was born out of 50 years of such activity. The science behind it was long known.[9] In 1884, Paul Nipkow patented in Germany a disk with a spiral of holes that would scan—and, in later versions, reproduce—pictures. The scanning wheel was a part of almost all early television and came close to being accepted, in the 1940s, as a standard component of color television in the United States. The Federal Communications Commission had to freeze all applications for new stations in the late 1940s while the decision was made whether to adopt the scanning wheel system from CBS or the all-electronic system proposed by RCA. Actually the CBS system at that time was thought to produce better color.

In 1908, when radio was still trying to change over from telegraphy to voice, Campbell-Swinton of England theorized a completely electronic system of television that would have worked if the equipment could have been made at the time. As early as 1907, Rosing in Russia had been able to produce a very faint television signal by using Braun's new cathode ray oscilloscope as a display tube. Thus people were already working on television when the idea itself was unknown to most of the world. In 1923 Charles Jenkins, an American, sent unmoving television silhouettes by wireless from Washington to Philadelphia. The same year Vladimir Zworykin patented the iconoscope camera tube, which became the key component of the RCA system and eventually of all completely electronic television systems. In other words, the fruit was ripe for picking. Just as someone other than Bell might have been first to demonstrate the telephone, so inventors in several countries in the mid-twenties might have gone down in history as first with television. But so far as we know the first demonstration of working television took place in the winter of 1925–1926. The place was London, and the inventor was John Baird. His apparatus was primitive. It used the scanning wheel and produced fuzzy pictures in black-and-white only. But it worked.

The date traditionally given for this event is January 26, 1926, although Baird had shown his machine to a few friends before that. It is interesting to read what some of the persons who saw the first formal demonstration had to say about it. W. C. Fox, a Press Association journalist, recalled:

> It was a cold January night and the members of the Royal Institution arrived in twos and threes. When they came out after the demonstration their remarks, such as I overheard, were much as one would expect. Some thought it was nothing worth consideration; others considered it the work of a young man who did not know what he was doing, while a few, a very few, thought there was something there capable of development. There was no realization of the fact that they had been present at the birth of a new science.
>
> The received image was admittedly crude, but was recognizable as—whatever it might be—a face, a vase of flowers, a book opened and shut or some simple article of everyday life. The image received was pinkish in color and tended to swing up and down. It was not possible to see much of the apparatus as it was covered by screens of one sort and another—extraneous light was not wanted and would interfere with the image.[10]

Two days after the demonstration a short account appeared in the *Times* of London. The *Times* described the new invention as

> . . . consisting of a huge wooden revolving disk containing lenses, behind which was a revolving shutter and a light sensitive cell. The head of a ventriloquist's doll was manipulated as the image to be transmitted, though the human face was also reproduced. First on a receiver in the same room as the transmitter and then on a portable receiver in another room, the visitors were shown recognizable reception of the movements of the dummy and of a person speaking. The image as transmitted was faint and often blurred, but substantiated a claim that through the "Televisor," as Mr. Baird has named

his apparatus, it is possible to transmit and reproduce instantly the details of movement, and such things as the play of expression on the face.[11]

That is all the record we have of that cold January night in England. And yet in a dozen countries engineers and inventors were galvanized into action. In a very short time, performance of "televisors" was dramatically improved—although the oldest surviving NBC picture, a picture of Krazy Kat, may not prove that point. Universities as well as electronic laboratories and factories began to work on the new device. I remember my own first experience with television. I had just come from Harvard to my first faculty position at the University of Iowa and, being young and vulnerable to flattery, accepted an invitation to make an experimental broadcast. I brought my fiancée to watch the broadcast. In a laboratory, I spoke into a hornlike microphone while a very bright light shone on my face. After I orated for about 30 minutes, the program time seemed to be over, and I inquired how much audience there might have been. The engineers explained they had only one receiver working at that time, but had placed it so that my future wife could watch it. Her account of the performance was somewhat less than complimentary. She said my face was a dark shadow—television at that time, as often later, was a "talking head"—that undulated from top to bottom. In fact, she laughed so hard that I almost lost the woman who has now been married to me for 50 years.

In 1936 BBC began regularly scheduled broadcasts of 405-line pictures from Alexandra Palace, London, comparing the Baird mechanical scanning system with the EMI-Marconi all-electronic system. Germany started broadcasts soon thereafter, using 180 lines. RCA began to demonstrate at the same time a 343-line scanning tube, which was, for that time, comparatively clear. But World War II started in 1939, and television had to wait until the late 1940s to begin the most sensational chapter in all media development.

That is no exaggeration. In 1956 a committee of the United States Senate tabulated how long it had taken certain prominent inventions to reach 34 million homes, which was approximately the total number in the United States at the time. It took the telephone 80 years to accomplish that feat. Electric wiring did it in 62 years, the automobile in 49 years, the electric washing machine in 47 years, and the refrigerator in 37 years. But television required only—what is your guess?—ten years! In 1945, the United States had one million receivers; in 1951, 10 million; in 1959, 50 million.[12]

The United States now has somewhere near 80 million receivers, 60 million or so receiving color. Over 30 million homes have more than one television set. Television is more common than bathtubs or indoor toilets, automobiles or refrigerators. Around it have grown industries for subsidiary products—electronic pre-programmed games that can be played on the television screen, cables that carry programs and other services to homes by means of wires, videocassettes to record programs, magazines that carry the week's program schedule, editors who comment on the programs, and so forth. And that is only the beginning.

We shall have more to say later about the early development of television. Here let us think back again to some of the accomplishments of that remarkable century between the first photograph, in 1826, and the first public demonstration of television in 1926. At the beginning of that century we had just moved from the age of stagecoaches and carriages into the age of the steam engine; at the end of it we had fast trains, steamships, automobiles, and airplanes. At the beginning of the century we could record neither sight nor sound, and certainly not moving sight; at the end of the century we could record all these. At the beginning we had the print media, but no more. At the end we had four additional media: motion pictures, sound recording, and radio and television just coming on stage. At the beginning of the century we had a post office and some couriers; at the end we had two powerful electronic communication channels, telegraph and telephone. We could talk with almost anyone in the world and send a message, electronically printed out, almost anywhere. We could snap a picture of almost anything we could see. It would be strange indeed if, after all those changes in transportation and communication, human life and human knowledge would be unchanged.

SUGGESTIONS FOR FURTHER READING

On the history of the telegraph, see G. Hubbard, *Cooke and Wheatstone and the Invention of the Electric Telegraph* (London: Routledge and Kegan Paul, 1965); R. L. Thompson, *Wiring a Continent: The History of the Telegraph Industry in the United States, 1832–1866* (New York: Arno Press, 1972); and *Encyclopaedia Britannica,* 14th ed., s. v. "Telegraph." Some of the most useful references on the telephone are J. Brooks, *Telephone: The First Hundred Years* (New York: Harper & Row, 1976); R. V. Bruce, *Alexander Graham Bell and the Conquest of Solitude* (Boston: Little, Brown, 1973); M. D. Fagan, ed., *A History of Engineering and Science in the Bell System. The Early Years, 1875–1925* (New York: Bell Telephone Laboratories, 1975); Ithiel de Sola Pool, ed., *The Social Impact of the Telephone* (Cambridge, Mass.: M.I.T. Press, 1977). On films: P. Rotha, *The Film Till Now: A Survey of World Cinema* (with additional sections by R. Griffith) (London: Spring Books, 1967); R. Griffith and A. Mayer, rev. ed., *The Movies* (New York: Simon & Schuster, 1970); G. Jowett, *The Democratic Art* (Boston: Little, Brown, 1976); and P. Cowie's chronological record of significant movies, *Eighty Years of Cinema* (South Brunswick, N.J.: A. S. Barnes, 1977). On radio and television, Erik Barnouw's important three volumes on *A History of*

Broadcasting in the United States (New York: Oxford University Press, 1966–1970) and his later book on television, *Tube of Plenty: The Evolution of American Television* (New York: Oxford University Press, 1875); Asa Briggs's three volumes on *The History of Broadcasting in the United Kingdom* (New York: Oxford University Press, 1961–1970); a readable text by C. H. Sterling and J. M. Kittross, *Stay Tuned: A Concise History of American Broadcasting* (Belmont, Calif.: Wadsworth, 1978); J. Greenfield, *Television: The First Fifty Years* (New York: Abrams, 1977); Radio and Television Culture Research Institute of NHK, *50 Years of Japanese Broadcasting* (Tokyo: The Institute, 1977); and E. Katz and G. Wedell, *Broadcasting in the Third World: Promise and Performance* (Cambridge, Mass.: Harvard University Press, 1978).

QUESTIONS TO THINK ABOUT

1. What are the differences between the talents of an inventor (like Edison) and a scientist (like Wheatstone or Maxwell)?
2. Of the developments in the electronic century (photography, telegraphy, telephone, recording, radio, television, etc.) it has been said that television has had the greatest impact upon society. Do you agree? If you do not, what is your nomination for the most influential communication product of that century?
3. If you could keep only three of these devices from the electronic century, which ones would you keep?
4. Most print before the nineteenth century had no pictures except illustrations that came from drawings. What is the strength of photography in printed materials?
5. How, if at all, has the telephone changed human life?

TIME CAPSULE

Daguerre and Niepce develop workable photographic process (about same time, Talbott develops photographic negatives)	1839
George Eastman develops first fast film (roll film in 1884)	1860
Alexander Graham Bell patents the telephone	1876
Thomas Alva Edison patents the electric light	1879
Edison invents the phonograph	1888
Motion pictures are made in laboratories	1889
Edison develops the kinetoscope	1891
Guglielmo Marconi transmits radio (in 1901, from Britain to Newfoundland)	1895
The Great Train Robbery—first movie with a plot	1903
De Forest vacuum tube makes sound possible—not merely telegraphic code—on radio	1906
Charles D. Herrold transmits several years of scheduled radio from homemade station in San Jose, California (station closed at beginning of war)	1912

Beginning of regularly scheduled and continuing radio—first station was
    probably KDKA, Pittsburgh   1920
Vladimir Zworykin invents iconoscope and kinescope, making television
    practical   1923
John L. Baird demonstrates television in London   1926
Edwin H. Armstrong invents FM radio   1933

NEW YORK, MONDAY, OCTOBER 31, 1938.

Radio Listeners in Panic, Taking War Drama as Fact

Many Flee Homes to Escape 'Gas Raid From Mars'—Phone Calls Swamp Police at Broadcast of Wells Fantasy

A wave of mass hysteria seized thousands of radio listeners throughout the nation between 8:15 and 9:30 o'clock last night when a broadcast of a dramatization of H. G. Wells's fantasy, "The War of the Worlds," led thousands to believe that an interplanetary conflict had started with invading Martians spreading wide death and destruction in New Jersey and New York.

The broadcast, which disrupted households, interrupted religious services, created traffic jams and clogged communications systems, was made by Orson Welles, who as the radio character, "The Shadow," used to give "the creeps" to countless child listeners. This time at least a score of adults required medical treatment for shock and hysteria.

In Newark, in a single block at Heddon Terrace and Hawthorne Avenue, more than twenty families rushed out of their houses with wet handkerchiefs and towels over their faces to flee from what they believed was to be a gas raid. Some began moving household furniture.

Throughout New York families left their homes, some to flee to near-by parks. Thousands of persons called the police, newspapers and radio stations here and in other cities of the United States and Canada seeking advice on protective measures against the raids.

The program was produced by Mr. Welles and the Mercury Theatre on the Air over station WABC and the Columbia Broadcasting System's coast-to-coast network, from 8 to 9 o'clock.

The radio play, as presented, was to simulate a regular radio program with a "break-in" for the material of the play. The radio listeners, apparently, missed or did not listen to the introduction, which was: "The Columbia Broadcasting System and its affiliated stations present Orson Welles and the Mercury Theatre on the Air in 'The War of the Worlds' by H. G. Wells."

They also failed to associate the program with the newspaper listing of the program, announced as "Today: 8:00-9:00—Play: H. G. Wells's 'War of the Worlds'—WABC." They ignored three additional announcements made during the broadcast emphasizing its fictional nature

Mr. Welles opened the program with a description of the series of

Continued on Page Four

The New York Times *reported the panic caused by Orson Welles's famous Halloween broadcast in 1938.*

LIVE PICTURES AND LIVE SOUNDS JOIN THE MASS MEDIA

Some say, what is the salvation of the Movies? I say, run 'em backward. It can't hurt 'em and it's worth a trial.

WILL ROGERS

I doubt if we will ever make any money. Of course, we have some hopes along that line, but I doubt if we will.

**MERLIN N. AYLESWORTH
PRESIDENT, NBC**

Never before in history had a single person been seen and heard by so many others at the same time.

LEO BOGART (on 1955 television program)

Movies, radio, and television came on the public stage at intervals of about 20 years, and each in turn was a sensation. In Chapter 12 we have already said something about the events that preceded the unveiling of movies—the picturesque experiment on Senator Stanford's farm in California and the almost accidental making of the first film in Edison's laboratory, among others.

THE MOVIES

People first became acquainted with movies by means of Edison's kinetoscope, a peep-show device that was placed in public places where viewers paid a few cents to peer through an eyepiece at a five-minute film. With a few exceptions, the content of these films did not make much impact, although *The Kiss,* the first close-up of a screen embrace, did succeed in arousing the wrath of clerics and others who feared it might ruin public morals. Other people first saw movies in the form of the real-life films and slapstick comedies made in the studios of the Lumière brothers in France. These films showed such events as a train arriving at a station or workers streaming out of a factory. The early comedies were such scenes as naughty boys stepping on a hose so that the gardener got a wet face. People got a good laugh out of these latter scenes, but the real impact of the pictures was not from the content but rather from the new medium itself—the fact that live movement could actually be captured, preserved, and shown. People who had learned to take still pictures of their children or the Arc de Triomphe or Niagara Falls could hardly fail to marvel when they saw such pictures actually move— children toddling and tumbling, spectators walking around the Arc, or water actually moving and clouds of spray rising from beneath the Falls. To repeat the sensation, people bought glass wheels bearing consecutive photographs; by twirling the wheels in front of a light they got the impression, for two or three seconds, of actually seeing motion.

Theater films began to replace the peep show, and in some countries, such as the United States, viewers began to pay five cents to go to the nickelodeon and hear a tinny piano playing while a film flickered on the screen.[1] Still it was a little while before movies began to attract people for the story they told rather than the marvelous optical way they told it. A number of countries found comedies the easiest way to begin. The example of the Lumières is a good one, but French filmmakers also put the Comédie Française and the great actress Sarah Bernhardt on the screen. English filmmakers experimented with pictures designed to carry a social message. American filmmakers had their Keystone Cop studios, whose most famous graduate was Charlie Chaplin. But the first movie in America, probably in the world, that demonstrated the ability of movies really to compete with the printed word and with the theater in telling a story was D. W. Griffith's *Birth of a Nation,* in 1915. Despite criticism of that picture because of its treatment of blacks, criticism that stung Griffith so much that he tried the following year to answer by making *Intolerance, Birth of a Nation* was a powerful picture and demonstrated what serious movies could be used for and what a great director like Griffith could do. Under Griffith's direction, even his critics admitted, actors became people on the screen, and consequently critics began to see the movies as a great medium.

Other countries began to make first-rate films about the same time or a little later. Examples were *The Cabinet of Dr. Caligari,* produced in Germany by Robert Wiene and released in 1919, and *Potemkin,* produced by the Russian director Serge Eisenstein and released in 1925. These were silent films, of course—sound films were a few years down the road—but they represent a mature stage of the film art. And to take an example where figures are readily available, by 1922 somewhere near 30 million Americans saw a movie at least once a week.

And then came radio.

RADIO JOINS THE MASS MEDIA

It apparently happened in 1906, although the exact time and most of the individuals involved are unknown.[2] But there is no doubt of the impact. Radio operators on ships, at shore stations, and in some private experimental sites reported that they heard voices in their earphones. Some of them heard operatic singers, some listened to instrumental music, and a few others heard voices reading the Bible. Not only was it startling to operators who were accustomed to hearing only Morse code (the dot-dash signals of wireless telegraphy) but it was also disturbing because it threatened to interfere with the emergency messages for which ship and shore stations were listening. At least one operator, so the story went, was afraid to tell his superior officer what he had heard, lest he be accused of drinking while on duty.

The explanation, however, gradually became known. Certain physicists and inventors were working on transmitting sound other than Morse code through the air. In 1902 Lee De Forest, an inventor who had earned a Ph.D. from Yale with a dissertation on wireless telegraphy, established the De Forest Wireless Telephone Company. Note the name of the company: *Telephone,* not *Telegraph.* He was working on transmitting voice and music by radio, and he had developed a small but powerful vacuum tube—the triode or audion tube—which proved to be an extraordinarily efficient amplifier for sound on radio broadcast. Therefore, some of the mysterious sounds on the air came from De Forest's experiments. Another inventor, Reginald Fessenden, a Canadian professor at the University of Pittsburgh, also demonstrated new circuits, and on Christmas Eve, 1906, broadcast a musical program from his experimental station in Massachusetts. He alerted ships' operators off the Atlantic coast and newspeople in New York. Because his program had been publicly scheduled and announced, it has a claim to be called the first public broadcast of voice radio.

Fessenden, De Forest, and others continued to broadcast experimental programs, some previously announced, some not. De Forest sometimes used phonograph records, sometimes live artists. With an eye to publicity, he aired in 1908 a program of phonograph records from the Eiffel Tower. The music was reported to have been heard as far as 500 miles from Paris. In 1910 he broadcast two operas starring Enrico Caruso live from the Metropolitan Opera in New York. So few were the receiving sets available, however, that the audience of those historic opera broadcasts may not have been more than 50 persons per program. But music and voice were heard more and more often on the air. Among frequent broadcasters was Charles D. Herrold, who operated a school of "engineering and wireless" in San Jose, California, and began to air regularly scheduled music and news in 1909 —at first one hour a day; later, three. In 1912 his station was officially licensed, and it operated until the beginning of World War I. Herrold's humble station therefore has a good claim to be called the first regularly operating broadcasting station in the United States, and probably in the world.

During the decade before 1920, radio began to receive rapidly increasing amounts of publicity. United States government time signals were broadcast from Arlington. Virginia, beginning in 1904, and more and more people set their watches to "Arlington." Radio brought the first news of the sinking of the *Titanic* in 1912. One of the young Marconi operators who transcribed the messages from the *Titanic* was David Sarnoff, who later became operating head, then president, of RCA.

From Events to Programs

Station KDKA, in Pittsburgh, has as good a claim as any to be called the first regularly and continuously programmed radio station on the air in the United States.[3] This claim has been vigorously disputed by others, such as station WWJ of Detroit. Furthermore, both a Dutch station, in 1919, and a Canadian station were broadcasting more or less regularly before KDKA. The question of primacy may never be completely settled. But Dr. Frank Conrad, assistant chief engineer of Westinghouse, assembled the necessary apparatus and in 1916 licensed station 8XK in the garage of his home. During World War I, Conrad used the apparatus for an assignment in designing new equipment for the navy. After the war he therefore had a working station. Chiefly he broadcast musical records, putting his microphone in front of a phonograph. A very large number of amateurs who were experimenting with coils and silicon crystals, and war veterans who had learned in the military services how to make receivers, heard these musical selections and wrote Conrad asking for their favorite numbers. Rather than respond to these requests individually, Conrad began to send out two hours of music every Thursday and Sunday evenings, occasionally adding baseball scores and other miscellany. The wide interest in these programs was not lost on Westinghouse. The company applied for a license on October 16, and received the license for station KDKA on October 27, 1920.

A studio covered by a tent was set up on the roof of one of the Westinghouse buildings. The setting was hardly luxurious; in fact, the radio employees told stories of stray dogs wandering into the tent and knocking down the microphone. But

KDKA went on the air. Its first program schedules bore a certain resemblance to the contents of the early newspapers—with the exception, of course, of KDKA's music. The station, according to a letter from its publicity department, opened in the morning with market quotations from the Chicago Board of Trade and updated them every half hour until 1:20 P.M. A few minutes of news plus a market summary followed at 2:15. At 3 P.M. lineups were read for professional baseball teams scheduled to play that day, and the scores of the games were reported each half hour thereafter. News, markets, and stock reports came again at 4:15 and 6:30, and summaries of the principal baseball games were heard again at 6:30 and 9:00. Beyond that, KDKA's first programs consisted of specials and targets of opportunity. The station soon began to broadcast a church service every Sunday morning. Political and other newsworthy events were broadcast or summarized when available. And live and recorded music became a more and more important part of the schedule.

There were no regular daily newscasts in the early years of radio. News was picked up from the newspapers, and special events were aired when that was possible. Thus, listeners became familiar even with reports of ships in trouble at sea. KDKA broadcast early bulletins of the 1920 election results, and in 1920 carried the two political conventions in detail. (In 1924 the Democratic party, deeply divided over its candidates, had to take 103 ballots, and "Alabama casts 24 votes for Oscar W. Underwood"—Alabama came first on the alphabetical list—was one of the most familiar phrases in the nation.) In 1925 the Scopes trial in Dayton, Tennessee, was carried in detail. This was the dramatic court case that pitted William Jennings Bryan against attorney Clarence Darrow on the question of whether public schools should teach that "man was descended from monkeys," as Darwin's concept of evolution was then commonly described. In October 1923, H. V. Kaltenborn, an assistant editor of the *Brooklyn Eagle,* was signed for a weekly news commentary over WEAF, New York. Kaltenborn, whose voice became familiar to radio listeners for more than 25 years thereafter, was the first such news "name" on radio, but David Lawrence and Frederick Wile were also giving radio commentaries once a week by the late 1920s. In 1930 Lowell Thomas went on NBC for 15 minutes a week, an arrangement that endured until 1976.

One of the early developments in radio that began to show an effect on news was the birth of the networks. RCA paid $1 million for station WEAF (New York) in 1926 and shortly thereafter incorporated the National Broadcasting Company (NBC). NBC issued advertising rate cards for *two* networks at the end of 1926—the Red Network, with WEAF as its anchor station, and the Blue Network, anchored by WJZ, also in New York. The Columbia Broadcasting System (CBS) started in 1927, after William Paley and his family purchased a majority interest in station WABC, New York, which became the anchor station of CBS. After a time RCA was compelled to sell the Blue Network (to avoid what was thought to be too much monopoly over the airwaves). The Blue became the American Broadcasting Company (ABC), the Red became the National Broadcasting Company (NBC), and these two along with CBS thenceforth dominated network broadcasting. Competition came for a time from the Mutual Broadcasting System, which actually had more member stations than the others, but NBC, CBS, and ABC had most of the clear-channel and high-power stations—and therefore the major part of the audience.

What the birth of the networks meant to radio news was that each network could furnish its own national news service to its member stations, the network stations could cooperate in covering stories, and the stage was set for the appearance of a number of broadcasters who became some of the best-known newspeople, in fact some of the best-known individuals, in the country—the network anchors and commentators.

In 1931 "The March of Time," a radio newsmagazine, made its debut. But the most exciting things on radio in the early years, in the United States and in other countries, were not commentaries or newsmagazines but rather reports of events. When Charles Lindbergh flew to Paris, radio carried frequent bulletins on his progress, on his arrival in France, and on his return to America. And when the Lindbergh baby was kidnapped and found dead, the trial of the supposed murderer, in 1935, monopolized the newspaper front pages and radio listening time for six weeks.

It took about five years to build up a nationally known cast of entertainers for American radio, although some attempts at networking were made as early as 1922. Much of the first radio entertainment was dance orchestras, usually broadcasting from hotel ballrooms. Thus, American listeners became familiar with the Coon-Sanders Nighthawks, broadcasting from Kansas City, the crooner Rudy Vallee, usually broadcasting from New York, at least one all-woman orchestra, and so forth. Some comedians and leading men and women came over from films to radio. And by 1930 radio had both networks and enough entertainment to fill them. In that year 618 stations were on the air in the United States, and 46 percent of all American homes had radio receivers.

A Note on Shortwave Radio

A feature of radio news in the 1920s that would not have been so familiar in later decades was the importance of shortwave transmissions. From the beginning of broadcasting, of course, many listeners built their own sets and, especially before the coming of networks, listened for distant stations both from within their own countries and from foreign countries. Listeners would clap on their earphones and

News made radio's great reputation. Top: *Lindbergh greeted on his return from the first solo flight across the Atlantic.* Right: *Edward VIII and his abdication speech, delivered in Windsor Castle.* Bottom: *George Herman "Babe" Ruth interviewed by Graham McNamee.*

compete for the distinction of tuning in Australia or England or Italy. This international news was for a time a significant part of the news intake of Americans, and especially in Europe, where foreign stations were relatively close, it brought events to listeners in other countries in a way that their own stations were hard put to match. Governments saw the advantage of this and inaugurated official news services, some of which, like BBC in England, came to be well known and trusted throughout the world.

Shortwave radio is less familiar in a country like the United States than it is in countries where the airwaves are not so full of medium waves that listeners have less incentive to tune in to shortwave, or than it was in the early years of broadcasting when it was a game to tune in distant stations. But in developing countries and sparsely settled areas, shortwave is important, and consequently listening to foreign broadcasts is more common. If in coming decades direct broadcasts from satellites are commonly received in homes, as some broadcast engineers think they will be, then shortwave may regain its popularity, and listening to direct broadcasts from foreign countries may once again become a common custom in such countries as the United States.

Germany began to broadcast radio (in Morse code) internationally in the 1920s. The Soviet Union in the 1920s began to broadcast shortwave voice radio in several languages, and soon upwards of a dozen countries were on the air with broadcasts intended for foreign audiences. The United States itself now broadcasts in 39 languages, but the real height of American shortwave development came in World War II when the country set up not only the Voice of America, which, by war's end, was broadcasting in 14 languages, but also stations such as Radio Free Europe and Radio Liberty (formerly Radio Liberation). These two stations had their headquarters in Munich and broadcast to the Soviet Union (Radio Liberty) and the countries of Eastern Europe (Radio Free Europe).

The extent of the world's shortwave broadcasting may come as a surprise to some Americans who are accustomed only to listening to their own country's medium-wave stations. There are approximately 4600 shortwave stations in the world and roughly one billion radio receivers, many of which can receive shortwave. Why is there so much interest in reaching foreign countries with shortwave radio? This activity is an aspect of what might be called international public relations—trying to get the broadcasting nation's side of the news out to other countries. Where there is less friendliness among the participating nations, the broadcasts are sometimes called propaganda (as were the broadcasts between the opposing sides in World War II). But there is no reason why international broadcasting should not also appeal to receiving countries for its own attractive qualities or be used to reveal the sending country's thinking about some world problem or development that is of wide interest. For instance, Great Britain's BBC has one of the largest shortwave audiences in the world, principally because it has built up a reputation for unbiased and reliable news and commentary.

Radio Goes on the Air in Other Countries

We have already noted that radio was broadcast from a station in the Netherlands beginning sometime in 1919 and from a Canadian station beginning in 1920, probably before KDKA. Australia inaugurated a station in Melbourne in 1921 and made an official start at national broadcasting in Sydney in 1923. France and the Soviet Union were on the air in 1922; Belgium, Czechoslovakia, Germany, and

Spain in 1923; Finland and Italy in 1924; Norway, Poland, Mexico, and Japan in 1925; and India, among others, in 1926.

Great Britain, which has had so much influence on broadcasting, was relatively slow in getting started. Two half hours, chiefly news and music, were broadcast daily by an experimental station in Chelmsford, Essex. The post office banned those broadcasts on the argument that they might encourage the commercialization of radio. But 4000 people had taken out licenses for receiving sets by that time, and doubtless they were not the only families listening. Consequently petitions were presented to the post office, which granted the Marconi Company permission to broadcast 15 minutes *a week*. That was obviously less than satisfactory to radio listeners, and the British Broadcasting Corporation (BBC) was founded in 1922.

For the first three years of its life, BBC was a private corporation, responsible to a governing board rather than to the British government, and supported by a 10 shilling license fee for receivers and a 10 percent royalty on the sale of receiving sets. In 1925, on recommendation of Parliament, the structure of radio in Britain was revised again. BBC became a public corporation, responsible to a board of governors which in turn reported to a committee of Parliament. This organization retained a monopoly on broadcasting until the creation of the Independent Television Authority in 1954. A limited arrangement for local commercial broadcasting began in the 1970s.

Both the great respect earned by BBC broadcasting and the strong guidance of Sir John Reith, the first governor general of the organization, helped lead many other countries to follow the organizational example of Britain. Reith had strong ideas about the advantages of broadcasting being operated by a public corporation. For this and other reasons, Sweden, Denmark, and a number of British commonwealth countries and British colonies, among others, followed the example of Britain. In France, at first, the national government and private-enterprise owners operated side by side until 1945, when the entire system was nationalized. In Germany, for a time the Ministry of Posts retained ownership of all technical materials and equipment; then, in 1932, all private broadcasting companies were nationalized.

On the other hand, a number of countries followed the example of the United States and adopted private-enterprise broadcasting, sometimes (as in the United States) with a provision also for public broadcasting, supported by universities or other nonprofit organizations without the aid of advertising. However, as broadcasting moved into the 1930s, its advertising income in the United States moved upward to $77 million, and Aylesworth's prediction about never making any money, quoted at the beginning of this chapter, deterred no one from entering commercial radio.

Years of Crisis

By the 1930s, radio was presenting a reasonably exciting daily program to its listeners. Its musical programs (in the United States alone) varied from Toscanini and the New York Philharmonic to Bing Crosby and the new "croon-tunes." Its personalities varied from Fred Allen, a truly outstanding radio comedian, to Franklin Delano Roosevelt, a truly outstanding radio political figure. By the middle of the decade, the bitter quarrel between radio and newspapers over access to news agency copy had been settled,[4] and regular newscasts took their place beside the commentaries and news bulletins. Sports from baseball to boxing began to be heard play by play or blow by blow over the air. Across the country, people drove with a barrage of news coming from their car radios. But so far as news was concerned, the great attraction of radio was its coverage of exciting events and great personalities.

If the networks had been choosing a president for his radio qualities, they could hardly have done better than Franklin D. Roosevelt, whose "fireside chats" represented probably the first sophisticated use of radio for national policy. The abdication of Edward VIII to marry Mrs. Simpson was a nonfiction soap opera almost made to order for radio, just as the coronation of George VI was a true-life spectacular made for radio (or, still better, for television). NBC is thought to have produced 460 news broadcasts about the Munich crisis alone. As World War II drew nearer, the reports of William Shirer from Berlin and Eric Sevareid from Paris were listened to almost as gospel. Kaltenborn was heard one day analyzing a broadcast prayer by the archbishop of Canterbury for evidence as to whether the archbishop had any inside information on the likelihood of war.

Even the nonpolitical news seemed to fit into the prewar news. One such event was the destruction of the dirigible *Hindenburg* in 1937. This was totally unexpected, and broadcasts might have missed the event if a Chicago radio man had not been at the airport in New Jersey to record the dirigible's arrival for the archives. It took only a minute or two for the gigantic balloon to catch on fire and crash to the ground in a mass of twisted steel and dead passengers. The dramatic part of the broadcast was less the event itself than the reaction of the broadcaster, who reflected as could never have been done in print the horror of what he was seeing. "Oh, the humanity," he sobbed. ". . . One of the worst catastrophes in the history of the world!" But still he did not lose control of himself to the extent that he was unable to stay at his microphone for half an hour and record what he was seeing. No radio fiction was ever more shocking.

When the war came, the CBS staff in particular brought its listeners close to the events in Europe. Edward R. Murrow, who was head of the staff, broadcast a vivid and moving series of accounts of what the war meant to a London under aerial attack.[5] Listeners not only heard the explosions of bombs but also learned what the war did to the daily lives of the people in the city. The phrase with which Murrow introduced his report each evening—"This is London"—became as well known to radio listeners as the eloquence of Roosevelt or Churchill. "For the first time," one critic wrote, "I now know what it's like!"

World War II was the first war to be brought so close to listeners far away. The surrender of the French army in the forest at Compeigne was broadcast directly by two enterprising newscasters. Kaltenborn broadcast one battle while hiding in a haystack. D-Day was carried with realism from the beaches of Normandy to 50 countries. But three things that were not directly a part of the war showed better than anything else what had happened to radio news since 1920.

First, between 1938 and 1939 the amount of news and commentary on radio almost exactly doubled—from a little over 6 percent to more than 12 percent of broadcast time. Second, the newspaper "extra"—a characteristic of newspaper publishing for a century—almost disappeared from the earth. Ten years after the war, a commentator described the situation with deep irony. "Even if we had the Second Coming today," he said, "we'd hear of it first on radio, and then run home to see it on television!"

Edward R. Murrow: "This is London."

A third piece of evidence was Orson Welles's 1938 broadcast of a radio adaptation of the H. G. Wells story *War of the Worlds.*[6] It was broadcast on Halloween: That itself should have been a hint. The announcer said frankly at the outset that the story was fiction—the incidents were a hoax. But listeners seemed not to notice that caveat. The program was done in the style of radio news. The action began with a dance band apparently playing in a hotel. An announcer interrupted the music to give a brief bulletin—radio audiences were accustomed to such news bulletins—a gas cloud had been observed on Mars. In much less time than it would have taken any known vehicle to come to Earth from Mars, things began to happen. A "large meteorite" was reported to have fallen near Grovers Mill, New Jersey. More music. Then a "noted astronomer" was called in to discuss the likelihood of life on Mars. Music again, again interrupted by the announcer. "Ladies and gentlemen," he said, "I have a grave announcement to make. Incredible as it may seem, both the observations of science and the evidence of our eyes lead to the inescapable assumption that those strange beings who landed in the Jersey farmlands tonight are the vanguard of an invading army from the planet Mars." Then the story built up in a series of news bulletins and on-the-scene reports. The gigantic Martians emerged from their spaceships and began to move on New York. The American military was being routed. The Martians sent their war machines out carrying poison gas. More and more reports of deaths and defeat. And so forth.

The important thing was not the script or the acting. It was the fact that tens of thousands of people in the eastern part of the country got into their automobiles and headed for the hills, making little if any attempt to check the validity of the news. In other words, the people listening to the Halloween broadcast had *learned to believe the news they heard on radio.* The radio newspeople were on the spot; they could be depended on to report what they saw.

The next day, when it was all over, there were a number of deeply embarrassed and rather angry listeners. The broadcasters apologized. But secretly they must have marveled at what had happened to a new medium in 20 years. Although no one was quoted as saying it, this seemed like the ideal time to use the quotation that Samuel Morse transmitted on the first telegraph program: "What hath God wrought?"

A FLOWERING OF ENTERTAINMENT TALENT

We must not lose sight of another contribution film and radio made to the decades beginning in 1930. Those years saw a truly remarkable flowering of entertainment talent that reached unprecedentedly large audiences through radio and film.

Of course, sound films were in the theaters by that time. Al Jolson's musical,

Orson Welles playing a Halloween trick in 1938. His broadcast unintentionally demonstrated the power of radio.

The Jazz Singer, in 1927, was not the first sound film but it was the first one that attracted wide attention. It pointed the way to later musicals like *The Sound of Music* and *West Side Story* that carried the magical sounds and sights of national theater to enormous numbers of people who had never seen Broadway (or, in other countries, the theatrical centers of Paris, London, Tokyo, Berlin, or Delhi).

Sound had another important impact on film: It required directors to solve the problem of how to handle the bulky technology of sound recording without losing the spatial freedom it had painfully won in earlier decades from the restrictions of a theatrical stage. Jolson's film was like a series of scenes shot on a stage, because it was too difficult to move the equipment very far. But René Clair in his French studio and his film *Sous les Toits de Paris* ("Under the Roofs of Paris") found how to move the camera around and regain the freedom of movement and airiness that had distinguished French films before films learned to talk.

Films like Clair's called attention to the appearance of a handful of highly skillful schools of film in countries other than the United States: In France, Clair and Jean Renoir, and much later, filmmakers like Jacques Tati (*Mr. Hulot's Holiday* was made in 1953); in England, cheerful comedies like *Kind Hearts and Coronets* (1949), the powerful documentaries of John Grierson and others, and the gripping films of Alfred Hitchcock; in Germany, a series of excellent sound films including Von Sternberg's *The Blue Angel,* with Emil Jannings, and Pabst's film version of Bertolt Brecht's *The Three-Penny Opera* (1931). Of course, in the Nazi years the big UFA film studio in Germany was used for propaganda, but some of those propaganda films also were powerful. The great Russian director Eisenstein made a few sound films (such as *Alexander Nevsky,* 1938), and his successors made many more. In more recent years we have come to know the Italian school through such directors as Frederico Fellini (for instance, *La Dolce Vita,* 1960), and Michelangelo Antonioni. Relatively little known in the United States until the 1950s was the Japanese school of filmmakers, which by the middle fifties actually produced more feature films than came out of Hollywood. Perhaps best known of the Japanese filmmakers is Kurosawa Akira, whose *Rashomon* (1950) was his first film to be widely seen outside Japan. And in this hurried film-seeing tour we must not neglect to mention the Indian group of filmmakers, led by Satyajit Ray, who made his famous *Apu* trilogy in the 1950s, but until recently has not been well known in the West. The output of Indian films compares well with that of Japan and the United States.

The story of Hollywood films in the middle years of the century is more complex than we can cover in these pages. Perhaps the best way to treat it is to mention a tiny sample of the men and women who helped bring Hollywood its reputation—directors like Ernst Lubitsch, Joseph von Sternberg, Cecil B. DeMille, Alfred Hitchcock (one of England's most talented directors, who came to work in Hollywood), and Walt Disney; and actors and actresses like Charlie Chaplin, John and Lionel Barrymore, Greta Garbo, Joan Crawford, Norma Shearer, Mickey Rooney, and Edward G. Robinson.

In its great years, Hollywood made many pictures in many genres; for example, the documentary form (like Pare Lorentz's *The Plow that Broke the Plains*), the western (like *The Ox-Bow Incident*), the light comedy *(Mr. Deeds Goes to Town),* the crime and gangster film, and too many others to classify. In what category, for instance, would we put Orson Welles's film *Citizen Kane,* which was modeled on the life of William Randolph Hearst, or Charlie Chaplin's picture *The Great Dictator,* which was a humorous and sensitive man's look around him at a threatening world?

Hollywood, during the middle years of the century, was called an entertainment factory. So also might commercial radio be called that in the same years. As the filmmakers were under obligation to attract theater audiences large enough to pay the salaries of the stars, so were the radio programmers obligated to attract large enough audiences to sell enough advertising to pay the cost of what went out on the air. Yet, both the media had an enormous amount of talent. Both of them were concerned with making art as well as making commercial money.

Take an example or two from the record of radio during the years we are talking about. One of the most popular program types on radio was the daytime serial—the soap opera, so called because soap companies sponsored so many of them. Two of these, "Helen Trent" and "Ma Perkins," went on the air in the early 1930s and remained there for nearly 28 years, holding their faithful audiences for the last dozen years or so even against the competition of television.

Soap operas that lasted so long, we may assume, became entertainment-factory products. Yet at the same time, radio was making a conscientious effort to put high levels of drama on the air. For example, CBS brought in Norman Corwin, Arch Oboler, Archibald MacLeish, and others to write serious plays that were broadcast with excellent casts, and many of them were published—which is something one cannot say of most of the soap operas. Unfortunately, they did not attract as many listeners as did the soap operas.

Another favorite program type on radio at the same time was the big band. Through this device, audiences met Paul Whiteman, Benny Goodman, the Dorsey brothers, and Glenn Miller. And a number of crooners. Some of these people, like Goodman, were excellent musicians, and yet their appeal, for the most part, was not to the same people who listened to the Metropolitan Opera broadcasts on Saturday afternoons. The opera broadcasts are still carried on radio in some parts of the country. Arturo Toscanini organized a symphony orchestra especially to play a series of classical music concerts on CBS. Leopold Stokowski later conducted a similar series. So although radio brought its audiences Rudy Vallee, it also brought them Enrico Caruso, Maria Callas, and Ezio Pinza.

A group of rather unusual comedians appeared in the later radio years. Fred Allen was not merely a funny man; he was also a satirist looking down his nose at the world around him. Bob Hope, Jack Benny, and the Marx brothers were among the talented stand-up comedians who for many years kept audiences laughing. Talk shows and quiz shows were another genre that was surprisingly popular. These were on every level from Major Bowes and his "Amateur Hour" to Lyman Byrson talking with his Columbia University faculty colleagues on Sunday mornings about great books by Plato, Montaigne, Tolstoy, or other authors whose names would not likely be mentioned on a soap opera.

One other type of radio content needs mentioning: That is education. In the

United States, the responsibility for educational broadcasting was delegated to state universities and educational systems, many of which had their own stations. They exchanged and broadcast class lessons and lectures for home use. In some other countries educational broadcasts were more important. Australia, for instance, used them to enable children in the outback, miles from any school, to study at home. Many countries used radio broadcasts to supplement the experiences of the classroom. Granted, this was broadcasting to a special audience, and no such huge audience as listened to the entertainment programs. And although no one would choose to teach by radio if television were available, radio for many years and in many places made education possible and effective for many persons who otherwise would not have been educated.

AND THEN CAME TELEVISION

England had been rather slow to start a major use of radio, but it was ahead of most of the rest of the world with television. Television was demonstrated publicly for the first time in London in 1926, and BBC was first in the world to initiate regularly scheduled television broadcasts, from Alexandra Palace in London, in 1936. Its first "spectacular" was the coronation of King George VI in 1937. English TV had to close down at the beginning of the war in 1939, just as the United States was getting into the act. After many experiments, American television was demonstrated publicly at the New York World's Fair in 1939, and a limited program of daily broadcasts was inaugurated in 1940. Then the growth of American television, like that of most other countries, was effectively halted by World War II.

The European countries and Japan had a hard time getting their television programs started again after the war, and the United States had a special problem in expanding its use of the new medium because it took about five years after 1945 to settle the fundamental problems of type of equipment and technical standards to be adopted.

In most industrialized countries, therefore, television made its real start in the early 1950s. By that time there were only about one million television sets in the United States—we say *only* because ten years later there were about 60 times as many. Indeed the impact of television on the two media that had immediately preceded it was one of the most dramatic chapters in media history.

By mid-century, media statistics were being recorded carefully, and perhaps the best way to indicate what happened in that decade is to sum up some of those figures.[7]

For one thing, what was the effect of television on the amount of use of radio?

In 1945, at the end of the war, about 33 million households in the United States had radio receivers, whereas the number of television homes was less than 10,000. By 1949, when the freeze on television was about to be lifted, the number of television homes had risen to nearly a million, while radio homes had reached 39 million. In 1950, when there were enough television homes to make it worthwhile to collect viewing times, the amount of time devoted to television in homes that had it was just a little more than the time devoted to radio in radio homes—between four and five hours a day. By 1955, however, listening time in an average radio household had declined by 50 percent (to 2 hours, 12 minutes), and in 1960 it was only 1:53.[8] Television, on the other hand, was turned on nearly five hours per day in 1955, and nearly six hours—three times as long as radio—in 1960. By 1960, of course, the number of television receivers in use had risen spectacularly, to 46 million (compared to 50 million radio receivers).

The result was much the same with the movie audience. More than 60 million were seeing at least one movie a week in 1950. In 1960 the comparable attendance was only about 15 million.

It is worth noting that radio needed 24 years (1922 to 1946) to reach 90 percent of American homes. The same climb took television just 14 years (1948 to 1962). Both media, of course, now reach practically all American homes; and radio, additionally, is in about 95 percent of American automobiles.

What Happens to Listening and Viewing When TV Comes

| Year | Daily Hours per Household | | |
	Radio	Television	Total
1931	4:04	—	4:04
1935	4:48	—	4:48
1943	4:48	—	4:48
1946	4:13	—	4:13
1950	4:06	4:35	8:41
1955	2:12	4:51	7:03
1960	1:53	5:59	7:32
1965	2:27	5:30	7:55
1971	2:52	5:56	8:48
1976	3:25	6:18	9:43
1981	3:19	6:45	9:64

SOURCE: C. H. Sterling and J. M. Kittross, *Stay Tuned: A Concise History of American Broadcasting* (Belmont, Calif.: Wadsworth, 1978), p. 220.

We should not assume that this was a lasting blow to radio's audience. Radio discovered in a decade or so what it could do best—bulletins, popular music, and background programming for audiences who were driving, working, or doing something else that kept them from watching a screen. Beginning about 1965, radio's time allocation relative to television began to climb. It rose again gradually to about three-fourths what it had been in the 1930s. But television still claimed about twice as much time. In the 1980s television's time margin was even a bit more.

The effect on movie use was a little different. Movie theater attendance came back somewhat after 1950—to nearly half what it had been. But movies made up some of the lost audience through television itself. The enormous TV appetite for programs led it to the motion picture archives for older films that deserved replaying, and then to the ordering of new films made especially for television. Consequently, Hollywood studios are now turning out a considerable part of their product for broadcast.

Several other effects of the television blitz, however, also were felt by the other media. In 1949 radio received 11 percent, and television only 1 percent, of all expenditures on broadcast advertising. In 1953 they received about the same amount each—8 percent. Since then, radio has fallen off slightly and television has risen greatly. In the 1980s, television has been receiving about 21 percent of the total, radio about 7 percent.

In 1952, radio and television received about the same amount of political advertising for the general election (about $3 million each). Now television receives about twice as much. In 1972 that was $24.6 million as against $13.5 million for radio.

In 1959, 34 percent of persons in a Roper survey said that radio was their most frequent source of news. In 1982 that had fallen to 18 percent. In those same years, television had risen from 51 to 65 percent, passing even newspapers, which had fallen as chief source, in the sixties and seventies, from 57 to 44 percent.

Striking results have been reported also from surveys that asked the question, "If you got conflicting reports on the same news story from radio, television, magazines and the newspapers, which of the four versions would you be most inclined to believe—the one on radio or television or magazines or newspapers?" On that question we have Roper organization surveys, with comparable samples and the same question repeated each year. The results can therefore be regarded seriously, although it has been argued by the printed media that the results would be different if the question were asked in different words. Here are the results (in percents) for five of the years during which the survey was made:

Year	Radio	TV	Mags	Newsprs	DK/NA
1959	12	29	10	32	17
1964	8	41	10	23	18
1968	8	44	11	21	16
1978	9	47	9	23	12
1982	6	53	8	22	11

SOURCE: Roper Organization, Inc., *Trends and Attitudes toward Television and Other Media* (New York: Television Information *Office,* annually since 1959).

Ignoring for the moment the possibility that the way the question is stated may affect the results, the most reasonable explanation for these data is that audiences tend to believe what they see. They believe the events and the newscasters that they can look at. This is television's advantage over a printed sentence or a faceless voice.

It would be hard to predict that a new medium, entering a society that already gives most of its spare time to mass media, could have an effect of such magnitude. It may be that television's impact was especially great in the United States. And yet the impact was certainly powerful in Japan. In some European countries, where we have solid evidence, the effect was apparently less than in the United States, though in the same direction. In Third World countries, economics and technology in some cases stood in the way of such a rapid and spectacular development of television, but the effects were of the same nature and the difference was in magnitude rather than direction.

The News on Television

When television swept the world in the 1950s, the effect on news was just as dramatic as the effect on home life. Only a few decades before, radio in the United States had been able to receive only grudging permission to broadcast a two-minute news bulletin or to make any use of wire news services. In the 1950s television started at once with a program of 15-minute newscasts, and in 1963 lengthened these to 30 minutes. A number of local stations scheduled their local evening news directly following the network cast, so that a full hour of news was available to any viewer who wanted it. Public television began to broadcast a news *hour* each evening (the McNeill-Lehrer program) with long interviews and detailed attention to the big stories of the day. Radio and television news stations sprang up in many cities. Between 1950 and 1980 the average amount of news time on television approximately tripled.

Whereas the outstanding memories of American radio news were individual voices—Kaltenborn, Lowell Thomas, Shirer in Berlin, Murrow in London—television paid as much attention to appearance as to voice, and TV preferred the news *team*. One of the first and best known of these teams was Chet Huntley and David Brinkley, who first worked together to cover the 1956 elections. That combination lasted until 1971, when Huntley retired because of illness. CBS for most of the time depended upon the single anchor. For 20 years this was Walter Cronkite, and when he retired from the job he was replaced by Dan Rather, who came from the team of investigative reporters on "60 Minutes." Even the larger local stations, however, tended to put in news teams, usually with an anchor, a specialist on sports, and sometimes a person to cover local news. In addition to these, the networks had overseas bureaus and stringers.

In certain respects television was blessed during its first three decades with news events that seemed almost made for it. For example, when Premier Khrushchev of the Soviet Union represented his country at the United Nations, the television cameras recorded him taking off one of his shoes and pounding it on his desk to express dissatisfaction, and his delegation of diplomats rather sheepishly taking off *their* shoes and following the leader's example. The murder of President John Kennedy was an unforgettable four-day period of tragedy and sorrow for those who followed it on television—about 93 percent of all Americans and many millions in other countries watched the funeral broadcast. Unforgettable, too, was the murder of Martin Luther King, Jr.

Not all the great television was tragic. The ten-year program for putting humans on the moon was an almost unequaled combination of adventure, danger, and experiences new to us—including our first views of our blue Earth from far space. Here is a transcript of how CBS covered the Apollo 11 moon landing, on July 20, 1969. Walter Cronkite was chief announcer for CBS.[9] "Capcom" is the NASA headquarters. "Eagle" is the lunar module. Schirra was in command of the spaceship that had released the module in which Armstrong and Aldrin were making the landing.

> CAPCOM: Eagle, you're looking great, coming up on nine minutes. We're now in the approach phase, everything looking good. Altitude, 5200 feet.
>
> CRONKITE: 5200 feet. Less than a mile from the moon's surface.
>
> EAGLE: Manual altitude control is good.
>
> CAPCOM: Roger. We copy. Altitude 4200 and you're go for landing. Over.
>
> EAGLE: Roger, understand. Go for landing. 3000 feet. Second alarm.
>
> CRONKITE: 3000 feet. Um-hmmm.

EAGLE: Roger. 1201 alarm. We're go. Hang tight. We're go. 2000 feet. 2000 feet, into the AGS. 47 degrees.

CRONKITE: These are space communications, simply for readout purposes.

CAPCOM: Eagle looking great. You're go.

HOUSTON: Altitude 1600. 1400 feet. Still looking very good.

CRONKITE: They've got a good look at their site now. This is their time. They're going to make a decision.

EAGLE: 35 degrees. 35 degrees. 750, coming down at 23. 700 feet, 21 down. 33 degrees.

SCHIRRA: Oh, the data is coming in beautifully.

EAGLE: 600 feet, down at 19. 540 feet down at 30—down at 15 . . . 400 feet, down at 9 . . . 8 forward . . . 350 feet down at 4 . . . 350 feet, down 3½ . . . 47 forward . . . 1½ down . . . 70 . . . got the shadow out there . . . 50, down at 2½ . . . 19 forward attitude-velocity lights . . . 3½ down . . . 220 feet . . . 13 forward . . . 11 forward. coming down nicely . . . 200 feet, 4½ down . . . 5½ down . . . 160, 6½ down . . . 5½ down, 9 forward . . . 5 per cent . . . quantity light 75 feet. Things still looking good, down a half . . . 6 forward . . . lights on . . . down 2½ . . . forward . . . 40 feet, down 2½, kicking up some dust . . . 30 feet, 2½ down, kicking up some dust . . . 30 feet, 2½ down . . . faint shadow . . . 4 forward . . . 4 forward, drifting to the right a little . . . 6 drifting right. . . .

CRONKITE: Boy, what a day.

CAPCOM: 30 seconds.

EAGLE: Contact light. O.K. engine stopped . . . descent engine command override off. . . .

SCHIRRA: We're home!

CRONKITE: Man on the moon!

EAGLE: Houston, Tranquility Base here. The Eagle has landed!

CAPCOM: Roger, Tranquility. We copy you on the ground. You've got a bunch of guys here about to turn blue. We're breathing again. Thanks a lot.

TRANQUILITY: Thank you!

CRONKITE: Oh, boy!

CAPCOM: You're looking good here.

CRONKITE: Whew! Boy!

SCHIRRA: I've been saying them all under my breath. That is really something. I'd love to be aboard.

CRONKITE: I know. We've been wondering what Neil Armstrong and Aldrin would say when they set foot on the moon, which comes a bit later now. Just to hear them do it. Absolutely with dry mouths.

CAPCOM: Roger, Eagle. And you're stay for T-1. Over. You're stay for T-1. . . .

TRANQUILITY: Roger. We're stay for T-1.

CAPCOM: Roger. And we see you getting the oc.

CRONKITE: That's a great simulation that we see here.

SCHIRRA: That little fly-speck is supposed to be the LM.

CRONKITE: They must be in perfect condition . . . upright, and there's no complaint about their position.

SCHIRRA: Just a little dust.

CRONKITE: Boy! There they sit on the moon! Just exactly nominal wasn't it . . . on green with the flight plan, all the way down. Man finally is standing on the surface of the moon. My golly!

CAPCOM: Roger, we read you Columbia. He has landed. Tranquility Base. Eagle is at Tranquility. Over.

Sports events (as large as the Olympics or as relatively small as a championship football game or a World Series baseball game) were surprisingly more vivid on television than on radio. A national political convention was even more exciting and more effective adult education on television than on radio. So too, throughout the world, was the parade of world leaders who moved before the television cameras. A parade of world-famous scientists and explorers led television audiences into places and experiences they would never otherwise have seen. And for the first time, a war—for the United States, a losing one—was seen in the world's living rooms. Vietnam had an effect not only on viewers' ideas of current political policies, but also on their ideas of war in general. The Watergate episodes, too, had a deep effect on viewers' attitudes toward politics and political behavior.

Other Television Programming

On the average, news in the last decade has filled about 15 percent of television time. This proportion varies considerably among countries and services. Japan and Britain, for example, have reported using considerably more than 15 percent of their general television services for news, current affairs, and information. It is apparent that such estimates are rather slippery because of different ideas of what should be included in the category of news. Countries that reported to UNESCO in 1982 were asked to differentiate between news and other informative programs.

Among those that did so, here are some examples of percentage of total television time said to be devoted to news and entertainment:

Country	News	Entertainment
United Kingdom	6%	37%
France	11	49
Czechoslovakia	15	54
Hungary	15	50
Australia	9	57
Ivory Coast	15	16
Canada	7	59
Brazil	8	59
Colombia	11	36
South Korea	14	48
Malaysia	11	38

SOURCE: Adapted from *UNESCO Statistical Annual* (Paris and New York, 1984), pp. 26, 36.

From this small sample, we can assume that news fills, on the average, somewhere around 12 percent, one minute out of eight, of present-day television. Half or a little more of this same television is given, on the average, to entertainment. Where there are exceptions, they are usually because television is dedicated to a special purpose; in the Ivory Coast, for example, where entertainment is estimated at only 16 percent, more than half of the national television is used for education. But in general the time devoted to entertainment is about four times that given news.

Another question that can be asked about television content is, What kind of entertainment is this that fills more than half of the television hours? The question is not easy to answer because general categories, such as plays, do not really describe the differences between national television in different countries. Nevertheless, we can say, from the same sample used before, that about half of TV entertainment time is given to films of various kinds, about one-quarter to plays (probably including serial comedies and other light plays as well as serious drama), and the remainder divided between music and sports.

THE BIG PICTURE

We might ask this question about the media we have been discussing: Where are these media? Dividing the world into regions and continents, what proportion of the world's books is printed, say, in Europe as compared to Asia or Africa? What proportion of the world's television receivers is in North America? What proportion of the world's newspaper circulation is in the Arab States as compared to Latin America? And so forth.

We can't answer these questions in as much detail as we would like, nor can we, from the data at hand, answer the more important question: How many hours in total are the people of a given continent or region devoting, every day or week or year, to each of these media? And for what kind of entertainment or information do they use one rather than another? But we can give at least some comparable figures from a large sample of countries about the distribution of the media in the world, and at the very least those figures will convey some idea of the amount of information that flows into a region through one channel as compared to others (see "For the Record" at the end of this chapter).

The measurements in the following table were gathered by UNESCO with the help of its member countries. The measure of book distribution is the number of titles, totalled by regions. The newspaper totals are the circulation of daily, general-interest newspapers. Films are measured by the number of long films (as distinguished from "shorts") in each region. For radio and television, UNESCO tried to arrive at the total number of radio or television receivers in a given region. Someday it may be possible to say accurately how much use is being made of each of the media—for example, how many of the theater seats are being occupied to watch what kinds of films, what television content is getting how much attention, and what effects it is having on its audiences. Pending such detailed information on the use of the media throughout the world, we shall have to be satisfied for the time being with information on where the media are available to persons who would like to use them.

Distribution of the World's Media

Region	Books	Newspapers	Films	Radio	TV
Africa	1.3%	1.0%	0.5%	2.7%	0.7%
Arab States	0.9	1.2	3.5	2.6	1.9
Asia	22.3	31.4	49.3	20.7	16.6
Europe	54.3	45.6	27.9	27.3	40.3
Latin America	6.1	6.4	6.5	8.1	7.3
Oceania	1.5	1.2	0.5	1.7	1.2
North America	13.6	13.2	11.7	35.8	32.1

SOURCE: UNESCO, *Statistical Annual* (Paris and New York: UNESCO, 1985), pp. VI, 3–10.

SOME NEWER MEDIA DEVELOPMENTS

The new media are so recent and so lively that we must expect their evolution to continue. And this is indeed what we have been seeing. Developments in general have been in the direction of finding more special uses for the media and putting the users more fully in charge of these uses.

The emerging importance of public television in the United States is not so much an innovation as an adaptation. Countries such as the United Kingdom started very early with public television, at least in the sense that they supported a television service without advertising, and it produced a very high average of programming. BBC has been likened to the London *Times* rather than the *Daily Mirror* or *News of the World,* although the *Times,* of course, depends on advertising whereas BBC subsists on government allocations which in turn are supported by license fees and social taxes. It is no accident that the Public Broadcasting Service (PBS) in the United States buys some of its better programs from BBC, for PBS too stands in relation to much commercial programming as the *Times* stands to the popular press. American public television, unlike other American television, accepts no advertising and depends partly on government grants but to a greater extent on gifts from viewers and commercial sources. It has been suggested that we may be moving toward an international network of high-quality programming, supplemented in each country by programs that fit particular local needs and interests. Language differences make this somewhat difficult. The next decade will probably tell whether the advantages can overcome the difficulties.

The special use of television for education is likewise not entirely a new thing, but rather a development of previous uses of films, radio, and television for that purpose. Educational films first made an impact on schools; then came educational radio stations, most of them operated in the United States by state universities and organized to carry educational radio programs to schoolrooms and home students. When television became available, teaching tapes began to replace teaching films, and educational television was made a part of numerous "distance teaching" activities, some of the most distinguished examples of which were "open" universities (such as the British Open University) for students who had to work full time while studying or who were unable for other reasons to continue their education on a campus. These universities may likewise take on greater importance in the future. The need for university education and for refresher training to keep up with rapidly advancing knowledge is becoming more widespread, and the cost of maintaining university campuses and high-quality teaching faculties is increasing. It has been suggested that higher education in the future may include for many students two or more years of home study, and only after that will the students who have proved their ability come to a campus to study. Only the future will tell about that, but it is already evident that refresher education will be increasingly necessary at several levels. For example, it has been suggested that, considering the speed of advance in many scholarly fields, a college graduate may have to take the equivalent of a fifth year in home study during the first four years after he or she graduates, in order to keep up with new knowledge.

Cable television has likewise become more and more popular during recent years as a supplement to the programs that come through networks and local stations. Cable systems can accept advertising but also live on monthly fees from users. Perhaps the major significance of cable services is that they make it possible for viewers to have more control over the kinds of programs they receive. That is, they can buy a general service, a service offering mainly movies, one that offers movies of a certain kind (for example, foreign films), or recorded Broadway shows, or a 24-hour news service, or a service specializing in sports, and so forth. Cable services also sometimes offer sports events that can be paid for individually and viewed live on a home receiver.

In one sense, therefore, cable simply provides alternatives to existing stations or networks. In a more important sense it offers the viewers more control over what they see. Viewer control has been a continuing trend in media development. Videotaped movies can be bought or rented for home use, whenever and however often the owners want to see them. Videocassette recorders that can be purchased for a few hundred dollars will record television programs for later viewing. Sound tape recorders, which have been available since mid-century, will keep a record of music or a lecture or business conversation or a child's first efforts at speech. Such recorders are used also to make "talking books" for persons with impaired sight or for others who simply like to hear prose or poetry expertly read. Home cameras of one kind or another are now inexpensive enough that many people can afford to make home movies or home television.

All these developments open the magic of using the media to individuals who neither are trained experts nor have a studio, station, or network to support them. Perhaps the most promising of all these developments is a combination of television, a telephone line, and a computer. Two versions of this are being experimented with in various places. The simpler one, called *teletext,* allows the user to call up on the television viewing screen some text that has been stored in the computer.

For example, by giving the right signal the user can read airplane schedules, baseball scores, a news summary, and the like. A more complex version, *videotex,* is a two-way circuit. It allows the viewer to communicate back and forth with the central computer, in order, for example, to shop by mail, answer questions in a home study course, or make reservations. We shall hear more about this new technology, because it brings the large and elaborate electronic media system down to the level of a single user.

SUGGESTIONS FOR FURTHER READING

A number of the titles suggested for reading in connection with the two preceding chapters also will make important contributions to Chapter 13. Among them are Asa Briggs's three-volume history of broadcasting, centering on Great Britain—*The History of Broadcasting in the United Kingdom* (London: Oxford, 1961–1970); Erik Barnouw's three volumes on American broadcasting—*A History of Broadcasting in the United States* (New York: Oxford, 1966–1970); and Barnouw's later book on television—*Tube of Plenty: The Evolution of American Television* (New York: Oxford, 1975). Also, *Fifty Years of Japanese Broadcasting,* compiled by the Radio and Television Culture Research Institute of NHK (Tokyo: The Institute, 1977); and E. Katz and B. Wedell, *Broadcasting in the Third World: Promise and Performance* (Cambridge, Mass.: Harvard University Press, 1973). Among the books on film are P. Rotha's *The Film till Now: A Survey of World Cinema* with additional sections by R. Griffith (London: Spring Books, 1957). Also, R. Griffith and R. Mayer, *The Movies* (New York: Simon & Schuster, revised ed., 1970). Also, several books by European filmmakers and theorists: among them, Sergei Eisenstein, *The Film Sense* (New York: Harcourt, Brace, 1942); and Siegfried Kracauer, *The Theory of Film* (New York: Oxford, 1960). Some of the most interesting books on the electronic and photographic media have been written by the performers and directors themselves. To give just one example, a collection of memorable scripts by Edward R. Murrow has been published under the title *In Search of Light: The Broadcasts of Edward R. Murrow, 1938–1961* (New York: Knopf, 1967). Unfortunately we know of no book that treats these three media and their interwoven impact.

QUESTIONS TO THINK ABOUT

1. For what kinds of news do you depend mostly on radio, for what kinds on television, and for what kinds on newspapers?
2. You have read answers to survey questions on whether you would trust newspaper or television news if the two media disagreed on the same story. How would you answer that question?
3. A criticism of broadcast news is that it very often does not furnish enough details so that the audience can really understand events. How do you feel about that?

4. Television has co-opted many movies for broadcast. Radio and the other news media have taken over the role of movies in presenting news. Yet no one doubts the power and attractiveness of movies as art and entertainment. Do you see a unique function, distinct from those of television and radio, that movies might fill in the next decades?
5. The mass media tables in this and the preceding chapter will repay your attention. For example, what can you conclude about the conditions that determine how the media are distributed throughout the world? Why does Africa lag behind other continents in the proportion of books, newspapers, films, radio, and television it produces? Why is Europe generally ahead of other regions in its proportion of printed media? Why is Japan unlike most of the other Asian countries in its very high use of all the media? Why does North America lead in the use of television and radio, rather than other media? As you consider questions like these, what characteristics of society—such as wealth, education, scientific development, national history, political relationships, and the like—would you say have most to do with the growth and development of media?

FOR THE RECORD

How Large Is Media Circulation?

The following table gives the number of radio receivers, daily newspapers in circulation, and television receivers, per 1000 persons. The figures are from UNESCO, and were published in 1985, meaning that the tabulations were probably made about 1983. UNESCO is not able to report totals for every country in every year, and this particular table does not include countries that have a population of less than 100,000 or in which the radio circulation is less than 2 percent (20 per 1000). The differences between countries in availability of these three principal media will be worth your attention.

Continent	Country	Radio	Newspapers	Television
Africa				
	Algeria	215	22	65
	Benin	78		
	Botswana	119	22	
	Burundi	40		
	Cameroon	49		
	Cape Verde	150		
	Central African Republic	57		
	Chad	219		
	Comoras	128		
	Congo	61		

Continent	Country	Radio	Newspapers	Television
	Djibouti	70		33
	Egypt	174	78	44
	Equatorial Guinea	303		
	Ethiopia	98		
	Gabon	91		
	Gambia	146		
	Ghana	173		
	Guinea	31		
	Guinea-Bissau	32		
	Ivory Coast	129		40
	Kenya	34		
	Lesotho	28	33	
	Liberia	185		
	Libya	223		66
	Malawi	48		
	Mauretania	101		
	Mauritius	211	68	86
	Morocco	163		39
	Mozambique	21		
	Niger	49		
	Nigeria	79		164
	Rwanda	63		
	Senegal	70		
	Sierra Leone	202		
	Somalia	25		
	South Africa	282		75
	Sudan	248		49
	Swaziland	154		
	Tanzania	20		
	Togo	214		
	Tunisia	163	41	54
	Uganda	22		
	Zaire	96		
	Zambia	27		
	Zimbabwe	45	21	
North and Central America				
	Bahamas	531	154	160
	Barbados	758	145	210

(continued)

Continent	Country	Radio	Newspapers	Television
	Belize	506		
	Canada	761	226	463
	Costa Rica	86	77	76
	Cuba	316	118	168
	Dominican Republic	201		92
	El Salvador	382		63
	Greenland	365		85
	Grenada	245		
	Guatemala	43		25
	Haiti	23		
	Honduras	49	61	
	Jamaica	394	46	89
	Mexico	290		111
	Netherlands Antilles	684		221
	Nicaragua	278	50	65
	Panama	180	61	122
	Puerto Rico	721	168	291
	St. Lucia	760	38	
	Trinidad and Tobago	300	149	261
	United States	2,043	269	790
South America				
	Argentina	540		699
	Bolivia	575	46	64
	Brazil	385	48	127
	Chile	304	215	116
	Colombia	133		98
	Ecuador	319	64	62
	Guyana	381	87	
	Paraguay	75		23
	Peru	160		49
	Surinam	627		121
	Uruguay	573		126
	Venezuela	405	186	126
Asia				
	Afghanistan	78		
	Bahrain	402		395
	Bangladesh	403		

Continent	Country	Radio	Newspapers	Television
	Brunei	188		138
	Burma	23		
	China	67	33	
	Cyprus	611		139
	Democratic Kampuchea	131		
	Democratic Yemen	61		
	Hong Kong	510		225
	India	61	21	
	Indonesia	138		22
	Iran	180		55
	Iraq	188		55
	Israel	270		256
	Japan	710	575	556
	Jordan	191		68
	Korea	461		175
	Kuwait	286	250	256
	Laos	95		
	Lebanon	797		296
	Thailand	146		
	Turkey	123		118
	United Arab Emirates	341		134
Europe				
	Albania	168	52	69
	Austria	530	453	311
	Belgium	468	224	303
	Bulgaria	235	235	189
	Czechoslovakia	270	318	280
	Denmark	392	356	309
	Finland	987	521	432
	France	860	191	375
	Germany (East)	384	535	358
	Germany (West)	401	408	360
	Greece	406		173
	Hungary	546	249	371
	Iceland	586	420	293
	Ireland	456	215	239
	Italy	255	62	243
	Luxembourg	531		255

(continued)

Continent	Country	Radio	Newspapers	Television
	Malta	398		265
	Netherlands	322	322	310
	Norway	412	483	319
	Poland	247	218	234
	Portugal	172	49	151
	Romania	143	186	173
	Spain	285	79	258
	Sweden	858	524	390
	Switzerland	364	381	378
	United Kingdom	993	421	470
	Yugoslavia	238		203
Oceania				
	Australia	1,301	334	423
	Fiji	597	102	
	New Zealand	890	325	288
	Solomon Islands	93		
	Tonga	721		
	Vanuata	242		
USSR				
	USSR	514	405	308
	Bylorussian SSR	235		229
	Ukrainian SSR	655		292

SOURCE: UNESCO, *Statistical Abstract* (Paris and New York: UNESCO, 1984).

Hours of Television Viewing per Week
in the United States

Audience Characteristics	Average Hours Viewing per Week		
	1960	1970	1980
Size of household			
1 or 2 members	33:01	36:31	39:25
3 or 4	39:20	49:03	54:30
5 or more	49:49	59:03	63:59

Audience Characteristics	Average Hours Viewing per Week		
	1960	1970	1980
Income level			
$5,000 or less*	42:42	42:55	43:43
$5,000 to $15,000*	44:36	45:35	50:28
$15,000 or more*	41:12	43:20	51:40
Educational level			
Grade school	—	48:14	52:13
High school	—	49:50	51:37
1 year of College or more	—	40:22	44:24
National average	40:02	45:41	49:14

*In 1980, income levels were changed to $10,000 or less, and $10,000 to $15,000.

SOURCE: Adapted from C. H. Sterling, *Electronic Media* (New York: Praeger, 1984), p. 241.

Number of Radio and Television Receivers in Use in the United States*

Year	Radio	Television	Year	Radio	Television
1922	400	—	1960	156,400	53,300
1930	13,000	—	1970	320,700	88,300
1940	51,000	—	1980	453,000	155,800
1950	85,200	4,000	1982	470,000	171,900

*All figures in thousands.

SOURCE: Adapted from Sterling, *Electronic Media,* p. 216.

"What Is Your Most Frequent Source of News?"*

Year	Radio	Television	Magazines	Newspapers	Other
1961	34	52	9	57	5
1972	21	64	6	50	4
1982	18	65	6	44	4

*Figures are percentage of those asked, and data were gathered for the Television Information Office. In this survey respondents were permitted to give more than one answer. Respondents are in the United States only.

SOURCE: Adapted from Sterling, *Electronic Media,* p. 158.

"What News Source Did You Use Yesterday?"

Years	Newspaper*	TV Newscast*	Radio Newscast*
1957	71	38	54
1965	71	55	58
1970	73	60	65
1973	70	62	59
1977	69	62	49

*Figures are percentage of those asked and are from the American Newspaper Publishers Association and are in the United States only.

SOURCE: Adapted from Sterling, *Electronic Media*, p. 160.

Top Ten Ranking Televised U.S. News Events, 1960–1980

Year	Event	Rating	Average Hours This Event Viewed
1963	Assassination of Kennedy	96.1	31:38
1969	Apollo moon landing	93.9	15:36
1965	Gemini IV "space walk"	92.1	4:47
1960	Kennedy-Nixon election returns	91.8	4:30
1964	Goldwater-Johnson election returns	90.6	2:51
1970	Abortive Apollo 13 mission	90.2	—
1968	Democratic convention	90.1	9:28
1976	Ford-Carter debates	90.0	5:45
1960	Kennedy-Nixon debates	89.8	4:00
1976	Democratic convention	88.5	27:16

SOURCE: Adapted from Sterling, *Electronic Media*, p. 248.

Top Ten Ranking U.S. Network Entertainment Episodes, 1960–1983

Program	Date	Network	Length*	Rating†
M*A*S*H (last episode)	Feb. 28, 1983	CBS	150	60.2
Dallas ("Who Shot J.R.?")	Nov. 21, 1980	CBS	60	53.3
Roots, Part VIII	Jan. 30, 1977	ABC	115	51.1
Super Bowl XVI	Jan. 24, 1982	CBS	213	49.1
Super Bowl XVII	Jan. 30, 1983	NBC	204	48.6

Program	Date	Network	Length*	Rating†
Gone with the Wind, Part 1	Nov. 7, 1976	NBC	179	47.7
Gone with the Wind, Part 2	Nov. 8, 1976	NBC	119	47.4
Super Bowl XII	Jan. 15, 1978	CBS	218	47.2
Super Bowl XIII	Jan. 21, 1979	NBC	230	47.1
Bob Hope Christmas Show	Jan. 15, 1970	NBC	90	46.6

*Duration in minutes of the episode.

†Rating is average percentage of total households.

SOURCE: Adapted from Sterling, *Electronic Media,* p. 246, based on Nielsen figures.

Charlie Chaplin in The Kid, *1921.*

INSTITUTIONS OF THE MASS MEDIA: ENTERTAINMENT

We have triumphantly invented, perfected, and distributed to the humblest cottage throughout the land one of the greatest technical marvels of history, television, and have used it for what? To bring Coney Island into every home.

ROBERT MAYNARD HUTCHINS

Entertainment—underestimated central function of communication.

HEINZ DIETRICH FISCHER

This instrument can teach, it can illuminate: yes, and even inspire. But it can do so only to the extent that humans are determined to use it to those ends. Otherwise it is merely wires and lights in a box.

EDWARD R. MURROW

*W*hy is Brooklyn so much less culturally productive than was Florence? Ernest Van den Haag asked that provocative question in one of his papers on culture.[1] At first sight, it doesn't seem very useful. After all, Brooklyn isn't comparable in many ways to Florence. The twentieth century isn't like the fifteenth. There is only one Michelangelo. We aren't likely to change those conditions. But in a book about communication, and a chapter on entertainment, perhaps the question is worth thinking about.

What exactly is Van den Haag asking? Certainly not why there is less *entertainment* in Brooklyn than there was in Renaissance Florence. All our evidence tells us there is *more* today. He is asking about a certain kind of entertainment, which we usually call high culture.

He is asking why Brooklyn has no Leonardo, no Michelangelo, no Donatello, no Raphael, no Dante, no Uffizi Gallery, no Pitti Palace, no Santa Croce. The list could be very long. But it provides a focus for some things we want to say about entertainment and cultural productivity.

Cultural production is shaped by a culture, and a culture is shaped by people. Let us begin, then, by talking about the people who are behind the culture that is behind the art.

THE RISE OF THE MIDDLE CLASS

Perhaps the most fundamental change in Western societies since the time of old Florence has been the rise of a middle class. Dante wrote for the well-educated people at the top of the political and clerical pyramid. The great painters of Italy worked mostly for patrons who supported the artists and then showed the best paintings in their galleries or their palaces. The first great European musicians composed music to be played at the royal palaces or the cathedrals. The kings and nobles themselves composed music and poetry, and sometimes joined the artists in performing music with, say, the king on the violin, and the composer at the harpsichord. It was not uncommon for patrons to read their own poetry with the other aristocrats and the greatest writers of the kingdom serving as critics. Every person in the group was a critic or a writer. The world of high culture was a cozy little in-group. Very few people had the money to support it or the talent to be invited into it. Nothing was farther from their thoughts than to make art for a mass audience.

Before the time of the middle class there had been chiefly masters and servants, aristocrats and workers, rich and poor. Then a new group of people moved between these traditional centers of power. The newcomers were merchants, traders, manufacturers, entrepreneurs, and politicians. They had money to spend—to buy education, to own land, to compete with the nobility for the services and products of the great artists. They had the numbers and the technology to take over power. And they did.

Mendelsohn, in a paper on the background of modern entertainment, described the kind of thing that began to happen after the middle class came in:[2]

- In 1606 Monteverdi's opera *Orfeo* was performed before a paying audience (not at court or in a palace).
- In 1613, in Venice alone, four theaters were offering musical entertainment to an audience that paid for its seats.

- By 1672, John Bannister was giving violin recitals in his home in London, to paying audiences.

- By 1730, or soon thereafter, secondhand bookstores, subscription libraries, reading clubs, and literary coffeehouses all were in existence.

- By the middle 1700s some London taverns were offering public entertainment by paid singers, musicians, and comedians. This entertainment foreshadowed music hall and variety shows of the next two centuries.

In other words, art and entertainment were becoming commodities to be bought and sold, to be enjoyed not merely by aristocrats but by anyone who wished to and could pay the tariff. Sales, as Mendelsohn pointed out, became a new criterion for entertainment. The artist survived not by pleasing one rich patron, but rather by giving the buying public what it wanted. A mass market for culture was growing up.

The mass media fit easily into this pattern. They provided the market, the talent, and reward for the talent. They made art and culture a spectator rather than a participant activity. The new type of artist produced entertainment largely for a relatively unskilled audience who did not take part in the performance, but only bought the right to choose the art they wanted and to enjoy it as they wished without concomitant creative or critical obligation. In a sense this kind of transaction was better than the old one for both parties: The audience had more choice, and the entertainer got more reward.

This new system assigned a much more important role to the entrepreneur, the manager, and the salesperson than they had played in the old days. They represented the artist and the audience. Truly, art had become a commodity and education a business.

Leo Lowenthal, in a study of biographical articles that appeared 40 years apart in two of America's most popular magazines, *Collier's* and *The Saturday Evening Post,* picked up some of the fallout from these changes.[3] In the earlier years the biographies dealt mostly with business and professional people and political leaders. When artists appeared in the biographies they were usually "serious" artists—opera singers, sculptors, concert pianists, and the like. Forty years later, not only were artists and entertainers written about more frequently than the titans of business and politics, but they were the heroes of *popular* rather than *high* culture. Instead of "serious" artists, *Collier's* and *The Saturday Evening Post* preferred to write about famous baseball players, popular singers, and movie stars.

What happened to entertainment as the mass media came into wide use, then, was not that the artists of high culture were any less respected or treated any less well, but rather that the popular artists were treated relatively much better than before. No longer did they have to perform for food and lodging, or pennies in the marketplace, or simply the applause of the townspeople. Movie stars could now look forward to the possibility of earning a million dollars a year (as Mary Pickford and Charlie Chaplin did). Storytellers could write books that would support them for the rest of their lives (as Charles Dickens and Mark Twain did). The difference was that the product of popular culture appealed to more people who were willing to pay for it. And that leads us to consider the relation of entertainment to changing culture.

HIGH CULTURE, POPULAR CULTURE, AND THE MASS MEDIA

Herbert Gans has written insightfully about the sociology of different kinds of culture in his volume *Popular Culture and High Culture*.[4] "I start with the basic assumption that all human beings have aesthetic urges," he said; "a receptivity to symbolic expression of their wishes and fears; a demand for both knowledge and wish fulfillment about their society; and a desire to spend free time, if such exists, in ways that diverge from their work routine. Therefore, every society must provide art, entertainment, and information for its members." However, he continued, "a society's art, information, and entertainment do not develop in a vacuum; they must have standards of form and substance which grow out of the society and the needs and characteristics of its members. Thus the aesthetic standards of every society can be related to others of its features. . . ." These choices, he emphasized, are not made randomly; they are related. Thus, "people who read *Harper's* or the *New Yorker* are also likely to prefer foreign movies and public television, to listen to classical (but not chamber) music, play tennis, choose contemporary furniture and eat gourmet food. Subscribers to the *Reader's Digest*, on the other hand, probably go to the big Hollywood films if they go to the movies at all, watch the family comedies on commercial television, listen to popular ballads or old Broadway musicals, go bowling, choose traditional furniture and representational art, and eat American homestyle cooking."

Thus he differentiates cultures in terms of their "taste publics." Each culture has its own "art, music, fiction, nonfiction, poetry, films, television programs . . . and so forth," and its own "writers, artists, performers, critics." He rigorously rejects the "dichotomy of high and popular culture," and particularly the idea that high culture "maintains aesthetic standards" while popular culture "exists for nonaesthetic reasons." He believes that there are actually many more than *two* cultures—exactly how many must be determined empirically. Thus he seems to think of the culture of old Florence as one end of a continuum and the culture of Brooklyn as perhaps somewhere in the middle of that continuum.

The idea of more than two cultures is not new. Perhaps the most famous division was a threefold one—highbrow, middlebrow, lowbrow—which came from Russell Lynes's book *The Tastemakers*. [5] My colleagues have sometimes speculated on how many dozens of cultures might be identified, at least theoretically, if we were to investigate this question empirically, taking into account not only individual taste choices but also all the other characteristics by which we distinguish each other: social class, age, sex, education, religion, ethnic background, economic status, occupation, personality, and so on. At least we can be sure that the map would be more complicated than the high-culture, popular-culture dichotomy or the highbrow, middlebrow, lowbrow triad. It would be easy to find more than two culture levels, more than one kind of popular culture, and different relationships of characteristics to tastes. Gans suggests that five might be a usable number. He calls them high, upper middle, lower middle, low, and "quasi-folk low." [6] The last is not very obvious nor is it developed very clearly. It seems to refer to "poor people" who are just emerging or have just emerged from "ethnic or rural folk culture." The other four levels, however, are relatively clear and seem to constitute a practicable set of index points.

If we want to think of taste cultures as divided into four levels—high, upper middle, lower middle, and low—that is a usable way of distinguishing them. *High* culture is like the culture of old Florence, a very small group (perhaps less than 5 percent of the people in the United States, for instance) who seek out "serious" art and are likely to practice it themselves. *Upper middle* is the taste culture of the majority of the upper middle class, probably the fastest-growing segment of society. *Lower middle* is the largest of these groups, usually considered the dominant force in determining media programming. *Low* culture is also a very large group, formerly the dominant one in setting taste (says Gans) until it was replaced in that position by the present lower-middle taste class.

Instead of using any group of named cultures, however, we might, as we have suggested, think of a continuum of cultures and tastes. In such a continuum, some individuals might straddle culture class barriers, take some characteristics from higher levels and some from lower, and thus create their own culture patterns which need not be given names at all.

It might be useful at this point to try to detail these taste cultures a bit more fully in an imaginary, rather lighthearted set of descriptions of people as they fit along such a cultural continuum. We shall try not to do violence to Gans's ideas (as the names of the people will indicate), but you should try to think of the people in this pattern as fitting along a continuum rather than belonging to culture classes.

CONTINUUM OF TASTE CULTURES

INCLUDING

Arthur High III, and his wife Priscilla
Elmer Upper, and his wife Cynthia
Louis Lower, and his wife Louise
Lawrence Low, and his wife Agnes

WHO WERE EDUCATED THUS

Arthur High went to Harvard. His wife Priscilla went to finishing school and then was sent to Lady Margaret Hall at Oxford. Arthur writes, and publishes quite a bit of it. Priscilla paints.

Elmer Upper went to a very good university, but changed to another one after two years because he wanted to get into their business school. His wife Cynthia went to one of the best private colleges for women.

Louis Lower went to the state university, which is where he met and married Louise. She finished two years of university work, then had to withdraw during her junior year to have their first baby.

Lawrence Low graduated from high school. His wife Agnes also was a high school graduate, but took a term of business school. They both are rather proud of having taken "practical" courses.

THEY WORK IN THESE JOBS

Mr. High teaches history. His wife worked for a time in the university president's office, but now does unpaid community work.

Mr. Upper is president of a bank. His wife knows she doesn't have to work, but gets a lot of enjoyment from serving as executive secretary of the state Republican party, where her main contribution is in public relations.

Mr. Lower is a salesman in one of the city's large stores. His wife sells, and does pretty well at selling, a line of cosmetics to women, house to house.

Mr. Low services refrigerators for a store that specializes in appliances. His wife is bookkeeper and secretary for the same store.

WHAT IS THEIR ATTITUDE TOWARD CULTURE?

The Highs take it for granted.

Mr. Upper wants to be cultured but frankly finds high culture rather uninteresting. Cynthia is somewhat more interested.

The Lowers aren't much interested.

The Lows aren't much interested either, in fact rather reject culture questions and opportunities. Lawrence finds the higher levels of culture rather dull and "effeminate."

THEIR TASTES IN ART

The Highs are proud to have old classics on their shelves. They also like newer experiments like atonal music and abstract art. They are more interested in fiction with good character development than with exciting plot. Priscilla's preferences run to graphic art and architecture; Arthur's to history and novels.

The Uppers, especially Elmer, like nonfiction. They like stories or articles about competition and upward mobility (which sound familiar to them!). They rely heavily on reviews, where possible, rather than exploring for new books and new authors.

The Lowers are likely to judge on substance rather than form. They like what they call "real" art—representational, rather than abstract paintings, sitcoms that remind them of the "ordinary" people they see every day, stories or articles that emphasize the traditional virtues.

The Lows used to be great moviegoers. Now that they are a bit older they spend more time with television, where they seek out "he-man" heroes and confrontations in which "right always wins."

SOME OF THEIR TYPICAL FAVORITES

The Highs really *like* great novels and classics of history and philosophy; it isn't just for show that they keep those books on their shelves. But they also like little magazines, foreign movies, seventeenth- and eighteenth-century music, Off-Broadway plays, abstract art, public TV, and radio. They take the *New York Times.*

The Uppers regularly read two or three newsmagazines, *Harper's, New Yorker, Vogue.* They like nineteenth-century music, but not much older than that. Elmer tries to keep up with the *Wall Street Journal,* the *Economist,* and, of course, professional journals.

The Lowers used to read *Life, Look,* and *The Saturday Evening Post* and were very sad when they were terminated. Now they read the *Reader's Digest.* They spend more and more time with television.

The Lows like westerns, on film or TV. They especially enjoy action films; actors and actresses like Lucille Ball, John Wayne, Red Skelton; and the "Beverly Hillbillies" and Lawrence Welk.

Remember that these people are imaginary, but note that they are *people,* not abstract classes. They don't wear uniforms, carry flags inscribed "Lower Middle" or something like that; their tastes are not completely uniform by families; they don't march in close rank toward a certain magazine, movie, television program.

But returning to the original question of what happened to cultural production between the time of old Florence and that of modern Brooklyn, it is apparent that the median point has moved down the continuum from the high culture of

Florence to some point in the popular culture of the mass media where it may last for a shorter time but in the meantime will reach more people. Therefore it may help to look at some of the relationships of entertainment and the mass media.

ENTERTAINMENT AND THE MASS MEDIA

Aside from the rise of the middle class, the other great event that helped change taste cultures and foreshadow the taste culture of our own time is the emergence of the mass media. In the great days of Florence there was hardly an example of media entertainment anywhere in Italy for artists and critics to marvel at or view with apprehension. Of course, popular culture was there, as it had been for centuries. People "talked story" to fill the time. Dancers performed without self-consciousness (or pay) on the village green. Wandering minstrels lived on the pennies tossed by a casual audience. Popular art must have been enjoyed then as now, but it had no way to draw very large audiences or pay performers much compensation. Minstrels and a few magicians or other semiprofessionals got around to nearby villages and a few village fairs, but on the whole the operation was as much amateur as professional and local rather than widespread, and its rewards were not very great either financially or critically.

In the latter half of the fifteenth century, the first books printed with the new movable metal type and the new kind of press began to appear. The first ones came from Mainz, but other print shops sprang up rapidly; some of the best of them, such as the shop of Aldus Manutius, were in Italy. Newspapers did not come along until the early 1600s, and then they were weeklies, or news books summarizing the year, or even news sheets. The electronic and photographic media were still three centuries down the road.

A man like Leonardo should have been fascinated by the new media, but he, like others, was probably unable to look ahead to the coming of the newer media. More solitary artists, like Dante and Raphael, would probably have been less excited than Leonardo. The people for whom the new media would make the greatest difference, the great popular audiences, were probably not fully aware of what the new printing houses meant for them.

To us, at this distance, it seems as though the mass media and popular art and entertainment were made for each other. But no one in the fifteenth century could have predicted that the new print shops were going to grow into what we call the media; that they would unchain the books from the monastery libraries and the nobles' collections and give them to the people; that the great writers like Dante and Shakespeare (who was becoming so popular in England that printers stole some of his plays from the dialogue they could copy in the theater) would soon become available to all who could read; and consequently that there would be a ground-swell of education so that most adults and all children could learn to read.

The first signs of the printed media that became available forecast neither a worldwide appearance of mass media nor a tidal wave of popular entertainment. The first book that came out of Mainz—the 42-line Bible—was a handsome volume, but it was issued only in 150 copies on rag paper and 50 on vellum, and it was a prestige volume rather than a piece of popular entertainment. The first news that came into European capitals was not especially entertaining; it was mostly price lists or political bulletins. The first magazines were news summaries or serious commentary, not mass entertainment. If it was going to take popular art or mass entertainment to start the tidal wave of mass-media growth, the starting energy was not immediately evident.

The tidal wave gathered strength slowly. In 1450 there were only a few tens of thousands of books in Europe, most of them block-printed or handwritten. There were some millions of printed books by the end of the fifteenth century, but even that number did not look like a tidal wave in Europe. News of other countries, which could be heard only from travelers or sailors in 1500, was heard in the coffeehouses or from news sheets on the streets in 1600. The stirring lines of the *Areopagitica* could be read, by those who wanted to read them, by 1644, and even though the circulation was not very large it was a forecast of the kind of political information that would make the media indispensable to the social change that was impending.

Perhaps it was the popularity of urban magazines such as Addison and Steele's *Spectator* together with the appearance of influential newspapers to help guide the revolutions of the seventeenth and eighteenth centuries that really set a map for the mass media: information, commentary, and entertainment.

Ralph Lowenstein used that triad of functions to help describe the trend in media development. He examined the content of the six major media—books, newspapers, magazines, film, radio, and television—and summarized the relative priorities they gave these functions, thus:[7]

Book	*Newspaper*	*Magazine*
1. Commentary	1. Information	1. Commentary
2. Entertainment	2. Commentary	2. Entertainment
3. Information	3. Entertainment	3. Information

Film	*Radio*	*Television*
1. Entertainment	1. Entertainment	1. Entertainment
2. Commentary	2. Information	2. Information
3. Information	3. Commentary	3. Commentary

We must read this list of priorities cautiously, as we should read any such wide-ranging summary. Obviously, media are different in different countries; for example, radio is relied upon in many developing countries today to carry news and information to the people, and in such cases it can hardly be called an entertainment rather than an information medium. Similarly, there may be as much difference *within* some media in some countries as *between* media; for instance, in the United States *TV Guide* and *National Geographic* exist mainly to carry information to their huge audiences, whereas Lowenstein feels (probably correctly) that magazines overall emphasize commentary. Again, books could legitimately be said to give priority to any of the three functions, depending on what books and where. But in general Lowenstein is probably justified in his rankings, and the priority he gives to entertainment for film, radio, and television is the least in doubt of all. Thus, he finds that the more recent the medium, the more likely it is to emphasize entertainment; and in particular the electronic and photographic media have turned out to be predominantly entertainment media.

The nineteenth century, then, was the turning point in the development of entertainment media. This was not only because the electronic and photographic media began to appear at the end of that century, but also because the print media, notably books and magazines, stood forth at that time as leaders in entertainment. It was a great century for fiction. For a few examples let us mention Dickens, Thackeray, and Hardy in England; Victor Hugo, Flaubert, and Balzac in France; Tolstoy and Dostoyevski in Russia; Thomas Mann (just at the turn of the century) in Germany; and Mark Twain in the United States. That outpouring of genius was enough to establish the novel, from at least that time, as the dominant form of literature. It became also the greatest magnet for reading audiences. The strength of this attraction was demonstrated by the lengths to which New York devotees of Dickens went to keep up with his writings. In those days, the novels of Dickens were published in installments of one or two chapters, usually every two weeks, and brought to New York by packet ship. The New York afficionados could not wait to pick up their installments at the bookstores. They would go out in small boats to meet the ship from England before it docked. There, in the harbor, they would shout up at the ship's officers and passengers, who would already have read that week's installment of the novel, questions like, "What happened to Little Nell?"

It would seem that this interest and affection could hardly be equaled, much less surpassed. But when films came into use, at the beginning of the twentieth century, and then were followed by radio and television at intervals of about 20 years, the magnetism of media entertainment was truly demonstrated. It was only a few years from the day when Thomas Edison filmed one of his laboratory employees sneezing within range of Edison's new camera until D. W. Griffith was filling large theaters with *Birth of a Nation* and audiences were laughing and crying with Charlie Chaplin. By 1922, approximately 30 million Americans saw a movie at least once a week. By 1947, movie attendance was 85 million a week. After that, television came into use and movie theater attendance fell off. But soon television discovered that it needed movies to build up its entertainment offerings, and so thousands of American moving pictures began to circulate to television stations throughout the world.

In some respects the story of radio's growth from a device that broadcast dots and dashes is even more picturesque than the story of the growth of motion pictures. In many respects its cast of people on the microphone was more spectacular even than that of television, and its coverage of news was more exciting. Although it could not carry pictures of events, it had the advantage of not having to restrict its items to those of which it could show pictures, and it had the advantage of a remarkable series of events to report—the Lindbergh story, the coming of a world war, a great depression, to name just a few. Radio came into regular use about 1920. In 1947 when, as we have noted, movie attendance in the United States was about 85 million, 93 percent of American homes had radio. Therefore we can estimate that in an average week, Americans were giving somewhere near 200 million hours per week to movies, somewhere over 3 *billion* hours to radio.

When television came into use (about 1950 in the United States) the result, as we have noted, was disastrous to both movies and radio. Perhaps the best way to show television's impact is to reproduce some figures.

Time Spent by Average Person in Minutes per Day

	Before Television Was Available	After Purchase of a Receiver
Magazines	17	10
Newspapers	39	32
Radio	122	52
Television	0	179

SOURCE: John F. Robinson, in Eli Rubenstein, et al., eds., *Television and Social Behavior* (Washington, D.C.: Institute of Mental Health, 1973), IV, p. 410.

Of course, both radio and television bounced back from their hard encounters with television. And it is worth noting that there was a comparatively small decline in newspaper use as a result of television's competition. The implication is that newspapers and TV serve mostly different functions for their audiences.

Just how much entertainment does television provide? UNESCO gathers figures every year on media and their audiences throughout the world. These reports for the newest of the media, radio and television, include the amount and kinds of material that each medium supplies to its audience. With a sample of countries throughout the world, we can see what proportion of television and radio content is reported by broadcasters as entertainment. Let us choose a sample of manageable size—say France and the United Kingdom from Western Europe, Czechoslovakia and the German Democratic Republic from Eastern Europe, Ghana from Africa, Egypt and Algeria from the Middle East, India and Japan from Asia, Brazil and Mexico from Latin America, and Australia from Oceania. Twelve countries. (Neither the United States nor the Soviet Union is covered fully by the UNESCO content figures.) The chief categories of content reported by the UNESCO countries are information (including news), education, culture, and entertainment. Here are the percentages of the radio and television broadcasts that these 12 countries say they are giving to each of the four main categories.

	Information	Education	Culture	Entertainment
Radio	17.1%	4.7%	10.7%	54.9%
TV	17.0	10.9	8.1	50.0

SOURCE: Adapted from UNESCO, *Statistical Annual* (Paris and New York: UNESCO, 1984), IX, pp. 16ff.

Thus, about one hour out of six, approximately the same on radio as on television, is used for information broadcasts. About twice the percentage of time on television as on radio goes for education; for television that is about one hour in ten. About one-tenth of the total broadcast time is devoted to cultural programs. And about *half* the total broadcast time—three times as much as the highest of the other categories—on television as well as radio goes for *entertainment.*

Thus the media that fill the bulk of our leisure time fill half of it with entertainment!

THE EFFECTS OF MEDIA ENTERTAINMENT ON AUDIENCES

There is little doubt that the mass media are providing an enormous amount of pleasure, relaxation, excitement, and relief from boredom for their audiences. Yet the taste cultures are normative, and as more and more people have joined the audiences for media entertainment, more and more questions have been asked about possibly undesirable effects of massive exposure to the entertainment media.

On three occasions during the last 50 years, groups of social scientists have been assembled to study the evidence on these questions. The first of these was the Payne Fund studies, in the early 1930s, in which a group of scholars, chiefly psychologists and educators, was gathered together to prepare books on the impact of radio. A second was the Hutchins Commission, another group of scholars, mostly political scientists, philosophers, and historians, that came together in the 1940s to examine modern challenges to the news media. This was a politically rather than a psychologically or educationally concerned group, and the books they wrote were directed to the effects of the news media on society rather than on the individual. These first two groups of studies were supported by private foundations. A third such activity, in the late 1960s and early 1970s, was financed by the United States government and named, after the department head in charge of it, the Surgeon General's Inquiry.

Unlike the earlier studies, this one recognized the continuing anxiety of the commercial media by permitting the media not only to nominate possible members of the Scientific Advisory Committee, but also to blackball proposed members of whom they did not approve. The members of this supervising committee and researchers chosen by them conducted studies, both experiments and field surveys, dealing mostly with the effects of television on children. The results of this activity, unlike those of the early activities, were aimed not so much at books by the individual participants (although there were a few of those as well as several volumes of summarized studies) but mainly at a summary report that appeared in 1972 under the title *Television and Growing Up: The Impact of Televised Violence*. The committee summarized its findings, with proper scholarly caution, as "a preliminary and tentative indication of a causal relation between viewing violence on television and aggressive behavior" (by the children who view it). However, the committee warned, this "causal relation operates only on some children (who are predisposed to be aggressive)," and "only in some environmental contexts." These conclusions, as the committee itself recognized, are "tentative and limited," but they represent the first time that a substantial case had been made against any part of the immensely popular entertainment media.[8]

The first American book on television and children had decided, "For some children, under some conditions, some television is harmful. For other children under the same conditions, or for the same children under other conditions, it may be helpful. For *most* children, under *most* conditions, most television is probably neither harmful nor particularly beneficial."[9] That is about where the later studies have left us, although the Surgeon General's Inquiry took the further steps of identifying some of the kinds of television content, some of the types of children, and some of the conditions that might create an undesirable effect. These conclusions are limited to children, to television, and to violence in entertainment programs. But they had the effect of warning viewers, parents, and television programmers that there are certain circumstances under which media entertainment may not be "good for you."

Studies like those of the Payne Fund, the Hutchins Commission, and the Surgeon General's Committee have apparently not brought about any striking changes in the media, although they have encouraged the making and revision of codes of performance. And they have at least stimulated a great deal of thinking about media entertainment.

For example, people have asked whether we are really prepared to distinguish entertainment from other kinds of communication content. Were the telecasts of Apollo 11 and the moon landing really entertainment or information? The answer is that they were probably both, and in different proportions for different viewers. Is the Super Bowl broadcast better classified as entertainment or information? Probably mostly entertainment, but there is also a component of information; otherwise the newspeople would have less to write about when they go back to their typewriters. In fact, can we say even that a certified card-carrying soap opera is used exclusively for entertainment? Herta Herzog demonstrated the difficulties of doing that in a study she published in 1944 under the title, "What We Really Know About Daytime Serial Listeners."[10]

Herzog confirmed by extensive survey data what was already believed to be known about these audiences—their large numbers, the impressive amount of time they use for listening to daytime serials, and so forth. Then to find out more about them she made a relatively small study—100 intensive interviews with women— to try to ascertain the gratifications they obtained from listening to the daytime serial programs. The women in the sample reported three main types of reward. One was emotional release—the "chance to cry," the chance to feel better from knowing that "other people have troubles too." A second kind of gratification was the opportunity to engage in "wishful thinking." For example, one woman listened to a certain serial for its funny episodes, so that she could pretend they had happened to herself and her husband, whose life together was not very funny or even very pleasant. Still another woman, whose daughter had run away from home to marry and whose husband "stays away five nights a week," listened to two certain serials because each portrayed a happy family life and a successful wife and mother. She enjoyed imagining herself in that situation. But an even more interesting finding was that such programs are used by many women as a source of *advice*. They "explain things," said one listener; and another reported that "if you listen to these programs and something turns up in your own life, you would know what to do about it." Half the women interviewed felt that the serials were helping them in their own lives—perhaps not as systematically as they might be helped by a lecture on family problems or a professional counseling session, but they felt they might remember the lesson longer because it came in story form.

It is thus clear that the rewards of mass-media entertainment are not always limited to the traditional ones we ascribe to entertainment: pleasure, relaxation, excitement, relief from boredom. For example, some people say they particularly enjoy the morning paper or the first newscast of the day because it is like returning from a trip and being able to find out what has happened in one's absence. Even bad news has a component of pleasure, especially because it happened to someone else, not you. Having something to listen to or read helps to combat loneliness. Some listeners or viewers say that after a while they come to think of the interesting people on the screen or in the loudspeaker as friends, and tuning them in is much the same kind of experience as seeing one's real-life friends in the flesh.

Bernard Berelson is one of the scholars who have tried empirically to understand these unexpected gratifications of entertainment.[11] During a newspaper strike in New York City he interviewed a number of persons in order to learn what missing the newspaper meant to them. They *did* miss the newspaper—they made that clear—and mostly they missed information about and interpretation of the day's events, as we might expect. But beyond that, they said in no uncertain terms that they missed

- Tools for daily living that could be obtained nowhere else quite as conveniently (at that time) as in the pages of the newspaper, for example, broadcast and film schedules, shoppers' advertisements, and weather forecasts.

- The respite and relaxation from everyday chores and boredom they are accustomed to obtain from sitting in a comfortable chair with the newspaper.

- The social prestige one gets from being able to be up-to-date on the news and discuss it with one's friends.

- The social contact derived from seeing the names of one's friends or acquaintances in the paper. For example, one might scan the obituaries and learn of the death of a friend or, less personally, read the news of well-known persons with whom one feels so well acquainted through the media that they seem almost like one's personal friends.

After the experience of these interviews, Berelson characterized the newspaper less as an impersonal force than as a "vehicle of social contact."

It is ironic that two of the most frequently used approaches to the study of entertainment during recent years have been theoretically so different. On one hand, a group of psychologists and communication scholars has been examining the widely held belief that television (and perhaps other media) may be teaching violent behavior to children by showing them violent behavior. On the other hand, another group of scholars has been examining the widely held belief that the function of mass-media entertainment is principally escape—as Van den Haag put it, to "distract men from life" rather than "having it revealed." These two avenues of investigation have not discredited the ideas that mass-media entertainment may have potential ill effects on children or that it may distract adult audiences from their real-life problems. Rather their effect has been to broaden knowledge of how people use entertainment, including both conditions under which television content may be copied with harmful results and the conditions under which it may contribute to happiness and understanding.

Herzog's look at the effect of soap operas is an example of the latter approach. So also is Emil Huizanga's book, *Homo Ludens: A Study of the Play Element in Culture,* and William Stephenson's *The Play Theory of Communication,* both of which try to understand the function of mass-media entertainment without equating it simply with escape.

Stephenson extends the theory even to news reading, and in so doing arrives at a conclusion distinctly different from Berelson's.[12] What has been overlooked "about newspaper reading is its essentially *play*-like character," he wrote. "What has to be explained about newsreading, fundamentally, is the *enjoyment* it engenders. Even bad news is enjoyed, in the sense that *afterwards,* upon reflection, we can say that it was absorbing, interesting, and enjoyed. So, also, *play* is enjoyed, though during the game we may be so intent upon winning that we are unaware of any feelings of pleasure. . . . Newsreading, in developed form, is substantive play."

Even the act of reading—the translation of letter symbols into pictures or meanings—may itself be experienced as a kind of play, he says. The voluntary surrender of one's own world of reality, for a time, in order to participate imaginatively in the events of the media is also a kind of play. And who is to say that one should not spend some of this time in play, or that it will not make ultimately for better mental health and happiness?

Perhaps we can end this chapter with a medical story that might not be accepted by a medical journal. Norman Cousins demonstrated how entertainment can contribute to both health and happiness, in curing himself of a supposedly mortal illness. Cousins is an indisputably serious thinker, who had been editor of the *Saturday Review,* and gained worldwide attention and applause by his efforts in behalf of the Hiroshima maidens, a group of young women who had been disfigured by the atomic bomb dropped on their city. When he was stricken by the supposedly incurable disease, and the doctors held out almost no hope, he took stock of himself and decided that he needed, so far as he could tell, to restore the kind of life he wanted to live. Later he wrote a book about the experience. The first action he took was to move out of the hospital. Then he designed a program of self-treatment. He began the treatment by ordering a large supply of old Marx brothers comedies that he could watch on his video recorder. He watched them with continuing amusement and an occasional guffaw. After this, he concocted other unorthodox prescriptions for entertainment and activities (even playing tennis despite a diagnosis of coronary occlusion) that used to amuse him. The conclusion to the story is that he apparently made a complete recovery from his deadly illness and is now living a quite normal life. "There is nothing like a good laugh!" he said.[13]

SUGGESTIONS FOR FURTHER READING

A good place to begin reading is with a book on which we have relied heavily in this chapter: Herbert J. Gans, *Popular Culture and High Culture* (New York: Basic Books, 1974). Two other volumes we have found useful were edited by Bernard Rosenberg and David Manning White: *Mass Culture: The Popular Arts in America* (New York: Free Press, 1957), and *Mass Culture Revisited* (New York: Van Nostrand Reinhold, 1971). Still another is Heinz-Dietrich Fischer's and Stefan R. Melnik's edited collection of chapters and articles, *Entertainment: A Cross-Cultural Examination* (New York: Hastings House, 1979). And yet another edited volume of papers is Percy Tannenbaum, ed., *The Entertainment Function of Television* (New York: Erlbaum, 1980). Many of the readings we have suggested in this book under the headings of films, television, radio, and advertising deal with mass-media entertainment; we shall not repeat those titles here. Among other related titles are Jay G. Blumler and Elihu Katz, *The Uses of Mass Communication* (Beverly Hills, Calif.: Sage, 1974); and Joffre Dumazdier, *Sociology of Leisure* (New York: Elsevier, 1974). On the concept of mass media use as "play," see William Stephenson, *The Play Theory of Mass Communication* (Chicago: University of Chicago Press, 1967); and Johan Huizinga, *Homo Ludens: A Study of the Play Element in Culture* (Boston: Beacon Press, 1950). A book that might well have been cited in an earlier chapter is Hortense Powdermaker, *Hollywood: The Dream Factory* (Boston: Little, Brown, 1964). We have said very little about comics. A good introduction to the history of comics is Jerry Robinson, *The Comics: An Illustrated History of Comic Strip Art* (New York: Putnam, 1974). Other treatments of the comics include Bill Blackbeard and Martin Williams, *The Smithsonian Collection of Newspaper Comics* (Washington, D.C.: Smithsonian Institution Press, 1977); George Perry and Alan Aldridge, *The Penguin Book of Comics* (Harmondsworth, England: Penguin, 1967); Pierre Couperie and Maurice C. Horn, *A History of the Comic Strip* (New York: Crown, 1968). The last two volumes mentioned devote more attention to comics outside the United States than do most of the other treatments of comic strips.

QUESTIONS TO THINK ABOUT

1. Do newspapers carry more entertainment material than they used to?
2. What media do you think of as offering especially high-quality entertainment of different kinds? For example, many viewers have been attracted to television since the 1950s because of the sports coverage; others spent many hours with radio during the thirties and forties because of the comedy and situation comedies. What other such examples can you think of?
3. How should entertainment radio and television be supported? Britain and Japan have presented consistently high-level programming on BBC and NHK and have supported them chiefly by license fees on receiving sets. Both countries, however, have introduced commercial broadcasting, supported by advertising, simultaneously with BBC and NHK. In the United States, a much higher fraction of broadcasting support is paid for by advertising; noncommercial radio and television, paid for largely by private grants and audience donations (that is, for Public Broadcasting and National Public Radio), receive a relatively small part of U.S. broadcasting support. What system for supporting entertainment broadcasting would you recommend to a new country just starting out in radio and television, and for what reasons?
4. One of the early goals set by commercial broadcasting in the United States was to make available everywhere in the country the same quality of art and entertainment as could be found in a large city such as New York. Has it succeeded in doing so?
5. What do you see as the future of film, TV, and radio, given the amount of competition among them and the rise in popularity of new delivery systems such as cable and home recorders?

TIME CAPSULE

Age of the nickelodeon	1900
Incubation of great comic talents—e.g., Charlie Chaplin—at studios like Mack Sennett's	1905–1915
Birth of a Nation, one of first "blockbuster" movies, starts films on their great popularity	1915
Chaplin, Mary Pickford paid a million dollars each per year	1920
First regularly scheduled radio	1920
Station WEAF begins selling ads on radio	1922
Radio networks begin to function	1923
First sound movie	1927
"One Man's Family," one of most popular soap operas of all time (continued 27 years—until 1959—before television forced it out of radio)	1932
TV demonstrated in England	1936
First U.S. commercial television stations licensed (but war and then administrative freeze kept them from doing much until 1950s)	1941

Movie attendance 85 million a week; radio in 85 percent of U.S. homes   1947

Great expansion of TV, with predictable impact on other entertainment media—radio listening time cut by half, movie audience from 85 to 25 million per week   1952–1960

Radio discovers how to appeal to audience (by specialized services) despite TV; film studios begin to sell movies to TV   1960–1970

Surgeon General's Committee report raises serious questions about effects of TV violence on young viewers   1972

Many of largest magazines—among them *Life, Look, Saturday Evening Post,* and *Colliers*—fold because of TV competition for general audience and advertising   1970–1980

TV in use 6 to 7 hours a day in average household, most frequent source of news for majority of viewers, earns $15 billion in advertising income per year   1982

The first postage stamp, printed in England in 1840, showing the profile of the young Queen Victoria.

THE STOREHOUSES AND COURIERS OF KNOWLEDGE

Knowledge and human power are synonymous.

FRANCIS BACON, NOVUM ORGANUM

He made man's talents a public possession.

PLINY (on Caesar's plan for a national library)

*T*he first president of the United States, in an extraordinary farewell address, which he never delivered but rather published in Claypoole's *Daily Advertiser* and which some of the brightest Americans of the time—Hamilton, Jefferson, and Madison among others—helped to write, left this advice for his compatriots: "Promote as an object of primary importance institutions for the general diffusion of knowledge."

He was neither the first nor the last national leader to advocate such a policy, but he was one leader whose people took his advice seriously. Within half a century the American wilderness was filling with public schools and public libraries. When I was a boy I attended a school named after that first president, in a small Ohio River town, and used as my chief source of reading material the Carnegie Library, named after a generous rich man who helped the taxpayers of my hometown erect a building for the public use of books. Thus a nation whose main problem was settling a wilderness followed not only the advice of its first president but also that of one of the greatest philosophers of the Renaissance, Francis Bacon, in trying to build power out of knowledge.

MONASTIC LIBRARIES

Schooling and libraries grow together, as the Babylonians reminded us when they left the clay tablets of their libraries beside the remains of their schools. In Europe it was mostly the monastic libraries that preserved a storehouse of knowledge through the Dark Ages. What did those libraries in the monasteries contain? The Scriptures, of course. The writings of the church fathers, and many commentaries on them. The works of philosophers such as St. Thomas Aquinas and Roger Bacon. Collections of history (for example, the works of the Venerable Bede). Chronicles of the times, put together with loving care by the monks. And usually a taste of the most respected secular literature—Cicero, Horace, Virgil, among others.

The monasteries almost always included a scriptorium, a room with desks or tables where some of the monks spent many of their working hours copying books to preserve them. Some of the more valuable texts were chained to their bookcases. Strict rules were laid down for the use of the library's volumes, and curses were sometimes invoked against any person who stole them. On the other hand, the rules were not so strict that some secular scholars were not permitted to come to the library to read, or that occasionally a book could not be lent out for use in another monastery or school or—after a deposit to guarantee its return—to an ordinary literate citizen.

RENAISSANCE LIBRARIES

In Europe, therefore, it was the monastic libraries that perhaps more than anything else bridged the gap between the book collections of classical times and those of Renaissance scholarship.[1] In the Renaissance, of course, the monastic collections became less essential. The libraries of rich and influential collectors began to be opened to the public. Petrarch wished to give his books to the city of Venice as a public library, but Cosimo de Medici got ahead of him by donating a similar but larger collection to Florence. And Cosimo's grandson, Lorenzo the Magnificent, who owned an even larger and more valuable collection of books, persuaded Michelangelo to design a suitably magnificent building for the collection, which still stands as a public library.

Philip II of Spain founded the great library of the Escorial in Madrid in 1584 around his own collection. This institution helped set a fashion for public libraries by doing away with the bays which provided a certain amount of privacy for users of the library. It kept the books on shelves along the wall and abandoned the custom of chaining valuable volumes to their shelves. As a matter of fact, the custom gradually became less necessary. As the new art of printing made books more readily available, wealthy nobles and a few wealthy commoners assembled libraries and gave them for public use, often with additional money to keep them up to date. One of the early predecessors of Andrew Carnegie as an endower of libraries was an English merchant named Humphrey Chetham, who bequeathed money in 1753 for two parish libraries (largely for the use of clerics) and a large public library that still stands in the city of Manchester. But the nobles were still more likely than commoners to be able to donate libraries. An example was Cardinal Mazarin, who collected one of the outstanding libraries in France and made it available to the public in 1691.

NEW CONCEPTS OF LIBRARIES

Cardinal Mazarin's collection was so extensive and varied that it required rethinking how such a large collection should be displayed and cataloged. The central purpose of the monastic libraries had been to defend the books against theft or loss, copy those that showed signs of falling to pieces, and add new volumes as they became available. Thus, the chief problem in managing monastic libraries was to preserve their contents rather than to make them easy to use. However, a large collection of books open to the public raised quite different problems. The librarian in charge of Mazarin's library was Gabriel Naude. When he faced the overwhelming problems of bringing a huge new library into use, he thought about it and wrote what has been called the first modern study of library management—*Avis pour dresser une Bibliothèque* ("Advice for Setting Up a Library") in 1627. This was widely translated and, perhaps more than any other volume, changed the concepts of librarianship in Europe.

One of the distinguished men who read it was Samuel Pepys, who organized his own library after Naude's pattern and gave it to Magdalene College, Cambridge, where it may still be seen. Another was the great philosopher, William Leibnitz, whose personal endorsement and scholarly additions contributed greatly to Naude's influence.

Naude's concept of a library was that it should cover the whole of recorded human knowledge, be systematically arranged, and be open to all scholars. Leibnitz added to this the stout belief that the purpose of a scholarly library is, above all, to keep communication open among scholars; they should be aware of all the work that has been done in their fields, and libraries should be organized to make this exchange easy and effective. He developed some of the theory of how knowledge should be organized and displayed in a library and advocated a national or international bibliographical organization to keep scholars and libraries in cooperative contact.

Another highly influential contributor to new ideas of the library was Antonio

Panizzui, who came to England as a political refugee from Italy, went to work for the library of the British Museum, and headed the library from 1856 to 1866. His greatest impact was on the cataloging of books. He set down a code of rules that has played a part in developing the catalogs of many of the great libraries of the world. Beyond this, however, he insisted both that a library face the question of what its function should be and that it be designed and organized to serve this function. Perhaps the outstanding monument to his thinking along this line is what has been accomplished by the British Museum library. What that library did to serve its function, as it saw that function, and the influence it exerted on other book collections have done much to shape and form today's scholarly libraries.

LIBRARIES IN THE NINETEENTH AND TWENTIETH CENTURIES

The nineteenth and twentieth centuries were a time for flowering of libraries. Among the largest of the national libraries that took shape in that period and are now serving the people of their countries is the V. I. Lenin State Library of the Soviet Union, in Moscow, which replaced the old Imperial Library in 1917 and is believed to have 25 million books and about 2.5 million manuscripts on its shelves. Another great national library is the Bibliothèque Nationale, in Paris, which has more than 6.5 million books and over 5 million manuscripts and prints. The British Museum Library, in London, has more than 8.5 million books and a very large additional collection of manuscripts, prints, drawings, coins, and medals. The largest library in the United States is the Library of Congress, in Washington, which began as a collection for the use of Congress only but was later opened to the general public. It now holds upwards of 15 million books, 29 million manuscripts, 3 million photographic negatives and slides, and a great number of prints and drawings.

Stupendous as the holdings of these national libraries may seem, they are by no means the only very large libraries in the world. Italy has seven national libraries, of which the one in Florence holds more than 4 million and the one in Rome more than 2 million books. Most of the European nations have national libraries, some of them very large and rich in their collections. The Deutsche Staatsbibliothek, which was taken over by East Germany after World War II, has more than 3 million books. Twenty-five nations of Asia have national libraries. Among them the National Diet Library, in Tokyo, and the National Library of China, in Beijing, have more than 2 million books each, and the National Library of India, in Calcutta, more than 1 million. The National Library of Brazil, in Rio de Janeiro, is the largest of these institutions in Central and South America, but every one of the major American nations has a national library.[2]

In some ways, the growth of university libraries has been as remarkable as that of the national libraries. The Harvard University Library, in Cambridge, Massachusetts, is the largest university library in the world; its 12 million-plus books and over 2 million microfilm units compare well with the Bibliothèque Nationale and the British Museum Library. Both Harvard University and its library grew out of John Harvard's gift of his personal library and 800 British pounds for endowment. The Bodleian Library at Oxford is also a very large and rich collection. But the size of university libraries throughout the United States is a source of wonder to librarians and scholars everywhere. At least 25 American university libraries, in addition to Harvard, have more than 1 million books each. Yale has over 7 million; the University of California (at Berkeley), Columbia, Michigan, and Illinois, over 5 million each; Stanford, Washington, Wisconsin, Chicago, Cornell, and the University of California (at Los Angeles), over 4 million each.

The public libraries and the public school libraries offer in some ways an even more remarkable record of growth than that of university libraries. The first city library in the United States to be supported by direct public taxation was the library of Boston, which is still one of the major public libraries in the country. Boston, New York, Chicago, and Los Angeles all have public libraries with 5 million or more books (New York many more than 5 million). But perhaps more interesting than these large-city book holdings is the number of books that smaller cities are able to offer to their citizens. To take one example, Dayton, Ohio, a city of a little over 200,000 people, has 1.4 million volumes in its public library. Akron, Ohio, which has a population only a bit higher than Dayton's, also has more than 1 million books in its public library. Small towns, in proportion, do even better. I grew up in a town of 15,000 people that had about 50,000 books for public use, in addition to perhaps 100,000 in a small college a few blocks away. Any town of 10,000 to 50,000 people may have 100,000 or more books in its library. These will probably include not only classics of literature and a supply of recreational reading, but also a considerable amount of reference material and books from which people can advance their knowledge of history, science, economics, and government. More and more libraries are providing materials in addition to books for home loan—for example, videocassettes, tapes and disks for music, music scores, study guides, and in some countries paintings and sculpture for borrowers who are willing to put down a deposit to guarantee safe return. Thus students can do a considerable part of their reading in the public library rather than depending wholly on the school library, which is probably smaller and more in demand. And public libraries contribute also to making the home an extension of the school, a place where all family members can satisfy their ambition to study by correspondence or extension or simply satisfy their curiosity.

The great growth of public libraries dates to about 1850, although there are many public libraries older than that. One example of the way schools and libraries learned to work together was in the early years of the nineteenth century, when the St. Louis public library began to stock pictures, charts, self-study material, and other things that would make it easier to introduce audiovisual teaching into the local classrooms. The success of these new methods helped encourage all schools to teach with audiovisual aids.

One of the many other ways in which librarians cooperated with scholars and schoolteachers was in the making of reference books, catalogs, scholarly journals, and abstract services. The scholars and teachers knew more about the content of these services and could encourage and guide their use; the librarians had special knowledge of the techniques required and could organize and display the materials when they were available. The techniques of abstracting and cataloging have, of course, taken giant strides in the years of electronic technology. One example is the kind of abstracting service illustrated by *Medlars,* which is intended to make the enormous product of medical research easily available to physicians and medical researchers. A few decades ago these abstracts of research would have been put on 3×5 cards or perhaps summarized in a reference book; now they are recorded by computers, so that someone who needs them can very quickly examine them on a screen or have an especially important abstract printed out in hard copy. Similar abstracting aids are provided in a number of other fields, although not always so extensively or so well. Chemistry, physics, law, even communication (the ERIC system) are among those in which the skills of abstracting and electronic technology are being used to do what Leibnitz dreamed of—keep scholars in touch with other scholars and their scholarship.

SCHOOLS AND THE MOVEMENT TO USE MASS MEDIA

It was the middle of the nineteenth century before schools really caught up with the growth of mass media—or, more accurately, with print and printed media, which were the only kind of mass media then in existence. How many children were in school before the day of Gutenberg is hard to estimate with any confidence now, except in two respects: that in Europe and its related countries the number of schools was certainly less than the number of monasteries and a few other religious organizations, and that the number of girls among the schoolchildren was very few indeed. A few families could hire tutors and a few school groups were supported by tuition, but by far the greater number of elementary schools were run by monasteries and entrance to them depended on both religious and intellectual tests.

If students wanted to go beyond elementary school, they ordinarily had to pay tuition, and the chief purposes of "high" school was to prepare students for the higher studies of the university. Medieval universities grew up around famous teachers—for example, Abelard, the doctors of Salerno, the lawyers of Bologna, the theologians of Paris. If a *group* of scholars, rather than one famous man, attracted the university students, the teachers elected their own chancellor and made their own rules. But in general, during the latter medieval centuries the school system was a small group of primary students usually taught without charge by a religious center, a much smaller group of elite students of high school age who had been selected as worthy candidates for university training, and a still smaller elite chosen from that elite to enter the severe individual and tutorial studies of a university.

The religious wars and disputations of the Renaissance and Reformation undermined the power as well as the contribution of the monastic schools. The availability of printed books made it possible, after 1450, to think of vastly larger numbers of children in school. But the general pattern of educational opportunity remained much the same—a fairly large enrollment in primary schools and sharply decreasing numbers at each level above that.

Two significant changes, in addition to the swift increase in number of books and the growth of individual and public library collections, became evident in the centuries after Gutenberg. For one thing, there was a growing tendency toward state or national support of primary schooling, although it was a very long time before this custom spread to include secondary education. In the second place, the rapid increase in number of books required some new thinking as to how those new resources should be handled, both in schools and in libraries. No longer were Abelard, two students, and a book considered a university, nor could primary school teachers in France or Germany be content to depend upon the old exercises in spelling and penmanship and a few old texts in moral theology. In other words, it was necessary now to examine questions about how and what to teach.

Given the emergence of absolutist states in Europe, and these states taking over from the church responsibility for primary education, certain pedagogical changes of broad importance began to appear in country after country. Some historians referred to them as reforms, others simply as developments. But their significance was recognized.

For one, Latin as a language of teaching was gradually replaced by the parent tongue. The significance of the parallel Latin and English columns of Comenius's illustrated textbook is sometimes ignored because the pictures themselves are so obviously a pedagogical innovation. But the English column beside the Latin says bluntly that primary school students were no longer being prepared primarily to read theology. Rather, they were now expected to take leadership in a world where business, politics, and social relations are primary and are conducted not in an ancient lingua franca but in a modern language that changes with society.

Second, science was entering the curriculum. Arithmetic had long been there, of course. But now astronomy, physics, chemistry, biology, and advanced mathematics were beginning to put down their feet where the Greek and Latin scientists and their Renaissance followers had suggested that footsteps might go. Furthermore, this new attention to exact science encouraged scholars to work on it—to keep in touch with each other on it. The foundations of the Industrial Revolution, and of the new science of the twentieth century, were being laid in the curricula of the seventeenth and eighteenth centuries.

Third, pedagogy itself was being recognized as a subject worth studying—not by the primary school students but by their teachers and the scholars who taught them.[3]

THE GROWTH OF POSTAL SERVICES

Schools and libraries worked together from the time humans learned to write. What the age of mass media contributed to this relationship was books and journals inexpensive enough to reproduce in large numbers and small enough to hold in one's hand, stack on shelves, or transport easily from place to place. The industrial and electronic centuries discovered how to exchange knowledge not merely in print but also digitally over wires or electronic waves. Thus the name *P.T.T.* (post, telegraph, telephone) is more accurately descriptive than *postal service*.[4]

We have already said something about the message-carrying systems of the ancient world. Message couriers were referred to in Egypt as early as 2000 B.C. China developed an elaborate system of wayside posthouses, where riders could change horses or rest. As a matter of fact the Chinese emperors maintained the system at least from the time of the Chou dynasty (1255–1122 B.C.) almost to the present. When Marco Polo returned from his trip to China in the fourteenth century, he reported just how elaborate the Chinese postal system was at that time: five routes, 16,000 post stations, staffed by 70,000 workers and 14,000 horses! Couriers were reported to cover 200 miles or more a day. Like most other early postal systems, the Chinese system was for official use only; private mail was accepted for the first time only about 1400.

Cyrus's Persian empire also maintained regular messenger routes, with posthouses about every 14 miles along the roads through the empire. The motto which appears on so many post offices today—"Neither snow nor rain, nor gloom of night stays these couriers from the swift completion of their appointed rounds"—

was written with reference to the Persian couriers. The author was the Greek historian Herodotus.

But Rome at the height of its power had probably the most extensive system of postal services, connecting the far corners of the empire to the capital city. The Appian Way was a kind of spinal cord for five trunk lines which were interconnected by smaller roads. Thousands of couriers rode these routes, on horseback or in chariots, keeping Rome in touch with every corner of its empire. This system peaked about the third century and thereafter gradually faded out, as did the empire.

Nothing like the Roman or the Persian postal systems survived those empires, although parts of the Europe and west Asian routes were in use for several centuries, serving the less extensive needs of lesser princes, municipalities, and organizations. It was the growth of commerce in the late Middle Ages, however, that began to restore postal services. In particular the merchants of Italy led this movement. They sent messengers on regular schedules to business centers and annual fairs and even maintained a regular route between Venice and Constantinople. German and other northern European merchants maintained a so-called Butcher Post (Metzger Post) which combined the carrying of commercial correspondence with traveling to buy or sell meat. In addition to these needs of merchants, monasteries found that they had to keep in touch with other monasteries and with the headquarters of their religious orders. When universities began to admit distant students, they found it useful to keep in touch with some of these students in their home countries. These needs encouraged the growth of the first large private message systems.

Some of these systems, such as that of the Paar family in Austria, covered a single country. Notable among the family organizations was the Taxis family who came originally from Italy but succeeded in developing a postal service that at its height used 20,000 couriers and covered most of Europe. The Taxis service lasted for nearly 500 years before it was absorbed by national states.

These national states not only believed in strong central government and tight control; they discovered also that postal services could be profitable, and the states were jealous about sharing the income. When William Dockwra set up a private municipal delivery service in London in 1680—simplifying the collection of charges by requiring that letters be prepaid and stamped—his "Penny Post" was so successful that he was prosecuted for infringing on the government monopoly. The government itself, however, reopened the service within a year or so.

The latter half of the eighteenth century was a period of extensive road building in England, and consequently stagecoaches could take the place of horseback couriers, carry more, and maintain regular schedules over long routes. In 1837 a remarkably prescient report by Rowland Hill, a British educator, advanced some recommendations that changed the shape and nature of postal services for a century. His studies told him that the cost of transit was not an important part of the cost of carrying mail; a rather more expensive part of the process was the cost of figuring charges, based on distance, and collecting them. Therefore, he proposed that users of the post be charged a uniform rate (he suggested one penny per half ounce) and that they pay for it by buying pieces of adhesive paper (called *stamps*) at a post office. Thus he would bring the cost of postage down to an affordable level, speed up the service, and simplify the operation by getting rid of an army of clerks and accountants who had to figure costs and collect from the receiver.

Hill's system was so simple and so relatively cheap that it was adopted not only in London but also in much of the rest of the world. Technological developments fitted neatly into it. Railroads immensely reduced delivery times. Automobiles, like railroads, speeded up delivery schedules and also made it possible to carry mail where no railroad tracks ran. The system was so much easier to operate that, for example, France could introduce variations on it—the postcard (in 1872, following the example of Austria in 1869), and parcels post (in 1881). Instead of using clerks to figure the charges on ordinary mail, it became possible to use the post offices for such ancillary services as money orders (which dated back to 1817), registered letters (1829), and postal savings accounts (1881).

From the early years of the nineteenth century, postal services have speeded up as transportation has. The stagecoach, the railroad, the automobile, all have carried mail faster and, in most cases, farther. Couriers on horseback and stagecoaches could cover about 9 miles an hour, 1500 miles a week. Using railway post offices in scheduled trains, railroads could deliver mail 400 miles away the morning after it was posted. Street corner mailboxes came into use (after a great deal of public opposition), and local post offices and collection and delivery systems were established (the first one in Paris in 1653). Local systems were ready for long-distance service.

Steamships and the opening of canals such as the Suez and the Panama helped the postal services bridge the miles between continents. A number of aerial bridges were tried, including balloons, pigeons, and German Zeppelins. But the real step forward came with air(plane) mail.

After tentative beginnings before World War I, the first scheduled international service (between Paris and London) started in 1919. Airmail was flown across the American continent in 1920, but regular service did not begin until four years later. At first, airmail planes could not fly at night, but that was overcome, and gradually airmail schedules extended from country to country. By mid-century it took one or two days to deliver mail across the Atlantic or the Pacific by air, as compared to a week or more by ship, and a day to span any continent rather than a week or two by train.

Thus, as each new form of transportation came into use it helped to speed up postal services. Yet let us not forget that the post has contributed to transportation also, by paying some of the overhead costs of the new transportation methods in return for their carrying the mail. Postal service was a dominant factor in railroad development for several decades. In our own time, the expansion of the airlines into new routes and new destinations has been made easier, place by place, by a load of mail that did not need the personal services or the meals expected by ticketed passengers.

THE U.S. POSTAL SYSTEM

The United States postal service is less remarkable for any pioneering it has done than for the size of it. It now handles almost half of all the world's mail. This adds up to more than 100 billion pieces of mail per year, and is approaching 500 pieces per year per resident of the country.

The totals themselves are less important than what they say about the use that has been made of what we call the storehouse of knowledge. When Benjamin Franklin in 1775 became the first postmaster general of the United States, the population of the country was not much over 3 million. There was very little settlement west of the Alleghenies. In other words, it was a great empty country which had necessarily to grow as a nation of immigrants. The great majority of the immigrants who streamed into it came from the poorer, less educated parts of their own populations. They had to settle a country where millions of square miles had no schools, no libraries, and, needless to say, no post offices.

Furthermore, Europe stood at that time on the threshold of the Industrial Revolution. A country that hoped to be competitive had to master the skills of industry and scientific agriculture, the understandings of law and politics, and for some of the citizens at least, the insights and theories of the hard sciences. Some of these were already in the storehouse of knowledge, and the supply of new and useful knowledge was constantly building up, but a way had to be found to unlock the storehouse and open the contents to the men and women—and, most important of all, to the children—who were going to build the new country.

These things are not accomplished by miracle. We have already said something about how the nation's libraries were assisted to grow and how the schools were helped to expand. The fact that half of the world's mail is now handled in the United States suggests that wise old Benjamin Franklin gave the country a good start in urging that news and knowledge as well as problems and solutions be exchanged. For a number of decades, the United States Congress was willing to incur an annual debt to make sure that newspapers could circulate at a postage rate they could afford to pay, that library books could be borrowed on loan, and that people who had problems could talk them over and perhaps get answers from other people who were a wilderness away.

This is not to glorify what the United States has done with its storehouses of knowledge and its message systems, and indeed a fuller account would show that it has done many things it should not have done. It is merely to say that given the raw materials of knowledge it is possible now, in this time of mass communication, to share them and use them—even in what may seem in retrospect to be a discouraging situation.

SOME ROADS AHEAD

Following Washington's guidelines to "promote institutions for the diffusion of knowledge," a few predictions are easy. We can expect to see some of the things that used to be printed with ink and a press now printed electronically. Electronic mail is already popular. Exchange of data and correspondence by computer and modem are coming into fashion. Similarly, abstract and summary services that used to be available to us on library catalog cards are now more likely to be on microfilm or microfiche, and soon they will be stored in computer memories with a great deal more detail than would otherwise have been possible. It will probably be a long time before we can print a library as inexpensively by computer as with paper and ink, but bear in mind what the Marquardt Corporation estimated—that all the knowledge arrived at since the beginning of time could be recorded (electronically) into a six-foot cube—and consider whether some of the rarer parts of our professional libraries may not some day be circulated on chip memories to be read when we need them rather than by visiting the British Museum. In today's schools we already have computers, expanded libraries, and self-study materials so that, as Lord Ashby said, "the teacher may teach less and the student may learn more."

In fact that might be a general prediction of how we will find ourselves using the storehouses of knowledge in future years. With better, easier access to knowledge, with better understanding of how self-study may be effectively accomplished, might we not expect that in the future more responsibility might fall upon our own shoulders for unlocking the storehouses of knowledge? More of our student life spent working by ourselves, perhaps with the aid of an open university or the equivalent? More of our study years after college, catching up with knowledge that threatens to outrun us? More of our learning time spent in command of ourselves, with our goals self-chosen, and the great ideas and findings where we need them when we need them? It is at least a challenging prospect.

SUGGESTIONS FOR FURTHER READING

Eisenstein's *The Printing Press as an Agent of Change,* listed with the readings for Chapter 8, is a useful bridge between what you have read on printed media and what you read in this chapter about libraries and postal services. Useful background information will be found in the *Encyclopaedia Britannica* articles "Publishing," "Postal Services," and "Libraries." A good introduction to libraries is by E. D. Johnson and M. H. Harris, *History of Libraries in the Western World,* 3rd ed. (New Jersey: Scarecrow Press, 1976). A similarly useful book on the post office and mail services is C. H. Scheele, *The Postal Services* (Washington, D.C.: Smithsonian Institution Press, 1970). Most books about the "Communication Revolution" or the "New Age of Information" discuss new ways to store and circulate information.

QUESTIONS TO THINK ABOUT

1. What do you know about who uses the library in your home city—age, education, frequency, purpose, etc.? Do you think public libraries today are more or less useful than they were at the beginning of this century, when they helped make up for lack of schooling and shortage of books in the home?
2. What, do you think, has been the effect of paperbacks on libraries?
3. We have already seen electronic mail in use. Do you believe that electronic services will be developed to provide information such as news summaries or materials to meet special reference needs?
4. Can you imagine a university today with only 22 books, the number Cambridge is supposed to have owned at one time around 1400? What do you know about the number of books in your college or university library? Your public library? If you increase the number of books or change the kind of books in either library, what changes might that make in the society served by the library?
5. Obviously developments in transportation have made enormous differences in postal services. What other social changes have significantly affected our posts and telegraphs, for example, the growth of commerce and foreign trade?
6. Has the telephone made for more or less use of postal services?

Franklin D. Roosevelt as he looked while giving a "fireside chat" in the 1930s. Roosevelt was one of the first to see that radio could be a powerful political tool.

INSTITUTIONS OF THE MASS MEDIA: PUBLIC OPINION

The basis of our government being the opinion of the people . . . if it were left to me whether we should have a government without newspapers, or newspapers without a government, I should not hesitate for a moment to prefer the latter.

THOMAS JEFFERSON

I fear three newspapers more than a hundred thousand bayonets.

NAPOLEON BONAPARTE

*T*homas Carlyle attributed to Edmund Burke one of the most famous of all quotations concerning the power of the press, and although no one has been able to show that Burke ever made that statement, it has been quoted again and again for the last century and a half. Carlyle wrote, "Burke said there were three estates in Parliament, but in the reporters' gallery sat a fourth estate more important far than they all." In the earlier years the three estates represented in the British Parliament were considered to be the clergy, nobles and knights, and commoners. Later, in Britain the term was more commonly used to include the royal government, the House of Lords, and the House of Commons. In the United States it is usual to refer to the government in terms of its three branches: executive, legislative, and judicial. Aleksandr Solzhenitsyn was referring to this latter pattern when he penned his barbed comment on the subject: "The Press has become the greatest power within Western countries, more powerful than the legislature, the executive, and the judiciary. One would then like to ask: By what law has it been elected? And to whom is it responsible?"[1]

THE EMERGENCE OF PUBLIC OPINION

The political power of the press is a relatively new phenomenon. It has been aided and abetted by printing, the growth of literacy, and the growing importance of public opinion. The appearance of single-page news sheets on the streets of Europe in the late sixteenth century made an impression on public opinion that can hardly be overestimated. As these sheets turned from trade news to political news and thence to political opinion and comment, the people of northern Europe found themselves in a different position relative to their most common sources of information and to the governments that were the chief sources of both their political knowledge and concerns. Now they were able to look beyond their primary and friendship groups, their coffeehouses and congregations, and consider problems and issues that included but far transcended local problems—that could be as large as the nation or even larger. In other words, the persons who read the news sheets found themselves invited to join with many other people in deciding how they stood on large issues. Although there may have been no such term as *public opinion* in the language as yet, these people in the sixteenth and seventeenth centuries were becoming part of public opinion on important issues and problems.

This was not lost on the brightest observers of politics. The importance of a convergence of political ideas and attitudes had been discussed by Plato and Aristotle 2000 years earlier. Machiavelli advised princes to take careful account of what people were feeling and thinking about government and law. Metternich was much concerned about public opinion. Rousseau, as one might expect, felt that all laws should be based on public opinion. He argued, as did many other leaders of thought in the seventeenth and eighteenth centuries, that "opinion of the people" was perhaps the ordinary person's greatest weapon against ruling authority.

It became apparent, though far from reassuring to those who held authority, that the news sheets and later the press were the chief tool, short of revolution itself, by which to steer and collect opinion. The more people who became involved in politics, the more clearly politicians and scholars saw that it was now necessary to take account of a political force that was neither an organized group (such as a political party, a craft guild, or a labor union) nor an undifferentiated one (such as a population). In a political situation, most people behave as though they were neither completely organized nor completely unorganized. They look around them to see how others are behaving—to learn what their friends, the people they especially respect, and even the majority of their fellow citizens think of the issues on which a decision is required. Thus, public opinion does not necessarily lead citizens to belong to something, but rather is something citizens use to lead them toward supportable positions and to support them when they have made their decisions.

What communication did in the late Renaissance was to bring public opinion, from farther away than previously, to bear upon an issue, a problem, or a political relationship. Public opinion in London had been little more than talk in a coffeehouse. When the news sheets began to appear for sale in the streets they expanded public opinion to other parts of the city, other parts of the country, other parts of Europe. A citywide or a nationwide sense of agreement became possible. What the French or the Germans, the Dutch or the Belgians were thinking about a problem was no longer a mystery, and therefore an international conception of public opinion became possible. As the more formal media replaced the news sheets, these media services began to report on what leaders were saying and on events (demonstrations, protests, strikes, jailings, and the like) from which public opinion could be deduced, and readers could decide whether to go along with it or not.

In the 1930s public opinion was so well recognized that people began to accept measurements of it in percentages of large totals. Once a year, once a month, or even once a week in election times newspapers carried the latest polls. Once a week or once a month people read what their fellow citizens were thinking and saying about issues or leaders, and even how they planned to vote on a candidate or a proposal. George Gallup was perhaps the first name widely connected with such information (he emerged from the University of Iowa in 1930 carrying his doctoral dissertation and already making polls), but there soon were others—Elmo Roper is an example—who made polls for the guidance of the general public; and others, more private pollsters, who surveyed opinions to guide policymakers and candidates. Thus public opinion emerged from the shadows; it was formalized and regularized, and recognized as something people wanted to know about.

THE EFFECT OF THE MEDIA ON PUBLIC OPINION

Walter Lippmann begins his classic book on public opinion with this story:

> There is an island in the ocean where in 1914 a few Englishmen, Frenchmen, and Germans lived. No cable reaches that island, and the British mail steamer comes but once in sixty days. In September it had not yet come and the islanders were still talking about the latest newspaper which told about the approaching trial of Madame Caillaux for the shooting of Gaston Calmette. It was, therefore, with more than usual eagerness that the whole colony assembled on the quay on a day in mid-September to hear from the captain what the verdict had been. They learned that for over six weeks now those of them who were French had been fighting in behalf of the sanctity of treaties against those of them who were Germans. For six strange weeks they had acted as if they were friends when in fact they were enemies.[2]

This poignant anecdote illustrates some characteristics of communication, public opinion, and politics that could hardly be conveyed in shorter space. For one thing, opinion relationships exist at all levels—from the community (even, perhaps, the family group) to national and global groups—and these different levels are not always in complete agreement. Just as the international politics of Europe interfered with the somewhat different opinions of an Atlantic island community, so the national backgrounds of husbands and wives sometimes interfered with the happiness of family life in those same years. And in many other years and other situations, public opinion gathered around relationships. The Germans on the island gathered together, defensively aware of the critical glances of some of their neighbors, and the French and English gathered together proudly pretending not to notice whether the Germans seemed to be feeling superior as their tanks rolled over France. The extraordinary thing about the whole scene is that no one on the island was experiencing the changed world conditions directly; everything they knew about what was happening in Europe came from long-distance communication—a newspaper, a small boat, a very late letter. That first night on the island must have been a strange one for the erstwhile friends, who asked themselves and sometimes their close companions, What is true? What is real? This friendly life we live here, or the deadly enmity into which the news has thrown us?

As distant relationships have become more important in our lives, so have the news media grown in power to shape those relationships. Of course, the watcher on the hill, new type or old type, has always had that kind of power. But the responsibility of present-day watchers, such as the media, is incomparably broader. What is really happening in Congress? In Cambodia? In El Salvador? In Afghanistan? In research laboratories? In the FBI? In the White House? In Soviet diplomatic planning? On the moons of Jupiter? The new watchers' tasks are to the ancient watchers' as 10^{10} is to 1.

The meaning of what we have been saying is what Lippmann calls the question of how "the pictures in our heads" get there, or what some other scholars call the organization of public opinion around a political issue or person. The point is that public opinion is now more likely to be determined through media of some kind than by personal experience. It is through such communication not only that we build up our pictures of environment, but also that we decide what in that environment is worth our attention.[3] It hardly needs saying that every element of life that comes to our attention becomes a part of our environment, no matter how we evaluate it. This is what a politician means when he or she tells a reporter, "Be sure to mention my name, whatever you call me. Just say who I am." Our working environment consists of all the people and things and ideas that stand out from the dark fog of things and people that *don't* come to our attention. Most of the elements that are politically or economically important to us now come through the media.

And it is through the media that we learn what corners of that dark fog we should peer into. What problems in Africa should concern us? Who are the important leaders in Japan? Who are the respected citizens of our community? Who are the candidates that might make good senators? Who were the promising candidates out of that large band of possible candidates for the Democratic presidential nomination in 1984—that amazing list: a former vice-president, our first astronaut, a group of senators, a black who is displaying real leadership qualities, and so on? How should we evaluate what Khomeini says? Or Gorbachev? Or one of our own leaders?

There has been an interesting line of political research in the last ten years on what Max McCombs and his colleagues call agenda-setting, meaning that the media are able to set topics of discussion and to some extent guide the direction of the discussion.[4] The individuals and events emphasized in the news are also likely to be emphasized in later talk. The situations depicted as threatening or promising are likely to be further considered. The individuals depicted as important are likely to enter into later thought or talk with the tag *important* on them. And so forth. ("Be sure to mention my name.") If the media associates a certain characteristic or bit of history with a person, that tag also is likely to remain with the individual. Thus one of the great powers of mass communication today is to have some control over what sights our windows will be opened to, what to recall in connection with a public figure or an event, what paths toward the future are worth looking down.

Therefore, what we are asking the mass media to do is to sit on the hill and look down the valley for us—just as we did with the watchers 15,000 years ago. We are asking them to look where we do not have the time or opportunity to see, to be alert *for us,* to learn more about our environment than we possibly could, to give us the little hints and suggestions that will help us make decisions more confidently. What a power we are delegating to the media!

THE PERSUADERS THAT HELP SHAPE PUBLIC OPINION

So far we have been talking about public opinion as though it were a tide washing up on the beach around us, leaving a perception of its dampness, its salt, and its coolness on us. But we know it isn't quite that simple; the content of mass media is not nature-made. Certain people have something to do with the perceptions that the mass media contribute to public opinion.

The title of a recent book, *The Selling of the President,* suggests what we are talking about.[5] That book is not primarily about advertising, but it suggests the advertising function of the media. Zechariah Chafee said that a newspaper is like a combination, in one organization, of a college and a large private business, the one devoted to educating the public, the other to making money for a few owners. And there is nothing essentially wrong, in our system, with that combination. For newspapers and broadcasters must be economically strong so that they can remain independent of government and report on it.

Mass media have achieved uncommon skill in selling. This became obvious a long time ago to the persons who were in charge of political campaigns as well as those in economic campaigns. The active, purposeful use of mass media in campaigns has become a hallmark of politics in the United States and other countries where the result of an election depends on the expression of public opinion through voting.

Almost every candidacy for a state, national, or large-city office now begins with the appointment of a campaign manager or information director who is usually a professional in public relations or political persuasion. Very early in the preparation of a campaign, public opinion is measured. An estimate is made of the issues likely to be most appealing to the voters, of what the voters know of the issues and the candidates, and of the groups and kinds of voters likely to be most or least favorable toward the candidate whose campaign it is. Then decisions can be made that are surprisingly like those of an advertising manager. What issues are most likely to produce votes and therefore should be emphasized? What aspects of the candidate should be held up before the public—what parts of his or her life-style or life history, what profiles or camera angles, what personality traits are most winning? Does the candidate need help with public speaking? As a matter of fact, should speaking or debating be allowed to enter into the campaigning at all? It is general opinion that ten minutes in an informal debate on television were largely responsible for the result of a mayoralty contest in a large capital city, in 1984, where the subject of the debate had very little to do with reasons for choosing one candidate or the other. An advertising manager would recognize what we are talking about: It is as necessary to "package" the candidate as to package other goods for sale. And therefore the most expensive segments of a television program are almost invariably the commercials—they are the most carefully researched, the most carefully put together, the most often rehearsed.

Nor are the mass media the only channels through which a candidate or an issue can be "sold." Direct mail, among other things, has now assumed considerable importance in political campaigns. The chairman of the Republican party's Senatorial Election Committee said recently that with the money and talent the party has now, it can achieve 90 percent visibility for almost anyone within a few months. In other words, a candidate who is all but unknown could become a well-known name and personality, in a few months, through the skillful use of mass media and direct-mail selling alone. The staff of a direct-mail operating center in the Washington area have claimed that they can get their mailing list to write a million letters to congresspeople, agencies, or media simply by sending out a "need now" letter for one of the right-wing causes that this organization typically espouses. During campaigns, therefore, voters are bombarded with skillfully planned and designed messages, by media and by mail, which add up to very large costs. In one of the smallest states (Hawaii), about $4 million was spent in 1982 on the gubernatorial election alone. Most of that money went for television and direct mail.

Yet some of the most effective results come less from money than from skill. In early 1985 President Reagan tossed the coin for the beginning of the Super Bowl, a ritual usually performed by the captains and the umpire, who were on the football field in Palo Alto, California, and could have tossed the coin as usual. Fans in the stadium and tens of millions of viewers watched the coin tossing, which was televised from the White House. The president even pointed out, in a graceful little speech, that he too had once played football and wanted to send especially good wishes to the players in the championship game. It was a nice touch. The fans liked it. The players liked it. And only a few people wondered, doubtless, whether the president's public relations staff had not decided that this would be an inexpensive and effective way to get their candidate some exposure before one of the year's largest audiences.

The transfer of the extraordinary skills and experience of advertising to the selling of candidates and issues is therefore one of the more obvious results of modern media politics. Another is the substitution of communication for campaign travel. The use of political communication to substitute for travel between places where a candidate needs to electioneer or otherwise show himself can perhaps be dated back to the Roosevelt "fireside chats" of the 1930s and early 1940s, or even to his radio talks as governor of New York in the 1920s. President Reagan's weekly radio talks are doubtless a lesson learned from those early precedents. John F. Kennedy had learned it, too. He made little use of campaign travel, limiting his efforts mostly to television, which showed him at his best, and to key speeches which, in most cases, drew television coverage also. Since his time, no presidential candidate has put much dependence on campaigning in the old style.

According to Dennis McQuail,

> Control over the mass media offers several important possibilities. First, the media can attract and direct attention to problems, solutions, or people in ways which can favour those with power and correlatively divert attention from rival individuals or groups. Second, the mass media can confer status and confirm legitimacy. Third, in some circumstances, the media can be a channel for persuasion and mobilization. Fourth, the media can help to bring certain kinds of public opinion into being and maintain them. Fifth, the media are a vehicle for offering psychic rewards and gratifications. They can divert and

Shot from a televised Kennedy–Nixon debate, 1960.

amuse and they can flatter. In general, mass media are very cost-effective as a means of communication in society; they are also fast, flexible, and relatively easy to plan and control. If we accept Etzioni's (1967) view that "to some degree power and communication may be substituted for each other," then mass communication is particularly well suited to the "stretching" of power in a society.[6]

As powerfully as the media can advance the cause of a candidate, they demand in return some power over the candidate. For one thing, they demand money. McQuail pronounces them "very cost-effective," and yet they raise the entire level of expectation in campaign costs. Certainly campaigning through the media is less expensive and immensely quicker than campaigning face-to-face with audiences of comparable size, but it is nevertheless far from inexpensive. In 1984 an impressive group of candidates ran toward the wire seeking the Democratic presidential nomination, but one by one they dropped out of the race—not because they had no stomach for competition but because those who had the least success in early rounds were no longer able to raise money from their friends and supporters to pay the mounting bills.

This phenomenon has little to do with news coverage; the media, without payment, will cover the most noteworthy speeches or other such campaign events. But there are relatively few of these. In order to exercise any considerable control over what themes and faces come into the campaign at what times, and how they are presented to the people, the candidates must put a large part of their resources into commercials of 30 seconds to one minute in length. In other words, as modern election campaigns have developed, the selling of the candidate is just as necessary as the selling of the president was, and many of the same techniques must be used as those used to sell food and household goods. This adds up to a fantastic total cost. We said earlier in this chapter that one of the smallest states in the Union recently spent $4 million on a gubernatorial primary alone. The combined cost of presidential primaries and the final election in 1984 may well exceed $100 million. If candidates and their supporters cannot raise a reasonable fraction of such costs, then they may as well give up the race. The media, then, have this rather alarming control over politics: They can bar from serious candidacy any person who cannot enter at the required monetary level, which is usually very high.

It is not simply a matter of money, of course. In addition to experience, demonstrated ability, and ideas sufficient to attract support, the candidate must make an attractive and impressive appearance on television. His or her campaign manager, communication director, makeup person, and speech writer will try to make sure that the candidate does. But in a modern campaign, voters will see a candidate much more frequently, more closely, and in greater detail on television than they could possibly see him or her face-to-face. If the candidate does not meet the requirements for a television appearance, money will not help much. In some ways it is ironic that election to high political office is coming to make many of the same demands of an individual as television entertainment makes. But it is a trade-off: Against the advantage of being presented in "living color" and real voice to more prospective voters than any candidate could possibly have reached at any time before 1950, the candidate must accept some of the mores of television that are not usually the concern of a political candidate.

William L. Rivers writes this of one president who has been able to meet the requirements of political television:

> Ronald Reagan walked onto the public stage with the security of a man who has been standing the boards successfully for more than 40 years. If his cue card of statistics, one-liners, and gibes are dog-eared and often simplistic and irrelevant, his voice, his timing, and his style have been honed over the years into a forceful instrument. Regardless of what Reagan is saying, he projects an easy confidence and determination and an appropriate modest certainty that he has a handle on the public good. That Ronald Reagan is a consummate public performer—and the first *professional* performer to attain the White House—is an unmistakable indication that the news media and television in particular have become the most powerful force in American politics.[7]

Total Costs and Broadcast Advertising Costs for General Elections in the United States, 1952–1972

	1952	1956	1960	1964	1968	1972
Total cost of election ($ million)	140	155	175	200	300	425
Total spent for broadcast advertising (percent)	4	6	8	13	13	9

SOURCE: Adapted from Sterling, *Electronic Media* (New York: Praeger, 1984), p. 166. Sterling's sources included Herbert Alexander, *Financing the 1968 Election* (Lexington, Mass.: Lexington Books, 1972), and *Financing the 1972 . . . 1976 . . . 1980 Election* (same publisher, same format, 1976, 1980, 1983). Also Federal Communication Commission, *Annual Report* (Washington, D.C.: FCC, 1973), p. 207.

Presidential Campaign Expenditures on Media, 1968–1980

Year and Candidate	Total Expenditures ($ million)	Percent on Media
1968		
Nixon	24.9	49.4
Humphrey	10.3	61.2
1972		
Nixon	61.4	13.4
McGovern	21.2	34.0
1976		
Ford	23.1	50.2
Carter	23.4	41.5
1980		
Reagan	34.0	52.3

SOURCE: Adapted from Sterling, *Electronic Media* (New York: Praeger, 1984), p. 167. Data supplied by Herbert Alexander, and national political committees.

Political scientists and historians have sometimes wondered whether Abraham Lincoln could have been elected to the presidency if there had been television in his time.

THE ADVERSARY RELATIONSHIP IN POLITICS AND PUBLIC OPINION

We began this chapter with a quotation from Thomas Jefferson which is one of the most often quoted statements about newspapers: If he had to choose between a government without newspapers, or newspapers without a government, he would not hesitate to prefer the latter. Jefferson wrote that in a letter to Edward Carrington in 1787. Twenty years later he wrote a letter to James Madison on the same subject. By that time Jefferson had been president and had experienced the kinds of contact that a chief executive has with his country's newspapers. And he wrote: "I shall never take another newspaper of any sort!"

That was not a momentary bit of irritation. He said it over and over again. In 1807 he wrote James Norvell, "Nothing can now be believed which is seen in a newspaper." In 1813 he wrote to Thomas Wortman, "At present it is disreputable to state a fact on newspaper authority; and the newspapers of our country by their abandoned spirit of falsehood, have more effectively destroyed the utility of the press than all the shackles devised by Bonaparte." And in another letter, "I do not take a single newspaper, nor read one a month, and I feel infinitely the happier for it."

Why the change? What happened in the dealings between a president and the chief channels of his country's public opinion to change his mind so completely?

Between press and president in a country such as the United States there is a built-in adversary relationship. The same thing exists between the press and other persons who move into important executive positions, but it is more extreme in the case of the American president because it is so much more easily visible. Not that some papers are not more favorable than others to the chief executive—of course, that is the case. But even editors who strongly supported the chief executive when he was only a candidate send to his office, after his inauguration, reporters who have been taught that one of the chief functions of the press is to *check on* government. These reporters represent their readers as well as their editors. If all is not well, it is their job to find it out and make it known.

As for the president, he too comes to his office the day after inauguration with certain additional burdens on his shoulders. Lippmann stated some of them bluntly: "Every official is to some degree a censor," he wrote. "Every leader is to some extent a propagandist."[8]

That is to say, every chief executive wants to control, as much as he legally and ethically can, what appears about his government. He wants the unfavorable things played down, the favorable ones emphasized. Above all he wants what he considers a fair report of his government and its stewardship to go out to the public whose opinion is essential to him.

It is not easy to exert this kind of control. Too many people have information and are willing to talk on the negative side of events. Too many reporters have become skillful at penetrating the information curtain and looking behind the flood of news releases and public appearances that come from every government. All too seldom does a reporter get to see the top man, and all too often are the underlings not permitted to talk about what they have not been told to talk about.

Here is an example. It is an imaginary transcript written by Ron Nessen, who was President Ford's press secretary, of the kind of press conference he sometimes had to conduct. This particular conference never occurred, of course, but some newspeople said it was "realer than real." Imagine a late evening in Beijing, China, when the president was meeting with Chinese leaders to talk about relations between the two countries. A roomful of reporters was impatient to get a lead for tomorrow's story. The president was in the meeting, and there was nobody to quiz except Nessen. And poor Nessen had been carefully instructed what news he could give out. Here, says Nessen, is how the conference might have gone:

> **QUESTION:** President Ford and the Chinese have been meeting for several hours. Have they made any progress toward further normalization or improvement of relations between the United States and the People's Republic of China?
>
> **NESSEN:** You can quote me as saying that the talks are continuing in a business-like and sincere atmosphere.
>
> **QUESTION:** Well, the Shanghai communiqué was going to be the subject of one of his latest talks. We know there are real obstacles as far as Taiwan is concerned. Are they going to issue something that will be part of the Shanghai communiqué, that will give a further understanding of the relationship between the People's Republic of China and the United States?
>
> **NESSEN:** I can't at this time tell you whether there will be a communiqué at the conclusion of these talks or not. In the past I have not said that there will be, or that there won't be. I don't want you to take this statement today to mean that there has been a decision one way or the other. I just don't know.
>
> **QUESTION:** As you do know, Ron, there are a number of people writing that the talks have failed, and there is a kind of showcase thing to bail out a couple of leaders of two countries who were rather shaky, and it seems to me that you are confirming it. Are you saying that the talks have failed?
>
> **NESSEN:** I'm saying that the talks are continuing in a businesslike and sincere manner. If you want a little more, I can tell you that this afternoon's meeting was for three hours and nineteen minutes. The two sides have met in the Great Hall of the People. The table was about twenty feet long and black lacquer. The representatives sat on one side. It was fairly warm in the room, and they took off their suit jackets and met in their shirt sleeves. Bottles were on the table.
>
> **QUESTION:** Now we are out here—we have come a long way. We are kind of captives here in this hotel. We are getting less from you than we are getting from the officials of the other groups—from the officials of China.
>
> **NESSEN:** All I can say is that the talks are continuing in a sincere manner.[9]

Obviously, the press secretary's instruction had been to tell the reporters that the talks were continuing "in a businesslike and sincere manner," until there was some news both countries were ready to announce. That did not please the newspeople very much, but it was part of the minuet that the executive office and the press must dance when the situation calls for it.

Frustration like this challenges the press corps, or some of it, to engage in investigative reporting. The Beijing incident was not the place for that, for a number of reasons. An investigative reporter, said Leonard Sellers, is one who "goes after information that is deliberately hidden because it involves a legal or ethical wrong." That was not the situation in Beijing. A better example is the star accomplishment of investigative reporting in recent years—the Woodward and Bernstein investigation of Watergate for the *Washington Post*.

Some aspects of that story are worth mentioning again here. For one thing, the investigative reporting was conducted not by the *Post*'s older and long-experienced political reporters, but by two young, little-known newsmen. Why? For one thing, they had everything to gain by breaking this story and few obligations to take them away from it. Again, they were relatively little known in Washington and had not obligated themselves to friends in the government. "If Ben Bradlee [the *Post*'s managing editor] had assigned this story to someone who called Haldeman by his first name, he wouldn't have gotten to first base," a fellow newsman said. In other words, there are obligations between important newspeople and important government officials, just as there are between other friends or cooperators. Woodward and Bernstein had to work from the outside, not the inside; find "little" people who knew important details, and put those details together; find people who could and would talk. They had to be willing to read and interpret tiny details rather than taking the big story from high spokespersons. Investigative reporting requires a reporter to work *around* the people who are supposed to deal with journalists. "For the press, progress is not news—trouble is news," Richard Nixon was quoted as saying. He might have added that for public officials news is more often about trouble than about progress. Any president wants his administration's progress, not its troubles, reported. But two bright and determined young newsmen were looking for evidence of troubles, and they brought down the president. *All the President's Men* tells the story.[10]

By no means were all the tensions in the Watergate investigation focused on Woodward and Bernstein. The *Post* and its chief editors were under great pressure, not only from the Nixon administration, but also from friends and political and economic allies. Some of the *Post*'s own top reporters found the situation embarrassing to them, and the government tried to make it so. Many government people who had to deal with reporters but were not in on the big story also found the situation difficult. It took a great deal of courage on the part of Bradlee and the owners of the *Post* to continue the investigation. Woodward and Bernstein themselves sometime wondered whether they were on a false trail.

"One of the chief dangers of most political reporting is that *too many* sources want to provide *too much* information that will serve their own interests," said William Rivers. "In contrast, the investigative reporter tends to walk into a lot of brick walls."[11]

So the relationship between press and political power is not an easy one, whether an investigative reporter is or is not involved. When Ronald Reagan was elected governor of California, his predecessor in that office, Edmund G. "Pat" Brown, wrote him a good-humored note that contained the following advice:

> There's a passage in *War and Peace* that every new Governor with a big majority should tack on his office wall. In it, young Count Rostov, after weeks as the toast of elegant farewell parties, gallops off on his first cavalry charge and finds real bullets snapping at his ears.
>
> "Why they're shooting at me," he says. "Me, whom everybody loves."
>
> Nothing worse will happen to you in the next four years. Learn to live with that; the rest is easy.
>
> . . . You will find that while both surgeons and reporters operate with professional detachment, there is one real difference between them. Surgeons make more money for cutting you up.
>
> But their motives are the same—to make sure everything is running properly. And in the case of the press they operate with a proxy from the voters.[12]

SUGGESTIONS FOR FURTHER READING

One of the classics of public opinion and communication study is Walter Lippmann, *Public Opinion* (New York: Harcourt Brace Jovanovich, 1922). On reporting political news, see John Hohenberg, *Foreign Correspondence: The Great Reporters and Their Times* (New York: Columbia University Press 1967); also Merriman Smith, *A White House Memoir* (New York: Norton, 1972); and S. Hess, *The Washington Reporters* (Washington, D.C.: Brookings Institution, 1981). More general books on the political press include William L. Rivers, *The Adversaries* (Boston: Beacon Press, 1970); Douglas Cater, *The Fourth Branch of Government* (Boston: Houghton Mifflin, 1959); J. D. Barber, *Race for the Presidency: The Media and the Nominating Process* (Englewood Cliffs, N.J.: Prentice-Hall, 1978). Also, Bernard C. Cohen, *The Press and Foreign Policy* (Princeton, N.J.: Princeton University Press, 1963). An appropriate chapter from *Voting: A Study of Opinion Formation in a Presidential Campaign,* by Bernard R. Berelson, Paul F. Lazarsfeld, and William McPhee (Chicago: University of Chicago Press, 1954) is "Political Processes: The Role of the Mass Media." See also Dan Nimmo, *The Political Persuaders* (Englewood Cliffs, N.J.: Prentice-Hall, 1970). On propaganda, see J. Ellul, *Propaganda* (New York: Knopf, 1965), and another volume that grew out of experience with World War II exchanges, Leonard Doob, *Propaganda and Public Opinion,* rev. ed. (New York: Holt, Rinehart and Winston, 1961). An old classic, still useful, is V. O. Key, *Public Opinion and American Democracy* (New York: Knopf, 1961), and a very good new volume is Gladys and Kurt Lang, *The Battle for Public Opinion: The President, the Press, and the Public During Watergate* (New York: Columbia University Press, 1983). Many of the same events are covered in Joseph C. Spear, *Presidents and the Press:*

The Nixon Legacy (Cambridge, Mass.: M.I.T. Press, 1984). Finally, a book that is useful in many aspects of the study of news: Daniel Boorstin, *The Image—A Guide to Pseudo-Events in America* (New York: Harper & Row, 1961).

QUESTIONS TO THINK ABOUT

1. What and how much do you think you learn, during a political campaign, (a) by talking to people about a candidate, (b) talking to the candidate, (c) reading about the candidate, (d) seeing the candidate on TV?
2. Do you feel that the media, during a campaign, are being used to bring you the "straight story" or to sway your opinion and vote?
3. What do you think about preelection debates?
4. What is your opinion of the so-called adversary relationship between press and government?
5. You have doubtless heard President Reagan in his short weekend radio addresses and some of his longer addresses on television. What are the qualities that make him so effective as a political broadcaster? If you have ever heard Franklin D. Roosevelt in one of his "fireside chats," compare Mr. Roosevelt and Mr. Reagan as political broadcasters.

The Health Jolting Chair
COPYRIGHT.

The most important Health Mechanism ever produced

A Practical Household Substitute for the Saddle-Horse.

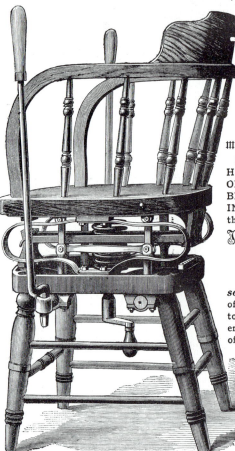

It affords a PERFECT means of giving EFFICIENT exercise to the ESSENTIALLY IMPORTANT NUTRITIVE ORGANS OF THE BODY in the most DIRECT, CONVENIENT, COMFORTABLE, and INEXPENSIVE manner.

Suitable for all ages and for most physical conditions.

INDISPENSABLE TO THE HEALTH AND HAPPINESS OF MILLIONS OF HUMAN BEINGS WHO MAY BE LIVING SEDENTARY LIVES through choice or necessity.

It preserves Health, cures Disease, and prolongs Life.

An *ingenious, rational, scientific, mechanical* means of overcoming those impediments to the taking of proper exercise, erected by the artificial methods of modern society.

For certain classes of invalids a veritable Treasure-Trove.

A CONSERVATOR of NERVOUS ENERGY.

No dwelling-house is completely furnished without The Health Jolting Chair.

USES OF THE HEALTH JOLTING CHAIR.

1st. It strengthens the action of the *heart*, and increases the force of the whole circulation.

2d. It increases the depth and frequency of the *respiratory* movements, promoting oxygenation.

3d. It affords a method of giving local exercise to those great and essentially important internal nutritive organs of the body, the *stomach, intestines, liver, kidneys,* etc. A nutritive stimulant.

4th. It strengthens the muscles of the whole of the trunk and neck ; and also especially develops those of the arms, shoulders, and chest, with a minimum strain on the heart and other muscles.

5th. It improves the *general nutrition* of the body in a remarkable manner, and is thus an invaluable PREVENTIVE OF DISEASE. Disease germs do not affect healthy tissues.

An advertisement that appeared in Harper's Weekly *in 1885.*

INSTITUTIONS OF THE MASS MEDIA: ADVERTISING AND PUBLIC RELATIONS

You can tell the ideals of a nation by its advertisements.

NORMAN DOUGLAS, SOUTHWIND

Advertising made me!

PHINEAS T. BARNUM

Never has anyone ruled on this earth by basing his rule on anything other than the rule of public opinion.

ORTEGA Y GASSETT

One day, several decades ago, when I was in a village of southern France I heard someone beating a drum. Beating is not a sufficient word: Someone was pounding the very stuffing out of that drum. People began to stream out of doors and down the street, all hurrying toward the commanding sound. I joined the procession. Around a corner, in a sort of public square, we came to the source of those sounds. A tall young man was responsible.

When he had a crowd around him he began to speak, in a wonderfully resonant far-carrying voice. And only then did I realize that I was seeing a town crier, a genuine member of a species that I had thought was no longer extant in a country like France. He had apparently ridden into town on a bicycle, the drum strapped behind him. I listened with care to his message. He had four items. Something was being done about taxes. Mendes-France had a message for the people. The mayor of a neighboring town was dead. And a farmer had a bull for sale.

I thought there was something oddly familiar about the form of the town crier's message, but it took a moment to realize what it was. Then it hit me: commercial radio! Short news items and advertising.

THE BEGINNINGS OF ADVERTISING

How old *is* this kind of communication? To put it less kindly, how long have people been beating the drum to attract attention and sell something? Written advertising is apparently almost as old as writing. Fryburger notes that an archaeologist, digging in ancient Thebes, found a written advertisement perhaps 3000 years old that offered "a whole gold coin" for the return of a runaway slave named Shem.[1] There were graffiti on the walls of Pompeii calling attention to items for sale. But it was too difficult to make multiple copies of commercial messages before printing, so whatever advertisements existed were mostly oral, or single-copy signs, until printing presses became widely available at the end of the fifteenth century. Then it was a wholly new day. Handbills could be printed. Signs could be printed and fastened up where people would see them. The newspaper passed through the stage of news sheet and news book to one-page weekly, and publishers found, then as now, that the sale of advertising would help pay the cost. Ads gained entrance even into the small weeklies. Fryburger records that the first advertisement in English weeklies for coffee is believed to have appeared in 1652, the first one for chocolate in 1657, and the first for tea in 1658.[2] As newspapers grew larger and more costly, and as the economy became more aggressive, the amount of advertising greatly increased. What Dr. Johnson wrote in *The Idler* just 100 years after the first English ad for tea has a highly modern sound: "Advertisements are now so numerous that they are very negligently perused, and it is therefore become necessary to gain attention by magnificence of promise and by eloquence sometimes sublime and sometimes pathetick."[3]

Neither the "sublime" nor the "pathetick" voices of advertising, however, were heard in full volume for another hundred years after that sour comment by Johnson. Meanwhile, when *The Times* of London was founded in 1788, its editor expressed a principle concerning the acceptance of advertising that was widely followed: "A News-Paper . . . ought to resemble an Inn, where the proprieter is obliged to give the use of his house to all travellers who are ready to pay for it and against whose person there is no legal or moral objection."[4] In the nineteenth century when much of the energy of society was turned to the manufacture of goods, merchants had to turn a corresponding amount of energy to the *sale* of

The notice believed to be the oldest printed advertisement in English. Printed by Caxton in 1477, it reads (in slightly modernized English): "If it please any man spiritual or temporal to buy any piece of two or three commemorations of Salisbury we printed after the form of this perfect letter which is well and truly correct, let him come to Westminster into the almonsry at the red pale and he shall have them good cheap." The handwritten note following the print merely translates the Latin phrase at the end of the advertisement.

goods. Two printed media, the daily press and the magazine, needed extra support at that time to keep subscription rates low. This was true in particular of the penny press, which staked its future on reaching a mass circulation and therefore looked toward a circularity of effects: high income from advertising to make possible low subscription rates to attract large audiences of readers which in turn would attract large amounts of advertising. For most penny papers in large cities the formula worked; almost all of them later had to raise their subscription rates to two cents, and later considerably more, but they did attract mass audiences and their advertising soon began to meet half or more of their operating costs.

Thus they paved the way for two newer media that, in free economies, had to meet most or all of their expenses from advertising. These were radio and television. They commandeered far more time than the print media, and their advertisers had to take a somewhat different approach to programming than did the advertisers in newspapers and magazines. The latter could concentrate on filling the space they bought and leave the news content entirely to the news staff. Radio and television advertisers, on the other hand, still had to make their advertising a kind of programming, an entertaining kind of broadcast that would fit smoothly into the other entertainment within the medium; and the nonadvertising entertainment beside which the advertising appeared was of the greatest concern to the advertiser because the more viewers who were attracted by this entertainment the more who would be likely to stay tuned for the commercials. This set the stage for the mercurial growth of advertising agencies.

ADVERTISING AGENCIES

The first advertising agency is thought to have been Reynell and Son, founded in London in 1812. The earliest agencies, such as Reynell and the first American agencies, chiefly sold space for newspapers and magazines. Manufacturers and retailers would go to an agency to buy space, and the agency then collected a percentage from the newspaper or magazine. But the real turning point in the growth of agencies was when they became agents of the buyer rather than the seller of advertising space or time.

N. W. Ayer & Son, which started in 1875 in Philadelphia, was set up chiefly to serve the buyers. Ayer published lists of rates actually charged by the media, and this helped not only in choosing media but also in designating the size of ads for the chosen medium. The next major step was to expand the services to the advertiser. In the late nineteenth and early twentieth centuries the emphasis was on the creation of skillful advertising copy. After copy services came art services, advertising production, and the selection of media. By 1920 most agencies could plan complete campaigns for their clients, including research and budgeting, and could also execute these campaigns by preparing the advertisements and arranging for their insertion in the various media, which soon came to include outdoor advertising and direct mail.[5]

This kind of service was so valuable to the buyers of advertising that agencies proliferated. There are now more than 4000 such agencies in the United States alone. England has about 500, other countries somewhat fewer. Only one agency outside the United States is listed currently as handling more than $100 million of business per year; that is in Japan. In the United States more than 30 agencies handle at least this amount.

As a matter of fact, somewhere in the neighborhood of 50 percent of all the advertising in the world is estimated to be placed and carried in the United States. *Advertising Age* estimated the total of U.S. advertising in 1980 to be about $55 billion. Of this amount, $15 billion (28 percent) went to newspapers, $11 billion (nearly 21 percent) to television, $7.5 billion to direct mail, nearly $4 billion to radio, and more than $3 billion to magazines. Thus the United States has been spending between $200 and $300 per capita for advertising.[6] Switzerland, West Germany, Sweden, and Japan are believed to be next in order. By way of contrast, the last report of the International Advertising Association in 1968 showed India spending only 16 cents per capita per year for advertising, Pakistan 14, and Nepal 5. These figures are doubtless somewhat higher now, but an enormous gap still exists between advertising in the richer and the poor countries.

Fryburger gives a very broad definition of advertising, which, he says, is "a form of communication intended to promote the sale of a product or service, to

Advertising Expenditures by Regions of the World

Region	Total 1982 Advertising Expenditures (in millions of U.S. $)	Per Capita Expenditures in Reporting Countries (in U.S. $)	Percent of World's Expenditures Made in Each Region
U.S. and Canada	70,249.9	272.82	56
Europe	29,089.9	72.77	23
Asia	13,009.0	9.28	10
Latin America	7,753.9	21.53	6
Australia and New Zealand	2,585.4	142.84	2
Middle East and Africa	2,246.4	6.72	2
Total world (84 countries)	124,934.5	45.09	100

SOURCE: Adapted from S. W. Dunn and A. M. Barban, *Advertising: Its Role in Modern Marketing,* 6th ed. (New York: Dryden Press, 1986); based on *World Advertising Expenditures,* 18th ed. (New York: Starch INRA Hooper, 1984). Reprinted by permission of original publisher and Dr. Dunn.

influence public opinion, to gain political support, to advance a particular cause, or to elicit some other response desired by the advertiser."[7] This seems to include some of the goals that most people would ascribe to public relations. (PR), so let us turn our attention for the moment to public relations.

PUBLIC RELATIONS: THE PERSUADER WITH A DIFFERENCE

Neither public relations people nor advertising professionals would argue with Fryburger's definition. Yet each group would emphasize a different part of it. The advertising people would say that their essential task is to sell goods; the public relations people, that their essential task is to create images. It is not that persons in advertising are not concerned with the images of their products held by the buying public, or that those in PR are unwilling to lend their skills to the sales program of a particular manufacturer or seller. But they emphasize different parts of the communication task.

Public relations has been accepted as a responsibility of elected and appointed officials and candidates, businesspeople, professionals, and activists of all sorts, as far back as history tells us anything about them. Shopkeepers, workers for hire, members of councils and parliaments, lawyers, physicians, bankers, and teachers all have been deeply concerned about what people think of them and their services. Political parties, religious organizations, and community organizations all have known it was essential to them to have a good image. Until about a century ago, however, public relations was considered one with the other duties of all persons who dealt with the public. Retailers, for example, felt it was part of their responsibility to maintain a shop that people wanted to come to, clerks they wanted to deal with, goods they could buy and be happy to have. It was the responsibility of owner or manager or both to make that happen. There was no thought, a century ago, of turning this responsibility over to a specialist in public relations. At that time, of course, there was less need to do so.

The first formal public relations department was established in 1889 as a part of the newly established Westinghouse Electric Company. It came about as a result of the battle over whether alternating current (AC) or direct current (DC) should be adopted for public use. The Edison General Electric Company used DC and wanted the public to adopt that rather than AC, which was offered by Westinghouse. To frighten purchasers and governments, rumors were circulated about the deadliness of AC, one example being the use of AC to execute criminals in electric chairs. About that time, the state of New York legalized electrocution. George Westinghouse, realizing that he had image trouble, hired a Pittsburgh newspaperman to make sure that the Westinghouse side of the story got to the public, and E. H. Heinrichs thus came to be the first public relations specialist heading a department in a major industry.[8]

This instance was, of course, not the first use of public relations by industry. In 1859 a promoter for the Burlington Railroad wrote, "We are beginning to find that he who buildeth a railroad west of the Mississippi must also find a population and build up business. We wish to blow as loud a trumpet as the merits of our position merit." In 1869 the Burlington hired "Professor J. D. Butler" to blow that trumpet. He was to promote settlement in Iowa and Nebraska, by means of "widely published entertaining and practical letters . . . well-concocted circulars, Posters, and a judicious amount of advertising."[9] So perhaps Butler more than Heinrichs deserves mention as pioneer in corporate public relations, although Butler worked individually, whereas Heinrichs established a department.

About the same time, the idea of corporate public relations was beginning to appear also in Europe. A German industrialist, Gustav Mevvissen, suggested not long after the middle of the nineteenth century that corporations should have public relations programs to counter criticism. The same idea was echoed by Alfred Krupp, the armament manufacturer, in 1866, but he was unable to find a satisfactory person to take on that job, and the Krupp program of public relations did not begin until Alfred Krupp's son, Friedrich Alfred, commissioned a public relations bureau in the 1890s. This became a part of the firm's organization in 1901.[10]

The turning point in the development of public relations came about the turn of the century, with the emergence of big governments, big business, big labor, big pressure groups of many kinds. Executives in these large organizations could no longer carry the responsibility for public relations along with their other duties.

Furthermore, the problem of building a public image was beginning to be seen as a specialized job. It was at this time that the first really famous names appeared in public relations. One of them was Ivy Lee, who was perhaps best known for his services to John D. Rockefeller, Jr. (and through him to his father, John D., Sr.), although he also served a number of Democratic party candidates and a still larger number of businesses.[11] Another was Edward Bernays, who was Sigmund Freud's nephew, and served a number of famous persons, including Enrico Caruso, as "public relations counsel" (a title coined by Bernays). He also wrote what is probably the first book on public relations, *Crystallizing Public Opinion,* in 1923. Later he edited a book entitled *The Engineering of Consent,* which made him less than popular among his fellow public relations counselors because of the title's connotations.

The task of public relations, modern practitioners are likely to say, is to assess, interpret, and modify public opinion. This has both an internal and an external aspect. The public relations department concerns itself with how employees feel about the organizations, and consequently what kind of image they present to outsiders and what kind of contribution they are likely to make to the organization. Among its external duties, the PR department must be prepared to interpret to the policymakers of the organization what the public thinks of it, its policies, and its products; and what kind of information needs to be circulated, in what form, and through what channels to make the external image more desirable. This may involve a great variety of communication tasks—advising on the probable reception of new policies and on opinion strategy, preparing news releases, writing speeches, issuing publications, planning special events of public interest, answering correspondence, maintaining friendly relations with the media, arranging publicity for persons or products—in fact, anything that has to do with the image presented by the employing organization to persons whose opinion it cares about.

But the details are generally wrapped in smaller boxes. One of these is the general responsibility for helping to create goodwill toward the employer— goodwill from the employees if it is a business or industry, or from the members if it is another kind of organization; from the communities in which the organization operates or has units; from stockholders or contributors; from the appropriate units of government; from the rest of the industry; from the customers, the voters, or whatever other individuals are depended upon for basic support. Another "box" in which public relations duties are often organized is responsibility for the public image of the employer or the organization, which includes finding ways to improve the image and handling changes that might threaten it.

The pattern is the same in general terms, though sometimes greatly different in detail, whether public relations is being managed for a financial institution like the Chase Manhattan Bank, a manufacturing center like Boeing or Chrysler, a retailer like Sears, Roebuck or Neiman-Marcus, the U.S. Departments of Defense or State, a large university, a political party, an activist group like the National Rifle Association, a religious organization like the Mormon Church, or, in short, any organization, formal or informal, commercial or not, public or private, whose image is important to it.

In general, the task of advertising is simpler than that of public relations. The advertiser designs and places an ad—in print, on a broadcast, on a signboard, on a sales package, on a T-shirt, or anywhere else it may be seen or heard with some likelihood of attracting potential buyers or users. The job becomes less simple and less direct when the advertiser is asked to "sell" a candidate or an issue to the voters. Actually, this kind of help is being asked more and more often of the advertising specialist, particularly for 30-second or one-minute ads on television to give exposure to a candidate or a point of view. Also it is becoming more and more common for a party or a candidate to buy time or space to make sure that its case gets to the public when and where that is most important. At this point in the persuasion process the responsibilities of the advertiser and the PR person overlap.

Suppose, for example, that a political party is going to buy 30 minutes of prime time or a series of one-minute spots for its candidate. The strategy has to involve much more than the time, the network, and the stations. Someone has to address such questions as what the candidate should say—in other words, What issues should be taken up at this point in the campaign and for this audience, and what references should be made to please or convince the audience? Who should be on the platform with the candidate or, if it is a spot, what visuals should be used for a background? What can be done to improve the impression the candidate will make by the way he or she speaks or looks? If the candidate is to answer questions, who should ask them and what should be asked? Perhaps we are giving the impression that a candidate is in somewhat the same position as a young child being worried about by a parent, and on the surface it may look that way; but *someone* has to worry about matters like these, and the candidate obviously doesn't have time to take care of all the details. Consequently, the public relations director, the campaign director, the political secretary, or someone else who is trusted by the candidate assumes those public relations responsibilities.

It hardly needs saying that one of the most important responsibilities of public relations is to get the client's viewpoint out. We have been talking about some of the ways this is accomplished in a political campaign. An industry, association, or organization that does not have election crises every two or four years nevertheless has the ongoing problem of keeping its voice heard and its position known. This requires, in some cases, publishing reports or journals. It requires providing news releases or interviews to the media. It requires public appearances by representatives of the company, surrounded by suitable publicity. It requires, from time to time, creating events that are newsworthy (and therefore covered by the news media) and also interesting (and therefore attended and read about by the general public). These "pseudo-events," as Daniel Boorstin called them because they are created for a purpose,[12] may be an exhibit, a meeting, an honorary degree or other honor bestowed on a member of the organization, a donation that will be suitably appreciated, an invitation to the press to see something new in the company, or anything else an imaginative public relations officer may dream up. Suffice it to say that a great deal of the coverage of any large business or other organization is likely to be this kind of event. Newspeople are aware of how such events come to be and do not much like the pattern, but if it is news it deserves to be covered.

Not all the duties of a public relations man or woman are as public and spectacular as the kind we have been mentioning. Some are as simple as writing letters—not necessarily policy letters for the people at the top, but personal letters to individuals whose friendship or understanding is important. One of the most skillful public relations men in the country will simply enclose with a letter a cartoon clipped from a journal that says not a word about the policy or viewpoint of the organization. But the cartoon will give the recipient a good laugh—and benevolent feelings—and the device has proved to be very effective.

Between 1900 and 1980 the number of persons professionally employed in the United States in public relations increased from approximately zero to about 120,000. From 1900 to 1950 alone, the growth in number of PR professionals was nearly 600 percent.[13]

Number of Public Relations Practitioners in the United States

Year	Number
1950	19,000
1960	31,141
1970	80,302
1980	120,037

SOURCE: U.S. Census.

Why are advertising and public relations so big in the United States? We have already spoken of the size of the advertising industry and the speed with which it developed in the nineteenth century. Public relations development came later, but the curve was nearly as steep. PR was practically an American invention, although it was practiced informally and without the name elsewhere as it was for a time here. The first countries outside the United States that went into it seriously were the United Kingdom and Canada. Then, soon after World War II, the number of public relations officers and counselors multiplied rapidly, especially in countries such as Japan, Norway, and Germany, and more gradually thereafter in other industrialized countries.

If there are so many PR men and women, why are there not PR agencies as large as the largest advertising agencies? Because the PR employees typically are in fairly small groups in a department of an industry, a company, or an agency of government, taking care of the image problems of their employers; buying advertising is not often the solution to most of these problems.

Why are advertising and public relations so big in the United States? Because it is a free economy, where prices and sales are little regulated by government and the proceeds of increased sales go to the sellers. Because it is an affluent economy, where people can afford to buy and therefore what people want determines in large part what goods are produced; consequently sales will depend on what people can be encouraged to decide they want. And because it is a relatively open political system, where public opinion matters a great deal and where both individuals and organizations can exert influence through the media and apart from government. The nature of the system makes a great deal of difference. It is noteworthy that there is relatively little advertising in the media of the Communist states, although the amount has been increasing lately; there is obviously some attention to public relations, but just how much is not always apparent on the surface.

THE GREAT PERSUADERS

Modern advertising and public relations are intertwined so intimately in fields such as politics that it is sometimes hard to draw a line between them. An agency that handles a state or national political campaign will have not only to prepare and buy advertising for the candidate but also to help write speeches, guide in the shaping of a public image, prepare news releases, and handle some contacts with organized groups. An organization that calls itself a public relations firm can handle the advertising assistance its clients need; and one that calls itself an advertising agency, if it takes on a political campaign, can handle the public relations requirements.

Together, advertising and public relations represent the great persuaders among the mass media. It is well at this point to ask some questions about the social effects of the persuaders. Of their broad effectiveness, of course, we can have little doubt. Advertising has clearly contributed to the prosperity of the business and industrial system; sales, manufacturing, production of foods and other raw materials, and all the subsidiary activities such as the service industries—all these are greater than they would have been without advertising. Similarly, large organizations and the public related to them could hardly get along so smoothly without attention to public relations. This applies to businesses, industries, political parties, universities and school systems, and all other kinds of organizations that must maintain relationships with a large public. More than one executive has said, "If we didn't have public relations, we'd have to invent it."

But there is a further question to ask: What has this diet of smooth persuasion meant to you and me as individuals? A question of this kind that has bothered many people is whether advertising makes goods cost more. The answer is not entirely clear. For the most part, the cost of advertising is passed on to the consumer. There is no doubt also that advertising and attractive packaging can be used to build up what advertisers call a brand name preference, so that a higher price can be charged for the preferred brand than might otherwise be acceptable. On the other hand, economists point out that advertising, by stimulating a mass market, makes possible mass production, where unit costs are less and retail costs can consequently also be reduced. To complicate the equation still more, however, the copyright laws grant an exclusive right to a brand name or trademark. Since the costs of national advertising are very high, only the largest firms can afford to use that kind of selling. Therefore, these firms can introduce new products and new brand names nationally and employ all the skills of advertising to gain a large share of the public mind for the belief that their specific brand is better. This may be simply because buyers hear and read about it more often, or because it really does appeal to customers' wants and needs. In any case, brand preference has to be balanced against mass production in deciding whether advertising is more likely to raise or lower retail prices. One case in point is the generic drug—the same drug without a brand name—which can be bought usually at a much lower price than the advertised product, if doctors will prescribe it. This is hopeful, but on the other hand there is little doubt that shoppers, in the midst of unfamiliar brands, are likely to buy the name they have heard of, which is likely to mean the brand they have seen advertised.

One situation in which the price effect of advertising can be clearly seen, however, is the fact that because of advertising we pay nothing for the programming on open-circuit television and radio, and perhaps only one-third as much as we would otherwise have to pay for the daily newspapers. The approximately $22 billion that goes into television each year and the $8 billion plus that goes to radio come almost wholly from the sale of advertising time; approximately 75 percent of newspapers' total annual income (approximately $30 billion) comes from advertising. Obviously, if this source of support were taken away, other support would have to be found, or else the content would have to be reduced and/or changed.

Critics point out, of course, that radio and television, in a country like the United States, are made up predominantly of popular culture rather than high culture because that is the way to generate large viewing audiences and consequently attract more advertising. They point out that Great Britain maintains one of the best television and radio services in the world without advertising—the British Broadcasting Corporation, which is supported by listener and viewer fees. On the other hand, even Britain found it necessary to introduce commercial television in addition to its distinguished BBC. When this happened, critics of newspapers charged that the printed media also were "going popular"—that is, introducing entertainment and feature material at a fast rate to compete with television for advertising support. In defense against that, it is argued that the newspaper provides a unique local service—local news and opinion, and advertising for local business that would not be able to advertise nationally. If advertising were taken away, both the local newspaper and much local business would necessarily become an endangered species. At least it is clear that, without advertising, the media would be considerably different.

About the social effects of public relations, also, there are conflicting opinions. On the one hand, news media often resent what they see as the effort of the PR people to get free advertising by creating pseudo-events that the news organs have to cover as news, or by providing releases that the news media have not asked for but often have to print because they *are* news. Needless to say, they are news the PR person wants to see in print or on the air. On the other hand, no experienced reporter will say that press releases from the PR department are not often useful to journalists. Even members of Congress who complain about the expenditures of the executive branch for "propaganda" or for lobbying will admit that they want to hear the viewpoints and the pertinent information from the executive branch before making up their minds on a new bill or a new policy. As much as they may resent what they consider executive propaganda, they are often grateful for it. Cutlip quotes Ernest K. Lindley, a veteran Washington reporter, as saying, "By and large the government information agencies have been invaluable to the Washington newsgatherers and therefore to the public. Without them, the comprehensive coverage of government affairs would be impossible."[14]

One of the situations that decreases the effectiveness of public relations is the suspicion that accompanies public use of it. When there is so much publicity, so much created news, so many pseudo-events, members of the audience tend to dismiss much of the news as "just PR." Robert Heilbroner, the economist, said,

> No one can quarrel with the essential function that public relations fills as a purveyor of genuine ideas and information. No one denies that many public relations men, working for corporations as well as for colleges and causes, honestly communicate things which are worth communicating. Nor can anyone absolve public relations for loading the communications channels with noise. We read the news and suspect that behind it lies the "news release." We encounter the reputation and ascribe it to publicity. Worst of all, we no longer

credit good behavior with good motives, but cheapen it to the level of "good public relations."[15]

Eric Sevareid noted wryly that Greshman's law has been operating in the news field: "Publicity Saints have been taking over the field from Great Men."[16]

Public relations, when it goes public, therefore operates with a built-in handicap making for suspicion and disbelief. The challenge to it is to live up to the rather idealized view that its apologists and interpreters have advanced. Leila Sussman, a social scientist rather than a PR person, held up this kind of ideal: "The job of the public relations man is to keep open a two-way channel of information so that no 'misunderstanding' can arise to disturb the true harmony of interests between the publics and management."[17] Scott Cutlip, a journalist before he wrote a book on public relations, held up this ideal to the PR person: "The profession has an important role to play in a nation that begs unity, a communion of purpose, and support among its people—in short, a sense of community."[18] Public relations, he went on to say, is a power device. "It can steadily advance toward a mature responsible profession," or it can decline toward what William Ernest Hocking called a "senseless publicity racket."

IF ADVERTISING STOPPED

Advertising and public relations have been for years favorite topics for jokes and stories. Most of us have heard, for instance, the often repeated story of Mark Twain and the spider. When Twain was a newspaperman in Missouri, his paper was said to have received a letter from a subscriber reporting that he had found a spider in his paper that day and wondered whether this was an omen of bad or good luck. Twain answered (so the story goes) that finding a spider in the paper means neither good nor bad luck. "The spider was merely looking over our paper to see which merchant was not advertising so that he could go to that store, spin his web across the door and lead a life of undisturbed peace ever afterward."

Among many public relations stories is the one about the small electric light company that decided it needed better public relations. Therefore, it invited some of its customers to a party at which the president of the company made a PR speech. After emphasizing how hard the company worked to be of use to the community, he climaxed his speech by saying, "Think of all the good this company has done. If I may be permitted to paraphrase a famous poem, it may well be said, 'Honor the Light Brigade!' " Whereupon a voice from the audience added, "Oh what a charge they made!"

In 1964 Lincoln Kirstein published in *The Nation* a delightful futuristic picture of what might happen on "The Day the Ads Stopped."[19] Kirstein images that a bill prohibiting advertising in the mass media had passed Congress. The margin in the Senate was only four votes, and this came only after one of the bitterest lobbying efforts in the history of the country. And next day, when the ads stopped, here is a summary of what he imagines took place:

> The *New York Times* (the story is set in New York), once one of the world's fattest newspapers, became very thin. The chief competing local newspaper went out of business. The price of a copy of the *Times* doubled.
>
> Driving to work, he saw workmen removing the billboards. An improvement, he thought, until he saw the houses that had been behind the signs.
>
> He turned on the car radio, and the music came through without commercial interruption, but only from the subscription station to which he had sent $30 dues. How long will listener loyalty last, he wondered?
>
> Absence of the familiar commercials, jingles, and songs led him to think what might be the result of *that?* Would his wife's lipsticks now cost half as much as before, or twice as much? What about razor blades and other nationally advertised articles?
>
> *Playboy* now cost $4 a copy, *Time* and *Newsweek* $2.75 each, he discovered. But *Consumer's Reports* was sold out, and *Reader's Digest* was announcing a "merchandise analysis" section next month to take the place of advertising.
>
> People were buying a lot of paperback books. Because newspapers and magazines were thin, paperbacks offered more pages for the money.
>
> Some people reported that television was now boring. Two channels had been assigned to (noncommercial) television. One was showing the ball game, the score of which was 8 to 0. The other showed the UN debating another African crisis.
>
> A visitor picked up a package of paper matches from Kirstein's desk. "They aren't giving these out free anymore," he said.

At least, that is the kind of thing Kirstein imagines would happen. So far there is no sign that the prohibition of advertising is imminent. But some readers—in addition to advertising and media heads, of course—didn't think Kirstein's ideas were very funny. They said he had missed the point.

Certain writers about media economics, however, take a somewhat different point of view.[20] They say that hostile critics of advertising tend to miss the point, which is that advertising is one of the lucky or prescient discoveries by means of which the Western press (and later the electronic media) have gained the ability to do the news job expected of them. Without economic support from advertising they would return to the restrictions they endured for two centuries in Europe. They would be pawns in the hands of power centers, unable to report freely on government, cover a story, or take an editorial position that might offend a patron. In other words, three centuries of struggle for a free press would mostly be lost. Without advertising or another ready source of income such as public licenses for broadcast reception, they would be unable to cover news in any such breadth or depth as people have become accustomed to: We would be back in the four-page newspaper age. Advertising, this ingenious discovery by the Western press, has not only put such economic strength behind the mass media that they can stand up to political controls and economic influences, but it has also contributed to the enormous growth of the whole society. A neat trick, said one critic, reviewing the history of the Western press. For now, if advertising stopped, it would shake all Western society.

SUGGESTIONS FOR FURTHER READING

Among many texts on advertising, perhaps the one in longest use is Otto Kleppner, *Advertising Procedure,* 7th ed. (Englewood Cliffs, N.J.: Prentice-Hall, 1978). This is now published as *Otto Kleppner's Advertising Procedure* (Englewood Cliffs, N.J.: Prentice-Hall, 1983), with new authors: Otto Kleppner, Thomas Russell, and Glenn Verrill. A newer text is S. W. Dunn and A. M. Barban, *Advertising: Its Role in Modern Marketing,* 6th ed. (New York: Dryden Press, 1986). A useful brief introduction is "Advertising" by V. R. Fry-burger, in the 13th and 14th editions of the *Encyclopaedia Britannica.* On the strategies and tactics of advertisers and their agents, see Martin Mayer, *Madison Avenue, U.S.A.* (New York: Macmillan, 1958); and on the economic basis of advertising, Neil M. Borden, *The Economic Effects of Advertising* (Homewood, Ill.: Irwin, 1947). On the area that advertising shares with public relations, useful readings are the case histories in Edward L. Bernays, *Public Relations* (Norman, Okla.: University of Oklahoma Press, 1979); Erik Barnouw, *The Sponsor* (New York: Oxford University Press, 1978); and Scott M. Cutlip and Allen H. Center, *Effective Public Relations,* 5th ed. (Englewood Cliffs, N.J.: Prentice-Hall, 1978). A recent text in public relations is Dennis L. Wilcox, Philip H. Ault, and Warren K. Agee, *Public Relations: Strategies and Tactics* (New York: Harper & Row, 1986). Advertising and public relations are described in a somewhat different tone in Vance Packard, *The Hidden Persuaders* (New York: Pocket Books, 1957). A good introduction to modern thinking about how advertising works is H. E. Krugman, "The Impact of Television Advertising: Learning without Involvement," in W. Schramm and D. F. Roberts, *The Process and Effects of Mass Communication,* rev. ed. (Urbana: University of Illinois Press, 1974), pp. 485ff.

QUESTIONS TO THINK ABOUT

1. What media are available to advertisers and public relations representatives now that were not available a century ago? In particular, what have been the effects on these activities of the coming into use of television and radio?
2. Why did advertising and public relations grow more rapidly, at least until the middle of this century, in the United States than anywhere else?
3. From what you can remember, or from old publications you have examined, how much and in what ways would you say advertising has changed in the last two or three decades?

4. Can you make a table of what advertising can do—for example, tell people that something is for sale and for how much; persuade possible buyers of the quality of a product; convince them that owning it would contribute to their prestige? Can you make a similar table of what public relations can do?
5. Is it your opinion that advertising has the effect of lowering or raising prices?
6. "You practice public relations all the time, but when you practice advertising you have to take formal steps to do so." Is this true?

TIME CAPSULE

Early advertising typically announces goods for sale; tablet offering one "whole gold coin" for the return of a runaway slave named Shem	1000 B.C.*
Probably the first advertising agency, Reynell and Son, London, founded	1812 A.D.
Volney Palmer, Philadelphia, first American advertising agency	1841
George P. Rowell, early agency, begins to sell large amount of space for weekly newspapers and other media	1865
N. W. Ayer & Son, Philadelphia, first agency to offer media a full line of marketing services	1875
Ivy Lee founds first modern public relations agency, in New York	1904
Of 4000 advertising agencies in the United States, each of 33 handles more than $100 million worth of billings for the current year	1970

*This date is approximate.

FOR THE RECORD

Ten Largest Advertising Agencies

Income Rank			Gross Income*		Billings*	
World	U.S.	Agency	World	U.S.	World	U.S.
1	1	Young & Rubicam	480	323	3,202	2,155
2	3	Ted Bates Worldwide	424	263	2,839	1,755
3	2	Ogilvy & Mather Int'l	421	271	2,888	1,804
4	5	J. Walter Thompson Co.	406	218	2,707	1,455
5	4	BBDO International	340	235	2,275	1,581

Income Rank			Gross Income*		Billings*	
World	U.S.	Agency	World	U.S.	World	U.S.
6	8	Saatchi & Saatchi Compton Worldwide	338	157	2,302	1,093
7	10	McCann-Erickson Worldwide	325	119	2,169	791
8	6	Foote, Cone & Belding Communications	269	197	1,802	1,324
9	7	Leo Burnett Co.	254	163	1,735	1,133
10	9	Grey Advertising	224	155	1,495	1,035

*In millions of dollars.

SOURCE: Adopted from S. W. Dunn and A. M. Barban, *Advertising: Its Role in Modern Marketing,* 6th ed. (New York: Dryden Press, 1986); based on data from *Advertising Age,* March 28, 1985. Reprinted by permission of original publisher and Dr. Dunn.

Advertising Expenditure by Medium (U.S.)

	Newspapers		Magazines		Radio		Television	
Year	$ Millions	%	$ Millions	%	$ Millions	%	$ Millions	%
1950	2,080	36.5	510	9.0	420	14.6		
1960	700	31.0	940	7.9	690	5.8	1,590	13.3
1970	5,850	29.7	1,320	6.7	1,290	6.5	3,600	18.6
1980	15,615	28.5	3,225	5.9	3,690	5.7	11,330	28.7

SOURCE: Adopted from Dunn and Barban, *Advertising,* p. 739; based on McCann-Erickson estimates. Reprinted by permission of authors.

Four practical scientists who had much to do with economic development in the United States and many other countries. From left to right they are Thomas A. Edison, John Burroughs, Henry Ford, and Harvey Firestone. They were photographed here during a camping trip. Were they, perhaps, talking about the electric light, scientific agriculture, the automobile, manufacturing rubber—or the old mill wheel? (Photo taken at Old Evans Mill waterwheel, Leadmine, West Virginia, in August 1918.)

COMMUNICATION AND DEVELOPMENT

All countries are developing countries. Development is the process through which a society moves to acquire the capability of enhancing the quality of life of its people.

EVERETT KLEINJANS

Social and economic development is development of people. It requires learning, motivation, and effective communication.

ITHIEL DE SOLA POOL

Very pretty, but what will it do for us?

CHIEF MINISTER OF A DEVELOPING COUNTRY (on viewing an exhibition of television)

*T*hroughout most of our history, the social changes we call economic and social development and the social process we call communication have moved forward, in long slow steps, together.

The early chapters of this book are full of such examples. After humans mastered the process of language they moved from hunting and gathering into agriculture, from caves and nomadic life to village life. To do this they had to create government and other devices for living together. When they learned to read they had the basis of a usable past. People kept records. They created the market, the school, the city, and the concepts of science and philosophy. When they invented printing they discovered the larger world through exploration, conquest, industry, and commerce, all based upon exchange of information. In their own times, these changes were usually not called development, but that, nevertheless, is what they were, just as truly as the settlement of the American West and the Industrial Revolution were development in our own time.

THE CHANGING PACE OF DEVELOPMENT

In recent years, some changes have taken place in the form and nature of development. For one thing, it has enormously speeded up. The economic and social history of the world before the Renaissance has been compared to walking the American plains from the Alleghenies to the Rockies. Only occasionally the road would lead past a hill (there was Athens, for example, Rome, the Chinese empires) but they were rather small hills in comparison to the endless plains, and were soon passed by. They represented development for a few. In Athens development was for the educated freeman, in Rome the rich, in China the courtiers. Only a few Athenians got to stroll in the groves of academe with Socrates; only a few Romans could consult the libraries that Cicero used; only a few Chinese lived in palaces. The good things of development were not spread among the mass of people until after the Renaissance. Then literacy and schooling became general in a few places on earth, and ordinary people took their political destinies into their own hands and made revolutions. A new system of land ownership, production, and marketing shared the wealth. Until that time, as we have suggested, economic and social history was like walking over the gently rolling plains; at the end of every day's walk the path would be a little higher in altitude, but the traveler would hardly notice it.

But at the end of the road were mountains. In the 80 years after 1700, the rate of growth in gross national product per decade in England was only about 2 percent; in the next 80 years it jumped to 13 percent and has never since been less. In Italy the growth rate as late as 1841 was zero. Then it jumped to 9 percent and since 1913 has been averaging about 16 percent per decade. In the United States the average rate of growth in real product per capita per decade before 1840 was less than 4 percent; for the 120 years before 1961 it averaged about 17 percent.[1] As Frey noted with a bit of wonderment "these striking and previously unknown rates of growth" in the economies of many nations have now been sustained for periods as long as two centuries![2]

And as the economic situation has changed, so has the way of life. The proportion of the population engaged in farming has steadily decreased, while that in industry, business, and service occupations has correspondingly increased. The middle class has dramatically risen both in numbers and affluence. In Europe, North

America, and a few other countries such as Japan, almost everyone is literate. Transportation and communication have expanded with what historians and sports writers call awesome speed. Equally remarkable have been the changes in social structure, values, and beliefs. Easterlin remarks that the developed countries have experienced in the last century "a greater advance in material well-being and a more sweeping change in way of life than occurred in any previous century of human history."[3]

These changes in the pace of development ("these conspicuous, unprecedented, and seemingly highly interrelated changes," Frey calls them) began in northern Europe, probably in Great Britain, in the late seventeenth or eighteenth century, and spread through much of Western Europe, then eastward as far as Russia and Japan, westward to North America and Australia and other lands settled by northern Europeans, and thence followed the paths of other European immigrants and colonists to the countries that have come to be called the Third World.[4] Thus in about two centuries, between the middle of the eighteenth and the middle of the twentieth century, development spread until it affected almost half of the world's people.

THE DEVELOPMENT IDEA

In the late nineteenth and early twentieth centuries, furthermore, people began to see development in a new light. What happened might be called a change from an evolutionary to a revolutionary viewpoint. Just where this started is not entirely clear, but it clearly came out of the political churnings and the industrial and technological advances that had been taking place. For centuries humans had taken a rather evolutionary view of the changes around them. As Addison said in *The Spectator,* things were thought to happen mostly "because they happened." The best one could do was to make the best possible life from what one had to work with, to ride the long, slow tide of change, adapting to it rather than trying to change it. But this attitude itself changed.

The human tenants of earth (particularly in northern Europe and North America) began to ask a new set of questions. Could they not take charge and direct some of these social changes themselves? Having proved that in some parts of the world they could settle a frontier, grow crops, make machines that would work for them (and, before long, fly them to the moon), extend participation in government to people who had no previous experience with that, and even change the form of government in some places to an arrangement they liked better—having done all this in a few centuries, they began to ask, could they not do more, for more people, and do it faster?

This has been called the *development idea*. It represented a hopeful, heady period in the history of earth's people.

CHALLENGE TO THE DEVELOPMENT IDEA

About this time some events occurred that squarely confronted the new vision of development. After World War II more than 50 new countries became independent, with new ambitions of their own, and with the example of industrialized countries to encourage them to try to develop toward their own goals. Most of three great continents—Asia, Africa, and Latin America—were hungry for the rewards of development. And just at that same time the second wave of mass media —the visual and electronic media—became readily available. The most attractive and apparently most effective of these new media was television (which was first demonstrated in 1926 but became generally available only about 1950), but films and radio also had demonstrated that people were attracted to them and could learn from them. The relation of efficient communication to development was widely recognized. This looked like an almost heaven-sent opportunity to carry the message of development where it was needed. With a need like that of the new countries, and available technology like that of the new media, the development idea suddenly looked as though it might become reality!

Therefore the new countries, the poor countries, looked to the older and richer ones for guidance. What had they learned in their own years of development that could be shared? What help could they give the newly developing states? And, unusual as it might seem in the ambitious and self-centered atmosphere of the mid-twentieth century, the developed countries responded.

THE NEW CAMPAIGN OF DEVELOPMENT AID

In future years this response may be read as a rather remarkable chapter in history. We do not mean to suggest that what the industrialized countries did about the development idea was wholly altruistic; the motive for much of it was simply self-interest—to produce raw materials and new markets in the developing countries. And yet there was a great deal of altruism in it too. The Marshall Plan, the first and still one of the greatest examples of foreign aid, by which the United States helped get its European allies back on the road to prosperity after the war, was more than self-interest. Japan, too, received some rather special help, if no more than being freed from the cost of defending itself. But these countries had merely to climb back to where they had been before 1939. The newer countries had a more difficult task, one that could not be solved only by a bit of financial aid. They had to climb the same economic and social mountains the so-called developed countries had climbed in earlier decades.

I have written elsewhere,

> As the men of war had crossed the seas in the late 1930s and 1940s, so the troops of development in the 1950s and 1960s moved toward the developing countries. Engineers, planners, industrialists, economists, agricultural scientists, extension service agents, successful farmers, successful small businessmen, skilled workers, educators, social scientists—yes, social scientists, for it was apparent that a great social movement would be taking place and therefore the social scientists should observe the changes, and determine what social processes were or were not working successfully. And from the developing countries, specialists and students of one kind or another crossed the ocean in the other direction to observe and study the skills they would need at home.[5]

What did these representatives of development carry with them by which to help the new countries accomplish their task? Certainly they had learned nothing that could bring about development instantaneously. Europe and North America had taken two centuries, or nearly that, to accomplish this task. Yet the new media were for the first time available to carry information about development. That put the problem in a new light: How much could the new media, coupled with the example of the already-developed countries, hurry up the process of learning, training, reorganization, mechanization, industry building, and so forth, that went into development? Therefore, one thing the developers carried with them was a sense of how communication had been used by developing countries elsewhere and how it *might* be used to contribute to the speed and effectiveness of development.

THEORIES OF DEVELOPMENT

The new countries had the beginning of social science theory of how development takes place. Asia, Latin America, and Africa were for the most part more deeply interested in what the industrialized countries had done to bring about development than in what scholars said about it, but they were interested in social theory too, and it will be interesting for us to review where the social science of development was in mid-twentieth century.

The chief advice that came from economists was that developing countries should save and invest. There was never a question about that: All the classical economists, from Adam Smith, David Ricardo, and John Stuart Mill to Karl Marx, had recommended it. There was a question as to where and how to invest. Nurske recommended a balanced growth; Hirschmann, on the other hand, argued for *un*balanced growth. Invest heavily in one area, he said, and let that area pull the others up by the bootstraps. Some countries followed the advice of one, some the other. But if investment was to be concentrated in one area, the most usual choice was industry.[6]

One of the most popular economic theories of development available for export in mid-century was the "stage model" of Walt Rostow, an economist at Yale.[7] Following some of the ideas of Max Weber and incorporating examples from aviation, he described economic development as taking place in five stages from "traditional society" to "development." The first step beyond traditional society, Rostow said, was a society in which the preconditions for "takeoff" had been met (in airplane language this happened when the plane was fueled, on the runway, and ready to go). Then came "takeoff" itself (meaning that the new country had developed to a point where it could move and steer itself). After that was a fourth stage, which Rostow called "drive toward maturity," and finally "development," when (going back to aviation language) the plane was ready to climb and fly on its chosen course without further help from outside.

The convenient feature of the Rostow model was that it provided a way to say how far along a country was on the scale of development. The usual measure was gross national product (GNP). In the 1960s, if GNP rose more than 5 percent that was regarded as good progress. A country that reached an annual GNP per capita of $300 was generally regarded as well on the way to development. (GNP per capita at that time in the developed countries was usually $1000 or more, whereas in many of the less fortunate countries it was still under $100.) Whereas the developing countries saw the logic of this model, some of them objected that the goal of development, in their opinion, was not only higher GNP, but rather concern for the quality of life. The economists, on the other hand, pointed out that it was necessary to pay for many of the quality aspects of life, and thus an economic measure was a basic one, although, they admitted, not the only one.

To many developers, the psychological theories of Everett Hagen and David McClelland were attractive. One of Hagen's most-quoted statements is that social structure is basically a function of personality.[8] That is, a traditional society is made up of traditional personalities; a developing society, of innovative personalities. For development to occur, therefore, something must happen to change personalities. How could a developing country do that? Hagen suggested that innovative personalities might be encouraged by certain developments in society—literacy, communication media, the growth of cities, and the appearance of nationalism and national pride. Thus, as other scholars noted, developing countries were asked to bring about social change that encouraged innovative personalities, and such personalities in turn would encourage further social change.

McClelland's psychological theory was built around the idea of *achievement motivation*.[9] This, like some aspects of Rostow's model, was influenced by Max

Weber, whose famous treatment of the Protestant ethic was useful to developers not for any theological reason, but because Weber concluded that Protestantism promoted among its followers a need for achievement. This is an important observation to scholars studying entrepreneurship and other such aspects of development. McClelland argued that need for achievement (n/Ach) encourages an individual to meet challenges, surmount opposition, and succeed in the face of difficulties. A society made up of achieving personalities, he said, is likely to be an achieving—and therefore a developing—society. Searching through history for parallels, he cited classical Greece, Renaissance Spain, England before the Industrial Revolution, and the United States during the century and a half after 1800 as states where a high level of achievement motivation apparently predicted high economic growth. By the same token, if achievement motivation appeared to be low in a country, this predicted an economic decline, or at least a lack of growth.

The psychologists, then, tended to build development theories on individual qualities within a developing country. Sociologists such as Talcott Parsons, on the other hand, interpreted development in terms of Durkheim's system theory or an equally broad view of social change.[10] Social change, as they saw it, could not be accomplished by a few interventions or measured on a few scales like GNP or n/Ach. It required society-wide programs and could be measured only by society-wide changes. Personality changes did not seem to be enough.

Perhaps the best-known sociological theory of communication was Daniel Lerner's.[11] Drawing on his studies of Middle Eastern countries, he developed a sort of stage theory for sociology. "Everywhere," he said in his best-known book, *The Passing of Traditional Society,* "increasing *urbanization* has tended to raise *literacy;* rising literacy has tended to increase *media exposure;* increasing media exposure has gone with wider *economic* and *political* participation." Lerner's linear scale was usually diagrammed U → L → M → E → P, and his advice to developers was interpreted in terms like these: First move more people into the cities; only after 10 percent of the population is urban will literacy begin to rise significantly; thereafter, literacy and urbanization increase together until they reach about 25 percent; thereafter media use increases with increasing literacy; and GNP and political participation (measured by proportion of people who vote) also increase. Scholars who used this scale found that it did not work as well in all countries as it had worked for Lerner in the Middle East—for instance, in a number of countries quite substantial increases in literacy occurred before urbanization reached 10 percent.[12] But the scale was interesting because it brought together a number of the chief elements in development.

Interpreting his findings, Lerner advanced what became possibly his best-known hypothesis—that development is basically the making of "modern man." The modern human, he said, has a "mobile personality," an ability to undertake new tasks and new experiences. Lerner's word was *empathy*—meaning that "modern man" can imagine himself in the role or place or responsibility of someone else, and also can form opinions on new problems and questions that "traditional man" would not think about. Modern humans, he argued, have empathy, and such a quality is basic to development.

These theories were obviously suggestive rather than prescriptive; that is, they suggested what might be happening in the process of development rather than telling developers exactly what to do about it. But they helped, among other things, to put together a recipe for development.

THE "OLD PARADIGM" OF DEVELOPMENT

From the available theories and, more importantly, from the experience of the developed countries, a model of development evolved that later came to be called the "old model" or the "old paradigm" of development. It served as a kind of general pattern to sum up what the older countries felt in mid-century they had to teach the newer ones. It was stated somewhat differently in different places, and different parts of it were emphasized more than others by different users, but it included these ideas:

1. The prime mover of the economy is industry. A major part of national investment must therefore go into industry, and a major part of national effort must go into providing raw materials, transportation, and equipment for it.
2. Industry requires specialists, and so do other sectors of a developing society. Therefore selection and training must be provided for each sector—manufacturing, service, farming, business, construction, health care, and so forth.
3. Beyond that, public education is needed to raise the capability of the whole work force and to encourage more citizens to take part in decisions, politics, planning, and other "modern" behaviors.
4. Effective communication is essential to development. All available channels should be used to diffuse necessary information and persuasion to the people. The mass media are therefore a necessary part of the system. Extension services; neighborhood specialists in such fields as agriculture, health, and education; organized groups; and cadres can be used to supplement the media.
5. For efficiency, planning should be centralized as much as possible. This does not imply, however, that local groups should not take part where possible in development decisions.
6. Profits from development activities, especially from centrally owned and managed industry, should be distributed in the population as evenly as possible. It was usually assumed that central profits would trickle down from the center to the periphery of the system—the industries and central

markets to the farms, the cities to the villages. This latter assumption proved to be one of the most questionable ones.

No one who participated in development planning or assistance in its early years would be entirely satisfied with either the completeness or all the specifics of that "model." But at least it gives some idea what critics talk about when they speak of the "old model," and what the developed countries felt in the mid-1950s they could teach the developing ones.

RESULTS OF THE DEVELOPMENT CAMPAIGN

National governments, international organizations (such as the UN, UNESCO, and the World Bank), aid agencies (such as US AID), schools and universities, churches, and other organizations contributed money, resources, experts, and effort to assist the almost worldwide effort to bring about national development. What were the results?

They were mixed. It would be nice to be able to say that everything worked satisfactorily, but that would not be true. Some projects worked well, some did not. Even in the United States, some of the new flagship projects had to give up on what they had started to do.

Take the example of educational television. In a number of cases it proved it could supplement classroom teaching and contribute to the depth and breadth of learning. Hagerstown, Maryland, for instance, found that it could connect all its schools by cable and use some of its best teachers to supplement instruction where teachers were not specialized. Institutions such as the Chicago Junior College found that they could offer a set of courses by television so that prospective students who worked or lived too far from the school could get their instruction at home. After a few years, however, both Hagerstown and Chicago abandoned their broadcasting and recorded their most useful programs on cassettes. In that way, the teachers in Hagerstown could decide what lessons they wanted their students to receive and when they were ready for them, rather than following a central schedule; and TV students in Chicago could go to libraries to use the cassettes when they felt ready and when it was convenient for them to do so. And one of the most innovative attempts in the United States to combine new technology with teaching—the Airborne project, which had an airplane flying lazy circles over the Midwest while it broadcast televised lessons that could be picked up in four states—also had to withdraw its services because school systems differed too much in the classes and schedules they used.[13]

On the other hand, some development innovations could be picked up and transferred directly to the new countries. For the most part, the kind of development communication that was in favor in the United States in mid-century was what has been called the diffusion model. The United States Agricultural Service furnished an example of that. Knowledge was to be diffused from the experts and the most widely experienced farmers to the others. Problems most in need of expert attention were sent up the line to the attention of the experiment farms, and the answers came down to the demonstration farms, where both the solutions and the results could be observed, and to extension agents where they could be explained. The "National Farm and Home Hour" helped explain them on a mass basis. And land-grant colleges like Iowa State were instrumental both in introducing such new products as hybrid corn and in studying the theory and tactics of bringing about the adoption of new practices in general.[14]

One of the innovations most appreciated throughout the world was the "open university" pattern, by which university study was offered by broadcast and print to large numbers of students who had to work during the day or for other reasons could not take advantage of campus study. This turned out in most places to be a great success. The Open University of Great Britain has become a truly distinguished university. China offered an opportunity for open university study and had 10 million applicants! Only about 500,000 could be accepted. But think what it would mean to a country whose young people are hungry for university education to be able, by establishing one central institution, to offer a complete university experience to half a million young people, and to do so without disrupting their work or having to move them to university campuses. The open university pattern is now in use in upwards of 50 countries worldwide.

As early as the 1930s, people interested in social change recognized the importance of groups in bringing about change. In the 1930s Kurt Lewin, the University of Iowa psychologist, was conducting pilot experiments on the use of groups in innovation and adoption. He was able to show that group commitment and group support are highly important in the adoption of new practices and attitudes.[15] Throughout the farming country, groups learned to meet and plan together, to select their extension agents by mutual opinion, and to benefit from exchange of experience. In the 1950s France was introducing "animation"—rural discussion groups presided over but by no means controlled by an *animateur* or discussion leader. These groups discussed farming, of course, but not only farming. They were concerned with how to develop their communities into good places to live. One of the best known of all the horizontal-plus-vertical communication devices of development was the radio rural forum, which originated in Canada in the 1940s but was soon adopted in India, and soon thereafter by at least 15 other developing countries. The forum used a radio broadcast to feed and stimulate group discussion and decision. The forum, or something like it, is now in use on every continent.

In most developing countries, the combination of broadcast with local study groups has turned out very well. For example, the Sutatenza program, under Father Salzedo, in Colombia, has now for several decades been teaching the skills of literacy and numeracy to thousands of campesinos, by means of radio broadcasts to study groups with volunteer leaders.[16] The ingenious directors of this program supplement the study opportunities of their students not only with easily readable books but also with an easy-to-read newspaper published especially for the program. Every year a certain number of the younger people who have just learned to read learn well enough so that they can enter the nearest public school and get a complete education rather than merely a course in reading.

We have been talking mostly about education. Development programs, of course, are much broader than that. The "green revolution," which taught the farmers of developing countries to plant newly developed and more hardy and productive strains of corn, rice, and wheat, was an admitted success. The development programs that operated through health centers concentrating on vaccination for smallpox have all but eliminated that disease from the developing nations. Presently a development program operating through health centers and other medical sources is having a comparable success in eliminating diarrhea, which is the greatest killer of children in the poor countries.

In general, the patterns that seemed to transfer most effectively from the developed countries were the media for carrying new knowledge, new ideas, superior teaching, and some of the devices built around them. Thus the impact of the specialists in various fields of development, such as the agriculture and health services, could be multiplied by the media. As we have seen, ideas and persuasion could be fed into the groups where developing people could meet, talk, and make plans and decisions together. Some of the group developments were very interesting indeed. For example, Kincaid and Yum reported on how a group of ambitious women in one of the poorest Korean villages, Oryu Li, took over what they thought the village government and the village men were failing to accomplish.[17] When the village was given a piglet, they assumed the task of raising it and using its progeny to start a small pig farm for food and for sale. They obtained free seedlings and planted these to beautify the village. They put their own wedding rings into a central fund with which they bought materials for a new village bathhouse and seeds for new grain crops. They planted and sold the crops, improved the school opportunities, formed a family planning club, and drew together first the women then some of the men into work groups to continue the tasks of development. The leader of the women was soon in demand to go to other villages and explain how they had done it.

This homely sort of approach to development often seemed to accomplish more than elaborate ones. For example, in the same country where the women of Oryu Li accomplished so much, plans were made to broadcast education from tethered balloons to the entire country, thus avoiding the expenses of microwave or satellite. But the balloons flew away, and the idea had to be abandoned. Similarly, one of the most elaborate educational television installations in the world, financed by United States sources to modernize the educational system of American Samoa, ultimately proved to be a disappointment.[18] The Samoan schools were given six open-circuit television stations and a core of experienced TV teachers from the States, so that every class in 12 grades could receive expert teaching by television while local teachers were retrained. For a time, the results were very impressive. But then problems appeared. For one thing, as the upper-grade teachers acquired more experience and training they became impatient with the timing and class outlines established by the central studios. They felt they knew better than the studio teacher what their own students needed to learn at a given time. And so, in effect, they rebelled. The result was that after a few years television was removed from the high schools and the upper grades of elementary school. Another early decision also caused more trouble in Samoa than anyone expected. To attract evening viewers to adult education programs, it was decided to add one commercial entertainment program each evening. These programs did indeed attract viewers, and soon the number of entertainment programs had to be multiplied many times. After 12 years, somewhat to the surprise of the original planners, half the stations were being used for entertainment programs rather than education.

THE LARGER EFFECTS

We have been talking mostly about single-purpose activities, many of which have scored resounding successes. But how about the broader development programs: How many of the new countries have followed Britain, France, Germany, Japan, and Canada up the ladder to the point where they, too, may be called developed countries?

Some, but not many. The comment which I heard the leader of a new country make at a demonstration of television—"Very pretty, but what will it do for us?" —came in some parts of the world to seem almost prophetic. In Asia, for instance, after two "development decades" (as proclaimed by UNESCO) only four of the new states—Singapore, Taiwan, South Korea, and Hong Kong—seem to be at or near the stage where they can be said to be developed. The two largest countries, India and China, are far from that stage, although China has recently been making encouraging steps toward it. It is hard to name more than one country in Latin America or even one country in Africa (except possibly South Africa) that can be called developed.[19]

In fact, to political and military leaders and scholars in parts of Asia and in

Latin America and Africa, the promise of development has proved disappointing. A well-known Latin American student of development, Luis Beltran, has summed up the situation in the developing countries as he saw it in 1980.[20] These countries, he said, in 1980 had amassed a foreign debt of about $440 billion; that debt in 1971 had been only $68 billion. Why had they borrowed so much? Because they were not satisfied with a few localized projects, like that of the Korean women or the Sutatenza schools. They were trying to move the whole country forward. Therefore they had to industrialize; they had to educate and train; they had to install what they needed for modernization and at the same time meet the needs of their people. Between 1971 and 1980 interest rates in these countries had grown by 800 percent. In 30 of the developing countries the per capita income was 80 cents a day or less; 800 million people, they estimated, were underfed; 140 developing countries, three-fourths of the world's population, about 3.2 billion people, accounted for only 20 percent of the world's gross product. These figures are obviously even more frightening to live through than to read about.

The spokespersons for the developing countries are less likely to blame communication for the failures of the program than to blame international political and economic relations. They feel, on the one hand, that the industrialized countries are making it hard for the new ones to industrialize. The developed countries tend to want to buy from the new countries raw materials rather than finished products. That does not help the developing states to industrialize. The new countries have to "sell cheap and buy dear." The recession of the seventies was even more devastating to the new countries than to the older ones, because it forced the new ones to borrow more and more, often at very high rates of interest. The result, as Beltran says, is "chronic trade imbalances, ever growing budgetary deficits, growing debts to the industrial nations, . . . higher interest and shorter repayment periods."[21] In Latin America, foreign debts rose from $67 billion in 1975 to almost $300 billion in 1982. Overwhelmed by their burden of debt, some countries feel they can only pay the interest while they try to renegotiate the basic debt. "Banks can wait," said the president of Peru, "hunger cannot."

The development program—the "old paradigm"—inherited from the developed countries has come in for its share of criticism too. For one thing, centralization of planning and management has not been entirely popular; many Third World critics have insisted that new countries should do it *their* way. Why not develop through agriculture rather than through industry, they have asked? Why not develop toward the quality of life they want, rather than toward a satisfying GNP? Why not put more of the planning and decisions in the hands of the little people rather than the central leaders? Why not divide the earnings of development among all the people rather than centralizing them in the industrialists and traders (the trickle-down concept has appeared not to be very successful)?

The new countries are happy to have better crops, to send their children to better schools, to rid their families of the curse of smallpox and children's diarrhea, but they are disappointed in the economic outlook of the development program and unhappy about being reminded that the European and North American countries took two centuries to travel the development road that they are trying to travel in much less time. Their greatest disappointment with the part communication plays in their development is that they had hoped the spectacular new media would cut down in an equally spectacular way the length of the long hard climb up from underdevelopment.

The slow pace of development in the less industrialized countries has caused some rethinking about the use of the mass media for social change and improving human life. As some historians have said, at no other time in human history have the media been so directly challenged to contribute to change that is generally and widely desired and visible. And because all the development story is so public and all the critics in the less developed states are so vocal, the favorable results have tended to be submerged and the less favorable results and interpretations more sharply emphasized.

THE INDONESIAN STUDY

Very few research studies of communication and development have been broad enough to focus on development in more than one respect (that is, effects not limited to education, agriculture, health, or some such single area of society) or in more than one small area (a whole country, for example, rather than a single village like Oryu Li). But one recent study has been able to cover the broad picture, and it may be instructive to look at that study.[22]

Dr. Godwin Chu, a communication researcher at the East-West Center in Honolulu, along with some of his colleagues, carried out a six-year study of satellite television in Indonesia, beginning in 1976. He was extremely fortunate in being able to choose that location and that time for the study. In 1976 Indonesia launched its Palapa satellite to broadcast to the rural regions of that large country, which had never before had television. The government was willing to space the ground rebroadcast stations so that some areas could receive the broadcasts, some not; and therefore it was possible to arrange control groups and compare viewers with nonviewers. Indonesia was strongly committed to a full test of television, and therefore before the satellite was launched had formed the ground organizations necessary to support the television programs—that is, community study and discussion groups, health centers, agriculture organizations, village cooperatives, and so forth. Because the study was to go on for six years it was possible to observe long-term as well as short-term results. The sample was large—2400 people, from five provinces of Indonesia, interviewed for one to two hours before, during, and after the six-year study. Furthermore, because Indonesia had only one television channel, everyone received the same programs; it was not possible, as it is in some other places, to tune away from the development television to an entertainment program. It was a carefully and solidly designed study, and the results are dependable.

What *were* the results? Perhaps the most impressive one was the enormous amount of learning that resulted from viewing television. During the six years of the study—to take one example—television viewers learned almost *three times* as much about Indonesia's eight primary development programs as did the people who did not view television. This is far from an academic finding. We are talking about a large fraction of 150 million people.

Note that we have been talking about learning, not adopting. In the process of adoption, communication of the basic information is usually necessary but not sufficient. Merely delivering information about a new development program will not of itself bring about adoption, although it will help. Besides the basic information that television can deliver, adopters usually need additional persuasion, encouragement, example. One of the best ways to get this is to join one of the village organizations. A television viewer who joins BIMAS (the large Organization for Mass Guidance) will find others who are considering the new programs; he or she can talk over the question with them, find out what their experience has been, draw encouragement from those who have decided to adopt, go to their fields to see the program in action. This is what happened in Indonesia.

The effect of the Indonesian development program on health care was little short of sensational. At the start of the Palapa study, in 1976, about 30 million Muslims in Indonesian villages were going to traditional untrained village doctors. In 1982, at the time of the postsurvey, two-thirds *fewer* people were using traditional medical practitioners. There was a parallel change in the use of untrained midwives as contrasted to the use of doctors and trained midwives for help in childbirth. In other words, the television viewers in Indonesian villages were turning more and more to modern medicine.

It might be expected that television would emphasize social differences—for example, emphasize the gap in adoption between the less and the more affluent, the better educated and those with less education. Other things being equal, of course, people who are more affluent or better educated are more likely to adopt new development practices. But the results of the Indonesian study were not at all what would have been expected. The Chu study showed convincingly that among television viewers there tended to be *less* difference in the amount of knowledge or the number of adoptions between high and low economic groups, or between high and low education groups, than there was among *non* viewers of television. In other words, television seemed to help even out development effects, to get rid of some of the educational disparities and economic inequalities. That is the implication of the Indonesian study.

It is clear also that television has made a considerable contribution to the speaking and reading of the national language, Bahasa Indonesia. This is one of Indonesia's prime development goals, because a national language will help integrate the country. In both written and spoken language, during the six years of the study, television viewers improved significantly more than nonviewers. This is not entirely surprising, because all the television is in Bahasa, and therefore viewing the program is automatic practice.

Another finding of the Chu study is that the Indonesian villagers who viewed television developed a geographically wider interest in news. This is probably because they got world news chiefly from television. Similarly, most of the village people reported that on development or adoption questions television had become their main source of information, next to the village head or the local specialist if there was one (the agricultural officer, the health officer, the bank, etc.).

One more item. The sample of villagers was asked, "What do you think is the main factor in, or reason for, success?" This question was deliberately made difficult in order to find out how the respondents thought about success. To answer the question the respondents had first to define success in their own terms, and then decide on the causes. Three answers were overwhelming choices—hard work, good luck, and planning. Both among viewers and nonviewers, and in 1976 as well as 1982, hard work stood first. That was recognized as an Indonesian norm, and the result was expected. However, in 1982, after six years, there had been a change in the relative position of hard work and good luck. More of the nonviewers voted for good luck, more of the viewers for planning. How did this happen? Because of what they saw on television, the villagers said.

We might mention in conclusion that the gross national product per capita in Indonesia almost exactly doubled between 1976 and 1981—from $275 to $547 (U.S.).

Therefore, the results of the Indonesian study read like a success story of a development program built around the mass media, especially television. Yet let us not overinterpret. Conditions in Indonesia were unusually favorable. Furthermore, the amount of control the government was willing to maintain over the program is not typical of all developing countries. Not many prospering countries of 150 million people would be willing to restrict their television to one channel. Not many of them would be willing, or politically able, to order commercials off the air when their influence on viewers and on development became suspect. There was a kind of single-minded determination in the government's attitude toward development and television that was far from usual. Furthermore, the oil income during the study years, 1976–1982, made development easier for everyone.

Let us say again that although Indonesia's rural regions in 1982 were clearly better informed and more concerned about development and national progress, more efficient in handling their business affairs, more involved in development and national progress—all signs of development—than they had been six years earlier, we cannot credit all that to the information input. Television was not the prime mover of development; it was the prime mover of information, and information exerted its influence on a society ready to develop. Television, as Chu said in summing up his own study, did not itself bring about development, but it "maximized effects."

Therefore, without claiming more than we have the right to claim for the impact of television, we have every reason to be somewhat impressed by what television and the other media, used well and under favorable conditions, can—or *could*—contribute to social change.

SUGGESTIONS FOR FURTHER READING

There is no current book that updates the history and status of development. Most nearly current introductions are likely to be found in reference books and periodicals, for example Erik Barnouw, ed., *International Encyclopedia of Communications* (New York and London: Oxford, in press) which carries summary articles on development by Beltran, Hornik, and Schramm. Slightly older but still helpful is David L. Sills, ed., *International Encyclopedia of the Social Sciences* (New York: Macmillan, 1968) which carries development-related articles by Hoselitz and Easterlin, among others. A 125-page article by Frey, in the *Handbook of Communication,* eds. Ithiel de Sola Pool and Wilbur Schramm (Boston: Houghton Mifflin, 1973), is itself a useful introduction.

Among older but still useful books in this field are *The Theory of Economic Development,* by Joseph A. Schumpeter (Cambridge, Mass.: Harvard University Press, 1934); Arno G. Huth, *Communication and Economic Development* (New York: Carnegie Endowment for International Peace, 1953); *Modernization among Peasants,* by Everett M. Rogers (New York: Holt, Rinehart and Winston, 1969); *Industrialization and Society,* eds. Bert J. Hoselitz and W. E. Moore (Paris: UNESCO, 1963), especially the article by Ithiel de Sola Pool,

"The Role of Communication in the Process of Modernization and Technological Change"; Lucian W. Pye, ed., *Communication and Political Development* (New Haven, Conn.: Yale University Press, 1963); Alex Inkeles and David H. Smith, *Becoming Modern* (Cambridge: Harvard University Press, 1974); Godwin Chu, *Radical Change through Communication in Mao's China* (Honolulu: University Press of Hawaii, for East-West Center, 1977); Majid Tehranian, et al., eds., *Communication Policy for National Development* (London: Routledge and Kegan Paul, 1977); and Wilbur Schramm, *Mass Media and National Development* (Stanford and Paris: Stanford University Press and UNESCO, 1964).

For the theoretical approaches mentioned in this chapter, see Walter W. Rostow, *The Stages of Economic Growth* (Cambridge, England: Cambridge University Press, 1960); Everett F. Hagen, *On the Theory of Social Change* (Chicago: Dorsey, 1962); David McClelland, *The Achieving Society* (New York: Van Nostrand, 1953); Talcott Parsons, *Structure and Process in Modern Societies* (New York: Van Nostrand, 1960); and Daniel Lerner, *The Passing of Traditional Society* (Chicago: Free Press, 1958).

Two collections of articles growing out of conferences that summed up the status of Asian development and communication in the mid-1960s and mid-1970s, respectively, are edited by Lerner and Schramm, *Communication and Change in the Developing Countries* (Honolulu: University Press of Hawaii, 1967 and 1976). Among publications critical of the existing development efforts are Goran Hedebro, *Communication and Change in Developing Nations: A Critical View* (Ames, Iowa: Iowa State College Press, 1982); Kaarle Nordenstreng and Herbert Schiller, eds., *National Sovereignty and International Communication* (Norwood, N.J.: Van Nostrand, 1979); and E. M. Rogers, "The Passing of the Dominant Paradigm," reprinted in Rogers, ed., *Communication and Development* (Beverly Hills, Calif.: Sage, 1976). Relevant statistical tables will be found in the annual UNESCO and UN *Statistical Yearbooks*.

QUESTIONS TO THINK ABOUT

1. Some scholars have suggested that *psychological* is just as appropriate a descriptive adjective for development as *economic and social,* and it might therefore be called *economic, social, and psychological development* or, as many do now call it, simply *development*. They cite the fact that Hagen, McClelland, and Lerner all describe it in psychological terms. What is your opinion about the use of *psychological* to help describe development?

2. Hagen uses *innovative personality,* McClelland *achievement motivation,* and Lerner *empathy* to describe persons and societies that are headed toward development. These terms are rather different. Which seems to you most useful? How would you measure them?

3. The most common measure of development is an economic one such as GNP. This is usually more meaningful to someone looking at the developing society from outside than from within. If you were in a developing society, how would you know whether or not you have "developed"?

4. Why was industrialization so successful in Europe, later in the United States and Japan, but apparently so difficult in most of the new countries of Asia, Latin America, and

Africa? Is this merely because we expect it to move faster? It has apparently moved along well in countries like Singapore, Taiwan, South Korea, and Hong Kong. What do those facts seem to imply concerning the requirements for industrial development?

5. The mass media are very effective in bringing about learning of development information, but less effective in encouraging adoption of development practices. How do you explain the difference?

What microelectronics means: a part of a logic circuit from an IBM computer, magnified 23,000 times.

THE NEW AGE OF INFORMATION

The major advances in civilization are processes that all but wreck the societies in which they occur.

ALFRED NORTH WHITEHEAD

*I*t is evident that something new is happening in communication. Some observers have called it a communication revolution; others, a new age of communication or a new age of information. The name doesn't matter. What matters is that every major development in human communication has begun with a major new development in communication technology. And therefore it is wise to read what the father of the communication satellite (as Arthur Clarke has every right to be called) has to say about what is happening to the technology of human technology:

> If you showed a modern diesel engine, an automobile, a steam turbine, or a helicopter to Benjamin Franklin, Galileo, Leonardo da Vinci, and Archimedes —a list spanning two thousand years in time—not one of them would have any difficulty in understanding how these machines worked. All four men would be astonished at the materials and the workmanship, but once they got over that surprise they would feel quite at home—as long as they did not delve too deeply into the auxiliary control and electrical systems.
>
> But now suppose they were confronted by a television set, an electronic computer, a nuclear reactor, a radar installation. Quite apart from the complexity of these devices, the individual elements of which they are composed would be incomprehensible to any man born before this century. Whatever his degree of education or intelligence, he would not possess the mental framework that could accommodate electron beams, transistors, atomic fission, waveguides, and cathode-ray tubes."[1]

EXTRA-TERRESTRIAL RELAYS

Can Rocket Stations Give World-wide Radio Coverage?

By ARTHUR C. CLARKE

ALTHOUGH it is possible, by a suitable choice of frequencies and routes, to provide telephony circuits between any two points or regions of the time, earth for a large part of the time, long-distance communication is greatly hampered by the peculiarities of the ionosphere, and there are even occasions when it may be impossible. A true broadcast service, giving constant field strength at all times over the whole globe would be invaluable, not to say indispensable, in a world society.

Unsatisfactory though the telephony and telegraph position is, that of television is far worse, since ionospheric transmission cannot be employed at all. The service area of a television station, even on a very good site, is only about a hundred miles across. To cover a small country such as Great Britain would require a network of transmitters, connected by coaxial lines, waveguides or VHF relay links. A recent theoretical study[1] has shown that such a system would require repeaters at intervals of fifty miles or less. A system of this kind could provide television coverage, at a very considerable cost, over the whole of a small country. It would be out of the question to provide a large continent with such a service, and only the main centres of population could be included in the network.

The problem is equally serious when an attempt is made to link television services in different parts of the globe. A relay chain several thousand miles long would cost millions, and transoceanic services would still be impossible. Similar considerations apply to the provision of wide-band frequency modulation and other services, such as high-speed facsimile which are by their nature restricted to the ultra-high-frequencies.

Many may consider the solution proposed in this discussion too far-fetched to be taken very seriously. Such an attitude is unreasonable, as everything envisaged here is a logical extension of developments in the last ten years—in particular the perfection of the long-range rocket of which V2 was the prototype. While this article was being written, it was announced that the Germans were considering a similar project, which they believed possible within fifty to a hundred years.

Before proceeding further, it is necessary to discuss briefly certain fundamental laws of rocket propulsion and "astronautics." A rocket which achieved a sufficiently great speed in flight outside the earth's atmosphere would never return. This "orbital" velocity is 8 km per sec. (5 miles per sec), and a rocket which attained it would become an artificial satellite, circling the world for ever with no expenditure of power—a second moon, in fact.

The German transatlantic rocket A10 would have reached more than half this velocity.

It will be possible in a few more years to build radio controlled rockets which can be steered into such orbits beyond the limits of the atmosphere and left to broadcast scientific information back to the earth. A little later, manned rockets will be able to make similar flights with sufficient excess power to break the orbit and return to earth.

There are an infinite number of possible stable orbits, circular and elliptical, in which a rocket would remain if the initial conditions were correct. The velocity of 8 km/sec. applies only to the closest possible orbit, one just outside the atmosphere, and the period of revolution would be about 90 minutes. As the radius of the orbit increases the velocity decreases, since gravity is diminishing and less centrifugal force is needed to balance it. Fig. 1 shows this graphically. The moon, of course, is a particular case and would lie on the curves of Fig. 1 if they were produced. The proposed German space-stations would have a period of about four and a half hours.

It will be observed that one orbit, with a radius of 42,000 km, has a period of exactly 24 hours. A body in such an orbit, if its plane coincided with that of the

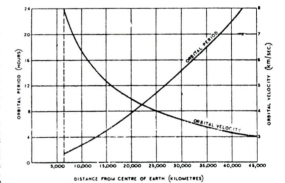

Fig. 1. Variation of orbital period and velocity with distance from the centre of the earth.

Much of the new technology Clarke was talking about came out of some remarkable years in the 1940s.

THREE YEARS THAT MADE THE DIFFERENCE

The movement in communication technology of which we are speaking grew mostly out of the publication of Clarke's own modest four-page article in the British radio journal, *Wireless World,* in 1945, which was entitled "Extra-Terrestrial Relays" and set forth with amazing foresight the idea and potential of the communication satellite.[2] In 1946 came the publication of John Von Neumann's historic monograph on the theory of the modern computer; every electronic computer built since then has followed in general Von Neumann's pattern.[3] The year 1947 saw the invention, at the Bell Telephone Laboratories, of the transistor. The inventors were Bardeen, Brattain, and Shockley. They won a Nobel Prize for it, and more important, out of their invention has grown a far-reaching series of developments in microelectronics, including the chip.

But be wary. Ages of humankind usually do not start on any given day, as we have said. The roots of the fourth age of information, if there is one now under way, undoubtedly include television, which in its primitive form dates to the late nineteenth century, and a great deal of other science not made into machines before the middle of our own century. There was even a small electronic computer operating at the Iowa State University in 1939, the invention of J. V. Atanassoff. Pioneer work in solid-state physics in the early twentieth century laid a basis for the transistor and the chip. So we have learned to restrain ourselves from decreeing birthdays for historical periods. For example, the day Columbus "discovered" America was apparently by no means the first day the continent was seen by Europeans. Therefore let us not announce that a new age of communication began in 1945 or 1946 or 1947, although we can confidently say that the communication discoveries of the 1940s are at the heart of modern change in the field.

We have never been very skillful at estimating the effect of new communication technology, in any case. Anthony Wedgwood Benn, when he was postmaster general of Great Britain, told the story of how a post office engineer testified before a committee of Parliament on the telegraph, which had just been demonstrated by Samuel Morse in the United States. "Let the Americans have their telegraph," he said. "They need it. We do not. We have plenty of boys to carry messages."[4]

Clarke passed on this story and jokingly related his own picture of how he imagined an evaluation committee might have performed in 1450 if set up to decide whether government funds should be committed to develop "Mr. Gutenberg's ingenious invention." Their recommendation, said Clarke, would undoubtedly have been, "No, because so few of the population can read."[5]

Actually the scientists of the 1940s whose inventions stood at the inauguration of what we suspect may be a new communication age were themselves too conservative in estimating the future of their ideas. Clarke wrote to the editor of the *Wireless World* that the communication satellite was really an idea whose time would probably not come before, say, half a century—in the 1990s. Actually, the first Sputnik was in orbit in 1957, only 12 years after Clarke published his article. The first large modern computers were being built within a year of Von Neumann's paper. Transistors were put to work almost at once to miniaturize electronic equipment, and within two decades Silicon Valley had grown in California to make use of the potential of the silicon chip.

Between 1957 and 1980, approximately 25,000 artificial satellites were launched into space. The Intelsat international communication system has more than 100 nation members. The number of regional and international, military and civilian, observation and relay satellite systems continues to grow. Satellites are in constant use for observing the surface of the earth, for forecasting weather, for helping aircraft navigate, and for many other purposes.

Computers in Von Neumann's time were building sized: The same output now is built into a machine the size of a desk.[6] The fifth-generation computer, when it comes into use, may do as much as the fourth-generation machine, with apparatus not much larger than a few chips. Speed of operation has increased inversely with size. The National Academy of Science estimated in 1970 that a building full of persons without calculators could make 125 million multiplications for about $12.5 million. Give them hand calculators and the job would cost about $2.5 million. On the first large electronic computer, 125 million multiplications would have cost no more than $130,000. And on the fastest computer available in 1970, the task would have cost—$4.00![7] Compared to the best of today's computers, the 1970 instruments moved at turtle speed. And the new generation of computers—perhaps in the 1990s—will have still vaster capabilities.

Chips, the tiny pieces of silicon that can hold hundreds or thousands of electronic instruments like transistors, switches, relays, and amplifiers, all in a space as big as the nail of one's little finger, now have in that small size much of the capability of the great machines of 20 years ago. More than anything else they are responsible for our new ability to do so much in electronics with so little. Ten years ago, the Astro Division of Marquardt Corporation estimated that with solid-state electronics all information recorded in the last 10,000 years could be stored, if one wanted to collect it, inside a single 6-foot cube—216 cubic feet.

How big, then, would an electronic cube have to be to store the 12 million books of the Library of Congress? A cubic inch or two, perhaps? What about the entire *Encyclopaedia Britannica?* Much less. Once I sat in London and played at calculating, with some of my friends, how long it would take to transfer the entire contents of the Bibliothèque Française in Paris to the British Museum in London. We estimated 7 to 17 minutes depending on the form the material could be put in and how many computer circuits one could get.

It is hard to make ourselves comprehend this post-1945 combination of distant communication made possible by the satellite, communication and calculation at the speed of light by means of the computer and other modern electronics, and great storage and manipulative capacity now possible in almost infinitely tiny space by the newest solid-state electronics. Small wonder, then, that we have trouble envisaging the potential these new developments offer us, and pondering what we shall do about them.

THE BEGINNING OF A NEW AGE

How did the people feel who stood at the end of the Middle Ages, looking ahead into the Renaissance? The chances are they had no idea that they were seeing anything remarkable. Historical ages are decreed by historians after the fact, usually long after the time, and they look different in perspective. If there was a day when the Middle Ages ended in Europe and the Renaissance began, it was probably much like the days before and after it. People may have been aware of some extraordinarily fine poetry coming from a man named Petrarch, or of a stirring of art and architecture in Italy. But if they knew they were facing into a new age, they did not say so. Time eddies around us like water around the ankles of a child wading in it. One bit of water is pretty much like another; one day like another. And yet how might the times have looked, what different things might people have looked for, if they had realized they stood at a border crossing in history where they could look back and look forward and see what might in the future be called a new age of humankind?

These speculations are of more than usual importance to us now because some of the people looking most seriously at these times tell us we do indeed stand at the beginning of a new age in which life and problems will be greatly different. Call it an age of information. Call it a communication revolution, as we have said. Whatever it is to be called, there is a surprising amount of agreement that something is beginning to happen that will change fundamentally what we know, how we think, how we live.

Let us not make too much of the idea of a communication *revolution*. It is easy to forget how many social "revolutions" have helped in the last 400 years to make modern times. A series of political revolutions has distributed power more widely than to a few privileged persons and has come near to making colonialism a thing of the past. An almost worldwide educational revolution has made it possible for most persons to learn to read and write and count, and for a high proportion of them, to go as far in school as their abilities justify. An agricultural revolution has divided land into economically efficient units, introduced new agricultural technology, and by producing more calories, released more farmers to industry and business. And finally, an industrial revolution in the late eighteenth and early nineteenth centuries has substituted new sources of energy for manual labor, speeded up production by using machines, and created fast transportation and long-range communication. Therefore, if we were now to name a part of tomorrow a communication revolution, it would probably be seen in the future as merely one of a number of such events and reorganizations that grew out of the Renaissance. If it were to result in what tomorrow's historians will call an age of information, that might very likely be interpreted not as a product of certain technology that came into being in the 1940s, but rather as a product of the combined revolutions we have passed through.

WHAT IS REALLY HAPPENING TO INFORMATION

Remember that what we are talking about is not primarily revolution, but information. We are looking toward a time when, as Daniel Bell predicted some years ago, knowledge would be the main factor in the economic growth of postindustrial society, and, as Peter Drucker wrote a little later, knowledge rather than capital would come to be both the "primary industry" and the "essential productive resource" of society. If we look around us now we see those things beginning to happen. Machlup surprised many people by his 1958 calculation that 29 percent of the compensation of the U.S. labor force went for information services.[8] A 1976 Stanford dissertation by Marc Porat raised that estimate to approximately 50 percent.[9] This is as striking a fact as that the proportion of the population working in agriculture has fallen in a century from 80 percent to less than 8 percent. Increasingly we see intelligent machines making machines by means of the information stored within them and the cybernetic control they can exert by exchanging information. Robots are replacing humans on assembly lines. Thus computers are building automobiles now in Japan, and they will doubtless be building chips and computers both in the United States and Japan. It is estimated that the "knowledge industry" has been growing at the rate of about 10 percent per year. Japan has been putting about 6 per cent of its gross national product into telecommunications and computers. The Canada Science Council estimated that in 1980 about 5 percent of Canada's GNP was going into computers alone. And in France the computer industry several years ago passed the automobile industry in size.

That trend will obviously intersect you and me, and we can hardly avoid asking what it will mean to us. That we shall have the opportunity and the problem of dealing with more information, coming faster, from farther away, doing more, is clear. More specifically we can expect that

1. More information will be available to us, expanding our horizons, offering us more knowledge with which to do what we want to do. But as the flow increases, it will also increase the chance of an overload.
2. Information will come faster, allowing us to make use sooner of findings and developments that would be helpful to us. But as it comes faster it will force us to create mechanisms and institutions to scan and sort and process it more quickly and efficiently.
3. A higher proportion of our information will come from farther away, allowing us to communicate by mass media or point-to-point communication anywhere on earth, to get in touch with virtually anyone anywhere we want to reach, and holding out the chance of relating people to people, culture to culture, in a way that the world has dreamed for a long time about doing.
4. More of the information flow will be point-to-point rather than point-to-mass, so individuals will have more control over what they receive and the channels they use. We see signs of this now as "narrow-casting" cuts into the domain of broadcasting, telephones ride satellite waves everywhere, and two-way use of radio and television channels becomes easier and less expensive.
5. Important tasks that would ordinarily be done by humans will be given to computers. An example is distant space travel.
6. Consequently, information is likely to be a source of power to those who have quick access to it, and can store, retrieve, and process it efficiently.

THE COMING COMBAT OF OPPORTUNITY VERSUS OVERLOAD

Thus, as many have observed, the stage is set for a battle between opportunity and overload. Increasingly in recent times, power has gone with information, perhaps even more with information than with resources. Japan, for example, is relatively short of resources, except its people, and their most valuable resource has been the information they have been able to gather. The nation that can scan, process, store, and retrieve information efficiently is likely now to have a power advantage such as came in previous ages with natural materials, industrial efficiency, and military strength. People who have their hands on information have a long advantage in competing with less informed neighbors.

On the other hand, the kind of information we are talking about is different from what circulated in the coffeehouses in 1600 or what children in a previously unschooled country learn in elementary school. It requires high technology. It requires a political and economic system geared up to a speed in processing and checking information never before asked of them.

What is the realistic chance of overload? For a nation, that question involves an amount of complexity we can hardly discuss here. For an individual, for the complex problem reduced to the level of you and me, the danger seems very real. Toffler takes it very seriously, indeed. He considers information overload one of the most likely conditions of "future shock." "Man has limited capacity to process information," he says. "Overloading the system leads to serious back down of performance."[10]

Take my own homely example. Presently I feel it necessary to become familiar with the contents of about 50 scholarly journals. These are the ones I *know* I should be familiar with; how many of the hundred thousand I do not know but should know, I am not prepared to say. To keep up professionally I should read several hundred books a year, and a large number of the preprints and manuscripts that circulate among scholars. I should also keep in touch with 50 or more scholars who are working on problems that interest me, and answer the letters of perhaps 100 students and scholars who write to ask about something I am supposed to know that interests them. What I have listed is already an impossible task, even if I had no need to sleep or to write my own books and papers. But it illustrates what the information explosion, at its present stage, means to one communication scholar; in some science fields, it must be still more formidable.

The most feasible solution currently available for that kind of problem is to share the task. That is why we have reviews, abstracts, indexes. They at least help scholars to decide what they themselves must read. In decades ahead, some persons may find it rewarding to make scanning and summarizing one of their chief scholarly tasks. And ultimately such a system will be moved to the computer line.

Take another example. The television installation in my home has 36 channels, almost all of which are presently occupied. Six of them are taken up by local stations. Others are "super stations," all-news stations, cable services of different kinds, religious stations, security cameras, and so forth. One channel is for local groups and organizations; another is an index to currently available programs. Ultimately, we expect *all* the channels to be in use. In fact, we anticipate that some day we shall have about 80 channels, many of them providing two-way service so that we can order up computerized study courses, ask for certain kinds of information, search data bases, and shop by television.

Looking forward to a choice of 80 channels is mind-boggling. Even now we have more than we can use. In such a situation any viewer is likely to change his or her habits. It is hard to think, any longer, of staying with a single channel all day, or even all evening. We are much more likely, even now, than we used to be, to plan our viewing in advance with the aid of program guides, rather than explore the dial. Suppose there is more than one program we would like to watch at a given hour. We can, of course, use the videocassette recorder (VCR), and record a second program while we watch our first choice. That leaves us only 22 or 23 channels we are unable to cover at a given time; it is rather awesome to think that if we had 80 channels we should have to leave 78 or 79 of them unused! If the average channel carries 18 hours a day, that would mean that 1440 hours of televised material of some kind would be coming into a home every day, out of which an average adult would choose about three hours, or, with a VCR, a few more. Given 1440 hours to choose from, will an individual assign more time to television? Or simply become frustrated?

Suppose that someone really wants to understand the complex and changing world we live in. That person will have available not only the usual radio and television news, but also shortwave radio to bring daily reports from at least 20 other countries. He or she will have the newspapers, newsmagazines, new books of which at least 1000 per year will surely have something important to say about the present world. The cable will offer additional services, like the news services of the *New York Times* or the *Washington Post,* the *New York Times Index,* and a passing parade of diplomats, scholars, travelers, and the like. In time we shall be able to have much of this flow of information printed out in our homes or offices, if we want to pay for it. How will we feel about that confrontation of opportunity with overload? Will we be grateful to have so much choice for the few hours we can devote each day to informing ourselves on the world? Or will we rather look fondly back to the quiet time when two newspapers a day, two magazines a month, an annual speech in town by our congressperson, a ten-minute stop every four years by one of the presidential campaign trains, and a week of lectures every year at summer chautauqua filled our window on the world?

Let us take an example less homely than the ones we have been looking at. George R. White, the Xerox engineer, has estimated with some rather fancy mathematics that an average human's total cerebral store of information probably increased about one order of magnitude after printing came into use, and another order of magnitude after the electronic revolution—in other words an increase of 100 times in 500 years. During that same time, he calculated, the total data available to humans increased two orders of magnitude as a result of

printing and another two orders since the coming of communication electronics
—10,000 times![11]

It isn't necessary to argue with White's counting or his mathematics. What if he is wrong by an order of magnitude, or even two orders, so that only 1000 or 100 times, rather than 10,000 times, as much information is now available to us as we had in 1450? The practical question is, what is a concerned citizen to do? Sample the available feast, and be frustrated? Give all waking hours to the pursuit of information—and still be frustrated? Or curse the age of information and tune in a soap opera?

THE EFFECTS OF THE INCREASING PACE OF INFORMATION

A word about the increasing pace of information. In 1805 it took Nelson's flagship crew 11 minutes to put out the flags that passed a brief but historic message from the admiral to the fleet at Trafalgar: "England expects every man will do his duty." Eleven minutes. Until the middle of the nineteenth century, distant messages could travel only as fast as transportation. In the time of the Mongol emperors, China had the fastest courier system in the world—about 100 miles a day. Baron Reuter's pigeons, carrying news bulletins across the English Channel, as we have said, could fly as fast as 60 miles an hour for a short distance. Then, of course, came the telegraph, and later radio, and still later the satellite, which has made distance relatively unimportant in the flow of information. After that the computer. It is not true, of course, that distance and speed are no longer matters of concern to us in handling information, for they will always be so; when the speed of light is within our power, we shall look for ways to carry knowledge still faster; when we can communicate easily around our own galaxy, we shall begin reaching toward more distant galaxies.

But the individual problems of an information revolution blend into societal problems. For example, how much better informed will the average person be as a result of meeting the flood tide of new information? Will people retreat from it, as Toffler predicted, and watch an "escape" program on entertainment television? Will they truly profit from it? Those people who learn the most are likely to be the ones who already have the most information, for in knowledge as in economics it seems to be a condition of development that the rich grow richer, and the poor relatively poorer. The information-rich will probably take time to learn the indexing devices. Just as "Sesame Street" apparently widened the knowledge gap between the children who already knew more and those who knew less, so is the information age likely to widen the gap within society. At least it will do so at first, although it will probably result ultimately in raising the general average of information in the population, as printing did. And inasmuch as there is some ceiling on the amount that even the information-haves can absorb, there is always the chance to bring the general average up closer to that ceiling and thus to reduce the differences within society if we want to make it a major policy to do so. We have the tools to accomplish such a thing. We have the tools to bring knowledge to people whether they are in the classroom, library, factory, city, village, or igloo. We have now learned to use mechanisms such as distance teaching (for example, the open university) and computerized instruction to offer life-long education. If a society really wants to distribute knowledge more widely, we can hardly say that there are no ways to do it.[12]

One trend in the revolutionary age of information will probably transfer to individuals more responsibility for use of the channels of information. The typewriter and the photocopy machine have in a sense already allowed people to be their own publishers; tape recorders, walkie-talkies, transceivers, citizens band radio, and so forth, have in a sense made it possible for all of us to play a part in broadcasting; movie cameras and VCRs, for us to make some of our own movies and television. Microcomputers are making it possible for individuals to share some of the capabilities of the great machines that are too costly for any individual. Point-to-point communication, as we have have suggested, promises to loom larger in the future than in the past, relative to mass communication. In other words, the day of big media and little human seems to be drawing toward a close.

National governments will have a similar problem in the age of communication. Information will come so fast that the traditional lead time of diplomacy will be reduced almost to zero. The general public will know what is happening almost as soon as their leaders do. This will be exaggerated by the new tendency of governments to speak directly to other nations through the media—as Iran chose to speak during the time when it held the U.S. hostages in the Teheran embassy. This makes an awkward situation for foreign offices, which traditionally have relied on a period of secrecy during which to read the cables, canvas the situation, and work out a policy before they go public. If their lead time disappears they will have to invent some new mechanisms for reality testing in order to decide quickly whether unofficial messages are true or false, rumor or fact, serious or manipulative. All of us, in truth, will have to develop quicker means of reality testing, in a time of very fast communication flow, in order to know what parts of that flow are worth our serious attention and concern.

Still another problem shared by government and citizens is privacy. Increasingly all the details of our lives will be recorded in computer memories which, as we are finding out from clever manipulation of bank accounts and credit card numbers, are far from impregnable. Any computer code can be cracked; and the contents of any record system can be made available to other government departments, to business that wants to check our credit, and in some cases to news and sales organizations. This makes us feel a bit uneasy, not only because someone might tell another organization whether we have overdue bills, but rather because of the extent to which the details of our lives can be paraded in front of people who really have no right to know. This is perhaps inevitable in a society that has so much need of the computer. The government must have ways to record a great deal of information. So also must private business, science, and education. There is little doubt that the computer will be the machine to do this. It will probably become the great communicating machine of the new age, because it is the only machine able to handle so much information.

THE PROBLEM OF A "THINKING MACHINE"

The computer raises another question that may be largely theoretical at the moment but may become very practical in the years ahead: the future of a "thinking machine" in human society.

Is the computer really a thinking machine? Can it think? The commonsense answer is that no machine can be more intelligent than its designers and builders. No machine can be expected to be imaginative or creative. Those are "human" qualities. Or are they?[13]

Let us approach this matter cautiously. Some of the scientists who know most about computers do not agree with the commonsense answer given above. The whole discipline of artificial intelligence that flourishes within the computer science departments of some of our greatest universities is built on the premise that the ability to think—or something so like it that we would have trouble finding the right words to discriminate between them—can, now or later, be built into advanced computers. Norbert Wiener, the M.I.T. mathematician, writes: "It is my thesis that machines can and do transcend some of the limitations of their designers. . . . It may well be that in principle we cannot make any machine, the elements of whose behavior we cannot comprehend sooner or later. This does not mean in any way that we shall be able to comprehend them in substantially less time than the operation of the machine, nor even within any given number of years or generations."[14] It has been pointed out, in other words, that even machines less intelligent than humans might escape from our control by sheer speed of operation.

Scientists like Wiener tend to agree on these points:

> Today's computers are "morons" in intelligence, although phenomenally fast in performing calculations and other operations with data.
>
> They can play a fairly good game of chess and compose a fairly interesting piece of music.

Some computers have been built that can learn from their mistakes and presumably never repeat them. (It has been remarked wryly that to learn from one's mistakes is human, but never to repeat them would be *super*human.)

Some computers have been built to search for proofs of logical theorems, and have been reported—although I have not myself seen this—sometimes to produce proofs that had not previously occurred to scholars.

Some computers have been built within artificial intelligence studies that are capable of revising their circuits to adapt to new requirements. As these machines become ever faster and more complex, it will probably become necessary to use computers to help design and program other computers.

When we reach this last stage we are perilously close to the borders of science fiction—the idea that computers are not so much machines as they are a species, able to reproduce and guide themselves and perhaps make their own future. It is not at all out of the question to envision spaceships driven by computers exploring the universe for us, inasmuch as computers are not inhibited from any amount of space travel by the need to eat or breathe oxygen, or see the doctor or the dentist, or by the limitations of human life span. Furthermore, we can build into a computer some sense organs a human does not have or cannot equal—senses that would allow it to detect radio waves, for example; eyes that see more and farther —infrared rays, for example; and ears that could hear a far wider range of frequencies than we hear. If we should create such a computerized pilot to represent us in space, we should certainly build into it not only capabilities for reporting back to us but also the ability to make some decisions of its own.

The computer is still in its stone age, its keepers admit. On the other hand, some experimental computers have promised to move far beyond that stage. Personal computers to help their owners overcome the decision overload may be a step or two up from the Neolithic. That is the key question: How much farther can computer scientists go toward giving their machines decision-making and reproductive capability? It is theoretically possible to build a computer to design another computer, or to make decisions on a much broader base than any computer has yet proved its ability to do, or to travel around the universe and report back to us. Yet there is no evidence as yet that encourages us to go as far as Clarke did: "The tools the ape-men invented enabled them to evolve into their successor, *Homo sapiens*. The tool *we* have invented *is* our successor."[15]

THE REAL CHALLENGE TO THE COMPUTER

We need not go as far as Clarke went in that statement, and still we can accept the likelihood that the computer has a special importance in the age of information, now probably just beginning. It is not only the most powerful information machine

Top: *First 600-scan-line photograph taken by the Surveyor I spacecraft on the moon's surface, 1966.* Bottom: *First photograph ever taken on the surface of Mars; it was transmitted by Viking I, 1976.*

ever built; it represents also the longest step yet taken to scale the supposedly unscalable barrier between thinking humans and machines. Human beings have never before had a machine capable of giving them the help a computer can, if used wisely.

Men and women in the years when they were learning to write may have had some of the same sense of excitement, of uncertain destiny, with opportunity and danger both standing along the path, as we are experiencing today. Perhaps our

Earth rising over the horizon of the moon. This is the view that scientists for many centuries dreamed of and that become possible for the first time in 1969 with the Apollo space flights. It is an appropriate symbol of the kind of experiences that modern science, modern transportation, and modern communication are bringing to earth dwellers. The picture is from NASA, was reprinted by Carl Sagan in his book Cosmos, *and has many times been shown on television. A picture taken on the moon, transmitted through 250,000 miles of space, shown on television, and printed in books is truly a long way from the footprints of prehumans that we saw in Chapter 2.*

present status can be summed up in a sentence: Humans, in this new age, are going to be responsible for their own intellectual destinies in a way that they have never been before.

It is almost impossible to believe that no other of the many billions of planets in the universe has developed an intelligent race of inhabitants. It has been asked, in complete seriousness, whether when such a race acquires the technical knowledge to blow itself up, it will not be likely to do so. This may be the reason, some scientists have suggested, why no message has ever come to us from the intelligent beings who can be assumed to exist on some of the planets outside our solar system. But surely human beings, those intelligent creatures who have learned to think and talk and write and print, who have created institutions like the city to make intensive use of communication and electronic technology to extend communication over the earth and reach toward the distant stars, can restrain their new control of natural forces sufficiently to avoid destroying themselves and their heritage. Let us hope that with the aid of our new technology, 500 years from now we ourselves may be exploring the universe and using the discoveries for our good, rather than leaving a burned-out planet for visitors from another solar system to inspect with pity and amazement.

SUGGESTIONS FOR FURTHER READING

This volume began with a quotation from William Shakespeare: "What's past is prologue." By this same token all the readings so far suggested in these chapters are prologue for reading about the coming age of information. A number of new books, however, are directly concerned with the age to come and are worth our attention. Notable among these is the literature on computers. There is not likely to be any shortage of readings in a field of science and technology growing as fast as this one, but the titles are likely to go rather soon out of date. Therefore, your reading list needs to be kept up. A good place to begin, with present books, is H. H. Goldstine, *The Computer from Pascal to Von Neumann* (Princeton, N.J.: Princeton University Press, 1972). Another good background book is J. R. Pierce, *Symbols, Signals, and Noise* (New York: McGraw-Hill, 1961). Bridging the gap between these machines and the societies that use them are titles like H. Sackman, *Computers, System Science and Evolving Society* (New York: Wiley, 1967); J. G. Kemeny, *Man and the Computer* (New York: Scribner, 1974); and C. J. Sippl and R. Bullen, *Computers at Large* (Indianapolis: Bobbs-Merrill, 1976). Sippl is also author of a useful article, "Computers," in *Encyclopaedia Britannica,* 14th ed.

On the social rather than the technical side are two interesting collections of papers: A. F. Weston, ed., *Information Technology in a Democracy* (Cambridge, Mass.: Harvard University Press, 1971); and George Gerbner, Larry P. Gross, and W. Melody, eds., *Communications Technology and Social Policy: Understanding the New "Cultural Revolution"* (New York: Wiley, 1973). Readings on the communication "revolution" or the "age of communication" include Daniel Bell, *The Coming of Post-Industrial Society* (New York:

Basic Books, 1976); Frederick Williams, *The Computer Revolution* (Beverly Hills, Calif.: Sage, 1982); Ben Bagdikian, *The Information Machines* (New York: Harper & Row, 1971); and a collection of conference papers edited by Alex S. Edelstein, J. E. Bowers, and S. N. Harsel, *Information Societies: Covering the Japanese and American Experience* (Seattle: University of Washington, International Communication Center, 1976). Anthony Smith's *Goodbye Gutenberg: The Newspaper Revolution of the 80s* (New York: Oxford University Press, 1980), and Wilson Dizard's *The Coming Information Age* (New York: Longman, 1982) are both easy-to-read introductions. On the economics of the coming age there is M. Porat's Department of Commerce publication, based on his Stanford dissertation, *The Information Economy* (New York: Elsevier Science Publishing Co., 1984); and M. Jussawala, *The Economics of Communication* (in press). And finally there is a futuristic volume with a rather grim title, built around a scenario which many futurists consider a realistic possibility for the coming age: P. and A. Ehrlich, *Extinction: The Causes and Consequences of the Disappearance of Species* (New York: Random House, 1981).

QUESTIONS TO THINK ABOUT

1. What signs, if any, of a new communication age have you yourself seen in the last decade or two?
2. We have now had five centuries with print, 50 to 100 years with the electronic media, about 35 years with electronic computers. What do you think historians in 2100 will say about the changes they have made in our lives and our society?
3. Imagine ahead 25 years. In what respects do you think the mass media will be different?
4. How do you see the information overload problem working out?
5. About $50 billion is spent in the United States each year on mass media and related information services, perhaps twice that much on education and libraries. These are conservative figures. Are we getting all that we should out of this expenditure?
6. In 1985 the average household in the United States devoted about 7 hours, 10 minutes a day to television, a little over 3 hours to radio. The average for films, magazines, and books would be somewhere around 1 hour per person per day, depending on age, education, and affluence. Corresponding figures a century ago when we had only the printed media would probably have been between 1 and 2 hours total per person. What have we replaced in our lives by this large modern time budget allocated to the media? And what future changes do you see likely in our allocations of time to information

TIME CAPSULE

Arthur C. Clarke sets down theory of communication satellite	1945
John Von Neumann sets down theory of electronic computer	1946
Three scientists at Bell Telephone Laboratories—Bardeen, Brattain, and Shockley—invent the transistor	1947
First large modern computers	1946–1950
Microprocessing begins to transform electronics	1947
First communication satellite, USSR Sputnik	1957

Fritz Machlup of Princeton calculates that 29% of compensation for
    U.S. labor force goes for information services   1958

U.S. Telstar satellite, first of a series of world communication
    instruments   .   1962

Portable video recorder   1968

Man on the moon   1969

Microelectronic chips in wide use   1970

Fiber optic transmission successfully developed   1975

Experiments with Videotext and similar machines   1978

First space shuttle flies   1981

Number of personal computers in the United States estimated to be
    more than one million   1984

R E F E R E N C E S

Chapter 1. THE DAWN YEARS

1. Geoffrey Bibby, *The Testimony of the Spade* (New York: Knopf, 1956), pp. 88–92.
2. See John E. Pfeiffer, *The Creative Explosion: An Inquiry into the Origins of Art and Religion* (New York: Harper & Row, 1982), especially Chapter 8.
3. For general background here, see Jacquetta Hawkes, *Prehistory* (New York: Harper & Row, 1963).
4. Maurice Fabre, *A History of Communications* (translated from French; New York: Hawthorn, 1963), pp. 15–17.

Chapter 2. HOW LONG IS A LONG TIME?

1. This chapter leans on Carl Sagan's brilliantly written *The Dragons of Eden: Speculations on the Evolution of Human Intelligence* (New York: Ballantine Books, 1977), especially the section on "The Cosmic Calendar," pp. 13–17.
2. See Chapter 1, "The Natural Stage," in Jacquetta Hawkes, *Prehistory* (New York: Harper & Row, 1963), pp. 61ff.
3. The quotation is from Hawkes, p. 47.
4. Sir Leonard Woolley, *The Beginnings of Civilization* (New York: Harper & Row, 1963), p. 379.
5. F. Soedjatmoko, "Communication and Cultural Identity," *Third World Quarterly* 1, no. 3 (July 1979): 86.

Chapter 3. THE BIRTH OF LANGUAGE

1. See Randall Harrison, "Nonverbal Communication," pp. 93–113, in Ithiel de Sola Pool and Wilbur Schramm (eds.), *Handbook of Communication* (Boston: Houghton Mifflin, 1976).
2. Edward T. Hall, *The Silent Language* (New York: Doubleday, 1959), pp. 196ff.
3. The quotation is from Mario Pei, *The Story of Language,* Rev. Ed. (Philadelphia: Lippincott, 1965), p. 11.
4. Pei, pp. 22–23.
5. One of Noam Chomsky's best known books on the structure of language is *Aspects of the Theory of Syntax* (Cambridge, Mass.: M.I.T. Press, 1965). See also *Chomsky Selected Readings,* edited by J. P. B. Allen (New York: Oxford, 1971).
6. Pei, *The Story of Language,* p. 19.
7. Pei, p. 20.
8. An article briefing Jaynes's presentation to the American Psychological Association is "The Evolution of Language," *APA Monitor* 1 (January 1976): 12–13.
9. See S. R. Harnad, H. D. Steklis, and Jane Lancaster, "From Hand to Mouth: Some Initial Steps in the Evolution of Language," *Annals of the New York Academy of Science* 280 (1975).
10. Gottfried Leibnitz, *New Essays on Human Understanding.* There have been many editions since the original publication in 1765. A recent edition has been published by the Cambridge University Press (1981), in which this topic is covered on pp. 282ff.

Chapter 4. THE INVENTION OF WRITING

1. On the growth of villages, see Jacquetta Hawkes, *Prehistory* (New York: Harper & Row, 1963), pp. 358–432, 395–398. Also see Gordon Childe, "Civilization, Cities, and Towns," *Antiquity* 121 (March 1957): 36ff; and Lewis Mumford, *The Culture of Cities* (New York: Harcourt, Brace and Co., 1938), pp. 285ff.
2. Maurice Fabre, *A History of Communications* (translated from French; New York: Hawthorn, 1963), p. 16.
3. Alex Haley, *Roots* (New York: Doubleday, 1976).
4. Good references on early astronomy are Leonard Woolley's *The Beginnings of Civilization* (New York: Harper & Row, 1963), especially pp. 418–432; and Carl Sagan's dramatically written volume *Cosmos* (New York: Random House, 1980), pp. 47ff, 170ff.
5. Lancelot Hogben, *From Cave Painting to Comic Strip* (New York: Chanticleer Press, 1948), pp. 40ff.
6. This quip is credited, perhaps apocryphally, to Shaw, and is consistent with his long interest in spelling reform.
7. Hogben, *From Cave Painting to Comic Strip.*
8. Fabre, *A History of Communications,* p. 26.
9. For a treatment of the Whorf–Sapir hypothesis, see J. B. Carroll (ed.), *Language, Thought, and Reality* (Cambridge, Mass.: M.I.T. Press, 1956).
10. Hogben, *From Cave Painting to Comic Strip,* p. 16.

Chapter 5. INSTITUTIONS OF COMMUNICATION: THE CITY

1. The quotation is from Lewis Mumford, *The Culture of Cities* (New York: Harcourt Brace Jovanovich, 1938), p. 3.
2. Mumford, p. 3.
3. Mumford, p. 5.
4. Leonard Woolley, *The Beginnings of Civilization* (New York: Harper & Row, 1963), p. 158.
5. Woolley, p. 169.
6. Ralph Turner, *The Great Cultural Traditions* (New York: McGraw-Hill, 1941), pp. 393–394.
7. S. N. Kramer, *From the Tablets of Sumer* (Indian Hills, Calif.: Falcon's Wing Press, 1956), pp. 3–9. See also Woolley's comments, *Beginnings,* pp. 393–399.
8. Turner, *Great Cultural Traditions,* p. 194.
9. Turner, pp. 194ff.
10. Turner, p. 432.
11. Woolley, *Beginnings,* p. 462.
12. Arnold J. Toynbee, *A Study of History* (London: Oxford, 3 vols., 1934), pp. 280ff.
13. See J. G. Dobson, *Ancient Education and Its Meaning to Us* (London: Oxford, 1935).
14. Turner, *Great Cultural Traditions,* p. 601.

Chapter 6. INSTITUTIONS OF COMMUNICATION: THE SCHOOL

1. See S. N. Kramer, *From the Tablets of Sumer* (Indian Hills, Calif.: Falcon's Wing Press, 1956).
2. See Leonard Woolley, *The Beginnings of Civilization* (New York: Harper & Row, 1963), pp. 467ff, for references to the scribe schools. Also Henri I. Marron, *Histoire de l'Education dans l'antiquité* (Paris: Editions du Seuil, 1948). An English translation has recently been issued by the University of Wisconsin Press (Madison, Wisconsin), 1982.
3. A useful introduction to the development of Chinese education is Ping Wen Kuo, *The Chinese System of Public Education* (New York: Columbia Teachers College, 1915). Also see Howard S. Galt, *A History of Chinese Educational Institutions* (London: A. Propthain, 1951).
4. Woolley, *Beginnings,* pp. 151–158.
5. The selection from the Upanishads is in *The Ten Principle Upanishads,* translated by Shri Purohit Swami and W. B. Yeats (London: A. P. Watts and Co., 1937), pp. 19–20.

6. For an introduction to education in Greece, see F. A. Beck, *Greek Education, 450–350 B.C.* (New York: Barnes & Noble, 1964), and John Emerson Baker's article in the *Encyclopaedia Britannica,* 14th ed., vol. 8, under "Education, History of."

7. The selection from Plutarch's "Life of Lycurgus" is from *Lives: The Dryden Plutarch,* revised by Arthur Hugh Clough (London: J. M. Dent, 1910), pp. 28–30.

8. See *Britannica,* 13th ed., pp. 323–324.

9. *Britannica,* 13th ed., pp. 323–324.

10. The "Dialogue on Women" is from Plato's *Republic,* Book 5, as translated by Benjamin Jowett, and published under several imprints.

11. From Aristotle's *The Art of Poetry,* Chapter 5, p. 1, as translated by Lane Cooper under the title *Aristotle on the Art of Poetry* (New York: Harcourt Brace Jovanovich, 1913), pp. 17–18.

12. For a helpful note on Roman education, see Baker's *Britannica,* 14th ed., article, under "Education, History of," pp. 522–523.

13. Adapted from Arthur O. Norton, *Readings in the History of Education—Medieval Universities* (Cambridge, Mass.: Harvard University Press, 1909), pp. 21–24.

14. Norton, pp. 21–24.

Chapter 7. A LANGUAGE FOR MATHEMATICS AND SCIENCE

1. See O. Kroehler, "The Ability of Birds to Count," in J. R. Newman, *The World of Mathematics* (New York: Simon & Schuster, 4 vols., 1956), pp. 489–498. Also Edna F. Kramer, *The Main Stream of Mathematics* (New York: Oxford, 1952), pp. 8–9.

2. Kramer, p. 12.

3. Kramer, p. 12.

4. Kramer, p. 13. Also see "From Numbers to Numerals and from Numerals to Computation" by D. E. Smith and J. Ginsburg, in Newman, *World of Mathematics,* vol. 1, pp. 442–464.

5. Newman, pp. 442–464.

6. Kramer, *Main Stream of Mathematics,* p. 13.

7. Kramer, p. 13.

8. The Whitehead quote is in Newman, *World of Mathematics,* vol. 1, p. 412.

9. Kramer, *Main Stream,* pp. 20–22.

10. For the reference to Laplace and the number zero, see Jacquetta Hawkes, *Prehistory* (New York: Harper & Row, 1963), pp. 7–9.

11. Carl Sagan, *Cosmos* (New York: Random House, 1980), pp. 175ff.

12. Sagan, pp. 175ff.

13. For the Democritus reference, see Sagan, pp. 180–181.

14. The Anaxagoras reference is in Sagan, p. 182.

15. See Sagan, pp. 209–210.

16. Sagan, p. 210.

17. Sagan, p. 210.

18. Whitehead quote appears in Newman, *World of Mathematics,* p. 411.

19. Whitehead quote in Newman, p. 412.

20. Whitehead quote in Newman, p. 411.

Chapter 8. THE DAY OF THE PRINTER

1. See T. F. Carter, *The Invention of Printing and Its Spread Westward* (revised by L. C. Goodrich; New York: Ronald Press, 1955), pp. 3–5.

2. Carter, p. 6.

3. All the books on early printing have sections on this topic. In addition to those mentioned, see T. L. DeVinne,

The Invention of Printing (New York: F. Hart, 1876; reprinted Detroit: Gale Research Co., 1969), and K. R. Burchard's article under "Printing," in the *Encyclopaedia Britannica,* 14th ed.

4. See Burchard; DeVinne; Carter, *Invention of Printing.*
5. DeVinne, pp. 67–68.
6. This appears in most of the books mentioned. A good introduction is by Burchard, in the *Encyclopaedia Britannica,* 13th ed., pp. 1051ff.
7. See Alfred W. Pollard, *The Fine Books* (New York: Putnam, 1912), p. 49.
8. Robert Lechene, in the *Encyclopaedia Britannica,* 15th ed., under "Printing," p. 1054.
9. Lechene, p. 1051.

Chapter 10. INSTITUTIONS OF THE MASS MEDIA: NEWS I

1. A useful note on early publishing is William Miller's article under "Publishing, History of," in the *Encyclopaedia Britannica,* 14th ed., pp. 223ff.
2. A good brief summary of the growth of the press is pp. 29–75 of P. M. Sandman, D. M. Rubin, and D. B. Sachsman, *Media: An Introductory Analysis of American Mass Communications,* 3rd ed. (Englewood Cliffs, N.J.: Prentice-Hall, 1982). See also E. Emery and M. C. Emery, *The Press and America,* 5th ed. (Englewood Cliffs, N.J.: Prentice-Hall, 1984), pp. 1–21; and, of course, Anthony Smith, *The Newspaper: An International History* (London: Thames and Hudson, 1979).
3. Smith, pp. 9–11.
4. Smith, pp. 24–25.
5. F. S. Siebert, *Freedom of the Press in England, 1476–1776* (Urbana: University of Illinois Press, 1952). Also R. Desmond, *The Newspaper Process* (Iowa City: University of Iowa Press, 1978).
6. Milton's *Areopagitica* has appeared in many editions. An easy place to find this passage is in Emery and Emery, *The Press and America,* p. 16.
7. Smith, *The Newspaper,* p. 48.
8. Smith, p. 30.
9. Smith, p. 105.

Chapter 11. INSTITUTIONS OF THE MASS MEDIA: NEWS II

1. Anthony Smith, *The Newspaper: An International History* (London: Thames and Hudson, 1979), p. 141.
2. See John C. Merrill and Harold A. Fischer, *The World's Great Dailies* (New York: Hastings House, 1980). Any of the standard histories of journalism will carry a section on the elite press.
3. See E. Emery and M. C. Emery, *The Press and America,* 5th ed. (Englewood Cliffs, N.J.: Prentice-Hall, 1984), pp. 141ff. Also Peter M. Sandman, David M. Rubin, David B. Sachsman, *Media: An Introductory Analysis of American Mass Communication* (Englewood Cliffs, N.J.: Prentice-Hall, 1972), p. 44.
4. This appeared in the *New York World,* May 11, 1883.
5. For a retelling of the "Yellow Kid" story, see Emery and Emery, *The Press in America,* pp. 285–286.
6. The *Encyclopaedia Britannica,* 14th ed., article "History of Publishing" will be useful here.
7. Emery and Emery, *The Press in America,* p. 316.
8. Paul S. Underwood in Merrill (ed.), *Global Journalism,* p. 101.
9. Underwood in Merrill, pp. 90–91.
10. For an even-handed discussion, see Jim Richstad and Michael H. Anderson (eds.), *Crisis in International News* (New York: Columbia University Press, 1981).
11. John Luter in Merrill, *Global Journalism,* p. 122.
12. See Victor Rosewater, *History of Cooperative News-Gathering in the United States* (New York: Appleton-Century-Crofts, 1930).
13. On the newsmagazines, see Emery and Emery, *The Press in America,* pp. 458–460.

Chapter 12. COMMUNICATION AND THE ELECTRONIC CENTURY

1. For some material on the scientists behind the Industrial Revolution, see C. Singer, "Science," in *British Science,* pp. 370–374.
2. See W. B. Brumit, "Photography," in *Encyclopaedia Britannica,* 14th ed., pp. 425–430.
3. For a brief account, see E. I. Green, "Telephone," in *Encyclopaedia Britannica,* 13th ed., pp. 83–86. On the telegraph, G. Hubbard, *Cooke and Wheatstone and the Invention of the Electric Telegraph* (London: Routledge and Kegan Paul, 1965). Also R. L. Thompson, *Wiring a Continent: The History of the Telegraph Industry in the United States, 1832–1866* (New York: Arno Press, 1972).
4. A convenient place to read Bell's letter is in Ithiel de Sola Pool (ed.), *The Social Impact of the Telephone* (Cambridge, Mass.: M.I.T. Press, 1977), pp. 156–157.
5. See H. E. Roys, "Phonograph," *Encyclopaedia Britannica,* 14th ed., pp. 901–909.
6. R. Griffith and S. W. Reed, "Motion Pictures," *Encyclopaedia Britannica,* 14th ed.
7. See O. Dunlap, *Marconi: The Man and His Wireless* (New York: Macmillan, 1937; reprinted by Arno Press, 1971).
8. C. H. Sterling and J. M. Kittross, *Stay Tuned: A Concise History of American Broadcasting* (Belmont, Calif.: Wadsworth, 1978).
9. Asa Briggs, *The History of Broadcasting in the United Kingdom* (London: Oxford, 1961–1970). Also, Erik Barnouw, *Tube of Plenty: The Evolution of American Television* (New York: Oxford, 1970).
10. G. Shiers, "Television 50 Years Ago," *Journal of Broadcasting* (Fall 1975): 393–394.
11. Shiers, 393–394.
12. *Television Inquiry. Part IV: Network Practices.* Committee on Interstate and Foreign Commerce, U.S. Senate, on Senate Resolutions 13 and 163 (June 12, 1956), p. 1707.

Chapter 13. LIVE PICTURES AND LIVE SOUNDS JOIN THE MASS MEDIA

1. A good start at reading on the early history of the films is Terry Ramsaye, *A Million and One Nights* (New York: Knopf, 1926, rep. 1960), and Paul Rotha and Richard Griffith, *Film Till Now,* 3rd ed. (New York: Twayne Publishers, 1960). Also Gerald Mast, *A Short History of the Movies* (New York: Simon & Schuster, 1971).
2. See Erik Barnouw, *A History of Broadcasting in the United States* (New York: Oxford University Press, 3 vols., 1966–1970).
3. For the KDKA story, a starting point is C. H. Sterling and J. M. Kittross, *Stay Tuned: A Concise History of American Broadcasting* (Belmont, Calif.: Wadsworth, 1978).
4. Concerning the press–broadcasting argument over news, start with Emery and Emery, *The Press and America,* 5th ed. (Englewood Cliffs, N.J.: Prentice-Hall, 1984), pp. 382–383. For the story from the broadcasters' side, see Sterling and Kittross, *Stay Tuned,* pp. 123, 133, 175.
5. On Murrow, see Alexander Kendrick, *Prime Time: The Life of Edward R. Murrow* (Boston: Little, Brown, 1969). Also sections on Murrow in Sterling and Kittross, and in Barnouw, *A History.*
6. On the Orson Welles broadcast, see Hadley Cantril, *The Invasion from Mars* (Princeton, N.J.: Princeton University Press, 1940).
7. See Barnouw, *A History,* and Sterling and Kittross, *Stay Tuned.*
8. The survey was made by the Roper organization and reported by the Television Information Office.
9. The transcript of the broadcast is reported in Sterling and Kittross, *Stay Tuned,* pp. 410–411. It appeared originally in *CBS Television News* (New York: CBS, 1970), pp. 76–78.

Chapter 14. INSTITUTIONS OF THE MASS MEDIA: ENTERTAINMENT

1. Bernard Rosenberg and David Manning White, (eds.), *Mass Culture: The Popular Arts in America* (Glencoe, Ill.: Free Press, 1957), p. 320.
2. Harold Mendelsohn and H. T. Spetnagel, "Entertainment as a Sociological Enterprise," in Percy Tannen-

baum, (ed.), *The Entertainment Function of Television* (Hillsdale, N.J.: Lawrence Erlbaum Associates, 1980), pp. 17ff.

3. Leo Lowenthal, "Historical Perspectives of Popular Culture," *Journal of Sociology* 55 (1950): 323–332.
4. Herbert Gans, *Popular Culture and High Culture* (New York: Basic Books, 1974), pp. 67ff.
5. Russell Lynes, *The Tastemakers* (New York: Harper and Brothers, 1954), Chapter 13.
6. Gans, *Popular Culture,* pp. 75ff.
7. Ralph L. Lowenstein, in Heinz Dietrich Fischer and Stefan Reinhard Melnik, *Entertainment: A Cross-Cultural Examination* (New York: Hastings House, 1979), p. 12.
8. Eli Rubinstein, et al., *Television and Social Behavior: Technical Report of the Surgeon General's Advisory Committee* (Washington, D.C.: National Institute of Mental Health, 1973) IV, p. 411.
9. Wilbur Schramm, Jack Lyle, and Edwin B. Parker, *Television in the Lives of Our Children* (Stanford, Calif.: Stanford University Press, 1961), pp. 1–2.
10. Herta Herzog, "What We Really Know about Daytime Serial Listeners," in Paul F. Lazarsfeld and Frank Stanton, (eds.), *Communication Research, 1942–1943* (New York: Duell, Sloan, and Pearce, 1944), pp. 3–33.
11. Bernard Berelson, "What Missing the Newspaper Means," in Paul F. Lazarsfeld and Frank Stanton, (eds.), *Communication Research, 1948–1949* (New York: Harper and Brothers, 1949), pp. 111–129.
12. William Stephenson, *The Play Theory of Mass Communication* (Chicago: University of Chicago Press, 1967), pp. 45ff.
13. Norman Cousins, *Anatomy of an Illness as Perceived by the Patient* (New York: Norton, 1979).

Chapter 15. THE STOREHOUSES AND COURIERS OF MODERN COMMUNICATION

1. See E. D. Johnson and M. H. Harris, *History of Libraries in the Western World,* 3rd. ed. (New Jersey: The Scarecrow Press, 1976).
2. See the *Encyclopaedia Britannica,* 14th ed., tabulation of principal libraries of the world, and the size of their collections ("Library," vol. 12, pp. 1054–1055).
3. See Wilbur Schramm, *Big Media Little Media* (Beverly Hills, Calif.: Sage, 1977), pp. 12–14.
4. C. H. Scheele, *The Postal Service—A Short History* (Washington, D.C.: Smithsonian Institute Press, 1970). The forthcoming article by Max R. Kenworthy ("Postal Services") in *The International Encyclopedia of Communications* (New York and London: Oxford and Annenberg, in press) will also be useful.

Chapter 16. INSTITUTIONS OF THE MASS MEDIA: PUBLIC OPINION

1. Aleksandr Solzhenitsyn, quoted in W. L. Rivers, *The Other Government* (New York: Universe Books, 1982), p. 7.
2. Walter Lippmann, *Public Opinion* (New York: Harcourt, Brace, 1922), p. 3.
3. See, for instance, P. F. Lazarsfeld, B. Berelson, and Hazel Gaudet, *The People's Choice* (New York: Harper & Row, 1944); B. Berelson, P. F. Lazarsfeld, and William McPhee, *Voting: A Study of Opinion Formation in a Presidential Election* (Chicago: University of Chicago Press, 1954).
4. See Maxwell E. McCombs and Donald Shaw, *The Emergence of American Political Issues: The Agenda-Setting Function of the Press* (New York, St. Paul: West Publishing Co., 1977).
5. J. McGinnis, *The Selling of the President* (New York: Trident Press, 1969).
6. Dennis McQuail, *Mass Communication Theory: An Introduction* (Beverly Hills, Calif.: Sage, 1982).
7. Rivers, *The Other Government,* pp. 47–48.
8. Lippman, *Public Opinion,* p. 247.
9. Rivers, *The Other Government,* pp. 110–111.
10. Bob Woodward and Carl Bernstein, *All the President's Men* (New York: Simon & Schuster, 1974).
11. Rivers, *The Other Government,* p. 118.
12. The letter from Governor Brown was published in the *San Francisco Chronicle,* February 27, 1967, p. 1.

Chapter 17. INSTITUTIONS OF THE MASS MEDIA: THE GREAT PERSUADERS

1. See V. R. Fryburger, "Advertising," in *Encyclopaedia Britannica,* 14th and 15th eds. under "Advertising."
2. Fryburger.
3. Fryburger.
4. Fryburger.
5. Fryburger.
6. C. H. Sterling, and T. R. Haight, *The Mass Media: Communication Industry Trends* (New York: Praeger, 1978).
7. Fryburger, "Advertising," *Britannica.*
8. Scott J. Cutlip, and Allen H. Center, *Effective Public Relations* (Englewood Cliffs, N.J.: Prentice-Hall, 1964), pp. 29–30.
9. Cutlip and Center.
10. Cutlip and Center, p. 36.
11. Cutlip and Center, pp. 46ff.
12. Daniel Boorstin, *The Image: A Guide to Pseudo-Events in America* (New York: Harper & Row, 1964).
13. U.S. Census, 1985.
14. Cutlip and Center, *Effective Public Relations,* p. 307.
15. Robert Heilbroner, "Public Relations: The Invisible Sell," *Harper's Magazine* 234 (June 1, 1957): 27–31.
16. In Sevareid's weekly column for June 10, 1963.
17. On this topic, see William L. Rivers, *The Adversaries* (Boston: Beacon Press, 1970). The Sussman quote is in her article entitled "The Personnel and Ideology of Public Relations," *Public Opinion Quarterly* 12 (Winter 1948): 697–708.
18. Cutlip and Center, *Effective Public Relations,* pp. 497–498.
19. Lincoln Kirstein, in *The Nation* (June 1, 1964): 555–557.
20. For an example of one economist's viewpoint, see Richard H. Holton, "The Use of Advertising," in *Advertising Age* (April 30, 1980).

Chapter 18. COMMUNICATION AND DEVELOPMENT

1. Richard A. Easterlin, "Economic Growth," in David L. Sills (ed.), *International Encyclopedia of the Social Sciences* (New York: Macmillan, 1968), pp. 395–408.
2. Frederick W. Frey, "Development," in Ithiel de Sola Pool and Wilbur Schramm (eds.), *Handbook of Communication* (Boston: Houghton Mifflin, 1973), pp. 339ff.
3. Easterlin, "Economic Growth." See also Neil J. Smyser, "The Modernization of Social Relations," in Myron Weiner (ed.), *Modernization: The Dynamics of Growth* (New York: Basic Books, 1966), pp. 110–121.
4. Frey, "Development."
5. Wilbur Schramm, "The Idea of Development," in Erik Barnouw (ed.), *International Encyclopedia of Communications* (London and Philadelphia: Oxford and Annenberg, in press).
6. Bert F. Hoselitz, "Noneconomic Aspects," in David L. Sills (ed.), *International Encyclopedia of the Social Sciences* (New York: Macmillan, 1968), IV, pp. 422–429.
7. Walt W. Rostow, *The Stages of Economic Growth* (Cambridge, England: Cambridge University Press, 1960).
8. Everett F. Hagen, *On the Theory of Social Change* (Chicago: Dorsey, 1962).
9. David C. McClelland, *The Achieving Society* (Princeton, N.J.: Van Nostrand, 1951).
10. Talcott Parsons, *Structure and Process in Modern Societies* (Chicago: Free Press, 1960).
11. Daniel Lerner, *The Passing of Traditional Society* (Chicago: Free Press, 1958).
12. See, for instance, Wilbur Schramm and W. Lee Ruggels, "How Mass Media Systems Grow," in Daniel Lerner and Wilbur Schramm (eds.), *Communication and Change in the Developing Countries* (Honolulu: University Press of Hawaii, 1967), pp. 55–75.
13. For these cases, see *New Educational Media in Action: Case Studies for Planners* (Paris: UNESCO, 3 vols., 1967).

14. For the Iowa State contribution, see the pioneering articles by Ryan and Gross, Bohlen and Beal, and the summary in Everett W. Rogers, *Diffusion of Innovations* (New York: Free Press of Glencoe, 1962).

15. See Alfred J. Marrow, *The Practical Theorist: The Life and Work of Kurt Lewin* (New York: Basic Books, 1969).

16. See *New Educational Media in Action*.

17. D. Lawrence Kincaid and June Ock Yum, "The Needle and the Ax: Communication and Development in a Korean Village," in Wilbur Schramm and Daniel Lerner (eds.), *Communication and Change: The Last Ten Years—and the Next* (Honolulu: University Press of Hawaii, 1976). Also, pp. 1–30 in Everett M. Rogers and D. Lawrence Kincaid, *Communication Networks* (New York: Macmillan, 1981).

18. The Samoa story will be found in Wilbur Schramm, Lyle M. Nelson, and Mere Betham, *Bold Experiment: The Story of Educational Television in American Samoa* (Stanford, Calif.: Stanford University Press, 1981).

19. See the World Bank annual report, 1985.

20. Luis Ramiro Beltran, "Another Pattern of Development—A Third World Viewpoint," in the *International Encyclopedia of Communications*.

21. Beltran.

22. Godwin C. Chu, *Palapa: Satellite Television Comes to the Indonesian Village* (in press).

Chapter 19. THE NEW AGE OF INFORMATION

1. Arthur C. Clarke, *Profiles of the Future* (London: Richard Clay, 1962; new ed., 1976), pp. 36–37.

2. Arthur C. Clarke, "Extra-Terrestrial Relays: Can Rocket Stations Give World-Wide Coverage?" *Wireless World* (October 1945): 305–308.

3. The first report was entitled "Preliminary Discussion of the Logical Design of an Electronic Computing Instrument," dated June 28, 1946, signed by A. W. Burks, H. H. Goldstine, and J. Von Neumann. The names are in alphabetical order; Burks and Goldstine were brought in by Von Neumann to assist him. For more information on these events, see Note 2, in H. H. Goldstine, *The Computer from Pascal to Von Neumann*, (Princeton, N.J.: Princeton University Press, 1972).

4. Arthur C. Clarke, "Beyond Babel," in W. Schramm and D. F. Roberts, *The Process and Effects of Mass Communication* (Urbana: University of Illinois Press, 1974), p. 953.

5. Clarke, p. 954. In this reference, Clarke credits Jean d'Arcy with the story.

6. Clarke.

7. H. Goldhamer, "Effects of Communication Technology," in Schramm and Roberts, *Process and Effects of Mass Communication*, p. 902.

8. F. Machlup, *The Production and Distribution of Knowledge in the United States* (Princeton, N.J.: Princeton University Press, 1962).

9. M. Porat, *The Information Economy* (Stanford University Ph.D. dissertation, Stanford, California, 1976).

10. A. Toffler, *Future Shock* (New York: Bantam Books, 1971), pp. 354–355.

11. G. R. White, "Graphic Systems," in G. Gerbner, et al. (eds.), *Communications Technology and Social Policy* (New York: Wiley, 1973), pp. 49–50.

12. See Machlup, *Production and Distribution of Knowledge;* Porat, *Information Economy;* and M. Jussawalla, *The Economics of Communication* (in press).

13. A. C. Clarke, *Profiles of the Future*, p. 232.

14. In J. C. Licklider and Robert W. Taylor, "The Computer as a Communicating Machine," *Science and Technology* (April 1968): 31.

15. A. C. Clarke, *Profiles of the Future*, p. 230.

I N D E X

Machlup, Fritz, 346, *357*
MacLeish, Archibald, 231
McLuhan, Marshall, 144
McNamee, Graham, *223*
McQuail, Dennis, 293–294
Madison, James, 297
Magazines, 160, *164, 165,* 184–185
  advertising in, 305, 306, *319*
  functions of, 261–262
  impact of television on, *271*
Magic, 7, 75–76
Mahavira, 87
Mainichi Shimbun (Japan), 181
Main Stream of Mathematics, The (Kramer), 106–107
Mann, Thomas, 262
Manutius, Aldus, *133,* 260
Mao Tse-tung, 175
Marathon races, 150
Marconi, Guglielmo, *203,* 207, *214*
Marconi Company, 225
Marco Polo, 120, 280
Marquardt Corporation, 344
Marshall Plan, 324
Marx, Karl, 167, 175
Marx brothers, 231
Mass media, 135–147. *See also* Magazines; Motion
  pictures; Newspapers; Radio; Television
  described, 136–138
  durability of, 140–141
  educational uses of, 231–232, 242–243, 278–280,
    314, 329, 332, 334–337
  entertainment and, 260–269
  growth of, 138–140
  impact of, 141–143
  importance of, 143–145
  levels of culture and, 256–260
  new developments in, 241–243
  relative international use of, 239–240, *240,*
    244–248, 263–264
  rise of middle class and, 255–256
Mathematics, 103–109, *114,* 190, 191
  counting in, 103–104, 112–113
  early Egyptian, 75, 105–107
  of early Greece, 106, 110, 111–113
  of Ionia, 112–113
  numbers in, 104–109, 190
  number symbol systems in, *105,* 106–108
  zero in, 106, 108–109
Mazarin, Cardinal, 275
Media. *See* Mass media and *specific media types*
Media codes, 34
Medici, Cosimo de, 274
Medicine, 75–76, 191
Medlars (abstracting service), 278
Mencken, H. L., *165*
Mendelsohn, Harold, 254–255
Mercurio, El (Chile), 178

Mercury, 153
Mergenthaler, Ottmar, *165*
Mesopotamia, education in, 85
Mevvissen, Gustav, 308
Mexico, *81,* 178, 225
Miami Herald, 187
Microchip, 29, 139, 343, 344
Microcomputers, 351, *358*
Microelectronics, 29, 139, *340,* 351, *357*
Microphone, 197
Microprocessing, 139, *357, 358*
Middle class, 254–256, 322
Middle East
  ancient postal service of, 280–281
  education in, 73–75, 84, 85, *100,* 139, 143
  Muslim universities of, 97
Middle Pleistocene Age, 41
Military service, in ancient Rome, 94–95
Miller, Glenn, 231
Milton, John, 157, *164,* 261
Minoan Crete, 59, 87
Mr. Deeds Goes to Town (movie), 230
Mr. Hulot's Holiday (movie), 230
Modifiers, earliest use of, 42
Monasteries
  Buddhist, 87
  libraries of, 274, 275
  need for postal services, 281
  schools of, 278, 279
Monde, Le (France), *165,* 168, *187*
Money orders, 282
Montagu, Ashley, 40, 44
Morse, Samuel F. B., 189, 195–196, *203,* 343
Morse code, 196, 207, 219
Motion pictures, 141, 203–205, 208, *214*
  development of talent for, 228–231
  functions of, 261–262
  growth of use of, 205, 217–219, 233, 262–263
  impact of sound on, 228–230
  impact of television on, 234
  international distribution of, 240, *240*
  invention of, 203–205, *214*
Mountains, formation of, *17, 26*
Movable type
  in China, 121–122, *132*
  growth of news media and, 151
  of Gutenberg, 123–127, *133*
Mumford, Lewis, 67–69
Murrow, Edward R., 226–227, *227,* 253
Musicals, 228–229
Muslims, 97, 120–121, 190
Mutual Broadcasting System, 222
Muybridge, Edweard, 203–204
Mycenaean civilization, 87

Naburianu, 107
Nación, La (Costa Rica), 178

United Press, *165,* 183
United Press International (UPI), 183
United States
    advertising agencies in, 306, *318–319*
    computers in, 346
    corporate public relations in, 308
    development aid of, 324, 329–332, 334–337
    economic growth of, 322
    elite newspapers of, 168
    libraries of, 276–278
    media circulation statistics, *246, 248–251*
    motion pictures of, 218, 230–231
    news agencies of, 184
    newspapers of, 156, 158–160, *164–165, 187. See also specific newspapers*
    postal service of, 283–284
    television use in, 232–238
U.S. News & World Report, 184
Universal, El (Venezuela), 178
Universities, 96–98, 191
    of China, 86
    early American, 98
    early European, 97–98
    growth of printing technology and, 123
    of India, 87, 96–97
    libraries of, 277
    list of early, *100*
    medieval, 279
    Muslim, 97
    need for postal services, 281
    "open," 241–242, 330
University of Paris, 97–98, *100,* 123
Upanishads, 86
Ur-language, 37

Vacuum tubes, *214,* 219
Valladilid University, *100*
Vallee, Rudy, 231
Van den Haag, Ernest, 253–254, 268
Vanguardia Española, La (Spain), *187*
Vatican City, newspaper, 187
Verbal communication
    earliest forms of, 26, 27, 41–43
    location of development of, 43–45
    origin of language and, 36–40
    predecessors to, 33–35
    reasons for development of, 35–36
    theory of development of, 40–43
Verhoeven, Abraham, 155–156
Videocassette recorder (VCR), 349
Videocassettes, 242, 277, 329
Videotapes, 242
Videotex, 243, *358*
Vietnam War, 238
Villages, 49–51, *64,* 67–71, 76
Violence, on television, 265
Vitascope, 205

Voice of America, 224
Vowels, 59

Wallace, DeWitt, *165*
Wall Street Journal, 168, *187*
Wang Cheng, 121
War of the Worlds, 216, 228, *229*
Washington, George, 273, 284
Washington Post, 168, *187,* 299
Watergate, 238, 299
Watson, Thomas, 197, 199
Watson, William, 196
Watt, James, 191
WEAF radio (New York), 221
Weber, Max, 326–327
Web-perfecting press, *165*
Welles, Orson, *216,* 228, *229,* 230
Wells, H. G., *216,* 228
Welt, Die (Germany), 168, *187*
West, Rebecca, 149
Western press
    American, 156, 158–160, *164–165,* 171–175, *187*
    birth of newspaper, 155–156
    development of early newspapers, 156–159
    elite newspapers, 168–169
    evolution of modern, 161–163
    freedom of, 159–160
    popular newspapers, 169–171
Western Union, 197–198
Westinghouse, George, 308
Westinghouse Electric Company, 220–221, 308
Wheatstone, Charles, 196–197
White, George R., 349
Whitehead, Alfred North, 107, 112, 113, 189, 341
White Lady (cave painting), 2, *3*
Whiteman, Paul, 231
Whorf, Benjamin, 33
Whorf-Sapir hypothesis, 63
Widow Jones, The (play), 205
Wiene, Robert, 218
Wiener, Norbert, 352
Wiener Zeitung (Austria), 158
Wile, Frederick, 221
Winnipeg Free Press (Canada), *187*
Wireless World (journal), 343, 344
Wisdom literature, 77
Wisner, George, 169
Wolff, Bernard, 182, 183
Women
    of early Athens, 80
    role in economic development, 331
    Socrates and, 92–93
Wood pulp paper, 130
Woodward, Bob, 299
Woolley, Leonard, 30, 69–70
World War II, 226–228, 324